EARTH MOVING PRAYERS

(PRAY UNTIL MIRACLE HAPPENS)

More Than 5300 Life Changing Prayer Points

Timothy Atunnise

TSA SOLUTION PUBLISHING
ATLANTA, GEORGIA

EARTH-MOVING PRAYERS

Copyright © 2013 by Timothy Atunnise

All rights reserved. No part of this book may be reproduced, copied, stored or transmitted in any form or by any means – graphic, electronic, or mechanical, including photocopying, recording, or information storage and retrieval systems without the prior written permission of TSA Solution Publishing except where permitted by law.

Unless otherwise specified, all Scripture quotations in this book are from The Holy Bible, King James Version. KJV is Public domain in the United States printed in 1987.

GLOVIM PUBLICATIONS
1096 Bethsaida Road
Riverdale, GA 30296 USA.
glovimpublications@gmail.com
www.glovimonline.org

TSA Solution Publishing
A division of Timat Store, LLC.
Atlanta, GA 30294
timatstore@yahoo.com

Cover Design: Tim Atunnise

Printed in the United States of America

DEDICATION

This book is dedicated to my spiritual parents, Apostle Alexander and Dr. Grace Bamgbola, thank you for your unconditional love and unending support. Your prayer, counsel and support are priceless, thank you for always being there.
May the Lord continue to increase your anointing, wisdom, and every knowledge in the name of Jesus Christ.

To my Lord Jesus Christ:
Thank you for the mercy and grace you extend
to someone like me.

IMPORTANT NOTICE

Deliverance is a benefit of the Kingdom, only for the children of God. If you have not accepted Jesus Christ as your personal Lord and Savior, this is the best time to do so.

Before you continue, you need to be sure you are in the right standing with God if you want to exercise authority and power in the name of Jesus Christ. The Bible says,

"Then he called his twelve disciples together, and gave them power and authority over all devils, and to cure diseases." - Luke 9:1

"And these signs shall follow them that believe; in my name shall they cast out devils; they shall speak with new tongues; they shall take up serpents; and if they drink any deadly thing, it shall not hurt them; they shall lay hands on the sick, and they shall recover." – Mark 16:17-18.

These are promises for the Children of God, not just for everyone. Why don't you give your life to Christ today and you will have access to the same promises. Food that is meant for the children will not be given to the dogs.

"But he answered and said, it is not meet to take the children's bread, and cast it to dogs" – Matthew 15:26.

If you really want to be delivered from any bondage of the wicked and be set free from any form of captivity, I ask you today to give your life to Christ. If you are ready, say this prayer with all your heart:

"Dear Heavenly Father, You have called me to Yourself in the name of Your dear Son Jesus Christ. I realize that Jesus Christ is the only Way, the Truth, and the Life.

I acknowledge to You that I am a sinner. I believe that Your only begotten Son Jesus Christ shed His precious blood on the cross, died for my sins, and rose again on the third day. I am truly sorry for the deeds which I have committed against You, and therefore, I am willing to repent (turn away from my sins). Have mercy on me, a sinner. Cleanse me, and forgive me of my sins.

I truly desire to serve You, Lord Jesus. Starting from now, I pray that You would help me to hear Your still small voice. Lord, I desire to be led by Your Holy Spirit so I can faithfully follow You and obey all of Your commandments. I ask You for the strength to love You more than anything else so I won't fall back into my old ways. I also ask You to bring genuine believers into my life who will encourage me to live for You and help me stay accountable.

Jesus, I am truly grateful for Your grace which has led me to repentance and has saved me from my sins. By the indwelling of Your Holy Spirit, I now have the power to overcome all sin which before so easily entangled me. Lord Jesus, please transform my life so that I may bring glory and honor to You alone and not to myself.

Right now I confess Jesus Christ as the Lord of my life. With my heart, I believe that God the Father raised His Son Jesus Christ from the dead. This very moment I acknowledge that Jesus Christ is my Savior and according to His Word, right now I am born again. Thank You Jesus, for coming into my life and hearing my prayer. I ask all of this in the name of my Lord and Savior, Jesus Christ. Amen".

I hereby congratulate and welcome you into the Kingdom. You hereby have full access to the benefits, promises and blessings of the Kingdom.

This book is loaded with blessings, you will not be disappointed as you continue to enjoy the goodness of the Lord.

INSTRUCTIONS

If you are new to this method of prayer, please follow this instruction carefully:

Step 1:

Spend enough time in praising and worshiping God not just for what He is about to do or what He has done, but WHO HE IS.

Step 2:

Unforgiveness will surely hinder your prayer, take time to remember all those who have done you wrong, and forgive them from the bottom of your heart. THIS IS VERY IMPORTANT BECAUSE YOUR DELIVERANCE DEPENDS ON IT.

Step 3:

Believe in your heart that God will answer your prayer when you call upon Him, and do not doubt in your heart.

Step 4:

Pray in the name of Jesus Christ alone.

Step 5:

Repeat each prayer point 25 to 30 times or until you are convinced that you receive answer before you go to the next prayer point. **Example:** When you take prayer point number 1, you say this prayer over and over again, 25 – 30 times or until you are convinced that you have an answer before you go to prayer point number 2.

Step 6:

It will be more effective if you can fast along with your prayer. If you want total deliverance from your bondage, take 3 days of sacrifice in fasting as you say your prayer aggressively, asking your situation to receive permanent solution and YOUR DELIVERANCE WILL BE MADE PERFECT IN THE NAME OF JESUS CHRIST. AMEN!

Table of Contents

Dedication 3
Important Notice.. 4
Instructions 7
Earth-moving prayer.. 13
Prayer to receive instant miracle 21
Let your Spirit come upon me 25
Pray before you travel 31
Pray before you pay your tithes.............................. 37
This is not just another day.................................... 42
Prayer when in a serious court case...................... 49
Prayer for the baptism of fire................................. 55
Prayer for business expansion/prosperity 61
Prayer for uncommon victory................................ 67
Let your angels locate my blessings...................... 75
Prayer when you desire to have a new story 85
Prayer for mercy to overcome judgment 91
Prayer to overcome stubborn situations.............. 97
Let the long distance be shortened 103
Prayer for sudden blessings 108
Prayer for God to fight your battle 114
Prayer for uncommon blessings 119
Prayer to release stolen blessings 124
Prayer to finish uncompleted project.................. 129
Jesus said, "It is finished" 132
Enter in by your blood O Lord 139
Prayer to get good result in test/examination 143
Prayer for God to showcase His power 149
Prayer to cancel evil transaction.......................... 155
Deliverance from your painful past 161

The valley of the shadow of death	165
Prayer to stop the activities of the enemy	169
Prayer to break annual evil cycle	175
This is the day	179
Prayer when you desperately need a change	186
Prayer for proseperity in time of recession	192
God can do anything	197
Prayer to fulfill purpose	203
Prayer for God to open door that is shut against you	207
Prayer to remove evil loads of infirmity	211
Prayer to experience a better day	215
Prayer for purification	218
Deliverance from addiction	225
When your situation needs urgent attention	228
Prayer for the storm victims	233
Total deliverance from Egyptian bondage	237
Upon mount Zion shall be deliverance	243
Prayer against evil agenda	246
Deliverance from unrepentant enemies	250
Prayer of deliverance from witchcraft attacks	258
Avenge me of my enemies	267
Prayer to break yokes and curses	275
Prayer to overcome obstacles in your way	280
Prayer to take your life back	287
Power for deliverance	294
Pray by the power in Jesus name	301
My life is built upon The Rock	307
New things that the enemy cannot stop	314
Father, stop them that want to stop me	320
Prayer for divine repositioning	329
Prayer to enter the solution room	336
Prayer to overcome fear	348

Prayer for rain of blessing	352
I am delivered	358
Prayer to know the plan of God	366
Prayer when you desire the best	372
Impossible is over	380
Prayer to open a new chapter in your life	386
Prayer to stop evil access to your life	393
Prayer to close evil chapter in your life	402
Prayer to destroy evil strongholds	407
Prayer for last minute miracle	414
Prayer to reject evil manifestation	420
Prayer to experience great things	427
Let my blessings come to me	430
Prayer to possess your throne	438
Divine relocation	445
Prayer to calm the storm of your life	450
For God nothing is impossible	456
Prayer for uncommon breakthrough	460
Never again	465
Deliverance prayer against evil patterns	469
Foundational deliverance	477
Prayer to purge your foundation	482
Prayer to break ancestral evil hold	488
Prayer for divine re-arrangement	497
Prayer against oppression at workplace	504
Prayer for unstoppable progress	508
Prayer to open the book of remembrance	513
Prayer for business and financial prosperity	517
Prayer to start the month of January	529
Prayer to start the month of February	535
Prayer to start the month of March	543
Prayer to start the month of April	550

Prayer to start the month of May 559
Prayer to start the month of June 567
Prayer to start the month of July 572
Prayer to start the month of August 581
Prayer to start the month of September 589
Prayer to start the month of October 595
Prayer to start the month of November 604
Prayer to start the month of December 611
Credits 618

Spiritual Warfare: Earth-Moving Prayer

"For though we walk in the flesh, we do not war after the flesh: For the weapons of our warfare are not carnal, but mighty through God to the pulling down of strongholds..." - 2 Corinthians 10:3-6

"And when they had prayed, the place was shaken where they were assembled together; and they were all filled with the Holy Ghost, and they spake the word of God with boldness." - Acts 4:31

Spiritual Warfare is the war or conflict between the forces of good and the forces of evil in the spiritual or invisible realm; it is the active battle between those representing God's kingdom and Satan's kingdom. Spiritual warfare is a powerful weapon that entails directly addressing Satan and his kingdom in offensive combat against the forces of evil. Mighty strategic weapons of war are available, through the power of earth-moving prayer, and may be used to defeat every enemy of the Church! Are you listed in God's book as one of the "Movers and Shakers" in the kingdom of God? Are you engaged effectively in Spiritual warfare: earth-moving prayer? Are you making a difference in our world?

EARTH-MOVING PRAYERS:

In the natural, when it is time to construct a path or road in undeveloped territory, a civil engineering technique referred to as "Earth-Moving" or "Cutting" is performed.

This construction process involves mechanically excavating or blasting (Earth-Moving) out soil or rock material from a hill or mountain to make way for a road, railway, etc, through the use of strategically placed explosives.

Allegorically, in the spiritual, when God's people render strategic prayer we can have explosive "mountain-moving faith," for Jesus said *"... whosoever shall say unto this mountain, Be thou removed, and be thou cast into the sea; and shall not doubt in his heart, but shall believe that those things which he saith shall come to pass; he shall have whatsoever he saith."* - Mark 11:23

Through dynamic "Earth-moving prayer," a way can be made where there seemeth no way!

INTERCESSORY EARTH-MOVERS:

When it is time to construct a building or structure in underdeveloped territory in the natural, heavy equipment is used such as an "Earthmover."

An Earthmover represents a machine, such as a bulldozer or backhoe that is used for digging or pushing (moving) earth. Psalms 99:1 says *"The LORD reigneth... let the earth be moved."*

Figuratively, in the spiritual realm through the power of intercessory prayer, the Church can "move Heaven and Earth."

The earth moved marking major Biblical events in history of humanity. The earth moved at Jesus' crucifixion (Matthew 27:54); it moved at His resurrection at the tomb (Matthew 28:2); it moved at midnight when Paul and Silas prayed and praised in prison *"...there was a great earthquake, so that the foundations of the prison were 'shaken:' and immediately all the doors were opened, and every one's bands were loosed"* Acts 16:26.

The earth moved in Acts 4:31 *"And when they had prayed, the place was 'shaken' ...."* The word *"shaken,"* displayed here having the Greek translation *"salĕuō"* is same word used in Acts 16:26, which means: to *move; to shake (together); to stir up; to rock; etc.*

When the disciples were "all together" they prayed (the place was *shaken)*, they were all filled with the Holy Ghost, and spake the Word with boldness. This was God's very presence empowering them "to speak the word with boldness." Let the earth move, as we intercede!

THE PURPOSE OF SPIRITUAL WARFARE:

The main objective of spiritual warfare is to enter in the Spirit and to pull down strongholds of the adversary and also the spiritual fortified gates of Hell with God's prevailing power and authority.

As we engage in spiritual warfare through intercession, God's kingdom is being established. Jesus and the Apostles both proclaimed the Kingdom of God. Jesus has commissioned us as disciples to likewise proclaim the Kingdom of God. (Luke 9:1-2)

One of the greatest prayers that one can pray is found in Matthew 6:10 *"Thy kingdom come. Thy will be done in earth, as it is in heaven."* Matthew 11:12 states, *"...the kingdom of heaven suffereth violence, and the violent takes it by force."*

Luke 12:31-32 says *"...seek ye the kingdom of God...and all these things shall be added unto you. Fear not, little flock; for it is your Father's good pleasure to give you the kingdom."*

A promise was made to Abraham by God ensuring that his "seed" would possess the gate of his enemies. We are the seed of Abraham. God said *"...I will bless thee...and multiply thy seed as the stars...and as the sand ...and thy seed shall possess the gate of his enemies."* Genesis 22:17

SOURCE OF SATANIC OPERATION:

One-third of the angels under Satan's authority joined him in his rebellion against God, and became organized fallen angels (demonic spirits or devils) when God cast them upon the earth, where Satan established a kingdom. Jesus said, *"And if Satan cast out Satan, he is divided against himself; how shall then his kingdom stand?"* (Matthew 12:26)

God created all things for mankind, but Man was created for God. The whole earth was under Adam's authority: *"The heaven, even the heavens are the LORD's: but the earth hath he given to the children of men"* (Psalm 115:16). God commanded Adam to take dominion over the earth and subdue it, but when he ate the forbidden fruit, he surrendered his right to rule the earth.

But through the sacrifice of Jesus at Calvary, and by the regeneration and redemption of Man through the new birth experience and through obedience the Word of God through the Spirit, redeemed Mankind (Church) can have access to the kingdom of God upon this earth.

PREPARING FOR THE BATTLE:

To effectively engage in Spiritual warfare, we must often first obtain victory in the battle fought within (internally) before we are successful in winning the battle fought without (externally). One must face their own internal fears of defeat, so that they will be able to fight the overall war and win in the conquest. *"For God hath not given us the spirit of fear; but of power, and of love, and of a sound mind."* (II Timothy 1:7) We must be solid in doctrinal truth and Biblical principles and we must be confident in God's ability through us! *"...greater is he that is in you, than he that is in the world."* I John 4:4

Some Main Battlefronts Confronted by Christians:

1. Self-inflicted – Problems arising from one's own personal negligence or mistakes. *Ex: Not paying bills that are due – electricity cut off; neglecting one's health – illness; not being responsible, etc.*

2. Human-inflicted – Problems surfacing from the attack of human spirits and carnal nature of others. *Ex:*

Persecution, sedition, strife, ridicule, physical attacks, abuse, envy, jealousy, bitterness, gossip, etc.

3. Satanic-inflicted – Problems launched directly by Satan/the forces of Hell to negatively affect you. *Ex: Severe mishaps, harassing spirits, demonic or devilish manifestations, possessed people or evil things, etc.*

4. Nature-inflicted – Problems occurring from the natural circumstances of life. *Ex: Health complications due to aging, vehicular mechanical problems, Adverse weather conditions, etc.*

RECOGNIZING THE ENEMY:

The mind is a battlefield of the soul, will and feelings; therefore, we must renew it daily with prayer. We cannot always avoid confrontation of the enemy, but we do not have to be a victim of circumstances and succumb to defeat. Once we recognize the schemes of Satan, we must prepare for the attack and then arm ourselves against him. We cannot sit idle and wait until he attacks; it may be too late then. We must know who Christ is and who we are in Christ! Satan is concerned about how we use the power that God has given to us. *The Spirit of God has "insight" with "eyesight."*

The Devil tries to get you close to failing with the "D" grade by instilling the following into your mind:

☐ Doubt – Provokes you to question God's Word and His support.

☐ Discouragement – Pressures you to focus on your problems instead of the Problem Solver/God.

☐ Diversion – Entices you towards ungodly endeavors instead of righteous matters.

☐ Delay – Influences you to exaggerate about your full commitment to God.

☐ Defeat – Makes you feel unaccepted, so you don't make an effort to succeed.

SATAN IS LIMITED:

He is a fallen angel and is not equal to God; He is not omnipresent (All places at once); He is not omniscient (All knowing); He is not omnipotent (All powerful); He is unaware of thoughts/mind.

The Power of Prayer over Satan:

From the headquarters of Hell demonic forces are sent on assignment by Satan to "kill, steal and destroy." The Bible says *"Be sober, be vigilant; because your adversary the devil, as a roaring lion, walketh about seeking whom he may devour."* (I Peter 5:8) Satan has power, but GOD HAS MORE! Jesus said, *"All power is given unto me in heaven and in earth."* (Matthew 28:18) Jesus also stated, *"...I beheld Satan as lightning fall from heaven. Behold, I give you power to tread on serpents, and scorpions and over ALL the power of the enemy: and nothing shall by any means hurt you."* (Luke 10:18-19)

THE WHOLE ARMOR OF GOD:

As you abide in Christ, and He in you, and you "put on Christ," you confidently can adorn yourself with the whole Armor of God and be able to fight in prayer, and war victoriously against the adversary!

Ephesians 6:10-12, 18-19 declares, *"...be strong in the Lord, and in the power of his might. Put on the whole armour of God, that ye may be able to stand against the wiles of the devil...For we wrestle not against flesh and blood, but against principalities, against powers, against the rulers of darkness of this world, against spiritual wickedness in high places...Praying always with all prayer and supplication in the Spirit...that utterance may be given...that I may open my mouth boldly, to make known the mystery of the gospel."*

PRAYER TO RECEIVE INSTANT MIRACLE

Passages To Read Before You Pray:
2 Kings 7:1-20, Mark 5:25-34, Psalms 103, 86, 30, 24

I have come today to fellowship with my heavenly Father, and make my requests and needs known unto Him. I cannot be hindered nor delayed because I know who I am in the Lord. I am a child of the Kingdom, born of the Spirit, redeemed by the blood of Jesus Christ. I walk in authority, living life without any apology because the power and authority has been given to me according to the Word of God in the book of Luke 9:1.

As I have come to pray today and to fellowship with my heavenly Father, I cover myself in the blood of Jesus Christ, and I put on the whole armor of God. I hereby come against every Prince of Persia that wants to hinder my prayer, I arrest you by the power in the blood of Jesus Christ, and I bind you and cast you down into the pit of hell.

I come against principalities and powers that wrestle with me and my prayers, I arrest you today by the power in the name of Jesus Christ, and I bind you and cast down into the pit of hell. I come against the rulers of the darkness of this world, against spiritual wickedness in high places, I arrest you all by the power in the name of Jesus Christ, and I bind you and cast you down into the pit of hell. I come against weakness and weariness, I arrest you today by the power in the name of Jesus Christ, and I bind you and cast you out of my life. I come against wondering

spirit and distractions, I arrest you today by the power in the name of Jesus Christ, and I bind you and cast you out of my life.

Today I receive the anointing to pray and get results, my prayers cannot be hindered nor delayed because Jesus is my Lord, I will pray today and get the desired results, I decree open heavens upon my prayers. I baptize myself in the fire of the Holy Ghost; therefore I have become too hot for the enemy to handle. My prayers today will attract divine intervention to every situation in my life; signs and wonders will follow my prayers today, testimonies will follow my prayers today and the name of God alone will be glorified, in Jesus name. Amen!

PRAYER POINTS:

1. O God my Father, thank you for being my God, my Father and my friend.
2. O God my Father, thank you for the privilege to know you and the power of the resurrection of Jesus Christ.
3. O God my Father, thank you for always being there for me and with me.
4. O God my Father, thank you for the great and mighty things that you are doing in my life.
5. O God my Father, thank you for your provision and protection over me and my household.
6. O God my Father, thank you for always answering my prayers.
7. I confess my sins before you today and I ask you to forgive me on the basis of your mercy, in the name of Jesus Christ.
8. Wash me clean today O Lord by the blood of Jesus Christ.

9. I cover myself and my household with the blood of Jesus Christ.
10. My prayers today will not go in vain; my prayers will produce the desired results in the name of Jesus Christ.
11. O God my Father, let every decision of the enemy against me be overturned in the name of Jesus Christ.
12. O God my Father, let every plan of the enemy to rob me of my joy be overturned in the name of Jesus Christ.
13. O God my Father, let every plan of the enemy to rob me of my testimonies be overturned in the name of Jesus Christ.
14. O God my Father let it be my turn to testify in the name of Jesus Christ.
15. O God my father let anything in my life robbing me of my testimonies, be destroyed by the fire of God.
16. O God my Father, release into my life today overnight miracles, in the name of Jesus Christ.
17. By this time tomorrow, I will surely have my testimonies in the name of Jesus Christ.
18. By this time tomorrow, I will surely have my miracles in the name of Jesus Christ.
19. By this time tomorrow, I will surely have answers to my prayers in the name of Jesus Christ.
20. By this time tomorrow, I will have abundance in my life instead of lack in the name of Jesus Christ.
21. By this time tomorrow, I will have testimonies concerning the promotions that I have been praying for, in the name of Jesus Christ.
22. By this time tomorrow, I will have testimonies concerning the breakthroughs that I am praying for, in the name of Jesus Christ.

23. By this time tomorrow, I will have testimonies concerning my business or career that I am praying for in the name of Jesus Christ.
24. By this time tomorrow, I will have surplus in every area of my life.
25. By this time tomorrow, I will celebrate my victory over the plan of the enemy.
26. Every hindrance to my breakthrough, be removed today by the fire of God.
27. Every obstacle to my progress, be removed today by the fire of God.
28. O God my Father, by this time tomorrow, you will give me every reason to testify.
29. O God my Father, it is my turn to testify, do something in my life today that will bring a complete turn-around.
30. O God my Father, it is my turn to testify, let there be a total transformation in every area of my life.
31. O God my Father, it is my turn to testify, you are permitted to move my life forward by force.
32. O God my Father, it is my turn to testify, you are permitted to change whatever needs to be changed in my life.
33. O God my Father, it is my turn to testify, you are permitted to destroy anything in my life that is holding me back from fulfilling purpose in the name of Jesus Christ.
34. By this time tomorrow, there must be a positive change in every area of my life to the glory of God.
35. O God my Father, it is my turn to testify, let there be a total restoration in every area of my life in the name of Jesus Christ.

LET YOUR SPIRIT COME UPON ME

Passages To Read Before You Pray:
1 Samuel 10:1-11, Ezekiel 37:1-14, Psalms 15, 19, 21, 30, 29, 42, 66

I have come today to fellowship with my heavenly Father, and make my requests and needs known unto Him. I cannot be hindered nor delayed because I know who I am in the Lord. I am a child of the Kingdom, born of the Spirit, redeemed by the blood of Jesus Christ. I walk in authority, living life without any apology because the power and authority has been given to me according to the Word of God in the book of Luke 9:1.

As I have come to pray today and to fellowship with my heavenly Father, I cover myself in the blood of Jesus Christ, and I put on the whole armor of God. I hereby come against every Prince of Persia that wants to hinder my prayer, I arrest you by the power in the blood of Jesus Christ, and I bind you and cast you down into the pit of hell.

I come against principalities and powers that wrestle with me and my prayers, I arrest you today by the power in the name of Jesus Christ, and I bind you and cast down into the pit of hell. I come against the rulers of the darkness of this world, against spiritual wickedness in high places, I arrest you all by the power in the name of Jesus Christ, and I bind you and cast you down into the pit of hell. I come against weakness and weariness, I arrest you today by the power in the name of Jesus Christ, and I

bind you and cast you out of my life. I come against wondering spirit and distractions, I arrest you today by the power in the name of Jesus Christ, and I bind you and cast you out of my life.

Today I receive the anointing to pray and get results, my prayers cannot be hindered nor delayed because Jesus is my Lord, I will pray today and get the desired results, I decree open heavens upon my prayers. I baptize myself in the fire of the Holy Ghost; therefore I have become too hot for the enemy to handle. My prayers today will attract divine intervention to every situation in my life; signs and wonders will follow my prayers today, testimonies will follow my prayers today and the name of God alone will be glorified, in Jesus name. Amen!

PRAYER POINTS:

1. O God my Father, thank you for being my God, my Father and my friend.
2. O God my Father, thank you for the privilege to know you and the power of the resurrection of Jesus Christ.
3. O God my Father, thank you for always being there for me and with me.
4. O God my Father, thank you for the great and mighty things that you are doing in my life.
5. O God my Father, thank you for your provision and protection over me and my household.
6. O God my Father, thank you for always answering my prayers.
7. I confess my sins before you today and I ask you to forgive me on the basis of your mercy, in the name of Jesus Christ.

8. Wash me clean today O Lord by the blood of Jesus Christ.
9. I cover myself and my household with the blood of Jesus Christ.
10. My prayers today will not go in vain; my prayers will produce the desired results in the name of Jesus Christ.
11. Today O Lord, open the eyes of my heart so that I may see you in your glory and majesty, in the name of Jesus Christ.
12. O God my Father, release upon my head today new anointing and fresh fire of the Holy Ghost in the name of Jesus Christ.
13. O God my Father, anoint me today to be the head and not the tail in the name of Jesus Christ.
14. O God my Father, anoint me today to be the head in my father's house in the name of Jesus Christ.
15. O God my Father, anoint me today to be the head among my friends in the name of Jesus Christ.
16. O God my Father, anoint me today to be the head among my co-workers and business partners, in the name of Jesus Christ.
17. O God my Father, let your Holy Spirit guide me in the way I should go so that I will not miss my way, in the name of Jesus Christ.
18. O God my Father, let your Holy Spirit guide me in the way I should go so that I will not work against your plan for my life, in the name of Jesus Christ.
19. O God my Father, let your Holy Spirit guide me in what I should do so that I will not disobey you, in the name of Jesus Christ.

20. No matter the situation around me, I am moving forward in the name of Jesus Christ.
21. No matter the plan and activity of the enemy against me, I am moving forward in life, in the name of Jesus Christ.
22. It doesn't matter what my present situation looks like, as long as I have Jesus Christ as my Lord, I am moving forward in life in the name of Jesus Christ.
23. It doesn't matter what people say or think about me, as long as I have Jesus Christ as my Lord, I will fulfill purpose in life in the name of Jesus Christ.
24. It doesn't matter what people say or think about me, as long as I have Jesus Christ as my Lord, I am more than a conqueror in the name of Jesus Christ.
25. It doesn't matter what people say or think about me, as long as I have Jesus Christ as my Lord, I will overcome every challenge that may come my way in the name of Jesus Christ.
26. It doesn't matter what people say or think about me, as long as I have Jesus Christ as my Lord, I will be what I was born to be in the name of Jesus Christ.
27. It doesn't matter what people say or think about me, as long as I have Jesus Christ as my Lord, my greatness will manifest without delay in the name of Jesus Christ.
28. It doesn't matter what people say or think about me, as long as I have Jesus Christ as my Lord, my breakthrough will manifest now without any delay in the name of Jesus Christ.
29. It doesn't matter what people say or think about me, as long as I have Jesus Christ as my Lord, I am born to rule and I will rule over nations and kingdoms in the name of Jesus Christ.

30. It doesn't matter what people say or think about me, as long as I have Jesus Christ as my Lord, I will enjoy the goodness of the Lord in the land of the living, in the name of Jesus Christ.
31. It doesn't matter what people say or think about me, I will make a positive impact in this generation and generations to come in the name of Jesus Christ.
32. It doesn't matter what people say or think about me, my prayers will bring a dramatic turn-around into every area of my life, in the name of Jesus Christ.
33. It doesn't matter what people say or think about me, my miracles will manifest now without any delay in the name of Jesus Christ.
34. It doesn't matter what people say or think about me now, they will all come together to celebrate with me when my miracles manifest in the name of Jesus Christ.
35. It doesn't matter what people say or think about me now, they will all come together to rejoice with me when my testimonies come in the name of Jesus Christ.
36. It doesn't matter what people say or think about me now, they will soon see the good hands of God upon my life and celebrate with me in the name of Jesus Christ.
37. O God my Father, bring people together today to contribute to my success in the name of Jesus Christ.
38. O God my Father, bring people together today and let them work together for my breakthrough in the name of Jesus Christ.
39. O God my Father, bring people together today and let them work together to make a way for me where there seems to be no way in the name of Jesus Christ.
40. O God my Father, let your Spirit come upon me today without measure in the name of Jesus Christ.

41. O God my Father, let your Spirit come upon me today and make me a new man in the name of Jesus Christ.
42. O God my Father, let your Spirit come upon me today and bring the best out of me, in the name of Jesus Christ.
43. O God my Father, let your Spirit come upon me today to transform my life in the name of Jesus Christ.
44. O God my Father, let your Spirit come upon me today and destroy anything that is not of God in my life in the name of Jesus Christ.
45. Today I receive the life of God and I will never be the same again, in the name of Jesus Christ.
46. Today I receive the life of God and I command every dead area of my life to come alive now, in the name of Jesus Christ.

PRAY BEFORE YOU TRAVEL

Passages To Read Before You Pray:
Psalms 121, 23, 91, 124, 125, 34

I have come today to fellowship with my heavenly Father, and make my requests and needs known unto Him. I cannot be hindered nor delayed because I know who I am in the Lord. I am a child of the Kingdom, born of the Spirit, redeemed by the blood of Jesus Christ. I walk in authority, living life without any apology because the power and authority has been given to me according to the Word of God in the book of Luke 9:1.

As I have come to pray today and to fellowship with my heavenly Father, I cover myself in the blood of Jesus Christ, and I put on the whole armor of God. I hereby come against every Prince of Persia that wants to hinder my prayer, I arrest you by the power in the blood of Jesus Christ, and I bind you and cast you down into the pit of hell.

I come against principalities and powers that wrestle with me and my prayers, I arrest you today by the power in the name of Jesus Christ, and I bind you and cast down into the pit of hell. I come against the rulers of the darkness of this world, against spiritual wickedness in high places, I arrest you all by the power in the name of Jesus Christ, and I bind you and cast you down into the pit of hell. I come against weakness and weariness, I arrest you today by the power in the name of Jesus Christ, and I bind you and cast you out of my life. I come against wondering spirit and distractions, I arrest you today by the power in the name of Jesus Christ, and I bind you and cast you out of my life.

Today I receive the anointing to pray and get results, my prayers cannot be hindered nor delayed because Jesus is my Lord, I will pray today and get the desired results, I decree open heavens upon my prayers. I baptize myself in the fire of the Holy Ghost; therefore I have become too hot for the enemy to handle. My prayers today will attract divine intervention to every situation in my life; signs and wonders will follow my prayers today, testimonies will follow my prayers today and the name of God alone will be glorified, in Jesus name. Amen!

PRAYER POINTS:

1. O God my Father, thank you for being my God, my Father and my friend.
2. O God my Father, thank you for the privilege to know you and the power of the resurrection of Jesus Christ.
3. O God my Father, thank you for always being there for me and with me.
4. O God my Father, thank you for the great and mighty things that you are doing in my life.
5. O God my Father, thank you for your provision and protection over me and my household.
6. O God my Father, thank you for always answering my prayers.
7. I confess my sins before you today and I ask you to forgive me on the basis of your mercy, in the name of Jesus Christ.
8. Wash me clean today O Lord by the blood of Jesus Christ.
9. I cover myself and my household with the blood of Jesus Christ.

10. My prayers today will not go in vain; my prayers will produce the desired results in the name of Jesus Christ.
11. O God my Father, I commit this journey into your able hand, keep me safe wherever I go in the name of Jesus Christ.
12. As I go on this journey, I cover myself with the blood of Jesus Christ.
13. As I go on this journey, I cover the road with the blood of Jesus Christ.
14. As I go on this journey, I cover the vehicle with the blood of Jesus Christ.
15. As I go on this journey, I reject any form of car malfunction or break-down, in the name of Jesus Christ.
16. Lord Jesus, I ask you to be the driver of the vehicle that I will use on this trip in the name of Jesus Christ.
17. As I go on this journey, I cover the air around with the blood of Jesus Christ.
18. As I go on this journey, I cover the aircraft with the blood of Jesus Christ.
19. I cover every part of the aircraft with the blood of Jesus Christ.
20. I reject any form of aircraft malfunction or break-down, in the name of Jesus Christ.
21. Lord Jesus, I ask you to be the pilot of this aircraft, in the name of Jesus Christ.
22. O God my Father, I commit my life into your able hands in the name of Jesus Christ.
23. O God my Father, let the Angel of the Lord go before me to make my way prosperous, in the name of Jesus Christ.
24. No weapon of the enemy fashioned against me shall prosper, in the name of Jesus Christ.

25. No weapon of the enemy fashioned against this trip shall prosper, in the name of Jesus Christ.
26. No weapon of the enemy fashioned against the purpose of this trip shall prosper, in the name of Jesus Christ.
27. By the power in the name of Jesus Christ, I cover all other passengers with the blood of Jesus Christ.
28. I paralyze, arrest and chain every demon of accident positioned to attack my journey by the power in the blood of Jesus Christ.
29. I cripple, arrest and bind every force assigned to the sea, air and road to cause accident in this period by the blood of Jesus Christ.
30. Though the road is full of death traps, I shall arrive at my destination safely in the name of Jesus Christ.
31. I arrest and bind all blood sucking demons assigned against this trip in the name of Jesus Christ.
32. I arrest and bind all blood sucking demons that will come across my path on this trip, in the name of Jesus Christ.
33. I arrest and bind all marine spirits assigned against this trip in the name of Jesus Christ.
34. I arrest and bind all marine spirits that will come across my path on this trip in the name of Jesus Christ.
35. I arrest and bind all accident causing demons on the highways, in the name of Jesus Christ.
36. I arrest and bind all accident causing demons in the air, in the name of Jesus Christ.
37. By the power in the name of Jesus Christ, I decree an accident free journey, in the name of Jesus Christ.
38. By the power in the name of Jesus Christ, I decree a problem free journey, in the name of Jesus Christ.

39. I decree that any co-passenger that has been condemned to die is delivered today for my sake, in the name of Jesus Christ.
40. I decree that any co-passenger that has been targeted for death is delivered today for my sake, in the name of Jesus Christ.
41. I release the blood of Jesus against powers assigned to cause delay on this journey, in the name of Jesus Christ.
42. Any power anywhere mandated by satan and his cohorts to trouble me and my fellow passengers, be destroyed by the fire of God before we begin this journey, in the name of Jesus Christ.
43. I command every bullet fired into the road, air and sea to hit me on this journey, to backfire in the name of Jesus Christ.
44. You spirit of fear released to fulfill the plans of my enemies on this journey, I bind and cast you into the pit of hell in the name of Jesus Christ.
45. By the grace and mercy of God, I shall not enter any plane, ship or car marked out for an accident, in the name of Jesus Christ.
46. Every sentence passed upon any passenger that is on this flight with me is revoked and nullified by the blood of Jesus Christ.
47. Every sentence passed upon any passenger that is in this car with me is revoked and nullified by the blood of Jesus Christ.
48. Every sentence passed upon any passenger that is on this ship with me is revoked and nullified by the blood of Jesus Christ.
49. I decree that this journey shall be a peaceful and fruitful one in the name of Jesus Christ.

50. I declare that I shall arrive and return safely to meet all that I left behind, in the name of Jesus Christ

PRAY BEFORE YOU PAY YOUR TITHE

Passages To Read Before You Pray:
Malachi 3:8-12, Deuteronomy 28:1-14, Joel 2:21-27, Psalms 1

I have come today to fellowship with my heavenly Father, and make my requests and needs known unto Him. I cannot be hindered nor delayed because I know who I am in the Lord. I am a child of the Kingdom, born of the Spirit, redeemed by the blood of Jesus Christ. I walk in authority, living life without any apology because the power and authority has been given to me according to the Word of God in the book of Luke 9:1.

As I have come to pray today and to fellowship with my heavenly Father, I cover myself in the blood of Jesus Christ, and I put on the whole armor of God. I hereby come against every Prince of Persia that wants to hinder my prayer, I arrest you by the power in the blood of Jesus Christ, and I bind you and cast you down into the pit of hell.

I come against principalities and powers that wrestle with me and my prayers, I arrest you today by the power in the name of Jesus Christ, and I bind you and cast down into the pit of hell. I come against the rulers of the darkness of this world, against spiritual wickedness in high places, I arrest you all by the power in the name of Jesus Christ, and I bind you and cast you down into the pit of hell. I come against weakness and weariness, I arrest you today by the power in the name of Jesus Christ, and I bind you and cast you out of my life. I come against wondering spirit and distractions, I arrest you today by the power in the name of Jesus Christ, and I bind you and cast you out of my life.

Today I receive the anointing to pray and get results, my prayers cannot be hindered nor delayed because Jesus is my Lord, I will pray today and get the desired results, I decree open heavens upon my prayers. I baptize myself in the fire of the Holy Ghost; therefore I have become too hot for the enemy to handle. My prayers today will attract divine intervention to every situation in my life; signs and wonders will follow my prayers today, testimonies will follow my prayers today and the name of God alone will be glorified, in Jesus name. Amen!

PRAYER POINTS:

1. O God my Father, thank you for being my God, my Father and my friend.
2. O God my Father, thank you for the privilege to know you and the power of the resurrection of Jesus Christ.
3. O God my Father, thank you for always being there for me and with me.
4. O God my Father, thank you for the great and mighty things that you are doing in my life.
5. O God my Father, thank you for your provision and protection over me and my household.
6. O God my Father, thank you for always answering my prayers.
7. I confess my sins before you today and I ask you to forgive me on the basis of your mercy, in the name of Jesus Christ.
8. Wash me clean today O Lord by the blood of Jesus Christ.
9. I cover myself and my household with the blood of Jesus Christ.

10. My prayers today will not go in vain; my prayers will produce the desired results in the name of Jesus Christ.
11. O God my Father, thank you for giving me a job/business from where I earn my income.
12. O God my Father, you gave me the opportunity to work, I recognize and worship you with this tithe as the source of all my income.
13. O God my Father, you gave me good health to work, I recognize and worship you with this tithe as the source of all my income.
14. O God my Father, you gave me the brain, wisdom and strength to work, I recognize and worship you with this tithe as the source of all my income.
15. Take this tithe O Lord as a symbol of my obedience to your commandments, in the name of Jesus Christ.
16. Take this tithe O Lord as a symbol of my submission to your divine omnipotence, in the name of Jesus Christ.
17. As Abraham paid tithe to Melchizedek, the high priest; Lord Jesus, I pay this tithe to your Priesthood today, in the name of Jesus Christ.
18. I do not give this tithe to my pastor or any mortal man, Lord Jesus, you are my High Priest.
19. Accept my tithe today O Lord and grant not the source of my income to run dry, in the name of Jesus Christ.
20. By this tithe, I hereby acknowledge that you are the possessor of heaven and earth, and things that dwell therein.
21. O God my Father, open the windows of heaven and release super-abundance into my life as you promised in your Word, in the name of Jesus Christ.

22. O God my Father, open the windows of heaven and release surplus into my finances, in the name of Jesus Christ.
23. O God my Father, open the windows of heaven and release breakthroughs into my business, in the name of Jesus Christ.
24. O God my Father, open the windows of heaven and let my miracles be released today in the name of Jesus Christ.
25. O God my Father, open the windows of heaven and grant me success in all my endeavors in the name of Jesus Christ.
26. O God my Father, open the windows of heaven and release so much blessings into my life that I will not have enough room to take it all, in the name of Jesus Christ.
27. O God my Father, arise and rebuke the devourer in every area of my life in the name of Jesus Christ.
28. O God my Father, arise and rebuke the devourer in my finances in the name of Jesus Christ.
29. O God my Father, arise and rebuke the devourer in my home in the name of Jesus Christ.
30. O God my Father, arise and rebuke the devourer in my business in the name of Jesus Christ.
31. O God arise and rebuke the devourer in my marriage in the name of Jesus Christ.
32. O God my Father, increase my income and reduce my expenses in a miraculous way, in the name of Jesus Christ.
33. O God my Father, block unnecessary spending and wastage in every area of my life, in the name of Jesus Christ.

34. O God my Father, baptize me with your favor and mercy in the name of Jesus Christ.
35. O God my Father, deliver me from any kind of loss and saturate my life with blessings that money cannot buy, in the name of Jesus Christ.
36. O God my Father, deliver me from any kind of loss and saturate my family with blessings that money cannot buy in the name of Jesus Christ.
37. O God my Father, deliver me from any kind of loss and saturate my ministry with blessings money cannot buy in the name of Jesus Christ.
38. O God my Father, deliver me from any kind of loss and saturate my business with blessings money cannot buy in the name of Jesus Christ.
39. O God my Father, I am a tither, let no man say they made me rich, in the name of Jesus Christ.
40. O God my Father, make me rich in every area as you did to your servant Abraham, in the name of Jesus Christ.

THIS IS NOT JUST ANOTHER DAY

Passages To Read Before You Pray:
1 Samuel 3:11, Isaiah 28:11, 29:14, Matthew 21:42, Psalms 118, 19, 78, 29, 126

I have come today to fellowship with my heavenly Father, and make my requests and needs known unto Him. I cannot be hindered nor delayed because I know who I am in the Lord. I am a child of the Kingdom, born of the Spirit, redeemed by the blood of Jesus Christ. I walk in authority, living life without any apology because the power and authority has been given to me according to the Word of God in the book of Luke 9:1.

As I have come to pray today and to fellowship with my heavenly Father, I cover myself in the blood of Jesus Christ, and I put on the whole armor of God. I hereby come against every Prince of Persia that wants to hinder my prayer, I arrest you by the power in the blood of Jesus Christ, and I bind you and cast you down into the pit of hell.

I come against principalities and powers that wrestle with me and my prayers, I arrest you today by the power in the name of Jesus Christ, and I bind you and cast down into the pit of hell. I come against the rulers of the darkness of this world, against spiritual wickedness in high places, I arrest you all by the power in the name of Jesus Christ, and I bind you and cast you down into the pit of hell. I come against weakness and weariness, I arrest you today by the power in the name of Jesus Christ, and I bind you and cast you out of my life. I come against wondering

spirit and distractions, I arrest you today by the power in the name of Jesus Christ, and I bind you and cast you out of my life.

Today I receive the anointing to pray and get results, my prayers cannot be hindered nor delayed because Jesus is my Lord, I will pray today and get the desired results, I decree open heavens upon my prayers. I baptize myself in the fire of the Holy Ghost; therefore I have become too hot for the enemy to handle. My prayers today will attract divine intervention to every situation in my life; signs and wonders will follow my prayers today, testimonies will follow my prayers today and the name of God alone will be glorified, in Jesus name. Amen!

PRAYER POINTS:

1. O God my Father, thank you for being my God, my Father and my friend.
2. O God my Father, thank you for the privilege to know you and the power of the resurrection of Jesus Christ.
3. O God my Father, thank you for always being there for me and with me.
4. O God my Father, thank you for the great and mighty things that you are doing in my life.
5. O God my Father, thank you for your provision and protection over me and my household.
6. O God my Father, thank you for always answering my prayers.
7. I confess my sins before you today and I ask you to forgive me on the basis of your mercy, in the name of Jesus Christ.
8. Wash me clean today O Lord by the blood of Jesus Christ.

9. I cover myself and my household with the blood of Jesus Christ.
10. My prayers today will not go in vain; my prayers will produce the desired results in the name of Jesus Christ.
11. This is not just another day, this is the day that you will bless me as promised, in the name of Jesus Christ.
12. This is not just another day, this is the day that you will promote me to another level in the name of Jesus Christ.
13. This is not just another day; this is the day for my miracles, in the name of Jesus Christ.
14. This is not just another day; this is the day for my testimonies, in the name of Jesus Christ.
15. This is not just another day; this is my day, the day for total deliverance in every area of my life in the name of Jesus Christ.
16. This is not just another day; this is the day for open heavens in every area of my life in the name of Jesus Christ.
17. This is not just another day, today there will be a release of abundance into every area of my life, in the name of Jesus Christ.
18. This is not just another day, today there will be a release of abundance into my business in the name of Jesus Christ.
19. This is not just another day, today there will be a release of abundance into my finances in the name of Jesus Christ.
20. This is not just another day, today there will be a release of heavenly blessings into my life in the name of Jesus Christ.

21. This is not just another day, today there will be a release of heavenly blessings into my home in the name of Jesus Christ.
22. This is not just another day, today there will be a release of heavenly blessings into my marriage in the name of Jesus Christ.
23. This is not just another day; this is my day, the day for supernatural breakthroughs in my life in the name of Jesus Christ.
24. This is not just another day; this is my day, the day for great achievements in every area of my life in the name of Jesus Christ.
25. This is not just another day, this is my day, the day that God has chosen to lift me up in the name of Jesus Christ.
26. This is not just another day, this is my day, the day that God has chosen to manifest His glory in every area of my life in the name of Jesus Christ.
27. This is not just another day, this is my day, the day that God has chosen to give me reasons to celebrate in the name of Jesus Christ.
28. This is not just another day, this is my day, the day that God has chosen to make me happy and given me joy in the name of Jesus Christ.
29. This is not just another day, this is my day, the day of Passover from slavery into total freedom in the name of Jesus Christ.
30. This is not just another day, this is my day, the day of Passover from poverty into prosperity in the name of Jesus Christ.
31. This is not just another day, this is my day, the day of Passover from trials into testimonies in the name of Jesus Christ.

32. This is not just another day, this is my day, the day that God has chosen to put an end to warfare in my life in the name of Jesus Christ.
33. This is not just another day, this is my day, the day that God has chosen to put an end to every trouble in my life in the name of Jesus Christ.
34. This is not just another day, this is my day, the day that God has chosen to put an end to frustration in my life in the name of Jesus Christ.
35. This is not just another day; this is my day, the day that God has chosen to advertise Himself in every area of my life in the name of Jesus Christ.
36. This is not just another day, this is my day, the day that my life will begin to reflect the glory of God in the name of Jesus Christ.
37. This is not just another day, this is my day, the day that God has chosen to provide solution to every situation in my life in the name of Jesus Christ.
38. This is not just another day, this is my day, the day that God will answer my prayers as He did in the days of Elijah in the name of Jesus Christ.
39. This is not just another day, this is my day, the day that my helpers will begin to locate me in the name of Jesus Christ.
40. This is not just another day, this is the day of my revelation in the name of Jesus Christ.
41. This is not just another day, this is my day, the day that God has chosen to open unto me His good treasures, in the name of Jesus Christ.
42. This is not just another day, this is my day, the day that God has chosen to release unto me the hidden riches of darkness in the name of Jesus Christ.

43. This is not just another day, this is the day that I will begin to enjoy the goodness of the Lord in the land of living in the name of Jesus Christ.
44. This is not just another day, this is the day that my harvest begins in the name of Jesus Christ.
45. This is not just another day, this is my day, the day that God has chosen to move me from glory to glory in the name of Jesus Christ.
46. This is not just another day; this is my day, the day that all things begin to work together for my good in the name of Jesus Christ.
47. This is not just another day; this is my day, the day that my friends and enemies begin to work together for my success in the name of Jesus Christ.
48. This is not just another day; this is my day, the day that my friends and enemies begin to work together for my promotion in the name of Jesus Christ.
49. This is not just another day; this is my day, the day that my friends and enemies begin to work together for my breakthrough in the name of Jesus Christ.
50. This is not just another day, this is my day, the day that God has chosen to give me rest in every area of my life in the name of Jesus Christ.
51. This is not just another day, this is my day, the day that God has chosen to take me from the valley of despair and place me on the mountain of testimonies in the name of Jesus Christ.
52. This is not just another day, this is my day, the day that God has chosen to open new doors of opportunity unto me in the name of Jesus Christ.

53. This is not just another day, this is my day, the day that God has chosen to release increase into my life in the name of Jesus Christ.
54. This is not just another day, this is my day, the day that God has chosen to release increase into my finances in the name of Jesus Christ.
55. This is not just another day, this is my day, the day that I will begin to receive uncommon favor from God and man in the name of Jesus Christ.
56. This is not just another day; this is day, the day that the season of celebration begins in every area of my life in the name of Jesus Christ.

PRAYER WHEN IN A SERIOUS COURT CASE

Passages To Read Before You Pray:
Isaiah 54:15, Isaiah 50:7-9, Isaiah 49:23, Romans 8:31-34,
Proverbs 21:1, Psalms 62, 46, 35

I have come today to fellowship with my heavenly Father, and make my requests and needs known unto Him. I cannot be hindered nor delayed because I know who I am in the Lord. I am a child of the Kingdom, born of the Spirit, redeemed by the blood of Jesus Christ. I walk in authority, living life without any apology because the power and authority has been given to me according to the Word of God in the book of Luke 9:1.

As I have come to pray today and to fellowship with my heavenly Father, I cover myself in the blood of Jesus Christ, and I put on the whole armor of God. I hereby come against every Prince of Persia that wants to hinder my prayer, I arrest you by the power in the blood of Jesus Christ, and I bind you and cast you down into the pit of hell.

I come against principalities and powers that wrestle with me and my prayers, I arrest you today by the power in the name of Jesus Christ, and I bind you and cast down into the pit of hell. I come against the rulers of the darkness of this world, against spiritual wickedness in high places, I arrest you all by the power in the name of Jesus Christ, and I bind you and cast you down into the pit of hell. I come against weakness and weariness, I arrest you today by the power in the name of Jesus Christ, and I bind you and cast you out of my life. I come against wondering

spirit and distractions, I arrest you today by the power in the name of Jesus Christ, and I bind you and cast you out of my life.

Today I receive the anointing to pray and get results, my prayers cannot be hindered nor delayed because Jesus is my Lord, I will pray today and get the desired results, I decree open heavens upon my prayers. I baptize myself in the fire of the Holy Ghost; therefore I have become too hot for the enemy to handle. My prayers today will attract divine intervention to every situation in my life; signs and wonders will follow my prayers today, testimonies will follow my prayers today and the name of God alone will be glorified, in Jesus name. Amen!

PRAYER POINTS:

1. O God my Father, thank you for being my God, my Father and my friend.
2. O God my Father, thank you for the privilege to know you and the power of the resurrection of Jesus Christ.
3. O God my Father, thank you for always being there for me and with me.
4. O God my Father, thank you for the great and mighty things that you are doing in my life.
5. O God my Father, thank you for your provision and protection over me and my household.
6. O God my Father, thank you for always answering my prayers.
7. I confess my sins before you today and I ask you to forgive me on the basis of your mercy, in the name of Jesus Christ.
8. Wash me clean today O Lord by the blood of Jesus Christ.

9. I cover myself and my household with the blood of Jesus Christ.
10. My prayers today will not go in vain; my prayers will produce the desired results in the name of Jesus Christ.
11. Today O Lord, I repent of any wrong-doing on this matter, I ask you to forgive me and show me mercy in the name of Jesus Christ.
12. On this case O Lord, let your mercy overcome every judgment against me in the name of Jesus Christ.
13. O God my Father, grant me an unusual favor in the sight of the judge assigned to this case, in the name of Jesus Christ.
14. O God my Father, grant me an unusual favor in the sight of the jury working on this case, in the name of Jesus Christ.
15. O God my Father, grant me an unusual favor in the sight of every law-enforcement officer working on this case, in the name of Jesus Christ.
16. O God my Father, grant me an unusual favor in the sight of every person involved in this case, in the name of Jesus Christ.
17. O God my Father, arise and turn this case around to favor me in the name of Jesus Christ.
18. O God my Father, let every decision made by the judge assigned to this case favor me, in the name of Jesus Christ.
19. O God my Father, let any conclusion reached by the jury working on this case favor me.
20. This is a wicked world! Lord, disappoint every plan of my adversaries to cover up the truth in the name of Jesus Christ.

21. O God my Father, arise and disappoint every plan of my adversaries to manipulate the truth concerning this case, in the name of Jesus Christ.
22. O God my Father, grant my lawyers grace and wisdom to paralyze all oppositions in the name of Jesus Christ.
23. Lord Jesus, you are my advocate, arise and work through my lawyers to turn this case around to my favor, in the name of Jesus Christ.
24. O God my Father let my adversaries make mistakes that will promote my case in the name of Jesus Christ.
25. O God my Father let my adversaries make mistakes that will bring me victory concerning this case in the name of Jesus Christ.
26. O God my Father let my adversaries make mistakes that will lead to my freedom in the name of Jesus Christ.
27. I release confusion into the camp of my adversaries during this case in the name of Jesus Christ.
28. Today I decree, no matter how smart my adversaries are, their evidence against me shall not hold in court in the name of Jesus Christ.
29. O God my Father, let all testimonies from the camp of my adversaries against me cause them to lose this case in the name of Jesus Christ.
30. I return to sender, arrow of disgrace that is targeted at me through this case in the name of Jesus Christ.
31. I return to sender, arrow of losses that is targeted at me through this case in the name of Jesus Christ.
32. I return to sender, arrow of dishonor that is targeted at me through this case in the name of Jesus Christ.
33. O God my Father, promote my life through this court battle in the name of Jesus Christ.

34. O God my Father, by your grace and mercy, I must win this court battle in the name of Jesus Christ.
35. I stand on the promise of God and I claim my deliverance now, in the name of Jesus Christ.
36. I withdraw this case from the hands of the enemy in the name of Jesus Christ.
37. By the authority in the name of Jesus Christ, I command the replacement of any evil judge assigned to this case, in the name of Jesus Christ.
38. By the authority in the name of Jesus Christ, I decree the replacement of every satanic agent among the jury working on this case, in the name of Jesus Christ.
39. By the authority in the name of Jesus Christ. I decree the replacement of any satanic agent among the law enforcement officers working on this case, in the name of Jesus Christ.
40. O God my Father, this case is too big for me, take it and fight for me as you fought Haman on behalf on the Jews, in the name of Jesus Christ.
41. O God my Father, let the expectation of my enemies on this case be disappointed, in the name of Jesus Christ.
42. O God my Father, let there be confusion of tongues in the camp of my adversaries, in the name of Jesus Christ.
43. O God my Father, let there be a great misunderstanding in the camp of my adversaries which will lead to my victory on this case, in the name of Jesus Christ.
44. Lord Jesus, you are the greatest lawyer, come and represent me on this case in the name of Jesus Christ.
45. Lord Jesus, you are the greatest lawyer, come and speak on my behalf in the name of Jesus Christ.
46. Lord Jesus, you are the greatest lawyer, fight for me and give me the victory in the name of Jesus Christ.

47. O God my Father, you are the righteous Judge, arise today and grant me victory in the name of Jesus Christ.
48. Today O Lord, clothe me with the garment of favor in the name of Jesus Christ.
49. I will walk out of the courtroom today victorious in the name of Jesus Christ.
50. I will walk out of the courtroom today with a song of thanksgiving, in the name of Jesus Christ.

PRAYER FOR THE BAPTISM OF FIRE

Passages To Read Before You Pray:
Acts. 1:4-8, 2:1-47, John 20:19-23, Psalms 19, 29, 42, Hebrews 12:29

I have come today to fellowship with my heavenly Father, and make my requests and needs known unto Him. I cannot be hindered nor delayed because I know who I am in the Lord. I am a child of the Kingdom, born of the Spirit, redeemed by the blood of Jesus Christ. I walk in authority, living life without any apology because the power and authority has been given to me according to the Word of God in the book of Luke 9:1.

As I have come to pray today and to fellowship with my heavenly Father, I cover myself in the blood of Jesus Christ, and I put on the whole armor of God. I hereby come against every Prince of Persia that wants to hinder my prayer, I arrest you by the power in the blood of Jesus Christ, and I bind you and cast you down into the pit of hell.

I come against principalities and powers that wrestle with me and my prayers, I arrest you today by the power in the name of Jesus Christ, and I bind you and cast down into the pit of hell. I come against the rulers of the darkness of this world, against spiritual wickedness in high places, I arrest you all by the power in the name of Jesus Christ, and I bind you and cast you down into the pit of hell. I come against weakness and weariness, I arrest you today by the power in the name of Jesus Christ, and I bind you and cast you out of my life. I come against wondering

spirit and distractions, I arrest you today by the power in the name of Jesus Christ, and I bind you and cast you out of my life.

Today I receive the anointing to pray and get results, my prayers cannot be hindered nor delayed because Jesus is my Lord, I will pray today and get the desired results, I decree open heavens upon my prayers. I baptize myself in the fire of the Holy Ghost; therefore I have become too hot for the enemy to handle. My prayers today will attract divine intervention to every situation in my life; signs and wonders will follow my prayers today, testimonies will follow my prayers today and the name of God alone will be glorified, in Jesus name. Amen!

PRAYER POINTS:

1. O God my Father, thank you for being my God, my Father and my friend.
2. O God my Father, thank you for the privilege to know you and the power of the resurrection of Jesus Christ.
3. O God my Father, thank you for always being there for me and with me.
4. O God my Father, thank you for the great and mighty things that you are doing in my life.
5. O God my Father, thank you for your provision and protection over me and my household.
6. O God my Father, thank you for always answering my prayers.
7. I confess my sins before you today and I ask you to forgive me on the basis of your mercy, in the name of Jesus Christ.
8. Wash me clean today O Lord by the blood of Jesus Christ.

9. I cover myself and my household with the blood of Jesus Christ.
10. My prayers today will not go in vain; my prayers will produce the desired results in the name of Jesus Christ.
11. Today O Lord, baptize me in the Holy Ghost in the name of Jesus Christ.
12. Anything in my life that will hinder me from receiving the baptism of the Holy Spirit, Father Lord, let it be destroyed today by the fire of God in the name of Jesus Christ.
13. I receive fresh fire of the Holy Spirit today; I will never be the same again in the name of Jesus Christ.
14. O God my Father let the fire of the Holy Spirit destroy the works of flesh manifesting in my life, in the name of Jesus Christ.
15. O God my Father, let the fire of the Holy Spirit consume all sinful desires in my heart and give me a new heart, in the name of Jesus Christ.
16. O God my Father let the fire of the Holy Spirit purify my life so that I may live a holy life in the name of Jesus Christ.
17. O God my Father let the fire of the Holy Spirit destroy the lust of the eyes manifesting in my life in the name of Jesus Christ.
18. O God my Father let the fire of the Holy Spirit destroy the lust of the flesh manifesting in my life in the name of Jesus Christ.
19. O God my Father let the fire of the Holy Spirit destroy the pride of life manifesting in my life in the name of Jesus Christ.

20. O God my Father, let the power of the Holy Ghost be released upon me today as promised in your Word, in the name of Jesus Christ.
21. O God my Father let the fresh anointing of the Holy Spirit be released upon me today in the name of Jesus Christ.
22. O God my Father let the anointing to function as a child of the Kingdom be released upon me today in the name of Jesus Christ.
23. O God my Father, let the anointing to heal the sick be released upon me today in the name of Jesus Christ.
24. O God my Father, let the anointing to cast out devils be released upon me today in the name of Jesus Christ.
25. O God my Father let the anointing to bind and to loose be released upon me today in the name of Jesus Christ.
26. O God my Father, let the anointing to destroy the works of the devil be released upon me today in the name of Jesus Christ.
27. O God my Father, let the anointing for signs and wonders be released upon me today in the name of Jesus Christ.
28. Today I shall experience the power of the Holy Spirit like on the day of Pentecost, in the name of Jesus Christ.
29. O God my Father let the mighty wind of the Holy Spirit encamp me around in the name of Jesus Christ.
30. O God my Father, fill me with the Holy Ghost in the name of Jesus Christ.
31. O God my Father, let your Holy Spirit give me a new revelation today in the name of Jesus Christ.
32. O God my Father, fill me with the Holy Spirit and let my fear go away forever in the name of Jesus Christ.

33. O God my Father, empower me with the Holy Spirit to confront and overcome my fears in the name of Jesus Christ.
34. O God my Father, empower me with the Holy Spirit to do great exploits in the name of Jesus Christ.
35. O God my Father, empower me with the Holy Spirit to succeed in the ministry in which you have called me in the name of Jesus Christ.
36. O God my Father, empower me with the Holy Spirit to lead the unsaved to the Kingdom of God in the name of Jesus Christ.
37. O God my Father, empower me with the Holy Spirit to fulfill my purpose as the light of the world in the name of Jesus Christ.
38. O God my Father, empower me with the Holy Spirit to fulfill my purpose as the salt of the earth in the name of Jesus Christ.
39. O God my Father, empower me with the Holy Spirit so that my life can be a wonderful epistle for the whole world to read, in the name of Jesus Christ.
40. O God my Father, empower me with the Holy Spirit so that I may do your will alone, in the name of Jesus Christ.
41. O God my Father, empower me with the Holy Spirit to overcome my weaknesses in every area of my life in the name of Jesus Christ.
42. O God my Father, empower me with the Holy Spirit so that I can become what you want me to be in the name of Jesus Christ.
43. O God my Father, baptize me in your fire in the name of Jesus Christ.

44. O God my Father, baptize me in your power in the name of Jesus Christ.
45. O God my Father, baptize me in your Shekinah glory in the name of Jesus Christ.
46. O God my Father, baptize me in your presence in the name of the Jesus Christ.
47. O God my Father, give me the grace to experience your presence today and forever in the name of Jesus Christ.
48. As I enter into your presence today O Lord, my heart will be filled with joy in the name of Jesus Christ.
49. As I enter into your presence today O Lord, I will never be same again in the name of Jesus Christ.
50. As I enter into your presence today O Lord, I will receive my miracles in the name of Jesus Christ.
51. As I enter into your presence today O Lord, there will be transformation in every area of my life in the name of Jesus Christ.
52. As I enter into your presence today O Lord, I receive fresh anointing in the name of Jesus Christ.
53. As I enter into your presence today O Lord, my mind will be renewed in the name of Jesus Christ.
54. As I enter into your presence today O Lord, my situation must change for the better in the name of Jesus Christ.
55. As I enter into your presence today O Lord, I must have every reason to testify to your goodness and mercy in the name of Jesus Christ.

PRAYER FOR BUSINESS EXPANSION/PROSPERITY

Passages To Read Before You Pray:
Philippians 4:19, Deuteronomy 8:18, Malachi 3:10, Psalms 1, 23, 115

I have come today to fellowship with my heavenly Father, and make my requests and needs known unto Him. I cannot be hindered nor delayed because I know who I am in the Lord. I am a child of the Kingdom, born of the Spirit, redeemed by the blood of Jesus Christ. I walk in authority, living life without any apology because the power and authority has been given to me according to the Word of God in the book of Luke 9:1.

As I have come to pray today and to fellowship with my heavenly Father, I cover myself in the blood of Jesus Christ, and I put on the whole armor of God. I hereby come against every Prince of Persia that wants to hinder my prayer, I arrest you by the power in the blood of Jesus Christ, and I bind you and cast you down into the pit of hell.

I come against principalities and powers that wrestle with me and my prayers, I arrest you today by the power in the name of Jesus Christ, and I bind you and cast down into the pit of hell. I come against the rulers of the darkness of this world, against spiritual wickedness in high places, I arrest you all by the power in the name of Jesus Christ, and I bind you and cast you down into the pit of hell. I come against weakness and weariness, I arrest you today by the power in the name of Jesus Christ, and I bind you and cast you out of my life. I come against wondering

spirit and distractions, I arrest you today by the power in the name of Jesus Christ, and I bind you and cast you out of my life.

Today I receive the anointing to pray and get results, my prayers cannot be hindered nor delayed because Jesus is my Lord, I will pray today and get the desired results, I decree open heavens upon my prayers. I baptize myself in the fire of the Holy Ghost; therefore I have become too hot for the enemy to handle. My prayers today will attract divine intervention to every situation in my life; signs and wonders will follow my prayers today, testimonies will follow my prayers today and the name of God alone will be glorified, in Jesus name. Amen!

PRAYER POINTS:

1. O God my Father, thank you for being my God, my Father and my friend.
2. O God my Father, thank you for the privilege to know you and the power of the resurrection of Jesus Christ.
3. O God my Father, thank you for always being there for me and with me.
4. O God my Father, thank you for the great and mighty things that you are doing in my life.
5. O God my Father, thank you for your provision and protection over me and my household.
6. O God my Father, thank you for always answering my prayers.
7. I confess my sins before you today and I ask you to forgive me on the basis of your mercy, in the name of Jesus Christ.
8. Wash me clean today O Lord by the blood of Jesus Christ.

9. I cover myself and my household with the blood of Jesus Christ.
10. My prayers today will not go in vain; my prayers will produce the desired results in the name of Jesus Christ.
11. O God my Father, it is your will that I prosper and succeed in life, arise today and promote my business in the name of Jesus Christ.
12. O God my Father, it is your will that I prosper and succeed in life, arise today and prosper the works of my hands in the name of Jesus Christ.
13. O God my Father, dispatch the angels of heaven to go from the highway to the sideway to market my business/products in the name of Jesus Christ.
14. O God my Father, dispatch the angels of heaven to go forth and bring me customers/clients in the name of Jesus Christ.
15. I am a giver and a tither; therefore, I rebuke every devourer in my life in the name of Jesus Christ.
16. I am a giver and a tither; therefore, I rebuke every devourer in my finances in the name of Jesus Christ.
17. I am a giver and a tither; therefore, I rebuke every devourer in my business in the name of Jesus Christ.
18. You spirit of laziness, I reject you and cast you out of my life, in the name of Jesus Christ.
19. Every spirit of stagnancy, I reject you and cast you out of my business, in the name of Jesus Christ.
20. Satan, I command you to remove your hands from my finances now, in the name of Jesus Christ.
21. I command money from the North, South, East and West to be released into my business now, in the name of Jesus Christ.

22. O God my Father, let the funds that I need to expand my business begin to come now, in the name of Jesus Christ.
23. O God my Father, grant me wisdom to know what business to do in the name of Jesus Christ.
24. O God my Father, grant me wisdom to know which sales to pursue or let go, in the name of Jesus Christ.
25. O God my Father, give me a discerning spirit to know which contract to pursue or let go, in the name of Jesus Christ.
26. O God my Father, cause and help all my debtors to pay back what they owe me, in the name of Jesus Christ.
27. O God my Father, increase my debtors' income and make provisions for them to meet their financial obligations, in the name of Jesus Christ.
28. O God my Father, withdraw the peace of the debtors that have the money but refuse to pay what they owe me, in the name of Jesus Christ.
29. My debtors will not rest until they pay all that they owe me, in the name of Jesus Christ.
30. O God my Father, open new door of opportunities for my business today in the name of Jesus Christ.
31. O God my Father, provide new markets for my business this week, in the name of Jesus Christ.
32. I decree that this week I will experience an unusual breakthrough that I have never seen before in my business, in the name of Jesus Christ.
33. Today O Lord, I bind and command the spirit of the tail to get out of my life, in the name of Jesus Christ.
34. Today O Lord, I claim big business and I command small business to become history in my life now, in the name of Jesus Christ.

35. I refuse to wear the garment of debt, in the name of Jesus Christ.
36. O God my Father, arise and deliver me from the bondage of debt and credit, in the name of Jesus Christ.
37. Today I decree that my business shall not fail because the Lord is the marketer, in the name of Jesus Christ.
38. Today I decree that my business shall not fail because I have made the Lord my business partner, in the name of Jesus Christ.
39. Today I decree that my business shall not fail because the Lord is my banker, in the name of Jesus Christ.
40. Today I decree that my business shall not fail because the Lord is the source of provision for me, in the name of Jesus Christ.
41. I hereby decree expansion into my business in the name of Jesus Christ.
42. My business shall expand to the North, to the South, to the East and to the West, in the name of Jesus Christ.
43. Today I decree that my business shall be big enough to become a source of strength to other businesses, in the name of Jesus Christ.
44. My business is planted by the side of the rivers of water which will never lack nourishment, in the name of Jesus Christ.
45. By the power in the name of Jesus Christ, I decree that my business shall flourish, in the name of Jesus Christ.
46. Every evil eye monitoring my business and finances, be destroyed by the fire of God, in the name of Jesus Christ.
47. Territorial spirit and power operating in my business location, I arrest you today, I bind and cast you out permanently, you are no longer welcomed in this location, in the name of Jesus Christ.

48. O God my Father, let every evil power driving away customers from my business be neutralized by your fire, in the name of Jesus Christ.
49. O God my Father, let every spiritual problem or trouble due to envy of my competitors come to an end now, in the name of Jesus Christ.
50. O God my Father, deliver me from financial mistakes in the name of Jesus Christ.
51. O God my Father, deliver me from business mistakes in the name of Jesus Christ.
52. O God my Father, make me a financial pillar in your house, in the name of Jesus Christ.
53. I command every strange money affecting my business to be neutralized now, in the name of Jesus Christ.
54. I command all unsold items to be sold this week, in the name of Jesus Christ.
55. I command unapproved contracts to be approved this week in the name of Jesus Christ.
56. O God my Father, let there be open heaven upon my business today in the name of Jesus Christ.
57. O God my Father, let the former and the latter rain be released upon my business now, in the name of Jesus Christ.
58. O God my Father, let my business prosper in the name of Jesus Christ.
59. O God my Father, let my business bring me joy and satisfaction, in the name of Jesus Christ.
60. O God my Father, bless and enlarge my business that I may leave a good inheritance for my children and my children's children according to your Word, in the name of Jesus Christ

PRAYER FOR UNCOMMON VICTORY

Passages To Read Before You Pray:
Isaiah 8:9-10, 48:22, 57:21, Genesis 11:1-9, 1 John 3:8,
Revelation 12:11, Psalms 109, 35, 68.

I have come today to fellowship with my heavenly Father, and make my requests and needs known unto Him. I cannot be hindered nor delayed because I know who I am in the Lord. I am a child of the Kingdom, born of the Spirit, redeemed by the blood of Jesus Christ. I walk in authority, living life without any apology because the power and authority has been given to me according to the Word of God in the book of Luke 9:1.

As I have come to pray today and to fellowship with my heavenly Father, I cover myself in the blood of Jesus Christ, and I put on the whole armor of God. I hereby come against every Prince of Persia that wants to hinder my prayer, I arrest you by the power in the blood of Jesus Christ, and I bind you and cast you down into the pit of hell.

I come against principalities and powers that wrestle with me and my prayers, I arrest you today by the power in the name of Jesus Christ, and I bind you and cast down into the pit of hell. I come against the rulers of the darkness of this world, against spiritual wickedness in high places, I arrest you all by the power in the name of Jesus Christ, and I bind you and cast you down into the pit of hell. I come against weakness and weariness, I arrest you today by the power in the name of Jesus Christ, and I bind you and cast you out of my life. I come against wondering

spirit and distractions, I arrest you today by the power in the name of Jesus Christ, and I bind you and cast you out of my life.

Today I receive the anointing to pray and get results, my prayers cannot be hindered nor delayed because Jesus is my Lord, I will pray today and get the desired results, I decree open heavens upon my prayers. I baptize myself in the fire of the Holy Ghost; therefore I have become too hot for the enemy to handle. My prayers today will attract divine intervention to every situation in my life; signs and wonders will follow my prayers today, testimonies will follow my prayers today and the name of God alone will be glorified, in Jesus name. Amen!

PRAYER POINTS:

1. O God my Father, thank you for being my God, my Father and my friend.
2. O God my Father, thank you for the privilege to know you and the power of the resurrection of Jesus Christ.
3. O God my Father, thank you for always being there for me and with me.
4. O God my Father, thank you for the great and mighty things that you are doing in my life.
5. O God my Father, thank you for your provision and protection over me and my household.
6. O God my Father, thank you for always answering my prayers.
7. I confess my sins before you today and I ask you to forgive me on the basis of your mercy, in the name of Jesus Christ.
8. Wash me clean today O Lord by the blood of Jesus Christ.

9. I cover myself and my household with the blood of Jesus Christ.
10. My prayers today will not go in vain; my prayers will produce the desired results in the name of Jesus Christ.
11. Every evil association working against my life, be scattered by the fire of God and never regroup again, in the name of Jesus Christ.
12. Every evil association hired to delay my progress, be scattered by the fire of God and never regroup again, in the name of Jesus Christ.
13. Every evil association hired to make my life miserable, be scattered by the fire of God and never regroup again in the name of Jesus Christ.
14. I command every evil association that is working against my prosperity to be broken in pieces in the name of Jesus Christ.
15. I command evil association that is blocking my miracles to be broken in pieces, in the name of Jesus Christ.
16. Every arrow of failure fired at me, return back to sender in the name of Jesus Christ.
17. Every arrow of untimely death fired at me, return back to sender in the name of Jesus Christ.
18. Every arrow of sickness fired at me, return back to sender in the name of Jesus Christ.
19. Every arrow of demotion fired at me, return back to sender in the name of Jesus Christ.
20. Every arrow of destruction fired at me, return back to sender in the name of Jesus Christ.
21. O God my Father, let the tongue of the enemy of my progress be divided and confused, in the name of Jesus Christ.

22. O God my Father, let the tongue of the enemy of my breakthrough be divided and confused, in the name of Jesus Christ.
23. O God my Father, let the tongue of the enemy of my success be divided and confused, in the name of Jesus Christ.
24. O God my Father, let the tongue of the enemy of my financial freedom be divided and confused, in the name of Jesus Christ.
25. I command the operation of the enemy in every area of my life to scatter by the fire of God, in the name of Jesus Christ.
26. I command the operation of the enemy against my finances to scatter by the fire of God in the name of Jesus Christ.
27. I command the operation of the enemy against my breakthrough to scatter by the fire of God in the name of Jesus Christ.
28. I command the operation of the enemy against my marriage to scatter by the fire of God, in the name of Jesus Christ.
29. I command the operation of the enemy against my business to scatter by the fire of God, in the name of Jesus Christ.
30. I command the operation of the enemy against my destiny to scatter by the fire of God, in the name of Jesus Christ.
31. I bind every evil activity in my environment and I command it to scatter by the fire of God in the name of Jesus Christ.
32. I bind every evil activity in my home and I command it to scatter by the fire of God in the name of Jesus Christ.

33. I bind every evil activity in my place of work and I command it to scatter by the fire of God in the name of Jesus Christ.
34. I bind every evil activity in my neighborhood and I command it to scatter by the fire of God in the name of Jesus Christ.
35. O God my Father, let me experience victory in every area of my life in the name of Jesus Christ.
36. By the power in the name of Jesus Christ, I claim victory today over evil manifestation in every area of my life, in the name of Jesus Christ.
37. By the power in the name of Jesus Christ, I claim victory today over every spiritual battle against my marriage.
38. By the power in the name of Jesus Christ, I claim victory today over every spiritual battle against my destiny.
39. By the power in the name of Jesus Christ, I claim victory today over every spiritual battle against my finances.
40. By the power in the name of Jesus Christ, I claim victory today over every spiritual battle against my dreams.
41. By the power in the name of Jesus Christ, I claim victory today over every spiritual battle against my purpose.
42. O God my Father, let all the enemies of my progress start their days with confusion and end it in destruction, in the name of Jesus Christ.
43. O God my Father, let all the enemies of my breakthrough start their days with confusion and end it in destruction, in the name of Jesus Christ.
44. O God my Father, let all the enemies of my financial freedom start their days with confusion and end it in destruction, in the name of Jesus Christ.

45. O God my Father, let all the enemies of my success start their days with confusion and end it in destruction, in the name of Jesus Christ.
46. O God my Father, let all the enemies of my promotion start their days with confusion and end it in destruction, in the name of Jesus Christ.
47. O God my Father, let all the enemies of my joy start their days with confusion and end it in destruction, in the name of Jesus Christ.
48. O God my Father, let every evil association working against my miracles be severely destabilized, in the name of Jesus Christ.
49. O God my Father, let every evil association working against my breakthrough be severely destabilized, in the name of Jesus Christ.
50. O God my Father, let every evil association working against my family be severely destabilized, in the name of Jesus Christ.
51. O God my Father, let every evil association working against the fulfillment of my dreams be severely destabilized, in the name of Jesus Christ.
52. O God my Father, let every evil association working against my promotion be severely destabilized, in the name of Jesus Christ.
53. O God my Father, let every evil association working against my business or career be severely destabilized, in the name of Jesus Christ.
54. O God my Father, let every evil association working tirelessly in order to put me to shame be severely destabilized, in the name of Jesus Christ.

55. O God my Father, let every evil association working tirelessly to hinder my prayers be severely destabilized, in the name of Jesus Christ.
56. O God my Father, let every evil association working tirelessly to block my success be severely destabilized, in the name of Jesus Christ.
57. O God my Father, let the wickedness of the wicked against my life return upon their own heads, in the name of Jesus Christ.
58. O God my Father, let the wickedness of the wicked against my family return upon their own heads, in the name of Jesus Christ.
59. O God my Father, let the wickedness of the wicked against my marriage return upon their own heads, in the name of Jesus Christ.
60. O God my Father, let the wickedness of the wicked against my finances return upon their own heads, in the name of Jesus Christ.
61. O God my Father, let the wickedness of the wicked against my joy return upon their own heads, in the name of Jesus Christ.
62. O God my Father, let the wickedness of the wicked against my children return upon their own heads, in the name of Jesus Christ.
63. O God my Father, let the wickedness of the wicked against my business return upon their own heads, in the name of Jesus Christ.
64. O God my Father, let the wickedness of the wicked against my breakthrough return upon their own heads, in the name of Jesus Christ.

65. O God my Father, let the wickedness of the wicked against my tomorrow return upon their own heads, in the name of Jesus Christ.
66. O God my Father, let the wickedness of the wicked against my calling return upon their own heads, in the name of Jesus Christ.
67. O God my Father, let the wickedness of the wicked against my helpers return upon their own heads, in the name of Jesus Christ.
68. O God my Father, let the wickedness of the wicked against my success return upon their own heads, in the name of Jesus Christ.
69. O God my Father, let the wickedness of the wicked against my dreams and goals return upon their own heads, in the name of Jesus Christ.
70. O God my Father, let the wickedness of the wicked against my destiny return upon their own heads, in the name of Jesus Christ.

LET YOUR ANGELS LOCATE MY BLESSINGS

Passages To Read Before You Pray:
Daniel 10:10-13, 1 Samuel 5:1-12, Hebrews 12:29, Psalms 3, 9, 59, 69, 86

I have come today to fellowship with my heavenly Father, and make my requests and needs known unto Him. I cannot be hindered nor delayed because I know who I am in the Lord. I am a child of the Kingdom, born of the Spirit, redeemed by the blood of Jesus Christ. I walk in authority, living life without any apology because the power and authority has been given to me according to the Word of God in the book of Luke 9:1.

As I have come to pray today and to fellowship with my heavenly Father, I cover myself in the blood of Jesus Christ, and I put on the whole armor of God. I hereby come against every Prince of Persia that wants to hinder my prayer, I arrest you by the power in the blood of Jesus Christ, and I bind you and cast you down into the pit of hell.

I come against principalities and powers that wrestle with me and my prayers, I arrest you today by the power in the name of Jesus Christ, and I bind you and cast down into the pit of hell. I come against the rulers of the darkness of this world, against spiritual wickedness in high places, I arrest you all by the power in the name of Jesus Christ, and I bind you and cast you down into the pit of hell. I come against weakness and weariness, I arrest you today by the power in the name of Jesus Christ, and I bind you and cast you out of my life. I come against wondering

spirit and distractions, I arrest you today by the power in the name of Jesus Christ, and I bind you and cast you out of my life.

Today I receive the anointing to pray and get results, my prayers cannot be hindered nor delayed because Jesus is my Lord, I will pray today and get the desired results, I decree open heavens upon my prayers. I baptize myself in the fire of the Holy Ghost; therefore I have become too hot for the enemy to handle. My prayers today will attract divine intervention to every situation in my life; signs and wonders will follow my prayers today, testimonies will follow my prayers today and the name of God alone will be glorified, in Jesus name. Amen!

PRAYER POINTS:

1. O God my Father, thank you for being my God, My Father and my friend.
2. O God my Father, thank you for the privilege to know you and the power of the resurrection of Jesus Christ.
3. O God my Father, thank you for always being there for me and with me.
4. O God my Father, thank you for the great and mighty things that you are doing in my life.
5. O God my Father, thank you for your provision and protection over me and my household.
6. O God my Father, thank you for always answering my prayers.
7. I confess my sins before you today and I ask you to forgive me on the basis of your mercy, in the name of Jesus Christ.
8. Wash me clean today O Lord by the blood of Jesus Christ.

9. I cover myself and my household with the blood of Jesus Christ.
10. My prayers today will not go in vain; my prayers will produce the desired results in the name of Jesus Christ.
11. I put on the whole armor of God.
12. By the power in the name of Jesus Christ, I overcome every attack of the enemy by the blood of Jesus Christ.
13. I overcome every spiritual conspiracy against me by the blood of Jesus Christ.
14. I overcome every joint operation of the enemy by the blood of Jesus Christ and I scatter them by the fire of God.
15. I overcome every covert operation of the enemy by the blood of Jesus Christ and I destroy them by the fire of God.
16. I scatter every satanic network working against me by the fire of God, in the name of Jesus Christ.
17. Any power anywhere that lets me see my blessings but will not allow me touch it, be destroyed today by the fire of God.
18. Any power anywhere that lets me see my blessings but will not allow me have it, be destroyed today by the fire of God.
19. Any power anywhere that lets me see my blessings but will not allow me enjoy the, be destroyed today by the fire of God.
20. Any power anywhere that lets me see my miracles but will not allow me touch them, be destroyed today by the fire of God.
21. Any power anywhere that lets me see my miracles but will not allow me have them, be destroyed today by the fire of God.

22. Any power anywhere that lets me see my miracles but not allow me enjoy them, be destroyed today by the fire of God.
23. Any power anywhere that lets me see the answers to prayers but will allow me have them, be destroyed today by the fire of God.
24. Any power anywhere that lets me see the answers to prayers but will not allow me enjoy them, be destroyed today by the fire of God.
25. Today O Lord, let every strategy of the enemy used against me, fail woefully in the name of Jesus Christ.
26. Today O Lord, let every strategy of the enemy used to rob me of my blessings, fail woefully in the name of Jesus Christ.
27. Today O Lord, let every strategy of the enemy used to hinder my prayers, fail woefully in the name of Jesus Christ.
28. Today O Lord, let every strategy of the enemy used to delay my miracles, fail woefully in the name of Jesus Christ.
29. Today O Lord, let every strategy of the enemy used to keep me in the bondage of poverty, fail woefully in the name of Jesus Christ.
30. Today O Lord, let every strategy of the enemy used to keep me in the dark, fail woefully in the name of Jesus Christ.
31. Today O Lord, let every strategy of the enemy used to intercept my breakthrough, fail woefully in the name of Jesus Christ.
32. Today O Lord, let every strategy of the enemy used to rob me of my joy, fail woefully in the name of Jesus Christ.

33. Today O Lord, let every strategy of the enemy used to take away my rest, fail woefully in the name of Jesus Christ.
34. Today O Lord, let every strategy of the enemy used to stop my progress, fail woefully in the name of Jesus Christ.
35. Today O Lord, let every strategy of the enemy used to quench the fire of God in me, fail woefully in the name of Jesus Christ.
36. Today O Lord, let every strategy of the enemy used to take away my rod of prayer, fail woefully in the name of Jesus Christ.
37. Today O Lord, let every strategy of the enemy used to make me work against myself, fail woefully in the name of Jesus Christ.
38. O God my Father, let my caged blessings break forth and come to me now in the name of Jesus Christ.
39. O God my Father, let my blessings in the hands of the enemy become the Ark of the Covenant and trouble them until they release my blessings, in the name of Jesus Christ.
40. O God my Father, arise and send your fire to destroy the camp of the enemy where my blessing is being held, in the name of Jesus Christ.
41. O God my Father, arise and send your fire to destroy the camp of the enemy where my miracle is being caged, in the name of Jesus Christ.
42. O God my Father, arise and send your fire to destroy the camp of the enemy where my breakthrough is being held in the name of Jesus Christ.

43. O God my Father, arise and send your fire to destroy the camp of the enemy where they are working against my finances in the name of Jesus Christ.
44. O God my Father, arise and send your fire to destroy the camp of the enemy where they are working against my progress, in the name of Jesus Christ.
45. O God my Father, arise and send your fire to destroy the headquarters of the enemy of my success, in the name of Jesus Christ.
46. O God my Father, arise and send your fire to destroy the headquarters of the enemy of my breakthrough, in the name of Jesus Christ.
47. O God my Father, arise and send your fire to destroy the headquarters of the enemy of my marriage, in the name of Jesus Christ.
48. O God my Father, arise and send your fire to destroy the headquarters of the enemy that want me to die struggling, in the name of Jesus Christ.
49. O God my Father, arise and send you or fire to destroy the headquarters of the enemy that want me to die poor, in the name of Jesus Christ.
50. O God my Father, dispatch your angels to search the whole earth to locate my blessing and bring it to me in the name of Jesus Christ.
51. O God my Father, dispatch your angels to search the heavens to locate my blessing and bring it to me in the name of Jesus Christ.
52. O God my Father, dispatch your angels to search the kingdom of darkness to locate my blessing and bring it to me in the name of Jesus Christ.

53. O God my Father, dispatch your angels to search the warehouse of the enemy to locate my blessing and bring it to me in the name of Jesus Christ.
54. O God my Father, dispatch your angels to search every satanic storage to locate my blessing and bring it to me in the name of Jesus Christ.
55. O God my Father, dispatch your angels to search the oceanic kingdom of darkness to locate my blessing and bring it to me, in the name of Jesus Christ.
56. O God my Father, dispatch your angels to search the kingdom of hell to locate my blessing and bring it to me, in theme of Jesus Christ.
57. O God my Father, dispatch your angels to search the marine kingdom of darkness to locate my blessing and bring it to me, in the name of Jesus Christ.
58. O God my Father, dispatch your angels to search every area where the enemy buries glory and destiny, to locate my blessing, and bring it to me in the name of Jesus Christ.
59. O God my Father, dispatch your angels to search every area where the enemy changes glory and destiny, to locate my blessing, and bring it to me in the name of Jesus Christ.
60. O God my Father, dispatch your angels to search every area where the enemy destroys people's life, to locate my blessing, and bring it to me in the name of Jesus Christ.
61. O God my Father, dispatch your angels to search the camp of my household wickedness to locate my blessing, and bring it to me in the name of Jesus Christ.
62. O God my Father, dispatch your angels to search the house of the strongman of my father's house to locate my blessing, and bring it to me, in the name of Jesus Christ.

63. O God my Father, dispatch your angels to search the house of the strongman of mother's house to locate my blessing and bring it to me, in the name of Jesus Christ.
64. O God my Father, dispatch your angels to search the house of the strongman of my place of birth to locate my blessing and bring it to me, in the name of Jesus Christ.
65. O God my Father, dispatch your angels to search the house of the strongman in the city where I live to locate my blessing and bring it to me in the name of Jesus Christ.
66. O God my Father, dispatch your angels to locate every satanic contractor working on my case to retrieve my blessing and bring it to me in the name of Jesus Christ.
67. O God my Father, dispatch your angels to locate every satanic contractor working on my case to retrieve my stolen miracle and bring it to me, in the name of Jesus Christ.
68. O God my Father, dispatch your angels to locate every satanic contractor working on my case to retrieve my stolen joy and bring it to me in the name of Jesus Christ.
69. O God my Father, dispatch your angels to locate every satanic contractor working on my case and let my stolen blessings be restored back to me in the name of Jesus Christ.
70. O God my Father, dispatch your angels to locate every satanic contractor working on my case and let stolen breakthrough be restored back to me in the name of Jesus Christ.
71. O God my Father, dispatch your angels to locate every satanic contractor working on my case and let my lost job be restored back to me in the name of Jesus Christ.

72. O God my Father, as from today, in the presence of my enemies I will enjoy the food that you have prepared for me in the name of Jesus Christ.
73. O God my Father, as from today, in the presence of enemies I will enjoy my breakthroughs in the name of Jesus Christ.
74. O God my Father, as from today, in the presence of my enemies I will have success in every area and enjoy it in the name of Jesus Christ.
75. O God my Father, I receive my miracle today with thanksgiving, and I will enjoy every bit of it in the name of Jesus Christ.
76. O God my Father, I receive my blessing today with thanksgiving and I will enjoy every bit of it in the name of Jesus Christ.
77. O God my Father, I receive my financial breakthrough today with thanksgiving, and I will enjoy every bit of it in the name of Jesus Christ.
78. O God my Father, I receive my promotion in every area today with thanksgiving, and I will enjoy every bit of it in the name of Jesus Christ.
79. O God my Father, I receive success in every area today with thanksgiving, and I will enjoy it in the name of Jesus Christ.
80. O God my Father, I receive the answer to my prayers today with thanksgiving, and it shall be permanent in the name of Jesus Christ.
81. O God my Father, I receive solution to my situations today with thanksgiving and it shall be permanent in the name of Jesus Christ.

82. O God my Father, I receive my healing today with thanksgiving and it shall be permanent in the name of Jesus Christ.
83. Every satanic bottle holding my blessings, break now by the fire of God in the name of Jesus Christ.
84. Every satanic bottle holding my miracles, break now by the fire of God in the name of Jesus Christ.
85. Every satanic bottle holding my success, break now by the fire of God in the name of Jesus Christ.
86. Every satanic bottle holding my finances, break now by the fire of God in the name of Jesus Christ.
87. Every satanic bottle holding the answer to my prayers, break now by the fire of God in the name of Jesus Christ.
88. Every satanic bottle holding my testimonies, break now by the fire of God in the name of Jesus Christ.
89. Every satanic bottle holding my progress, break now by the fire of God in the name of Jesus Christ.
90. Every satanic bottle holding my joy, break now by the fire of God in the name of Jesus Christ.
91. O God my Father, enough is enough, I shall never labor in vain again in the name of Jesus Christ.
92. O God my Father, enough is enough, I shall never lack again in the name of Jesus Christ.
93. O God my Father, enough is enough, I shall never fail again in the name of Jesus Christ.
94. O God my Father, enough is enough, I shall never endure shame again in the name of Jesus Christ.

PRAYER WHEN YOU DESIRE TO HAVE A NEW STORY

Passages To Read Before You Pray:
Luke 8:43-48, Mark 10:46-52, John 9:1-41, 1 Samuel 30:1-8, Psalms 3, 9, 59, 69

I have come today to fellowship with my heavenly Father, and make my requests and needs known unto Him. I cannot be hindered nor delayed because I know who I am in the Lord. I am a child of the Kingdom, born of the Spirit, redeemed by the blood of Jesus Christ. I walk in authority, living life without any apology because the power and authority has been given to me according to the Word of God in the book of Luke 9:1.

As I have come to pray today and to fellowship with my heavenly Father, I cover myself in the blood of Jesus Christ, and I put on the whole armor of God. I hereby come against every Prince of Persia that wants to hinder my prayer, I arrest you by the power in the blood of Jesus Christ, and I bind you and cast you down into the pit of hell.

I come against principalities and powers that wrestle with me and my prayers, I arrest you today by the power in the name of Jesus Christ, and I bind you and cast down into the pit of hell. I come against the rulers of the darkness of this world, against spiritual wickedness in high places, I arrest you all by the power in the name of Jesus Christ, and I bind you and cast you down into the pit of hell. I come against weakness and weariness, I arrest you today by the power in the name of Jesus Christ, and I bind you and cast you out of my life. I come against wondering

spirit and distractions, I arrest you today by the power in the name of Jesus Christ, and I bind you and cast you out of my life.

Today I receive the anointing to pray and get results, my prayers cannot be hindered nor delayed because Jesus is my Lord, I will pray today and get the desired results, I decree open heavens upon my prayers. I baptize myself in the fire of the Holy Ghost; therefore I have become too hot for the enemy to handle. My prayers today will attract divine intervention to every situation in my life; signs and wonders will follow my prayers today, testimonies will follow my prayers today and the name of God alone will be glorified, in Jesus name. Amen!

PRAYER POINTS:

1. O God my Father, thank you for being my God, my Father and my friend.
2. O God my Father, thank you for the privilege to know you and the power of the resurrection of Jesus Christ.
3. O God my Father, thank you for always being there for me and with me.
4. O God my Father, thank you for the great and mighty things that you are doing in my life.
5. O God my Father, thank you for your provision and protection over me and my household.
6. O God my Father, thank you for always answering my prayers.
7. I confess my sins before you today and I ask you to forgive me on the basis of your mercy, in the name of Jesus Christ.
8. Wash me clean today O Lord by the blood of Jesus Christ.

9. I cover myself and my household with the blood of Jesus Christ.
10. My prayers today will not go in vain; my prayers will produce the desired results in the name of Jesus Christ.

11. Long time problems manifesting in my life, receive solution today, in the name of Jesus Christ.
12. Long time problems manifesting in my home, receive solution today, in the name of Jesus Christ.
13. Long time problems attacking my finances, receive solution today in the name of Jesus Christ.
14. Long time problems attacking my health, receive solution today in the name of Jesus Christ.
15. Long time problems attacking my marriage, receive solution today in the name of Jesus Christ.
16. Long time problems manifesting in my business, receive solution today in the name of Jesus Christ.
17. Long time problems manifesting in the life of my spouse, receive solution today in the name of Jesus Christ.
18. Long time problems manifesting in the life of my children, receive solution now in the name of Jesus Christ.
19. Long time problems challenging the power of God in my life, receive solution now in the name of Jesus Christ.
20. Long time problems posing a threat to my future, receive solution now in the name of Jesus Christ.
21. Any power anywhere attacking my mind, you will not escape the judgment of God, in the name of Jesus Christ.
22. Any power anywhere attacking my home, you will not escape the judgment of God, in the name of Jesus Christ.

23. Any power anywhere attacking my finances, you will not escape the judgment of God, in the name of Jesus Christ.
24. Any power anywhere attacking my joy, you will not escape the judgment of God, in the name of Jesus Christ.
25. Any power anywhere attacking my destiny, you will not escape the judgment of God, in the name of Jesus Christ.
26. Any power anywhere attacking my family, you will not escape the judgment of God, in the name of Jesus Christ.
27. Any power anywhere attacking my health, you will not escape the judgment of God, in the name of Jesus Christ.
28. Any power anywhere attacking my efforts, you will not escape the judgment of God, in the name of Jesus Christ.
29. Any power anywhere attacking my marriage, you will not escape the judgment of God, in the name of Jesus Christ.
30. Any power anywhere attacking my testimony, you will not escape the judgment of God, in the name of Jesus Christ.
31. Any power anywhere attacking my breakthrough, you will not escape the judgment of God, in the name of Jesus Christ.
32. Any power anywhere attacking my harvest, you will not escape the judgment of God, in the name of Jesus Christ.
33. Any power anywhere attacking my progress, you will not escape the judgment of God, in the name of Jesus Christ.
34. Any power anywhere attacking my fruitfulness, you will not escape the judgment of God, in the name of Jesus Christ.

35. Any power anywhere attacking the work of my hands, you will not escape the judgment of God, in the name of Jesus Christ.
36. Any power anywhere attacking the sources of my income, you will not escape the judgment of God, in the name of Jesus Christ.
37. Any power anywhere trying to close the doors of my blessing, you will not escape the judgment of God, in the name of Jesus Christ.
38. Any power anywhere trying to close the doors of opportunity against me, you will not escape the judgment of God in the name of Jesus Christ.
39. I cover myself in the blood of Jesus Christ, I enter into the strong room of the devil and claim back my stolen glory, in the name of Jesus Christ.
40. I cover myself in the blood of Jesus Christ, I enter into the strong room of the devil and claim back my stolen blessings, in the name of Jesus Christ.
41. I cover myself in the blood of Jesus Christ, I enter into the strong room of the devil and claim back my stolen miracles, in the name of Jesus Christ.
42. I cover myself in the blood of Jesus Christ, I enter into the strong room of the devil and claim back my stolen prosperity, in the name of Jesus Christ.
43. I cover myself in the blood of Jesus Christ, I enter into the strong room of the devil and claim back my stolen progress, in the name of Jesus Christ.
44. I cover myself in the blood of Jesus Christ, I enter into the strong room of the devil and claim back my stolen testimony, in the name of Jesus Christ.

45. I cover myself in the blood of Jesus Christ, I enter into the strong room of the devil and claim back my stolen achievement, in the name of Jesus Christ.
46. I cover myself in the blood of Jesus Christ, I enter into the strong room of the devil and claim back my stolen breakthrough, in the name of Jesus Christ.
47. I cover myself in the blood of Jesus Christ, I enter into the strong room of the devil and claim back my stolen joy, in the name of Jesus Christ.
48. I cover myself in the blood of Jesus Christ, I enter into the strong room of the devil and claim back answers to all my prayers, in the name of Jesus Christ.
49. I cover myself in the blood of Jesus Christ, I enter into the strong room of the devil and claim back my stolen money, in the name of Jesus Christ.
50. I cover myself in the blood of Jesus Christ, I enter into the strong room of the devil and claim back my promotion, in the name of Jesus Christ.
51. I cover myself in the blood of Jesus Christ, I enter into the strong room of the devil and claim back my success, in the name of Jesus Christ.
52. I cover myself in the blood of Jesus Christ, I enter into the strong room of the devil and claim back my stolen harvest, in the name of Jesus Christ.
53. I cover myself in the blood of Jesus Christ, I enter into the strong room of the devil and claim back all good things that the enemy has stolen from me, in the name of Jesus Christ.

PRAYER FOR MERCY TO OVERCOME JUDGMENT

Passages To Read Before You Pray:
James 2:8-13, Proverbs 3:3, Psalms 51, 57, 6, 31, 78, 19, 42, 46

I have come today to fellowship with my heavenly Father, and make my requests and needs known unto Him. I cannot be hindered nor delayed because I know who I am in the Lord. I am a child of the Kingdom, born of the Spirit, redeemed by the blood of Jesus Christ. I walk in authority, living life without any apology because the power and authority has been given to me according to the Word of God in the book of Luke 9:1.

As I have come to pray today and to fellowship with my heavenly Father, I cover myself in the blood of Jesus Christ, and I put on the whole armor of God. I hereby come against every Prince of Persia that wants to hinder my prayer, I arrest you by the power in the blood of Jesus Christ, and I bind you and cast you down into the pit of hell.

I come against principalities and powers that wrestle with me and my prayers, I arrest you today by the power in the name of Jesus Christ, and I bind you and cast down into the pit of hell. I come against the rulers of the darkness of this world, against spiritual wickedness in high places, I arrest you all by the power in the name of Jesus Christ, and I bind you and cast you down into the pit of hell. I come against weakness and weariness, I arrest you today by the power in the name of Jesus Christ, and I bind you and cast you out of my life. I come against wondering

spirit and distractions, I arrest you today by the power in the name of Jesus Christ, and I bind you and cast you out of my life.

Today I receive the anointing to pray and get results, my prayers cannot be hindered nor delayed because Jesus is my Lord, I will pray today and get the desired results, I decree open heavens upon my prayers. I baptize myself in the fire of the Holy Ghost; therefore I have become too hot for the enemy to handle. My prayers today will attract divine intervention to every situation in my life; signs and wonders will follow my prayers today, testimonies will follow my prayers today and the name of God alone will be glorified, in Jesus name. Amen!

PRAYER POINTS:

1. O God my Father, thank you for being my God, My Father and my friend.
2. O God my Father, thank you for the privilege to know you and the power of the resurrection of Jesus Christ.
3. O God my Father, thank you for always being there for me and with me.
4. O God my Father, thank you for the great and mighty things that you are doing in my life.
5. O God my Father, thank you for your provision and protection over me and my household.
6. O God my Father, thank you for always answering my prayers.
7. I confess my sins before you today and I ask you to forgive me on the basis of your mercy, in the name of Jesus Christ.
8. Wash me clean today O Lord by the blood of Jesus Christ.

9. I cover myself and my household with the blood of Jesus Christ.
10. My prayers today will not go in vain; my prayers will produce the desired results in the name of Jesus Christ.

11. O God my Father, let your mercy triumph over every judgment that is against me in the name of Jesus Christ.
12. O God my Father, let your mercy triumph over the judgment of lack that is against me, in the name of Jesus Christ.
13. O God my Father, let your mercy triumph over the judgment of stagnancy that is upon my life in the name of Jesus Christ.
14. O God my Father, let your mercy triumph over the judgment of backwardness that is upon my life in the name of Jesus Christ.
15. O God my Father, let your mercy triumph over the judgment of vain labor that is upon my life in the name of Jesus Christ.
16. O God my Father, let your mercy triumph over the judgment of poverty that is upon my life in the name of Jesus Christ.
17. O God my Father, let your mercy triumph over the judgment of slavery that is upon my life in the name of Jesus Christ.
18. O God my Father, let your mercy triumph over the judgment of affliction that is upon my life in the name of Jesus Christ.
19. O God my Father, let your mercy triumph over the judgment of hard labor that is upon my life in the name of Jesus Christ.

20. O God my Father, let your mercy triumph over the judgment of loneliness that is upon my life in the name of Jesus Christ.
21. O God my Father, let your mercy triumph over the judgment of frustration that is upon my life in the name of Jesus Christ.
22. O God my Father, let your mercy triumph over the judgment of infirmities that is upon my life in the name of Jesus Christ.
23. O God my Father, let your mercy triumph over the judgment untimely death upon my life in the name of Jesus Christ.
24. O God my Father, let every judgment against me be satisfied by the blood of Jesus Christ that was shed on the cross, in the name of Jesus Christ.
25. O God my Father, let every judgment against my bloodline be satisfied today because I have given my life to you in the name of Jesus Christ.
26. O God my Father, let every judgment against my future generation be satisfied today because you died on the cross of Calvary, in the name of Jesus Christ.
27. O God my Father, let your mercy triumph over every judgment inherited from my ancestors, in the name of Jesus Christ.
28. O God my Father, let your mercy triumph over every judgment that is upon my life because of the people that I work with, in the name of Jesus Christ.
29. O God my Father, let your mercy triumph over every judgment that comes upon my life because of the place where I live, in the name of Jesus Christ.

30. O God my Father, let your mercy triumph over every judgment that comes upon me because of people that I do business with, in the name of Jesus Christ.
31. O God my Father, let your mercy triumph over every judgment that comes upon me because of my parents mistakes, in the name of Jesus Christ.
32. O God my Father, let your mercy triumph over every judgment that comes upon me because of my place of birth in the name of Jesus Christ.
33. O God my Father, let your mercy triumph over every judgment that comes upon me as a result of my past mistakes, in the name of Jesus Christ.
34. O God my Father, let your mercy triumph over every judgment affecting my children because of my sins and mistakes, in the name of Jesus Christ.
35. O God my Father, let your mercy triumph over every judgment that comes upon me because of my lack of self-control, in the name of Jesus Christ.
36. O God my Father, let every judgment pronounced upon me by the enemy be reversed by the power in the name of Jesus Christ.
37. O God my Father, let every judgment pronounced upon me by the kingdom of darkness by reversed today by the authority in the name of Jesus Christ.
38. Today I am released from any judgment pronounced against me by the household wickedness, in the name of Jesus Christ.
39. O God my Father, let your mercy triumph over the judgment of failure that is against me, in the name of Jesus Christ.
40. Today I am discharged from every judgment that is against me in the name of Jesus Christ.

41. Today I am discharged from every judgment that is against my marriage in the name of Jesus Christ.
42. Today I am discharged from every judgment that is against my finances in the name of Jesus Christ.
43. Today I am discharged from every judgment that is against my destiny in the name of Jesus Christ.
44. By the order of the King of kings, the Ancient of Days, I am discharged and totally free from every judgment that is against me and my household, in the name of Jesus Christ.

PRAYER TO OVERTURN STUBBORN SITUATIONS

Passages To Read Before You Pray:
Ezekiel 21:27, Isaiah 43:18-19, Psalms 34, 86, 40, 70, Jeremiah 32:36-43, 33:14, 1 John 3:8,

I have come today to fellowship with my heavenly Father, and make my requests and needs known unto Him. I cannot be hindered nor delayed because I know who I am in the Lord. I am a child of the Kingdom, born of the Spirit, redeemed by the blood of Jesus Christ. I walk in authority, living life without any apology because the power and authority has been given to me according to the Word of God in the book of Luke 9:1.

As I have come to pray today and to fellowship with my heavenly Father, I cover myself in the blood of Jesus Christ, and I put on the whole armor of God. I hereby come against every Prince of Persia that wants to hinder my prayer, I arrest you by the power in the blood of Jesus Christ, and I bind you and cast you down into the pit of hell.

I come against principalities and powers that wrestle with me and my prayers, I arrest you today by the power in the name of Jesus Christ, and I bind you and cast down into the pit of hell. I come against the rulers of the darkness of this world, against spiritual wickedness in high places, I arrest you all by the power in the name of Jesus Christ, and I bind you and cast you down into the pit of hell. I come against weakness and weariness, I arrest you today by the power in the name of Jesus Christ, and I bind you and cast you out of my life. I come against wondering

spirit and distractions, I arrest you today by the power in the name of Jesus Christ, and I bind you and cast you out of my life.

Today I receive the anointing to pray and get results, my prayers cannot be hindered nor delayed because Jesus is my Lord, I will pray today and get the desired results, I decree open heavens upon my prayers. I baptize myself in the fire of the Holy Ghost; therefore I have become too hot for the enemy to handle. My prayers today will attract divine intervention to every situation in my life; signs and wonders will follow my prayers today, testimonies will follow my prayers today and the name of God alone will be glorified, in Jesus name. Amen!

PRAYER POINTS:

1. O God my Father, thank you for being my God, my Father and my friend.
2. O God my Father, thank you for the privilege to know you and the power of the resurrection of Jesus Christ.
3. O God my Father, thank you for always being there for me and with me.
4. O God my Father, thank you for the great and mighty things that you are doing in my life.
5. O God my Father, thank you for your provision and protection over me and my household.
6. O God my Father, thank you for always answering my prayers.
7. I confess my sins before you today and I ask you to forgive me on the basis of your mercy, in the name of Jesus Christ.
8. Wash me clean today O Lord by the blood of Jesus Christ.

9. I cover myself and my household with the blood of Jesus Christ.
10. My prayers today will not go in vain; my prayers will produce the desired results in the name of Jesus Christ.
11. O God my Father, let every judgment against me be overturned by your power, in the name of Jesus Christ.
12. O God my Father, it is high time, let every unpleasant situation in my life be overturned by the power in the name of Jesus Christ.
13. O God my Father, let every satanic decree against me be overturned today in the name of Jesus Christ.
14. O God my Father, let every satanic decree against my family be overturned today in the name of Jesus Christ.
15. O God my Father, let every satanic decree against my destiny be overturned today in the name of Jesus Christ.
16. O God my Father, let every satanic decree against my future be overturned now in the name of Jesus Christ.
17. O God my Father, let every satanic decree against my children be overturned now in the name of Jesus Christ.
18. O God my Father, let every satanic decree against my marriage be overturned now in the name of Jesus Christ.
19. O God my Father, let every satanic decree against my business be overturned now in the name of Jesus Christ.
20. O God my Father, let every satanic decree against my finances be overturned now in the name of Jesus Christ.
21. Any decision made anywhere against the plan of God for me, be overturned now by the fire of God in the name of Jesus Christ.
22. Any decision made anywhere in contrary to the plan of God my future, be overturned now by the fire of God in the name of Jesus Christ.

23. Any decision made anywhere in contrary to the divine agenda for my marriage, be overturned now in the name of Jesus Christ.
24. Any decision made anywhere in contrary to the divine plan for my children, be overturned now by the fire of God in the name of Jesus Christ.
25. Any decision made anywhere to make my life miserable, be overturned by the fire of God in the name of Jesus Christ.
26. Any decision made anywhere to frustrate my life, be overturned now by the fire of God in the name of Jesus Christ.
27. Any decision made anywhere to make me labor in vain, be overturned now by the power in the name of Jesus Christ.
28. Any decision made anywhere to make my life a living hell, be overturned now by the power in the name of Jesus Christ.
29. Any decision made anywhere to rob me of my blessings, be overturned now by the authority in the name of Jesus Christ.
30. Any decision made anywhere to rob me of my miracles, be overturned now by the authority in the name of Jesus Christ.
31. O God my Father, let every evil pronouncement against my life be overturned now until it shall be no more, in the name of Jesus Christ.
32. O God my Father, let the spirit and power of poverty that want to take over my life be overturned now until it shall be no more, in the name of Jesus Christ.

33. O God my Father, let the power of stagnancy over my life be overturned now until it shall be no more, in the name of Jesus Christ.
34. O God my Father, let the situation that makes me cry be overturned and overturned until it shall be no more, in the name of Jesus Christ.
35. O God my Father, let the problem that challenges my faith in you be overturned and overturned until it shall be no more, in the name of Jesus Christ.
36. O God my Father, let inherited failure in my life be overturned and overturned until it shall be no more, in the name of Jesus Christ.
37. O God my Father, let inherited sickness in my life be overturned and overturned until it shall be no more, in the name of Jesus Christ.
38. O God my Father, let every work of the devil in my life be overturned and overturned until it shall be no more, in the name of Jesus Christ.
39. O God my Father, let every power that causes me to make mistake at the edge of breakthrough be overturned and overturned until it shall be no more, in the name of Jesus Christ.
40. O God my Father, let the expectation of the enemy over my life be overturned and overturned until it shall be no more, in the name of Jesus Christ.
41. O God my Father, Let my shame be overturned and overturned today until it shall be no more, in the name of Jesus Christ.
42. O God my Father, let my ridicule be overturned and overturned today until it shall be no more, in the name of Jesus Christ.

43. O God my Father, let inherited curses upon my life be overturned and overturned today until it shall be no more, in the name of Jesus Christ.
44. O God my Father, let the situation that sets limit on my success be overturned and overturned today until it shall be no more, in the name of Jesus Christ.

LET THE LONG DISTANCE BE SHORTENED

Passages To Read Before You Pray:
Proverbs 13:12, Numbers 21:4, Psalms 73:3, 83, 19, 22, 78

I have come today to fellowship with my heavenly Father, and make my requests and needs known unto Him. I cannot be hindered nor delayed because I know who I am in the Lord. I am a child of the Kingdom, born of the Spirit, redeemed by the blood of Jesus Christ. I walk in authority, living life without any apology because the power and authority has been given to me according to the Word of God in the book of Luke 9:1.

As I have come to pray today and to fellowship with my heavenly Father, I cover myself in the blood of Jesus Christ, and I put on the whole armor of God. I hereby come against every Prince of Persia that wants to hinder my prayer, I arrest you by the power in the blood of Jesus Christ, and I bind you and cast you down into the pit of hell.

I come against principalities and powers that wrestle with me and my prayers, I arrest you today by the power in the name of Jesus Christ, and I bind you and cast down into the pit of hell. I come against the rulers of the darkness of this world, against spiritual wickedness in high places, I arrest you all by the power in the name of Jesus Christ, and I bind you and cast you down into the pit of hell. I come against weakness and weariness, I arrest you today by the power in the name of Jesus Christ, and I bind you and cast you out of my life. I come against wondering spirit and distractions, I arrest you today by the power in the name of Jesus Christ, and I bind you and cast you out of my life.

Today I receive the anointing to pray and get results, my prayers cannot be hindered nor delayed because Jesus is my Lord, I will pray today and get the desired results, I decree open heavens upon my prayers. I baptize myself in the fire of the Holy Ghost; therefore I have become too hot for the enemy to handle. My prayers today will attract divine intervention to every situation in my life; signs and wonders will follow my prayers today, testimonies will follow my prayers today and the name of God alone will be glorified, in Jesus name. Amen!

PRAYER POINTS:

1. O God my Father, thank you for being my God, my Father and my friend.
2. O God my Father, thank you for the privilege to know you and the power of the resurrection of Jesus Christ.
3. O God my Father, thank you for always being there for me and with me.
4. O God my Father, thank you for the great and mighty things that you are doing in my life.
5. O God my Father, thank you for your provision and protection over me and my household.
6. O God my Father, thank you for always answering my prayers.
7. I confess my sins before you today and I ask you to forgive me on the basis of your mercy, in the name of Jesus Christ.
8. Wash me clean today O Lord by the blood of Jesus Christ.
9. I cover myself and my household with the blood of Jesus Christ.

10. My prayers today will not go in vain; my prayers will produce the desired results in the name of Jesus Christ.

11. O God my Father, with you nothing is impossible, let the distance between me and my promise land be shortened, in the name of Jesus Christ.

12. O God my Father, with you nothing is impossible, let the distance between me and my breakthrough be shortened, in the name of Jesus Christ.

13. O God my Father, with you nothing is impossible, let the distance between me and my success be shortened in the name of Jesus Christ.

14. O God my Father, with you nothing is impossible, let the distance between me and my harvest be shortened in the name of Jesus Christ.

15. O God my Father, with you nothing is impossible, let the distance between me and my miracle be shortened in the name of Jesus Christ.

16. O God my Father, with you nothing is impossible, let the distance between me and my testimony be shortened in the name of Jesus Christ.

17. O God my Father, with you nothing is impossible, let the distance between me and the answers to my prayers be shortened in the name of Jesus Christ.

18. O God my Father, with you nothing is impossible, let the distance between me and my promotion be shortened in the name of Jesus Christ.

19. O God my Father, with you nothing is impossible, let the distance between me and my time of joy be shortened in the name of Jesus Christ.

20. O God my Father, with you nothing is impossible, let the distance between me and the time of my celebration be shortened in the name of Jesus Christ.
21. O God my Father, with you nothing is impossible, let the distance between me and the time of my open heavens be shortened in the name of Jesus Christ.
22. O God my Father, with you nothing is impossible, let the distance between me and the fulfillment of your promise in my life be shortened in the name of Jesus Christ.
23. O God my Father, with you nothing is impossible, let the distance between me and my time of revelation be shortened in the name of Jesus Christ.
24. O God my Father, with you nothing is impossible, let the distance between me and my appointed time be shortened in the name of Jesus Christ.
25. O God my Father, with you nothing is impossible, let the distance between me and my time of restoration be shortened in the name of Jesus Christ.
26. O God my Father, with you nothing is impossible, let the distance between me and my time of victory be shortened in the name of Jesus Christ.
27. O God my Father, with you nothing is impossible, let the distance between me and my time of increase be shortened in the name of Jesus Christ.
28. O God my Father, with you nothing is impossible, let the distance between me and the new things you promised me be shortened in the name of Jesus Christ.
29. O God my Father, I know you can do all things, let the distance between now and the time you have chosen to rearrange my life for breakthrough be shortened in the name of Jesus Christ.

30. O God my Father, I know you can do all things, let the distance between now and the time you have chosen to promote be shortened in the name of Jesus Christ.
31. O God my Father, I know you can do all things, let the distance between now and the time you have chosen to manifest your glory in my life be shortened in the name of Jesus Christ.
32. O God my Father, I know you can do all things, let the distance between now and the time you have chosen to enlarge my coast be shortened in the name of Jesus Christ.
33. O God my Father, I know you can do all things, let the distance between now and the time you have chosen to demonstrate your power in my life be shortened in the name of Jesus Christ.
34. O God my Father, I know you can do all things, let the distance between me and the time of my great achievement be shortened in the name of Jesus Christ.
35. O God my Father, I know you can do all things, let the distance between now and the time you have chosen to send me divine help be shortened in the name of Jesus Christ.

PRAYER FOR SUDDEN BLESSINGS

Passages To Read Before You Pray:
2 Kings 6:8-23, 7:1-20, Joel 2:21, Habakkuk 1:5, Psalms 29, 61, 30, 42, 55

I have come today to fellowship with my heavenly Father, and make my requests and needs known unto Him. I cannot be hindered nor delayed because I know who I am in the Lord. I am a child of the Kingdom, born of the Spirit, redeemed by the blood of Jesus Christ. I walk in authority, living life without any apology because the power and authority has been given to me according to the Word of God in the book of Luke 9:1.

As I have come to pray today and to fellowship with my heavenly Father, I cover myself in the blood of Jesus Christ, and I put on the whole armor of God. I hereby come against every Prince of Persia that wants to hinder my prayer, I arrest you by the power in the blood of Jesus Christ, and I bind you and cast you down into the pit of hell.

I come against principalities and powers that wrestle with me and my prayers, I arrest you today by the power in the name of Jesus Christ, and I bind you and cast down into the pit of hell. I come against the rulers of the darkness of this world, against spiritual wickedness in high places, I arrest you all by the power in the name of Jesus Christ, and I bind you and cast you down into the pit of hell. I come against weakness and weariness, I arrest you today by the power in the name of Jesus Christ, and I bind you and cast you out of my life. I come against wondering

spirit and distractions, I arrest you today by the power in the name of Jesus Christ, and I bind you and cast you out of my life.

Today I receive the anointing to pray and get results, my prayers cannot be hindered nor delayed because Jesus is my Lord, I will pray today and get the desired results, I decree open heavens upon my prayers. I baptize myself in the fire of the Holy Ghost; therefore I have become too hot for the enemy to handle. My prayers today will attract divine intervention to every situation in my life; signs and wonders will follow my prayers today, testimonies will follow my prayers today and the name of God alone will be glorified, in Jesus name. Amen!

PRAYER POINTS:

1. O God my Father, thank you for being my God, my Father and my friend.
2. O God my Father, thank you for the privilege to know you and the power of the resurrection of Jesus Christ.
3. O God my Father, thank you for always being there for me and with me.
4. O God my Father, thank you for the great and mighty things that you are doing in my life.
5. O God my Father, thank you for your provision and protection over me and my household.
6. O God my Father, thank you for always answering my prayers.
7. I confess my sins before you today and I ask you to forgive me on the basis of your mercy, in the name of Jesus Christ.
8. Wash me clean today O Lord by the blood of Jesus Christ.

9. I cover myself and my household with the blood of Jesus Christ.
10. My prayers today will not go in vain; my prayers will produce the desired results in the name of Jesus Christ.

11. O God my Father, let my miracle come suddenly that the enemy will not be able to see or hinder it, in the name of Jesus Christ.
12. O God my Father, let my testimony come suddenly that the enemy will not be able to see or hinder it, in the name of Jesus Christ.
13. O God my Father, let my breakthrough come suddenly that the enemy will not be able to see or hinder it, in the name of Jesus Christ.
14. O God my Father, let my promotion come suddenly that the enemy will not be able to see or hinder it. In the name of Jesus Christ.
15. O God my Father, let my success come suddenly that the enemy will not be able to see or hinder it, in the name of Jesus Christ.
16. O God my Father, let my financial freedom come suddenly that the enemy will not be able to see or hinder it, in the name of Jesus Christ.
17. O God my Father, let my blessings come suddenly that the enemy will not be able to see or hinder it, in the name of Jesus Christ.
18. O God my Father, let my progress come suddenly that the enemy will not be able to see or hinder it, in the name of Jesus Christ.
19. O God my Father, let the answers to my prayers come suddenly that the enemy will not be able to see or hinder it, in the name of Jesus Christ.

20. O God my Father, let my harvest come suddenly that the enemy will not be able to see or hinder it, in the name of Jesus Christ.
21. O God my Father, let my increase come suddenly that the enemy will not be able to see or hinder it, in the name of Jesus Christ.
22. O God my Father, let my great achievement come suddenly that the enemy will not be able to see or hinder it, in the name of Jesus Christ.
23. O God my Father, let new things begin to manifest in my life without the knowledge of my enemies, that they will not be able to see or hinder it, in the name of Jesus Christ.
24. O God my Father, let restoration begin to happen in every area of my life without the knowledge of my enemies, that they will not be able to see or hinder it, in the name of Jesus Christ.
25. O God my Father, let my business begin to grow without the knowledge of the enemy, that they will not be able to see or hinder it, in the name of Jesus Christ.
26. O God my Father, let the divine help locate me now without the knowledge of the enemy, that they will not be able to see or hinder it, in the name of Jesus Christ.
27. O God my Father, let there be a sudden divine repositioning in my life, that the enemy will not be able to see or hinder it, in the name of Jesus Christ.
28. O God my Father, let there be a sudden divine rearrangement in my life, that the enemy will not be able to see or hinder it, in the name of Jesus Christ.
29. O God my Father, let my time of celebration come suddenly that the enemy will not be able to see or hinder it, in the name of Jesus Christ.

30. O God my Father, let there be a sudden fulfillment of your promises in my life, that the enemy will not be able to see or hinder it, in the name of Jesus Christ.
31. O God my Father, let there be a sudden manifestation of your glory upon my life, that the enemy will not be able to see or hinder it, in the name of Jesus Christ.
32. O God my Father, let my fruitfulness come suddenly that the enemy will not be able to see or hinder it, in the name of Jesus Christ.
33. O God my Father, let there be sudden increase in every area of my life, that the enemy will not be able to see or hinder it, in the name of Jesus Christ.
34. O God my Father, let there be sudden expansion in every area of my life, that the enemy will not be able to see or hinder it, in the name of Jesus Christ.
35. O God my Father, let there be sudden demonstration of your power in my life, that the enemy will not be able to see or hinder it, in the name of Jesus Christ.
36. O God my Father, let there be sudden move of the Holy Spirit in every area of my life, that the enemy will not be able to see or hinder it, in the name of Jesus Christ.
37. O God my Father, let my miracles take my enemies by surprise, that they will have no choice but to celebrate with me, in the name of Jesus Christ.
38. O God my Father, let my promotion take my enemies by surprise that they will have no choice but to celebrate with me, in the name of Jesus Christ.
39. O God my Father, let my great achievement take my enemies by surprise that they will have no choice but to celebrate with me, in the name of Jesus Christ.

40. O God my Father, let the answers to my prayers take my enemies by surprise that they will have no choice but to celebrate with me, in the name of Jesus Christ.
41. O God my Father, let my testimonies take my enemies by surprise that they will have no choice but to celebrate with me in the name of Jesus Christ.
42. O God my Father, let the fulfillment of your promise in my life take my enemies by surprise that they will have no choice but to celebrate with me in the name of Jesus Christ.
43. O God my Father, let my breakthrough take my enemies by surprise that they will have no choice but to celebrate with me in the name of Jesus Christ.
44. O God my Father, let the season of my harvest take my enemies by surprise that they will have no choice but to celebrate with me in the name of Jesus Christ.

PRAYER FOR GOD TO FIGHT YOUR BATTLE

Passages To Read Before You Pray:
Psalm 68, 97, 35, 109, 1 Samuel 17:48-51, Isaiah 50:7-9

I have come today to fellowship with my heavenly Father, and make my requests and needs known unto Him. I cannot be hindered nor delayed because I know who I am in the Lord. I am a child of the Kingdom, born of the Spirit, redeemed by the blood of Jesus Christ. I walk in authority, living life without any apology because the power and authority has been given to me according to the Word of God in the book of Luke 9:1.

As I have come to pray today and to fellowship with my heavenly Father, I cover myself in the blood of Jesus Christ, and I put on the whole armor of God. I hereby come against every Prince of Persia that wants to hinder my prayer, I arrest you by the power in the blood of Jesus Christ, and I bind you and cast you down into the pit of hell.

I come against principalities and powers that wrestle with me and my prayers, I arrest you today by the power in the name of Jesus Christ, and I bind you and cast down into the pit of hell. I come against the rulers of the darkness of this world, against spiritual wickedness in high places, I arrest you all by the power in the name of Jesus Christ, and I bind you and cast you down into the pit of hell. I come against weakness and weariness, I arrest you today by the power in the name of Jesus Christ, and I bind you and cast you out of my life. I come against wondering spirit and distractions, I arrest you today by the power in the name of Jesus Christ, and I bind you and cast you out of my life.

Today I receive the anointing to pray and get results, my prayers cannot be hindered nor delayed because Jesus is my Lord, I will pray today and get the desired results, I decree open heavens upon my prayers. I baptize myself in the fire of the Holy Ghost; therefore I have become too hot for the enemy to handle. My prayers today will attract divine intervention to every situation in my life; signs and wonders will follow my prayers today, testimonies will follow my prayers today and the name of God alone will be glorified, in Jesus name. Amen!

PRAYER POINTS:

1. O God my Father, thank you for being my God, my Father and my friend.
2. O God my Father, thank you for the privilege to know you and the power of the resurrection of Jesus Christ.
3. O God my Father, thank you for always being there for me and with me.
4. O God my Father, thank you for the great and mighty things that you are doing in my life.
5. O God my Father, thank you for your provision and protection over me and my household.
6. O God my Father, thank you for always answering my prayers.
7. I confess my sins before you today and I ask you to forgive me on the basis of your mercy, in the name of Jesus Christ.
8. Wash me clean today O Lord by the blood of Jesus Christ.
9. I cover myself and my household with the blood of Jesus Christ.

10. My prayers today will not go in vain; my prayers will produce the desired results in the name of Jesus Christ.

11. O God my Father, visit me today as a mighty man in battle and fight my battle for me in the name of Jesus Christ.

12. I refuse to lose the battle of life, no matter the situation I will win and not lose, in the name of Jesus Christ.

13. O God my Father, let the captain of my enemy's army fall today by the fire of God, in the name of Jesus Christ.

14. O God my Father, let your mercy be withdrawn from my enemies that they may know that you are my God and Savior, in the name of Jesus Christ.

15. Any power behind my stubborn situation, be knocked down today and never rise again in the name of Jesus Christ.

16. Any power behind my problems, be knocked down today and never rise again in the name of Jesus Christ.

17. Any power behind my financial failure, be knocked down today and never rise again in the name of Jesus Christ.

18. Any power behind my marital problems, be knocked down today and never rise again in the name of Jesus Christ.

19. Any power anywhere fueling my problems, be knocked down today and never rise again in the name of Jesus Christ.

20. O God my Father, let the fire of the Holy Ghost pursue my enemies to the point of no return, in the name of Jesus Christ.

21. O God my Father, send the man or woman behind my problems on a journey of no return, in the name of Jesus Christ.
22. O God my Father, send the man or woman that doesn't want me to enjoy my life on a journey of no return, in the name of Jesus Christ.
23. O God my Father, send the man or woman that doesn't want me to have peace on a journey of no return in the name of Jesus Christ.
24. O God my Father, send the man or woman troubling my life on a journey of no return in the name of Jesus Christ.
25. O God my Father, arise and fight my battles until my enemies are no more in the name of Jesus Christ.
26. O God my Father, arise and fight for me until my household wickedness are no more in the name of Jesus Christ.
27. O God my Father, release your fire and destroy the plan of the enemy concerning my life in the name of Jesus Christ.
28. O God my Father, release your fire and destroy the plan of the enemy concerning my destiny in the name of Jesus Christ.
29. O God my Father, release your fire and destroy the plan of the enemy concerning my marriage, in the name of Jesus Christ.
30. O God my Father, release your fire and destroy the plan of the enemy concerning the life of my children, in the name of Jesus Christ.
31. O God my Father, release your fire and destroy the plan of the enemy concerning my finances in the name of Jesus Christ.

32. Any power anywhere attacking my marriage, receive the arrow of destruction, in the name of Jesus Christ.
33. Any power anywhere attacking my joy, receive the arrow of destruction in the name of Jesus Christ.
34. Any power anywhere attacking my finances, receive the arrow of destruction in the name of Jesus Christ.
35. Any power anywhere attacking the plan of God for me, receive the arrow of destruction in the name of Jesus Christ.
36. Any power anywhere attacking my quiet enjoyment, receive the arrow of destruction in the name of Jesus Christ.
37. Any power anywhere attacking my progress, receive the arrow of destruction in the name of Jesus Christ.
38. O God my Father, arise and trouble those that trouble me in the name of Jesus Christ.
39. O God my Father, arise and fight those that fight against me in the name of Jesus Christ.
40. O God my Father, arise and fight those that fight against my marriage in the name of Jesus Christ.
41. O God my Father, arise and fight those that fight against my family in the name of Jesus Christ.
42. O God my Father, arise and let my enemies be scattered in the name of Jesus Christ.
43. O God my Father, arise and let the enemies of my progress be scattered in the name of Jesus Christ.
44. O God my Father, demonstrate your power in my life, that my enemies may know that you rule the affairs of men in the name of Jesus Christ.

PRAYER FOR UNCOMMON BLESSINGS

Passages To Read Before You Pray:
Isaiah 61:1-3, Joshua 5:9, Psalms 115, 24, 30, 42, 29, 78, 9

I have come today to fellowship with my heavenly Father, and make my requests and needs known unto Him. I cannot be hindered nor delayed because I know who I am in the Lord. I am a child of the Kingdom, born of the Spirit, redeemed by the blood of Jesus Christ. I walk in authority, living life without any apology because the power and authority has been given to me according to the Word of God in the book of Luke 9:1.

As I have come to pray today and to fellowship with my heavenly Father, I cover myself in the blood of Jesus Christ, and I put on the whole armor of God. I hereby come against every Prince of Persia that wants to hinder my prayer, I arrest you by the power in the blood of Jesus Christ, and I bind you and cast you down into the pit of hell.

I come against principalities and powers that wrestle with me and my prayers, I arrest you today by the power in the name of Jesus Christ, and I bind you and cast down into the pit of hell. I come against the rulers of the darkness of this world, against spiritual wickedness in high places, I arrest you all by the power in the name of Jesus Christ, and I bind you and cast you down into the pit of hell. I come against weakness and weariness, I arrest you today by the power in the name of Jesus Christ, and I bind you and cast you out of my life. I come against wondering spirit and distractions, I arrest you today by the power in the name of Jesus Christ, and I bind you and cast you out of my life.

Today I receive the anointing to pray and get results, my prayers cannot be hindered nor delayed because Jesus is my Lord, I will pray today and get the desired results, I decree open heavens upon my prayers. I baptize myself in the fire of the Holy Ghost; therefore I have become too hot for the enemy to handle. My prayers today will attract divine intervention to every situation in my life; signs and wonders will follow my prayers today, testimonies will follow my prayers today and the name of God alone will be glorified, in Jesus name. Amen!

PRAYER POINTS:

1. O God my Father, thank you for being my God, my Father and my friend.
2. O God my Father, thank you for the privilege to know you and the power of the resurrection of Jesus Christ.
3. O God my Father, thank you for always being there for me and with me.
4. O God my Father, thank you for the great and mighty things that you are doing in my life.
5. O God my Father, thank you for your provision and protection over me and my household.
6. O God my Father, thank you for always answering my prayers.
7. I confess my sins before you today and I ask you to forgive me on the basis of your mercy, in the name of Jesus Christ.
8. Wash me clean today O Lord by the blood of Jesus Christ.
9. I cover myself and my household with the blood of Jesus Christ.

10. My prayers today will not go in vain; my prayers will produce the desired results in the name of Jesus Christ.

11. O God my Father, release your power today to turn my life around for good, in the name of Jesus Christ.
12. O God my Father, release your power today to turn my situation around for good, in the name of Jesus Christ.
13. O God my Father, release your Spirit upon me today like on the day of Pentecost, turn my mourning to dancing in the name of Jesus Christ.
14. O God my Father, release your Spirit upon me today like on the day of Pentecost, turn my crying to laughter in the name of Jesus Christ.
15. O God my Father, let your Spirit rest upon me today and release me from any form of captivity in the name of Jesus Christ.
16. Today I decree that this year shall be my year of uncommon favor, in the name of Jesus Christ.
17. Today I decree that this year shall be my year of uncommon miracles, in the name of Jesus Christ.
18. Today I decree that this year shall be my year of uncommon success, in the name of Jesus Christ.
19. Today I decree that this year shall be my year of uncommon breakthrough, in the name of Jesus Christ.
20. Today I decree that this year shall be my year of uncommon testimonies, in the name of Jesus Christ.
21. Today I decree that this year shall be my year of uncommon laughter, in the name of Jesus Christ.
22. Today I decree that this year shall be my year of uncommon victory, in the name of Jesus Christ.
23. Today I decree that this year shall be my year of uncommon fruitfulness, in the name of Jesus Christ.

24. Today I decree that this year shall be my year of uncommon harvest, in the name of Jesus Christ.
25. Today I decree that this year shall be my year of uncommon promotion, in these of Jesus Christ.
26. O God my Father, let my wasted efforts be restored and begin to bring forth harvest, in the name of Jesus Christ.
27. Today O Lord, roll away the reproach of unfruitfulness that is upon my life, in the name of Jesus Christ.
28. Today O Lord, roll away the reproach of fruitless hard work that is upon my life, in the names of Jesus Christ.
29. Today O Lord, roll away the reproach of financial embarrassment that is upon my life, in the name of Jesus Christ.
30. Today O Lord, roll away the reproach of backwardness that is upon my life, in the name of Jesus Christ.
31. Today O Lord, roll away the reproach of inherited failure that is upon my life in the name of Jesus Christ.
32. Today O Lord, roll away the reproach of stagnancy that is upon my life, in the name of Jesus Christ.
33. Today O Lord, I claim my uncommon testimony, I will testify before the end of this prayer program in the name of Jesus Christ.
34. O God my Father, let signs and wonders follow this prayer program in my life, in the name of Jesus Christ.
35. O God my Father, let testimonies follow this prayer program in my life in the name of Jesus Christ.
36. O God my Father, surprise me with great and favorable surprises in the name of Jesus Christ.
37. O God my Father, surprise me with financial breakthrough as a result of this prayer program, in the name of Jesus Christ.

38. O God my Father, surprise me with uncommon breakthrough as a result of this prayer program in the name of Jesus Christ.
39. O God my Father, surprise me with great testimonies as a result of this prayer program in the name of Jesus Christ.
40. O God my Father, do something in my life today that will make my greatest fear go away forever, in the name of Jesus Christ.
41. O God my Father, do something in my life today that will make my situation turn around permanently for good, in the name of Jesus Christ.
42. O God my Father, do something in my life today that will make everyone around me to celebrate with me, in the name of Jesus Christ.
43. O God my Father, do something in my life today that will make me dance a new dance, in the name of Jesus Christ.
44. O God my Father, do something in my life today that will make me laugh a new laugh, in the name of Jesus Christ.
45. O God my Father, do something in my life today that will make me sing a new song, in the name of Jesus Christ.

PRAYER TO RELEASE STOLEN BLESSINGS

Passages To Read Before You Pray:
Psalms 115, 24, 23, 31, 1 Corinthians 3:21, Genesis 1:29-30

I have come today to fellowship with my heavenly Father, and make my requests and needs known unto Him. I cannot be hindered nor delayed because I know who I am in the Lord. I am a child of the Kingdom, born of the Spirit, redeemed by the blood of Jesus Christ. I walk in authority, living life without any apology because the power and authority has been given to me according to the Word of God in the book of Luke 9:1.

As I have come to pray today and to fellowship with my heavenly Father, I cover myself in the blood of Jesus Christ, and I put on the whole armor of God. I hereby come against every Prince of Persia that wants to hinder my prayer, I arrest you by the power in the blood of Jesus Christ, and I bind you and cast you down into the pit of hell.

I come against principalities and powers that wrestle with me and my prayers, I arrest you today by the power in the name of Jesus Christ, and I bind you and cast down into the pit of hell. I come against the rulers of the darkness of this world, against spiritual wickedness in high places, I arrest you all by the power in the name of Jesus Christ, and I bind you and cast you down into the pit of hell. I come against weakness and weariness, I arrest you today by the power in the name of Jesus Christ, and I bind you and cast you out of my life. I come against wondering spirit and distractions, I arrest you today by the power in the name of Jesus Christ, and I bind you and cast you out of my life.

Today I receive the anointing to pray and get results, my prayers cannot be hindered nor delayed because Jesus is my Lord, I will pray today and get the desired results, I decree open heavens upon my prayers. I baptize myself in the fire of the Holy Ghost; therefore I have become too hot for the enemy to handle. My prayers today will attract divine intervention to every situation in my life; signs and wonders will follow my prayers today, testimonies will follow my prayers today and the name of God alone will be glorified, in Jesus name. Amen!

PRAYER POINTS:

1. O God my Father, thank you for being my God, my Father and my friend.
2. O God my Father, thank you for the privilege to know you and the power of the resurrection of Jesus Christ.
3. O God my Father, thank you for always being there for me and with me.
4. O God my Father, thank you for the great and mighty things that you are doing in my life.
5. O God my Father, thank you for your provision and protection over me and my household.
6. O God my Father, thank you for always answering my prayers.
7. I confess my sins before you today and I ask you to forgive me on the basis of your mercy, in the name of Jesus Christ.
8. Wash me clean today O Lord by the blood of Jesus Christ.
9. I cover myself and my household with the blood of Jesus Christ.

10. My prayers today will not go in vain; my prayers will produce the desired results in the name of Jesus Christ.

11. O earth, you are a warehouse where God has deposited blessings for me, everything that my destiny is in need of, release it now in the name of Jesus Christ.
12. O earth, you are a warehouse where God has deposited blessings for me, anything that will move my life forward, release it now in the name of Jesus Christ.
13. O earth, you are a warehouse where God has deposited blessings for me, I have come today to claim my breakthrough in the name of Jesus Christ.
14. O earth, you are a warehouse where God has deposited blessings for me, I have come today to claim my uncommon success in the name of Jesus Christ.
15. O earth, you are a warehouse where God has deposited blessings for me, I have come today to claim my testimonies in the name of Jesus Christ.
16. O earth, you are a warehouse where God has deposited blessings for me, I have come today to claim my financial freedom in the name of Jesus Christ.
17. O earth, you are a warehouse where God has deposited blessings for me, I have come today to claim my double promotion in the name of Jesus Christ.
18. O earth, you are a warehouse where God has deposited blessings for me, everything my family needs to breakthrough in life, release it now in the name of Jesus Christ.
19. O earth, you are a warehouse where God has deposited blessings for me, everything I need to fulfill purpose, release it now in the name of Jesus Christ.

20. First quarter of this year, release blessing deposited in you for me now, in the. Name of Jesus Christ.
21. First quarter of this year, release promotion deposited in you for me now, in the name of Jesus Christ.
22. First quarter of this year, release breakthrough deposited in you for me now, in the name of Jesus Christ.
23. First quarter of this year, release success deposited in you for me now, in the name of Jesus Christ.
24. First quarter of this year, release abundance deposited in you for me now, in the name of Jesus Christ.
25. First quarter of this year, release answers to my prayers now, in the name of Jesus Christ.
26. First quarter of this year, release victory deposited in you for me now, in the name of Jesus Christ.
27. First quarter of this year, release solution deposited in you for me now, in the. Name of Jesus Christ.
28. First quarter of this year, release progress deposited in you for me now, in the name of Jesus Christ.
29. O God my Father, let my delayed blessings be released now before the end of this month, in the name of Jesus Christ.
30. O God my Father, let my hindered breakthroughs be released now before the end of this month, in the name of Jesus Christ.
31. O God my Father, let my stolen miracles be released to me now in the name of Jesus Christ.
32. O God my Father, let my delayed testimonies be released now in the name of Jesus Christ.
33. Any power anywhere holding my miracle, release it now in the name of Jesus Christ.
34. Any power anywhere holding my breakthrough, release it now in the name of Jesus Christ.

35. Any power anywhere holding my progress, release it now in the name of Jesus Christ.
36. Any power anywhere holding my blessing, release it now in the name of Jesus Christ.
37. Any power anywhere holding my promotion, release it now in the name of Jesus Christ.
38. I am moving forward and I refuse to leave my blessings behind in the name of Jesus Christ.
39. I am moving forward and I refuse to leave my testimonies behind in the name of Jesus Christ.
40. I am moving forward and I refuse to leave my miracles behind in the name of Jesus Christ.
41. I am moving forward and I refuse to leave my breakthroughs behind in the name of Jesus Christ.
42. I am moving forward and I refuse to leave my family behind in the name of Jesus Christ.
43. I am moving forward and I refuse to leave my promotion behind in the name of Jesus Christ.

PRAYER TO FINISH UNCOMPLETED PROJECT

Passages To Read Before You Pray:
Zechariah 4:6-10, Philippians 1:6, Habakkuk 1:5, Psalms 126

I have come today to fellowship with my heavenly Father, and make my requests and needs known unto Him. I cannot be hindered nor delayed because I know who I am in the Lord. I am a child of the Kingdom, born of the Spirit, redeemed by the blood of Jesus Christ. I walk in authority, living life without any apology because the power and authority has been given to me according to the Word of God in the book of Luke 9:1.

As I have come to pray today and to fellowship with my heavenly Father, I cover myself in the blood of Jesus Christ, and I put on the whole armor of God. I hereby come against every Prince of Persia that wants to hinder my prayer, I arrest you by the power in the blood of Jesus Christ, and I bind you and cast you down into the pit of hell.

I come against principalities and powers that wrestle with me and my prayers, I arrest you today by the power in the name of Jesus Christ, and I bind you and cast down into the pit of hell. I come against the rulers of the darkness of this world, against spiritual wickedness in high places, I arrest you all by the power in the name of Jesus Christ, and I bind you and cast you down into the pit of hell. I come against weakness and weariness, I arrest you today by the power in the name of Jesus Christ, and I bind you and cast you out of my life. I come against wondering

spirit and distractions, I arrest you today by the power in the name of Jesus Christ, and I bind you and cast you out of my life.

Today I receive the anointing to pray and get results, my prayers cannot be hindered nor delayed because Jesus is my Lord, I will pray today and get the desired results, I decree open heavens upon my prayers. I baptize myself in the fire of the Holy Ghost; therefore I have become too hot for the enemy to handle. My prayers today will attract divine intervention to every situation in my life; signs and wonders will follow my prayers today, testimonies will follow my prayers today and the name of God alone will be glorified, in Jesus name. Amen!

PRAYER POINTS:

1. O God my Father, thank you for being my God, my Father and my friend.
2. O God my Father, thank you for the privilege to know you and the power of the resurrection of Jesus Christ.
3. O God my Father, thank you for always being there for me and with me.
4. O God my Father, thank you for the great and mighty things that you are doing in my life.
5. O God my Father, thank you for your provision and protection over me and my household.
6. O God my Father, thank you for always answering my prayers.
7. I confess my sins before you today and I ask you to forgive me on the basis of your mercy, in the name of Jesus Christ.

8. Wash me clean today O Lord by the blood of Jesus Christ.
9. I cover myself and my household with the blood of Jesus Christ.
10. My prayers today will not go in vain; my prayers will produce the desired results in the name of Jesus Christ.

11. I will not be an uncompleted project in the hands of God.
12. I am a project in the hands of God, and He that has began a good work in my life will complete it in the name of Jesus Christ.
13. You are the one who laid the foundation of my life O Lord, continue to be the pillar in my life in the name of Jesus Christ.
14. No matter what my enemies are saying concerning my life, I will not be an uncompleted project in the hands of my God.
15. O God my Father, complete the project of my life so that your name may be glorified.
16. Today I decree the end of uncompleted projects in my life in the name of Jesus Christ.
17. Every project entrusted into my hands by God must be completed now.
18. Anyone around me causing me to be distracted and causing my project to remain uncompleted be removed by your fire in the name of Jesus Christ.
19. O God my Father, give me the grace to complete this project in the name of Jesus Christ.
20. O God my Father, let your mighty hands finished the mighty works that you have begun in my life, in the name of Jesus Christ.

JESUS SAID, "IT IS FINISHED"

Passages To Read Before You Pray:
John 19:30, Colossians 2:14-15, 2 Timothy 3:9, Psalms 68, 35, 9

I have come today to fellowship with my heavenly Father, and make my requests and needs known unto Him. I cannot be hindered nor delayed because I know who I am in the Lord. I am a child of the Kingdom, born of the Spirit, redeemed by the blood of Jesus Christ. I walk in authority, living life without any apology because the power and authority has been given to me according to the Word of God in the book of Luke 9:1.

As I have come to pray today and to fellowship with my heavenly Father, I cover myself in the blood of Jesus Christ, and I put on the whole armor of God. I hereby come against every Prince of Persia that wants to hinder my prayer, I arrest you by the power in the blood of Jesus Christ, and I bind you and cast you down into the pit of hell.

I come against principalities and powers that wrestle with me and my prayers, I arrest you today by the power in the name of Jesus Christ, and I bind you and cast down into the pit of hell. I come against the rulers of the darkness of this world, against spiritual wickedness in high places, I arrest you all by the power in the name of Jesus Christ, and I bind you and cast you down into the pit of hell. I come against weakness and weariness, I arrest you today by the power in the name of Jesus Christ, and I bind you and cast you out of my life. I come against wondering spirit and distractions, I arrest you today by the power in the name of Jesus Christ, and I bind you and cast you out of my life.

Today I receive the anointing to pray and get results, my prayers cannot be hindered nor delayed because Jesus is my Lord, I will pray today and get the desired results, I decree open heavens upon my prayers. I baptize myself in the fire of the Holy Ghost; therefore I have become too hot for the enemy to handle. My prayers today will attract divine intervention to every situation in my life; signs and wonders will follow my prayers today, testimonies will follow my prayers today and the name of God alone will be glorified, in Jesus name. Amen!

PRAYER POINTS:

1. O God my Father, thank you for being my God, my Father and my friend.
2. O God my Father, thank you for the privilege to know you and the power of the resurrection of Jesus Christ.
3. O God my Father, thank you for always being there for me and with me.
4. O God my Father, thank you for the great and mighty things that you are doing in my life.
5. O God my Father, thank you for your provision and protection over me and my household.
6. O God my Father, thank you for always answering my prayers.
7. I confess my sins before you today and I ask you to forgive me on the basis of your mercy, in the name of Jesus Christ.
8. Wash me clean today O Lord by the blood of Jesus Christ.
9. I cover myself and my household with the blood of Jesus Christ.

10. My prayers today will not go in vain; my prayers will produce the desired results in the name of Jesus Christ.

11. O God my Father, reveal yourself unto me today like never before in the name of Jesus Christ.
12. Today I carry my pain to Calvary and nail it to the cross of Jesus, it is finished, in the name of Jesus Christ.
13. Today I carry my shame to Calvary and nail it to the cross of Jesus, it is finished in the name of Jesus Christ.
14. Today I carry my disappointment to Calvary and nail it to the cross of Jesus, it is finished in the name of Jesus Christ.
15. Today I carry my failure to Calvary and nail it to the cross of Jesus, it is finished in the. Name of Jesus Christ.
16. Today I carry my weakness to Calvary and nail it to the cross of Jesus, it is finished in the name of Jesus Christ.
17. Today I carry my poverty to Calvary and nail it to the cross of Jesus, it is finished in the name of Jesus Christ.
18. Today I carry all curses upon my life to Calvary and nail it to the cross of Jesus, it is finished in the name of Jesus Christ.
19. Today I carry stagnation upon my life to Calvary and nail it to the cross of Jesus, it is finished in the name of Jesus Christ.
20. Today I carry backwardness in my life to Calvary and nail it to the cross of Jesus, it is finished in the name of Jesus Christ.
21. Today I carry barrenness in my life to Calvary and nail it to the cross of Jesus, it is finished in the name of Jesus Christ.

22. Today I carry all evil pronouncements upon my life to Calvary and nail it to the cross of Jesus, it is finished in the name of Jesus Christ.
23. Today I carry all evil manifestations in my life to Calvary and nail it to the cross of Jesus, them is finished in the name of Jesus Christ.
24. Today I carry the spirit of non achievement in my life to Calvary and nail it to the cross of Jesus, it is finished in the name of Jesus Christ.
25. Today I carry all works of the enemy in my life to Calvary and nail them to the cross of Jesus, it is finished in the name of Jesus Christ.
26. Today I carry sickness in my body to Calvary and nail it to the cross of Jesus, it is finished in the name of Jesus Christ.
27. Today I carry unpleasant situations in my life to Calvary and nail them to cross of Jesus, it is finished in the name of Jesus Christ.
28. Today I carry my problems to Calvary and nail them to the cross of Jesus, it is finished in the name of Jesus Christ.
29. Today I carry my frustration to Calvary and nail it to the cross of Jesus, it is finished in the name of Jesus Christ.
30. Today I carry all my troubles to Calvary and nail them to the cross of Jesus, it is finished in the name of Jesus Christ.
31. Today I carry satanic delay in my life to Calvary and nail it to the cross of Jesus, it is finished in the name of Jesus Christ.
32. Today I carry all hindrances on my way to Calvary and nail them to the cross of Jesus, it is finished in the name of Jesus Christ.

33. Any power anywhere hindering my blessings, I carry you to Calvary and nail you to the cross of Jesus, it is finished in the name of Jesus Christ.
34. Any power anywhere delaying my miracles, I carry you to Calvary and nail you to the cross of Jesus, it is finished in the name of Jesus Christ.
35. Unrepentant Pharaoh of my life, I carry you to Calvary and nail you to the cross of Jesus, it is finished in the name of Jesus Christ.
36. Any power anywhere reminding me of my painful past, I carry you to Calvary and nail you to the cross of Jesus, it is finished in the name of Jesus Christ.
37. Long time problems in my life, I carry you to Calvary today and nail you to the cross of Jesus, it is finished in the name of Jesus Christ.
38. Any power anywhere attacking my finances, I carry you to Calvary and nail you to the cross of Jesus, it is finished in the name of Jesus Christ.
39. Any power anywhere attacking my marriage, I carry you to Calvary and nail you to the cross of Jesus, it is finished in the name of Jesus Christ.
40. Any power anywhere attacking my family, I carry you to Calvary and nail you to the cross of Jesus, it is finished in the name of Jesus Christ.
41. Any power anywhere attacking my health, I carry you to Calvary and nail you to the cross of Jesus, it is finished in the name of Jesus Christ.
42. Any power anywhere posing a threat to my future, I carry you to Calvary and nail you to the cross of Jesus, it is finished in the name of Jesus Christ.

43. Any power anywhere attacking my efforts, I carry you to Calvary and nail you to the cross of Jesus, it is finished in the name of Jesus Christ.
44. Any power anywhere challenging the power of God in my life, I carry you to Calvary and nail you to the cross of Jesus, it is finished in the name of Jesus Christ.
45. Any power anywhere closing the door of opportunity against me, I carry you to Calvary and nail you to the cross of Jesus, it is finished in the name of Jesus Christ.
46. Any power anywhere attacking my harvest, I carry you to Calvary and nail you to the cross of Jesus, it is finished in the name of Jesus Christ.
47. Any power anywhere attacking my progress, I carry you to Calvary and nail you to the cross of Jesus, it is finished in the name of Jesus Christ.
48. Any power behind my financial failure, I carry you to Calvary and nail you to the cross of Jesus, it is finished in the name of Jesus Christ.
49. Any power behind my marital problems, I carry you to Calvary and nail you to the cross of Jesus, it is finished in the name of Jesus Christ.
50. You strongman of my father's house. I carry you to Calvary and nail you to the cross of Jesus, it is finished in the name of Jesus Christ.
51. All challenges of life confronting my life, I carry you to Calvary and nail you to the cross of Jesus, it is finished in the name of Jesus Christ.
52. All impossibilities in my life, I carry them to Calvary and nail them to the cross of Jesus, it is finished in the name of Jesus Christ.

53. Today I carry every satanic plan against me to Calvary and nail it to the cross of Jesus, it is finished in the name of Jesus Christ.

ENTER IN BY YOUR BLOOD O LORD!

Passages To Read Before You Pray:
Hebrews 9:11-15, Hebrews 12:24, Revelation 12:11

I have come today to fellowship with my heavenly Father, and make my requests and needs known unto Him. I cannot be hindered nor delayed because I know who I am in the Lord. I am a child of the Kingdom, born of the Spirit, redeemed by the blood of Jesus Christ. I walk in authority, living life without any apology because the power and authority has been given to me according to the Word of God in the book of Luke 9:1.

As I have come to pray today and to fellowship with my heavenly Father, I cover myself in the blood of Jesus Christ, and I put on the whole armor of God. I hereby come against every Prince of Persia that wants to hinder my prayer, I arrest you by the power in the blood of Jesus Christ, and I bind you and cast you down into the pit of hell.

I come against principalities and powers that wrestle with me and my prayers, I arrest you today by the power in the name of Jesus Christ, and I bind you and cast down into the pit of hell. I come against the rulers of the darkness of this world, against spiritual wickedness in high places, I arrest you all by the power in the name of Jesus Christ, and I bind you and cast you down into the pit of hell. I come against weakness and weariness, I arrest you today by the power in the name of Jesus Christ, and I bind you and cast you out of my life. I come against wondering spirit and distractions, I arrest you today by the power in the name of Jesus Christ, and I bind you and cast you out of my life.

Today I receive the anointing to pray and get results, my prayers cannot be hindered nor delayed because Jesus is my Lord, I will pray today and get the desired results, I decree open heavens upon my prayers. I baptize myself in the fire of the Holy Ghost; therefore I have become too hot for the enemy to handle. My prayers today will attract divine intervention to every situation in my life; signs and wonders will follow my prayers today, testimonies will follow my prayers today and the name of God alone will be glorified, in Jesus name. Amen!

PRAYER POINTS:

1. O God my Father, thank you for being my God, my Father and my friend.
2. O God my Father, thank you for the privilege to know you and the power of the resurrection of Jesus Christ.
3. O God my Father, thank you for always being there for me and with me.
4. O God my Father, thank you for the great and mighty things that you are doing in my life.
5. O God my Father, thank you for your provision and protection over me and my household.
6. O God my Father, thank you for always answering my prayers.
7. I confess my sins before you today and I ask you to forgive me on the basis of your mercy, in the name of Jesus Christ.
8. Wash me clean today O Lord by the blood of Jesus Christ.
9. I cover myself and my household with the blood of Jesus Christ.

10. My prayers today will not go in vain; my prayers will produce the desired results in the name of Jesus Christ.
11. Lord Jesus, enter in at once by your blood and deliver me from the ancestral bondage that is about to destroy my destiny, in the name of Jesus Christ.
12. Lord Jesus, enter in at once by your blood and deliver me from the ancestral bondage contending with your plan for my life, in the name of Jesus Christ.
13. Lord Jesus, enter in at once by your blood and deliver me from the ancestral bondage that wants me to suffer like my ancestors in the name of Jesus Christ.
14. Lord Jesus, enter in at once by your blood and deliver me from the ancestral curse trying to recreate my life in the name of Jesus Christ.
15. Lord Jesus, enter in at once by your blood and deliver me from the ancestral curse trying to redesign my future in the name of Jesus Christ.
16. Lord Jesus, enter in at once by your blood and deliver me from every work of the devil manifesting in my life, in the name of Jesus Christ.
17. O God my Father, arise and release my blessings today by the blood of Jesus Christ.
18. O God my Father, arise and destroy every evil assignment given for my sake by the blood of Jesus Christ.
19. O God my Father, arise and destroy every evil contract signed for my sake or on my behalf by the blood of Jesus Christ.
20. O God my Father, arise and scatter every evil work completed against my life and destiny, in the name of Jesus Christ.

21. O God my Father, arise and scatter every evil work completed against my finances, in the name of Jesus Christ.
22. O God my Father, arise and scatter every evil work completed against my home, in the name of Jesus Christ.
23. O God my Father, arise and scatter every evil work completed against my marriage, in the name of Jesus Christ.
24. O God my Father, arise and scatter every evil work completed against my future, in the name of Jesus Christ.
25. O God my Father, arise and scatter every evil work completed against my business, in the name of Jesus Christ.
26. O God my Father, arise and scatter every evil work completed against my success, in the name of Jesus Christ.
27. O God my Father, arise and scatter every evil work completed against my dreams, in the name of Jesus Christ.
28. Today I claim victory over every attack of the enemy by the blood of Jesus Christ.
29. Today I claim victory over every satanic plan against my life in the name of Jesus Christ.
30. Today I claim victory over every battle against my life in the name of Jesus Christ.
31. Today I claim victory over the problems manifesting in my life by the blood of Jesus Christ.
32. Today I claim victory over every unpleasant situation in my life by the blood of Jesus Christ.
33. Today I claim victory over the wickedness of the wicked manifesting in my life, in the name of Jesus Christ.

PRAYER TO GET GOOD RESULT IN TEST / EXAMINATION

Passages To Read Before You Pray:
Isaiah 11:2, Psalms 1, 71, 19, 29, 86, Daniel 1

I have come today to fellowship with my heavenly Father, and make my requests and needs known unto Him. I cannot be hindered nor delayed because I know who I am in the Lord. I am a child of the Kingdom, born of the Spirit, redeemed by the blood of Jesus Christ. I walk in authority, living life without any apology because the power and authority has been given to me according to the Word of God in the book of Luke 9:1.

As I have come to pray today and to fellowship with my heavenly Father, I cover myself in the blood of Jesus Christ, and I put on the whole armor of God. I hereby come against every Prince of Persia that wants to hinder my prayer, I arrest you by the power in the blood of Jesus Christ, and I bind you and cast you down into the pit of hell.

I come against principalities and powers that wrestle with me and my prayers, I arrest you today by the power in the name of Jesus Christ, and I bind you and cast down into the pit of hell. I come against the rulers of the darkness of this world, against spiritual wickedness in high places, I arrest you all by the power in the name of Jesus Christ, and I bind you and cast you down into the pit of hell. I come against weakness and weariness, I arrest you today by the power in the name of Jesus Christ, and I bind you and cast you out of my life. I come against wondering

spirit and distractions, I arrest you today by the power in the name of Jesus Christ, and I bind you and cast you out of my life.

Today I receive the anointing to pray and get results, my prayers cannot be hindered nor delayed because Jesus is my Lord, I will pray today and get the desired results, I decree open heavens upon my prayers. I baptize myself in the fire of the Holy Ghost; therefore I have become too hot for the enemy to handle. My prayers today will attract divine intervention to every situation in my life; signs and wonders will follow my prayers today, testimonies will follow my prayers today and the name of God alone will be glorified, in Jesus name. Amen!

PRAYER POINTS:

1. O God my Father, thank you for being my God, my Father and my friend.
2. O God my Father, thank you for the privilege to know you and the power of the resurrection of Jesus Christ.
3. O God my Father, thank you for always being there for me and with me.
4. O God my Father, thank you for the great and mighty things that you are doing in my life.
5. O God my Father, thank you for your provision and protection over me and my household.
6. O God my Father, thank you for always answering my prayers.
7. I confess my sins before you today and I ask you to forgive me on the basis of your mercy, in the name of Jesus Christ.

8. Wash me clean today O Lord by the blood of Jesus Christ.
9. I cover myself and my household with the blood of Jesus Christ.
10. My prayers today will not go in vain; my prayers will produce the desired results in the name of Jesus Christ.
11. O God my Father, as I prepare for this test/examination, grant me divine understand that I may have better understand of my studies in the name of Jesus Christ.
12. O God my Father, as I prepare for this test/examination, lead me to the area which I need to focus my study on in the name of Jesus Christ.
13. I hereby come against the spirit of failure, I bind you and cast you out of my life in the name of Jesus Christ.
14. You spirit of ancestral failure, I command you to loose your hold upon me in the name of Jesus Christ.
15. O God my Father, as I prepare for this test/examination, I uproot all foundational arrow of failure, in the name of Jesus Christ.
16. O God my Father, as I prepare for this test/examination, I stop all arrows of sickness sent to stop me in the name of Jesus Christ.
17. O God my Father, as I prepare for this test/examination, I stop all arrows of confusion sent to stop me in the name of Jesus Christ.
18. O God my Father, as I prepare for this test/examination, I stop all arrows of distraction sent to stop me in the name of Jesus Christ.
19. The spirit arrogance, you are not allowed to stop me as I prepare to take this test/examination, in the name of Jesus Christ.

20. Over-confidence, you will not stop me as I prepare to take this test/examination, in the name of Jesus Christ.
21. O God my Father, as I prepare for this test/examination, I come against laziness in my studies in the name of Jesus Christ.
22. Today O Lord, I release the fire of God to destroy all arrows of heaviness sent to stop me from preparing, in the name of Jesus Christ.
23. By the power in the name of Jesus Christ, I cancel every plan of enemy to make me end up in the hospital instead of the test center/examination hall, in the name of Jesus Christ.
24. O God my Father, on the basis of your mercy, guide me in whatever I need to do to pass this test/examination in the name of Jesus Christ.
25. O God my Father, complete the good works that you have started in me concerning this test/examination, in the name of Jesus Christ.
26. I decree today that I shall be the head and not the tail among those that have ever taken or will ever take this test/examination, in the name of Jesus Christ.
27. I decree that the Spirit of counsel, wisdom and might, rest upon me now in the name of Jesus Christ.
28. The God that made Daniel 10 times better than his colleagues is doing the same for me now and in this test/examination in the name of Jesus Christ.
29. I cancel my name from the register of failure concerning this test/examination in the name of Jesus Christ.
30. O God my Father, open my eyes of understanding today, as I prepare for this test/examination in the name of Jesus Christ.

31. O God my Father, bring to my remembrance all that I have learned in class concerning this test/examination, in the name of Jesus Christ.
32. O God my Father, bring to my remembrance all that I have studied concerning this test/examination in the name of Jesus Christ.
33. O God my Father, bring to remembrance anything that will help me to pass this test/examination in the name of Jesus Christ.
34. O God my Father, as I am going in to the test center for this test/examination, I cover myself in the blood of Jesus Christ.
35. I cover the test center with the blood of Jesus Christ, in the name of Jesus Christ.
36. I arrest every evil manifestation at this test center in the name of Jesus Christ.
37. I charge the atmosphere of the test center with wisdom and understanding, in the name of Jesus Center, in the name of Jesus Christ.
38. The situation that makes people to experience black-outs in the middle of testing, I am not your candidate, in the name of Jesus Christ.
39. The situation that makes people to forget everything they have studied, I am not your candidate, in the name of Jesus Christ.
40. Satanic attack in the middle of testing, I am not your candidate, in the name of Jesus Christ.
41. By the power in the name of Jesus Christ, I receive a sound mind.
42. I command all evil powers that operate in the test center/examination hall to bow at the name of Jesus Christ.

43. As I go in for the testing, I surround myself with angels of the Living God, and I will come out with thanksgiving in the name of Jesus Christ.
44. By the power in the name of Jesus Christ, I arrest every evil plan to seize, manipulate or distort my test results in the name of Jesus Christ.
45. My results shall not be misplaced or replace in the name of Jesus Christ.
46. O God my Father, grant me patience to understand each question of the test before I answer it, in the name of Jesus Christ.
47. I come against nervousness, I received confidence from the Lord in the name of Jesus Christ.
48. I receive the grace of God to do better than expected in this test/examination, in the name of Jesus Christ.
49. O God my Father, let the best that you have deposited in me manifest in this test/examination, in the name of Jesus Christ.
50. I decree today, that the result of this test/examination will take me to the next level in life, in the name of Jesus Christ.

PRAYER FOR GOD TO SHOWCASE HIS POWER

Passages To Read Before You Pray:
Isaiah 43:18-19, 2 Kings 2:1-18, John 11:1-48, Psalms 46, 19, 126

I have come today to fellowship with my heavenly Father, and make my requests and needs known unto Him. I cannot be hindered nor delayed because I know who I am in the Lord. I am a child of the Kingdom, born of the Spirit, redeemed by the blood of Jesus Christ. I walk in authority, living life without any apology because the power and authority has been given to me according to the Word of God in the book of Luke 9:1.

As I have come to pray today and to fellowship with my heavenly Father, I cover myself in the blood of Jesus Christ, and I put on the whole armor of God. I hereby come against every Prince of Persia that wants to hinder my prayer, I arrest you by the power in the blood of Jesus Christ, and I bind you and cast you down into the pit of hell.

I come against principalities and powers that wrestle with me and my prayers, I arrest you today by the power in the name of Jesus Christ, and I bind you and cast down into the pit of hell. I come against the rulers of the darkness of this world, against spiritual wickedness in high places, I arrest you all by the power in the name of Jesus Christ, and I bind you and cast you down into the pit of hell. I come against weakness and weariness, I arrest you today by the power in the name of Jesus Christ, and I bind you and cast you out of my life. I come against wondering

spirit and distractions, I arrest you today by the power in the name of Jesus Christ, and I bind you and cast you out of my life.

Today I receive the anointing to pray and get results, my prayers cannot be hindered nor delayed because Jesus is my Lord, I will pray today and get the desired results, I decree open heavens upon my prayers. I baptize myself in the fire of the Holy Ghost; therefore I have become too hot for the enemy to handle. My prayers today will attract divine intervention to every situation in my life; signs and wonders will follow my prayers today, testimonies will follow my prayers today and the name of God alone will be glorified, in Jesus name. Amen!

PRAYER POINTS:

1. O God my Father, thank you for being my God, my Father and my friend.
2. O God my Father, thank you for the privilege to know you and the power of the resurrection of Jesus Christ.
3. O God my Father, thank you for always being there for me and with me.
4. O God my Father, thank you for the great and mighty things that you are doing in my life.
5. O God my Father, thank you for your provision and protection over me and my household.
6. O God my Father, thank you for always answering my prayers.
7. I confess my sins before you today and I ask you to forgive me on the basis of your mercy, in the name of Jesus Christ.

8. Wash me clean today O Lord by the blood of Jesus Christ.
9. I cover myself and my household with the blood of Jesus Christ.
10. My prayers today will not go in vain; my prayers will produce the desired results in the name of Jesus Christ.
11. In the presence of those who are waiting to mock me, O God my Father, demonstrate your power that they may know that you are my God, in the name of Jesus Christ.
12. In the presence of those who are waiting to celebrate my failure, O God my Father, grant immeasurable success that they may know you are my God, in the name of Jesus Christ.
13. In the presence of those who are waiting to see what will become of me, O God my Father, demonstrate your power that they may know you are my God, in the name of Jesus Christ.
14. In the presence of those who are waiting to mock the outcome of my prayers, O God my Father, answer my prayer by fire that they may know you are my God, in the name of Jesus Christ.
15. O God my Father, in the presence of those who are waiting to see what you can do for me, demonstrate your power that they may know that you can do all things, in the name of Jesus Christ.
16. O God my Father, in the presence of those who are waiting to see me fall, demonstrate your power that they may know that you are my God, in the name of Jesus Christ.
17. O God my Father, in the presence of those who are waiting to point evil fingers at me, demonstrate your

power that they may know you are my God, in the name of Jesus Christ.
18. My helpers, wherever you are, I command you to come forth in the name of Jesus Christ.
19. My glory, wherever you are, I command you to come forth in the name of Jesus Christ.
20. My financial freedom, wherever you are, I command you to come forth, in the name of Jesus Christ.
21. My miracles, wherever you are, I command you to come forth, in the name of Jesus Christ.
22. My blessings, wherever you are, I command you to come forth, in the name of Jesus Christ.
23. My financial breakthrough, wherever you are, I command you to come forth in the name of Jesus Christ.
24. My success, wherever you are, I command you to come forth in the name of Jesus Christ.
25. People that will show me the way, wherever you are, I command you to come forth in the name of Jesus Christ.
26. People that will lead me to the top, wherever you are, I command you to come forth in the name of Jesus Christ.
27. People that God sent to support me, wherever you are, I command you to come forth in the name of Jesus Christ.
28. People that will show me how to make it, wherever you are, I command you to come forth in the name of Jesus Christ.
29. People that will contribute to my success, wherever you are, I command you to come forth in the name of Jesus Christ.
30. People that will show me how to get to the next level, wherever you are, I command you to come forth in the name of Jesus Christ.

31. People that will connect me to those that will help me, wherever you are, I command you to come forth in the name of Jesus Christ.
32. O God my Father, I am tired of being the same, let transformation begin to happen in every area of my life in the name of Jesus Christ.
33. O God my Father, I am tired of being the same, let the new things begin to happen in every area of my life in the name of Jesus Christ.
34. O God my Father, I am tired of being the same, begin to showcase your power in my life in the name of Jesus Christ.
35. O God my Father, I am tired of being the same, let extraordinary things begin to happen in my life in the name of Jesus Christ.
36. O God my Father, I am tired of being the same, let there be supernatural breakthrough in every area of my life in the name of Jesus Christ.
37. O God my Father, I am tired of being the same, take me from where I am to where you want me to be in the name of Jesus Christ.
38. O God my Father, I am tired of being the same, catapult me into greatness in the name of Jesus Christ.
39. O God my Father, I am tired of being the same, catapult me into double promotion in the name of Jesus Christ.
40. O God my Father, I am tired of being the same, take me to the next level of your power in the name of Jesus Christ.
41. O God my Father, I am tired of being the same, take me to the next level of your glory in the name of Jesus Christ.

42. O God my Father, I am tired of being the same, take me to the next level of prosperity in the name of Jesus Christ.
43. O God my Father, I am tired of being the same, take me to the place of fulfillment in the name of Jesus Christ.
44. O God my Father, I am tired of being the same, take me to the land that is flowing with milk and honey in the name of Jesus Christ.
45. O God my Father, I am tired of being the same, transfer me from the valley to the mountain top, in the name of Jesus Christ.
46. O God my Father, I am tired of being the same, let the great and mighty things that you promise begin to happen in my life, in the name of Jesus Christ.
47. O God my Father, I am tired of being the same, give me reasons to sing a new song in the name of Jesus Christ.
48. O God my Father, I am tired of being the same, give me reasons to dance a new dance in the name of Jesus Christ.
49. O God my Father, I am tired of being the same, let your power bring the best out of me in the name of Jesus Christ.
50. O God my Father, I'm tired of being the same, give me reasons to laugh a new laugh in the name of Jesus Christ.

PRAYER TO CANCEL EVIL TRANSACTION

Passages To Read Before You Pray:
John 2:13-17, I Corinthians 3:16-17, Psalms 83, 30, 86, 3,
Jeremiah 1:1-19

I have come today to fellowship with my heavenly Father, and make my requests and needs known unto Him. I cannot be hindered nor delayed because I know who I am in the Lord. I am a child of the Kingdom, born of the Spirit, redeemed by the blood of Jesus Christ. I walk in authority, living life without any apology because the power and authority has been given to me according to the Word of God in the book of Luke 9:1.

As I have come to pray today and to fellowship with my heavenly Father, I cover myself in the blood of Jesus Christ, and I put on the whole armor of God. I hereby come against every Prince of Persia that wants to hinder my prayer, I arrest you by the power in the blood of Jesus Christ, and I bind you and cast you down into the pit of hell.

I come against principalities and powers that wrestle with me and my prayers, I arrest you today by the power in the name of Jesus Christ, and I bind you and cast down into the pit of hell. I come against the rulers of the darkness of this world, against spiritual wickedness in high places, I arrest you all by the power in the name of Jesus Christ, and I bind you and cast you down into the pit of hell. I come against weakness and weariness, I arrest you today by the power in the name of Jesus Christ, and I bind you and cast you out of my life. I come against wondering

spirit and distractions, I arrest you today by the power in the name of Jesus Christ, and I bind you and cast you out of my life.

Today I receive the anointing to pray and get results, my prayers cannot be hindered nor delayed because Jesus is my Lord, I will pray today and get the desired results, I decree open heavens upon my prayers. I baptize myself in the fire of the Holy Ghost; therefore I have become too hot for the enemy to handle. My prayers today will attract divine intervention to every situation in my life; signs and wonders will follow my prayers today, testimonies will follow my prayers today and the name of God alone will be glorified, in Jesus name. Amen!

PRAYER POINTS:

1. O God my Father, thank you for being my God, my Father and my friend.
2. O God my Father, thank you for the privilege to know you and the power of the resurrection of Jesus Christ.
3. O God my Father, thank you for always being there for me and with me.
4. O God my Father, thank you for the great and mighty things that you are doing in my life.
5. O God my Father, thank you for your provision and protection over me and my household.
6. O God my Father, thank you for always answering my prayers.
7. I confess my sins before you today and I ask you to forgive me on the basis of your mercy, in the name of Jesus Christ.

8. Wash me clean today O Lord by the blood of Jesus Christ.
9. I cover myself and my household with the blood of Jesus Christ.
10. My prayers today will not go in vain; my prayers will produce the desired results in the name of Jesus Christ.
11. Every satanic trader buying and selling in my life, I bind you and cast you out of my life by the power and authority in the name of Jesus Christ.
12. Any spirit or power buying and selling in my life, your time is up, come out with all your merchandise in the name of Jesus Christ.
13. Any spirit or power trying to exchange my glory for something else, you are not allowed to tamper with my glory, in the name of Jesus Christ.
14. Any spirit or power trying to change my destiny for something else, you are not allowed to tamper with my destiny, in the name of Jesus Christ.
15. Any spirit or power trying to change my future for something else, you are not allowed to tamper with my future in the name of Jesus Christ.
16. Any spirit or power stealing my blessing to sell for profit, you are no longer allowed and you will not escape the judgment of God in the name of Jesus Christ.
17. O God my Father, let my stolen blessings begin to torment them in the camp of my enemy until they return it back to me in the name of Jesus Christ.
18. Every satanic merchandise in my temple/life, I set you on fire in the name of Jesus Christ.

19. Every satanic merchandise in the life of my spouse, I set you on fire in the name of Jesus Christ.
20. Every satanic merchandise in the life of my children, I set you on fire in the name of Jesus Christ.
21. Every satanic merchandise in this church, I set you on fire in the name of Jesus Christ.
22. Every satanic merchandise in my home, I set you on fire in the name of Jesus Christ.
23. O God my Father, let every evil transaction concerning my life be cancelled in the name of Jesus Christ.
24. O God my Father, let every evil transaction concerning my spouse be cancelled in the name of Jesus Christ.
25. O God my Father, let every evil transaction concerning my children be cancelled in the name of Jesus Christ.
26. O God my Father, let every evil transaction concerning my marriage be cancelled in the name of Jesus Christ.
27. O God my Father, let every evil transaction concerning my destiny be cancelled in the name of Jesus Christ.
28. O God my Father, let every evil transaction concerning my future be cancelled in the name of Jesus Christ.
29. O God my Father, let every evil transaction concerning my dreams be cancelled in the name of Jesus Christ.
30. Satanic agent of change, you cannot change my destiny, my destiny is covered in the blood of Jesus Christ.

31. Satanic agent of change, you cannot change the destiny of my spouse, my spouse's destiny is covered in the blood of Jesus Christ.
32. Satanic agent of change, you cannot change my children's destiny, my children's destiny is covered in the blood of Jesus Christ.
33. Satanic agent of change, you cannot change the plan of God for my life, it is done and sealed by the blood of Jesus Christ.
34. Satanic agent of change, you cannot change my future, my future is in the hands of God in the name of Jesus Christ.
35. Any power anywhere trying to turn my life into a shopping mall for the enemy, loose your hold upon my life now in the name of Jesus Christ.
36. Any power anywhere trying to turn my life into a satanic drive through, you will not escape the judgment of God in the name of Jesus Christ.
37. Today I drive out any spirit or power buying and selling in my life, in the name of Jesus Christ.
38. Today I drive out every satanic agent of change residing in my life, in the name of Jesus Christ.
39. Every satanic merchandise dumped in my life, I set it on fire in the name of Jesus Christ.
40. O God my Father, let there be a total cleansing in every area of my life in the. Name of Jesus Christ.
41. Today I overthrow every satanic establishment that is troubling my life, in the name of Jesus Christ.
42. Today I overthrow every satanic king and kingdom working against me, in the name of Jesus Christ.

43. Today I overthrow every satanic king and kingdom working against my marriage in the name of Jesus Christ.
44. Today I overthrow every satanic king and kingdom working against my children in the name of Jesus Christ.
45. Today I overthrow every satanic king and kingdom working against my progress in the name of Jesus Christ.
46. Today I overthrow every satanic king and kingdom working against the will of God for my life in the name of Jesus Christ.

DELIVERANCE FROM YOUR PAINFUL PAST

Passages To Read Before You Pray:
Isaiah 43:1-19, Psalms 59, 69, 44, Joel 2:21-27

I have come today to fellowship with my heavenly Father, and make my requests and needs known unto Him. I cannot be hindered nor delayed because I know who I am in the Lord. I am a child of the Kingdom, born of the Spirit, redeemed by the blood of Jesus Christ. I walk in authority, living life without any apology because the power and authority has been given to me according to the Word of God in the book of Luke 9:1.

As I have come to pray today and to fellowship with my heavenly Father, I cover myself in the blood of Jesus Christ, and I put on the whole armor of God. I hereby come against every Prince of Persia that wants to hinder my prayer, I arrest you by the power in the blood of Jesus Christ, and I bind you and cast you down into the pit of hell.

I come against principalities and powers that wrestle with me and my prayers, I arrest you today by the power in the name of Jesus Christ, and I bind you and cast down into the pit of hell. I come against the rulers of the darkness of this world, against spiritual wickedness in high places, I arrest you all by the power in the name of Jesus Christ, and I bind you and cast you down into the pit of hell. I come against weakness and weariness, I arrest you today by the power in the name of Jesus Christ, and I bind you and cast you out of my life. I come against wondering spirit and distractions, I arrest you today by the power in the name of Jesus Christ, and I bind you and cast you out of my life.

Today I receive the anointing to pray and get results, my prayers cannot be hindered nor delayed because Jesus is my Lord, I will pray today and get the desired results, I decree open heavens upon my prayers. I baptize myself in the fire of the Holy Ghost; therefore I have become too hot for the enemy to handle. My prayers today will attract divine intervention to every situation in my life; signs and wonders will follow my prayers today, testimonies will follow my prayers today and the name of God alone will be glorified, in Jesus name. Amen!

PRAYER POINTS:

1. O God my Father, thank you for being my God, my Father and my friend.
2. O God my Father, thank you for the privilege to know you and the power of the resurrection of Jesus Christ.
3. O God my Father, thank you for always being there for me and with me.
4. O God my Father, thank you for the great and mighty things that you are doing in my life.
5. O God my Father, thank you for your provision and protection over me and my household.
6. O God my Father, thank you for always answering my prayers.
7. I confess my sins before you today and I ask you to forgive me on the basis of your mercy, in the name of Jesus Christ.
8. Wash me clean today O Lord by the blood of Jesus Christ.
9. I cover myself and my household with the blood of Jesus Christ.

10. My prayers today will not go in vain; my prayers will produce the desired results in the name of Jesus Christ.
11. O God my Father, deliver me from my past and prepare me for a great tomorrow, in the name of Jesus Christ.
12. O God my Father, I am tired of living in the past, deliver me today from the bondage of the past, in the name of Jesus Christ.
13. I refuse to think about my past failures, I am moving forward by the power in the name of Jesus Christ.
14. Anything in my life holding me captive to my past, I command you, loose you hold over my life now, in the name of Jesus Christ.
15. O God my Father, help me to forget what my past looked like so I can focus on your plan for me, in the name of Jesus Christ.
16. O God my Father, separate me from every unfriendly friend reminding me of my past, in the name of Jesus Christ.
17. O God my Father, deliver me from every situation reminding me of my past, in the name of Jesus Christ.
18. O God my Father, do something wonderful in my life today that will make me forget my past pain, in the name of Jesus Christ.
19. O God my Father, do something marvelous in my life today that will make me forget my past disappointment, in the name of Jesus Christ.
20. O God my Father, do something miraculous in my life today that will make me forget my past failure, in the name of Jesus Christ.

21. O God my Father, do something miraculous in my life today that will make me forget my past rejection, in the name of Jesus Christ.
22. Whatever it is that made me cry in the past, the same shall make me laugh today in the name of Jesus Christ.
23. Wherever I have been rejected in the past, I will be accepted today with honor in the name of Jesus Christ.
24. Every mouth that have said No to me in the past shall call me back and say Yes with respect in the name of Jesus Christ.
25. Any situation that has given me so much pain in the past, the same shall give me great joy today in the name of Jesus Christ.
26. I refuse to allow my past to affect my future in the name of Jesus Christ
27. Any situation that has brought me misfortune in the past, the same shall be a great source of breakthrough for me in the name of Jesus Christ.
28. O God my Father, let all my pitfalls in the past become stepping stones to greatness today in the name of Jesus Christ.
29. O God my Father, let all my past mistakes become sources of miracle for me today in the name of Jesus Christ.

THE VALLEY OF THE SHADOW OF DEATH

Passages To Read Before You Pray:
Psalms 23, 27, 56, 118, John 11:1-45, Isaiah 50:7-9

I have come today to fellowship with my heavenly Father, and make my requests and needs known unto Him. I cannot be hindered nor delayed because I know who I am in the Lord. I am a child of the Kingdom, born of the Spirit, redeemed by the blood of Jesus Christ. I walk in authority, living life without any apology because the power and authority has been given to me according to the Word of God in the book of Luke 9:1.

As I have come to pray today and to fellowship with my heavenly Father, I cover myself in the blood of Jesus Christ, and I put on the whole armor of God. I hereby come against every Prince of Persia that wants to hinder my prayer, I arrest you by the power in the blood of Jesus Christ, and I bind you and cast you down into the pit of hell.

I come against principalities and powers that wrestle with me and my prayers, I arrest you today by the power in the name of Jesus Christ, and I bind you and cast down into the pit of hell. I come against the rulers of the darkness of this world, against spiritual wickedness in high places, I arrest you all by the power in the name of Jesus Christ, and I bind you and cast you down into the pit of hell. I come against weakness and weariness, I arrest you today by the power in the name of Jesus Christ, and I bind you and cast you out of my life. I come against wondering spirit and distractions, I arrest you today by the power in the name of Jesus Christ, and I bind you and cast you out of my life.

Today I receive the anointing to pray and get results, my prayers cannot be hindered nor delayed because Jesus is my Lord, I will pray today and get the desired results, I decree open heavens upon my prayers. I baptize myself in the fire of the Holy Ghost; therefore I have become too hot for the enemy to handle. My prayers today will attract divine intervention to every situation in my life; signs and wonders will follow my prayers today, testimonies will follow my prayers today and the name of God alone will be glorified, in Jesus name. Amen!

PRAYER POINTS:

1. O God my Father, thank you for being my God, my Father and my friend.
2. O God my Father, thank you for the privilege to know you and the power of the resurrection of Jesus Christ.
3. O God my Father, thank you for always being there for me and with me.
4. O God my Father, thank you for the great and mighty things that you are doing in my life.
5. O God my Father, thank you for your provision and protection over me and my household.
6. O God my Father, thank you for always answering my prayers.
7. I confess my sins before you today and I ask you to forgive me on the basis of your mercy, in the name of Jesus Christ.
8. Wash me clean today O Lord by the blood of Jesus Christ.
9. I cover myself and my household with the blood of Jesus Christ.

10. My prayers today will not go in vain; my prayers will produce the desired results in the name of Jesus Christ.
11. When I find myself in the valley of the shadow of death, I receive boldness from the Lord and I will not be afraid, for the Lord is with me.
12. I receive wisdom to neutralize the plan, techniques and strategies of the enemy in the valley of the shadow of death in the name of Jesus Christ.
13. I release the fire of God to destroy every stronghold of the enemy planning to attack me in the name of Jesus Christ.
14. O God my Father, release the warring angels to make a way for me even in the valley of the shadow of death in the name of Jesus Christ.
15. I receive wisdom and power to overcome my archenemy trying to turn my life into hell on earth, in the name of Jesus Christ.
16. O God my Father, surround me with strong and fearless people that will go with me to conquer the battle of the valley of the shadow of death in the name of Jesus Christ.
17. O God my Father, let the valley of the shadow of death be converted to a mountain of testimony in the name of Jesus Christ.
18. O God my Father, when I walk through the valley of the shadow of death, command your angels to carry me in their hands so that the enemy will not be able to harm me in the name of Jesus Christ.
19. O God my Father, when I walk through the valley of the shadow of death, surround me with your fire, so that the enemy will not be able to touch me.

20. O God my Father, when I walk through the valley of the shadow of death, give me courage to move forward without fear no matter the activity of the enemy in the name of Jesus Christ.
21. O God my Father, arise and fight for me, I must win the battle of the valley of the shadow of death in the name of Jesus Christ.
22. Any power anywhere trying to divert my journey to go through the valley of the shadow of death, you will not escape the judgment of God in the name of Jesus Christ.

PRAYER TO STOP THE ACTIVITIES OF THE ENEMY

Passages To Read Before You Pray:
2 Timothy 3:9, 2 John 3:8, Psalms 3, 9, 35, 109, 68, 69

I have come today to fellowship with my heavenly Father, and make my requests and needs known unto Him. I cannot be hindered nor delayed because I know who I am in the Lord. I am a child of the Kingdom, born of the Spirit, redeemed by the blood of Jesus Christ. I walk in authority, living life without any apology because the power and authority has been given to me according to the Word of God in the book of Luke 9:1.

As I have come to pray today and to fellowship with my heavenly Father, I cover myself in the blood of Jesus Christ, and I put on the whole armor of God. I hereby come against every Prince of Persia that wants to hinder my prayer, I arrest you by the power in the blood of Jesus Christ, and I bind you and cast you down into the pit of hell.

I come against principalities and powers that wrestle with me and my prayers, I arrest you today by the power in the name of Jesus Christ, and I bind you and cast down into the pit of hell. I come against the rulers of the darkness of this world, against spiritual wickedness in high places, I arrest you all by the power in the name of Jesus Christ, and I bind you and cast you down into the pit of hell. I come against weakness and weariness, I arrest you today by the power in the name of Jesus Christ, and I bind you and cast you out of my life. I come against wondering

spirit and distractions, I arrest you today by the power in the name of Jesus Christ, and I bind you and cast you out of my life.

Today I receive the anointing to pray and get results, my prayers cannot be hindered nor delayed because Jesus is my Lord, I will pray today and get the desired results, I decree open heavens upon my prayers. I baptize myself in the fire of the Holy Ghost; therefore I have become too hot for the enemy to handle. My prayers today will attract divine intervention to every situation in my life; signs and wonders will follow my prayers today, testimonies will follow my prayers today and the name of God alone will be glorified, in Jesus name. Amen!

PRAYER POINTS:

1. O God my Father, thank you for being my God, my Father and my friend.
2. O God my Father, thank you for the privilege to know you and the power of the resurrection of Jesus Christ.
3. O God my Father, thank you for always being there for me and with me.
4. O God my Father, thank you for the great and mighty things that you are doing in my life.
5. O God my Father, thank you for your provision and protection over me and my household.
6. O God my Father, thank you for always answering my prayers.
7. I confess my sins before you today and I ask you to forgive me on the basis of your mercy, in the name of Jesus Christ.

8. Wash me clean today O Lord by the blood of Jesus Christ.
9. I cover myself and my household with the blood of Jesus Christ.
10. My prayers today will not go in vain; my prayers will produce the desired results in the name of Jesus Christ.
11. The works of the household wickedness in my life shall proceed no further, in the name of Jesus Christ.
12. The works of the household wickedness in the life of my spouse shall proceed no further, in the name of Jesus Christ.
13. The works of the household wickedness in the life of my children shall proceed no further, in the name of Jesus Christ.
14. The works of the household wickedness against my finances shall proceed no further, in the name of Jesus Christ.
15. The works of the household wickedness against my success shall proceed no further, in the name of Jesus Christ.
16. The works of the household wickedness against my marriage shall proceed no further, in the name of Jesus Christ.
17. The works of the household wickedness against my dreams shall proceed no further, in the name of Jesus Christ.
18. The works of the household wickedness against my business shall proceed no further, in the name of Jesus Christ.

19. The works of the household wickedness against my destiny shall proceed no further, in the name of Jesus Christ.
20. The works of the household wickedness to change my destiny shall proceed no further, in the name of Jesus Christ.
21. All the activities of the enemies in my life shall proceed no further, in the name of Jesus Christ.
22. All the activities of the enemies in the life of my spouse shall proceed no further, in the name of Jesus Christ.
23. All the activities of the enemies in the life of my children shall proceed no further, in the name of Jesus Christ.
24. All the activities of the enemies against my finances shall proceed no further, in the name of Jesus Christ.
25. Any power anywhere that has been delaying the move of God in my life, it shall proceed no further, in the name of Jesus Christ.
26. Any power anywhere that has been hindering my prayers, your work in my life shall proceed no further in the name of Jesus Christ.
27. Any power anywhere challenging the power of God in my life, your efforts in my life shall proceed no further in the name of Jesus Christ.
28. Any power anywhere hindering my miracles, your work in my life shall proceed no further in the name of Jesus Christ.
29. Any spirit or power assigned to put me to shame, your work in my life shall proceed no further, in the name of Jesus Christ.

30. Any spirit or power assigned to frustrate my life, your work in my life shall proceed no further, in the name of Jesus Christ.
31. Any spirit or power assigned to make my life miserable, your work in my life shall proceed no further, in the name of Jesus Christ.
32. Any spirit or power assigned to devour my finances, your work in my life shall proceed no further, in the name of Jesus Christ.
33. Any spirit or power assigned to inflict me with sickness, your work in my life shall proceed no further, in the name of Jesus Christ.
34. Any spirit or power assigned to take away the peace or joy out of my marriage, your work in marriage shall proceed no further, in the name of Jesus Christ.
35. Any spirit or power assigned to attack my relationship, your work in my life shall proceed no further, in the name of Jesus Christ.
36. Any spirit or power assigned to create confusion in my life, your work in my life shall proceed no further, in the name of Jesus Christ.
37. Clouds of unbelief in my life that has been hindering my blessings, you will proceed no further in the name of Jesus Christ.
38. With all authority I declare today, all battles against me shall proceed no further in the name of Jesus Christ.
39. With all authority I declare today, all satanic attacks against me shall proceed no further in the name of Jesus Christ.
40. With all authority I declare today, failure in any area of my life shall proceed no further in the name of Jesus Christ.

41. With all authority I declare today, all evil effects of evil covenant in my life shall proceed no further in the name of Jesus Christ.
42. With all authority I declare today, all evil effects of past mistakes in my life shall proceed no further, in the name of Jesus Christ.
43. With all authority I declare today, all evil effects of satanic arrows fired at me shall proceed no further in the name of Jesus Christ.
44. With all authority I declare today, all evil effects of negative words I have spoken against myself in the time of ignorance shall proceed no further, in the name of Jesus Christ.
45. With all authority I declare today, all evil effects of evil pronouncement against me shall proceed no further, in the name of Jesus Christ.
46. With all authority I declare today, the works of every satanic virus released into my life shall proceed no further, in the name of Jesus Christ.
47. With all authority I declare today, any plan of darkness to pollute my prayer altar shall proceed no further, in the name of Jesus Christ.
48. With all authority I declare today, every satanic virus released to corrupt the anointing of God upon my life, your work in my life shall proceed no further in the name of Jesus Christ.
49. Every serpentine spirit assigned to attack me, your plan shall proceed no further in the name of Jesus Christ.
50. With all authority I declare today, barrenness in any area of my life shall proceed no further in the name of Jesus Christ.

PRAYER TO BREAK ANNUAL EVIL CYCLE

Passages To Read Before You Pray:
Deuteronomy 2:1-3, Mark 5:25-34, Psalms 30, 55, 46, 70

I have come today to fellowship with my heavenly Father, and make my requests and needs known unto Him. I cannot be hindered nor delayed because I know who I am in the Lord. I am a child of the Kingdom, born of the Spirit, redeemed by the blood of Jesus Christ. I walk in authority, living life without any apology because the power and authority has been given to me according to the Word of God in the book of Luke 9:1.

As I have come to pray today and to fellowship with my heavenly Father, I cover myself in the blood of Jesus Christ, and I put on the whole armor of God. I hereby come against every Prince of Persia that wants to hinder my prayer, I arrest you by the power in the blood of Jesus Christ, and I bind you and cast you down into the pit of hell.

I come against principalities and powers that wrestle with me and my prayers, I arrest you today by the power in the name of Jesus Christ, and I bind you and cast down into the pit of hell. I come against the rulers of the darkness of this world, against spiritual wickedness in high places, I arrest you all by the power in the name of Jesus Christ, and I bind you and cast you down into the pit of hell. I come against weakness and weariness, I arrest you today by the power in the name of Jesus Christ, and I bind you and cast you out of my life. I come against wondering spirit and distractions, I arrest you today by the power in the name of Jesus Christ, and I bind you and cast you out of my life.

Today I receive the anointing to pray and get results, my prayers cannot be hindered nor delayed because Jesus is my Lord, I will pray today and get the desired results, I decree open heavens upon my prayers. I baptize myself in the fire of the Holy Ghost; therefore I have become too hot for the enemy to handle. My prayers today will attract divine intervention to every situation in my life; signs and wonders will follow my prayers today, testimonies will follow my prayers today and the name of God alone will be glorified, in Jesus name. Amen!

PRAYER POINTS:

1. O God my Father, thank you for being my God, my Father and my friend.
2. O God my Father, thank you for the privilege to know you and the power of the resurrection of Jesus Christ.
3. O God my Father, thank you for always being there for me and with me.
4. O God my Father, thank you for the great and mighty things that you are doing in my life.
5. O God my Father, thank you for your provision and protection over me and my household.
6. O God my Father, thank you for always answering my prayers.
7. I confess my sins before you today and I ask you to forgive me on the basis of your mercy, in the name of Jesus Christ.
8. Wash me clean today O Lord by the blood of Jesus Christ.
9. I cover myself and my household with the blood of Jesus Christ.

10. My prayers today will not go in vain; my prayers will produce the desired results in the name of Jesus Christ.
11. O God my Father, the annual event that is causing me to cry, I command it to permanently stop now in the name of Jesus Christ.
12. O God my Father, the annual event that is causing me to lose faith, I command it to permanently stop now.
13. O God my Father, the annual event that is causing me to lose hope, I command it to permanently stop now.
14. The annual event that is causing me to question the power of God, I command it to permanently stop now.
15. The annual event that is causing me to question my faith in God, I command it to permanently stop now.
16. The annual event that is causing me to be sorrowful, I command you to stop now.
17. The annual event that has turned to an evil cycle in my life, I command it to permanently stop today.
18. The annual event that causes people to challenge the power of God in me, I command it to permanently stop today.
19. The annual event that causes people to ask if my God can or cannot deliver me, O God my Father, for your name sake, let it stop today permanently.
20. The annual event that always brings ridicule in my life, Father Lord, for your name sake, let it stop today permanently.
21. The annual event that always reminds me of my past pain and sorrow, I command it to permanently stop today.
22. The annual event that always reminds me of my past failure, I command it to permanently stop today.

23. The annual event that always reminds me of my past disappointment, I command it to permanently stop today.
24. The annual event that always rewind the clock of my life, I command you to permanently stop today.
25. The annual event that is causing my life to go backward, I command you to permanently stop today.
26. O God my Father, let the memory of my past failure be permanently erased today.
27. O God my Father, let the memory of my past disappointment be permanently erased today.
28. O God my Father, let the memory of any bad occurrence in my past be permanently erased today.
29. O God my Father, let the memory of painful events in my life be permanently erased today.
30. Today I decree, I shall cry no more in the name of Jesus Christ.

THIS IS THE DAY

Passages To Read Before You Pray:
Isaiah 10:27, Isaiah 29:14, Jeremiah 33:14, Psalm 35, 3, 9, 86

I have come today to fellowship with my heavenly Father, and make my requests and needs known unto Him. I cannot be hindered nor delayed because I know who I am in the Lord. I am a child of the Kingdom, born of the Spirit, redeemed by the blood of Jesus Christ. I walk in authority, living life without any apology because the power and authority has been given to me according to the Word of God in the book of Luke 9:1.

As I have come to pray today and to fellowship with my heavenly Father, I cover myself in the blood of Jesus Christ, and I put on the whole armor of God. I hereby come against every Prince of Persia that wants to hinder my prayer, I arrest you by the power in the blood of Jesus Christ, and I bind you and cast you down into the pit of hell.

I come against principalities and powers that wrestle with me and my prayers, I arrest you today by the power in the name of Jesus Christ, and I bind you and cast down into the pit of hell. I come against the rulers of the darkness of this world, against spiritual wickedness in high places, I arrest you all by the power in the name of Jesus Christ, and I bind you and cast you down into the pit of hell. I come against weakness and weariness, I arrest you today by the power in the name of Jesus Christ, and I bind you and cast you out of my life. I come against wondering spirit and distractions, I arrest you today by the power in the name of Jesus Christ, and I bind you and cast you out of my life.

Today I receive the anointing to pray and get results, my prayers cannot be hindered nor delayed because Jesus is my Lord, I will pray today and get the desired results, I decree open heavens upon my prayers. I baptize myself in the fire of the Holy Ghost; therefore I have become too hot for the enemy to handle. My prayers today will attract divine intervention to every situation in my life; signs and wonders will follow my prayers today, testimonies will follow my prayers today and the name of God alone will be glorified, in Jesus name. Amen!

PRAYER POINTS:

1. O God my Father, thank you for being my God, my Father and my friend.
2. O God my Father, thank you for the privilege to know you and the power of the resurrection of Jesus Christ.
3. O God my Father, thank you for always being there for me and with me.
4. O God my Father, thank you for the great and mighty things that you are doing in my life.
5. O God my Father, thank you for your provision and protection over me and my household.
6. O God my Father, thank you for always answering my prayers.
7. I confess my sins before you today and I ask you to forgive me on the basis of your mercy, in the name of Jesus Christ.
8. Wash me clean today O Lord by the blood of Jesus Christ.
9. I cover myself and my household with the blood of Jesus Christ.

10. My prayers today will not go in vain; my prayers will produce the desired results in the name of Jesus Christ.
11. Today is the day O Lord, let it be known that you are my God.
12. Today is the day O Lord, let it be known that you are able to deliver me from any form of bondage, in the name of Jesus Christ.
13. Today is the day O Lord, let it be known that you have power to transform lives and change situation for good, in the name of Jesus Christ.
14. Today is the day O Lord, arise and prove yourself as the Almighty God in my life in the name of Jesus Christ.
15. Today is the day O Lord, arise and deliver me from the bondage of the wicked, in the name of Jesus Christ.
16. Today is the day O Lord, arise and deliver me from poverty in the name of Jesus Christ.
17. Today is the day O Lord, arise and deliver me from stagnancy I want to move forward in life, in the name of Jesus Christ.
18. Today is the day O Lord, arise and deliver me from backwardness, I am tired of going backward in life, in the name of Jesus Christ.
19. Today is the day O Lord, arise and deliver me from any form of sickness, you are my healer, in the name of Jesus Christ.
20. Today is the day O Lord, arise and deliver me from any form of ailment and infirmity, you are the Greatest Physician, in the name of Jesus Christ.
21. Today is the day O Lord, arise and deliver me from the hands of household wickedness in the name of Jesus Christ.

22. Today is the day O Lord, arise and rescue me from the pit of hopelessness, in the name of Jesus Christ.
23. Today is the day O Lord, arise and deliver me from every form of slavery in the name of Jesus Christ.
24. Today is the day O Lord, arise and deliver me from the hands of the power that wants to kill my dreams, in the name of Jesus Christ.
25. Today is the day O Lord, arise and deliver me from the mouth of satanic lion trying to swallow me in the name of Jesus Christ.
26. Today is the day O Lord, arise and deliver me from hatred and jealousy around me that I may live a fulfilled life in the name of Jesus Christ.
27. Today is the day O Lord, arise and fight against any power fighting against me, in the name of Jesus Christ.
28. Today is the day O Lord, arise and trouble any spirit or power troubling me, in the name of Jesus Christ.
29. Today is the day O Lord, arise and deliver me from the hands of any spirit or power refusing to let me move forward, in the name of Jesus Christ.
30. Today is the day O Lord, arise and deliver me from the spirit of fear in the name of Jesus Christ.
31. Today is the day O Lord, arise and destroy every yoke of sickness upon my life in the name of Jesus Christ.
32. Today is the day O Lord, arise and destroy every yoke of spiritual laziness upon my life in the name of Jesus Christ.
33. Today is the day O Lord, arise and destroy every plan of the enemy concerning my life in the name of Jesus Christ.
34. Today is the day O Lord, arise and set me free from any trouble that I put myself in, in the name of Jesus Christ.

35. Today is the day O Lord, arise and deliver me from the hands of the power that is holding my life back, in the name of Jesus Christ.
36. Today is the day O Lord, arise and destroy every satanic embargo placed upon my life, in the name of Jesus Christ.
37. Today is the day O Lord, arise and rescue me from drowning in debt, in the name of Jesus Christ.
38. Today is the day O Lord, arise and turn my situation around for good, in the name of Jesus Christ.
39. Today is the day O Lord, arise and change my story for the better, in the name of Jesus Christ.
40. Today is the day O Lord, arise and transfer me from the bottom to the top, in the name of Jesus Christ.
41. Today is the day O Lord, arise and relocate me from the valley to the mountain top, in the name of Jesus Christ.
42. Today is the day O Lord, arise and grant me favor in every area and wherever I go in the name of Jesus Christ.
43. Today is the day O Lord, arise and complete the good work that you have started in my life, in the name of Jesus Christ.
44. Today is the day O Lord, arise and remove all impossibilities in every area of my life, in the name of Jesus Christ.
45. Today is the day O Lord, proceed to do a marvelous work in my life, in the name of Jesus Christ.
46. Today is the day O Lord, proceed to do a marvelous work in my home, in the name of Jesus Christ.
47. Today is the day O Lord, proceed to do a marvelous work in the life of my spouse in the name of Jesus Christ.

48. Today is the day O Lord, proceed to do a marvelous work in the life of my children in the name of Jesus Christ.
49. Today is the day O Lord, proceed to do a marvelous work in my business, in the name of Jesus Christ.
50. Today is the day O Lord, proceed to do a marvelous work in my finances in the name of Jesus Christ.
51. Today is the day O Lord, proceed to a marvelous work in my marriage and relationship, in the name of Jesus Christ.
52. Today is the day O Lord, proceed to do wonders in my life according to your word, in the name of Jesus Christ.
53. Today is the day O Lord, proceed to do wonders in my home according to your word in the name of Jesus Christ.
54. Today is the day O Lord, proceed to do wonders in my finances in the name of Jesus Christ.
55. Today is the day O Lord, proceed to do wonders in my business in the name of Jesus Christ.
56. Today is the day O Lord, proceed to do wonders in my household in the name of Jesus Christ.
57. Today is the day O Lord, arise and perform the good things that you have promised me, in the name of Jesus Christ.
58. Today is the day O Lord, arise and perform the good things that you have promised to do concerning my finances, in the name of Jesus Christ.
59. Today is the day O Lord, arise and perform the good things that you have promised to do in marriage, in the name of Jesus Christ.

60. Today is the day O Lord, arise and perform the good things that you have promised to do in my business, in the name of Jesus Christ.
61. Today is the day O Lord, arise and perform the good things that you have to do in the life of my spouse, in the name of Jesus Christ.
62. Today is the day O Lord, arise and perform the good things that you have promised to do in the life of my children, in the name of Jesus Christ.
63. Today is the day O Lord, arise and perform the good things that you have promised to do concerning my dreams and goals, in the name of Jesus Christ.
64. Today is the day O Lord, arise and perform the good things that you have promised to do concerning my destiny and purpose in life, in the name of Jesus Christ.
65. Today is the day O Lord, arise and take me to the next level, in the name of Jesus Christ.

PRAYER WHEN YOU DESPERATELY NEED A CHANGE

Passages To Read Before You Pray:
Isaiah 43:18-19, Jeremiah 32:27, Jeremiah 33:14, Joel 2:21-24

I have come today to fellowship with my heavenly Father, and make my requests and needs known unto Him. I cannot be hindered nor delayed because I know who I am in the Lord. I am a child of the Kingdom, born of the Spirit, redeemed by the blood of Jesus Christ. I walk in authority, living life without any apology because the power and authority has been given to me according to the Word of God in the book of Luke 9:1.

As I have come to pray today and to fellowship with my heavenly Father, I cover myself in the blood of Jesus Christ, and I put on the whole armor of God. I hereby come against every Prince of Persia that wants to hinder my prayer, I arrest you by the power in the blood of Jesus Christ, and I bind you and cast you down into the pit of hell.

I come against principalities and powers that wrestle with me and my prayers, I arrest you today by the power in the name of Jesus Christ, and I bind you and cast down into the pit of hell. I come against the rulers of the darkness of this world, against spiritual wickedness in high places, I arrest you all by the power in the name of Jesus Christ, and I bind you and cast you down into the pit of hell. I come against weakness and weariness, I arrest you today by the power in the name of Jesus Christ, and I bind you and cast you out of my life. I come against wondering

spirit and distractions, I arrest you today by the power in the name of Jesus Christ, and I bind you and cast you out of my life.

Today I receive the anointing to pray and get results, my prayers cannot be hindered nor delayed because Jesus is my Lord, I will pray today and get the desired results, I decree open heavens upon my prayers. I baptize myself in the fire of the Holy Ghost; therefore I have become too hot for the enemy to handle. My prayers today will attract divine intervention to every situation in my life; signs and wonders will follow my prayers today, testimonies will follow my prayers today and the name of God alone will be glorified, in Jesus name. Amen!

PRAYER POINTS:

1. O God my Father, thank you for being my God, my Father and my friend.
2. O God my Father, thank you for the privilege to know you and the power of the resurrection of Jesus Christ.
3. O God my Father, thank you for always being there for me and with me.
4. O God my Father, thank you for the great and mighty things that you are doing in my life.
5. O God my Father, thank you for your provision and protection over me and my household.
6. O God my Father, thank you for always answering my prayers.
7. I confess my sins before you today and I ask you to forgive me on the basis of your mercy, in the name of Jesus Christ.

8. Wash me clean today O Lord by the blood of Jesus Christ.
9. I cover myself and my household with the blood of Jesus Christ.
10. My prayers today will not go in vain; my prayers will produce the desired results in the name of Jesus Christ.

11. I am tired of talking about my failure, Father Lord, change my story in the name of Jesus Christ.
12. I am tired of talking about my defeat, Father Lord, give me a better story to tell in the name of Jesus Christ.
13. I am tired of talking about my disappointment, Father Lord, change my story in the name of Jesus Christ.
14. I am tired of complaining, Jehovah God, give me a new and better story to share in the name of Jesus Christ.
15. I am tired of talking about how things are not going well, Jehovah God, give me a new and better story to tell in the name of Jesus Christ.
16. I am tired of talking about my loss, Father Lord, give me a better story to tell in the name of Jesus Christ.
17. I am tired of sharing old testimonies, Father Lord, do something new in my life, in the name of Jesus Christ.
18. I am tired of talking about how great you were in my life, Jehovah God, proof yourself once again a Great God in my life in the name of Jesus Christ.
19. I am tired of talking about mighty things you did in my life years ago, Father Lord, do something new in my life today in the name of Jesus Christ.
20. I am tired of talking about miracles that you did in my life years ago, Father Lord, I need fresh miracles in the name of Jesus Christ.

21. It is written, without signs and wonders people will not believe, Father Lord, let there be signs and wonders in my life that people may believe that I serve a mighty God, in the name of Jesus Christ.
22. I am tired of thinking about my situation, Jehovah God, do something new in my life that will make me forget my present situation, in the name of Jesus Christ.
23. O God my Father, let there be a change in my situation, take me from where I am to where you want me to be, in the name of Jesus Christ.
24. O God my Father, let there be a change in my situation, take me from the bottom and place me at the top of the ladder, in the name of Jesus Christ.
25. O God my Father, give me the grace to share a better story than the story of defeat, in the name of Jesus Christ.
26. O God my Father, give me the grace to share a better story than the story of poverty, in the name of Jesus Christ.
27. O God my Father, give me the grace to share a better story than the story of unanswered prayers, in the name of Jesus Christ.
28. O God my Father, give me the grace to share a better story than the story of Jabez, in the name of Jesus Christ.
29. O God my Father, give me the grace to share a better story than the sorry of Job, in the name of Jesus Christ.
30. O God my Father, give me the grace to share a better story than the story about my sufferings, in the name of Jesus Christ.
31. Today O Lord, give me reasons to share a new story of prosperity in the name of Jesus Christ.

32. Today O Lord, give me reasons to share a new story of victory, in the name of Jesus Christ.
33. Today O Lord, give me reasons to share a new story of abundance, in the name of Jesus Christ.
34. Today O Lord, give me reasons to share a new story of breakthroughs, in the name of Jesus Christ.
35. Today O Lord, give me reasons to share a new story of uncommon success, in the name of Jesus Christ.
36. Today O Lord, give me reasons to share a new story of unbelievable miracles, in the name of Jesus Christ.
37. Today O Lord, give me reasons to share a new story of how you made a way for me where there was no way, in the name of Jesus Christ.
38. Today O Lord, give me reasons to share a new story of how you opened the heavens and released abundance into my life, in the name of Jesus Christ.
39. Today O Lord, give me reasons to share a new story of how you opened the heavens and released the former and the latter rain upon my life, in the name of Jesus Christ.
40. Today O Lord, give me reasons to share a new story of how you increased my harvest, in the name of Jesus Christ.
41. Today O Lord, give me reasons to share a new story of how you healed me from sicknesses and infirmities, in the name of Jesus Christ.
42. Today O Lord, give me reasons to share a new story of how you connected me with Kings and Priests, in the name of Jesus Christ.
43. Today O Lord, give me reasons to share a new story of how you made room for me in every area, in the name of Jesus Christ.

44. Today O Lord, give me reasons to share a new story of how you healed my land, in the name of Jesus Christ.
45. Today O Lord, give me reasons to share a new story of how you demonstrated your power in every area of my life, in the name of Jesus Christ.

PRAYER FOR PROSPERITY IN TIME OF RECESSION

Passages To Read Before You Pray:
Genesis 26:1-16, Joel 2:21-24, Leviticus 26:5, Deuteronomy 30:9, Isaiah 30:23, Philippians 4:19

I have come today to fellowship with my heavenly Father, and make my requests and needs known unto Him. I cannot be hindered nor delayed because I know who I am in the Lord. I am a child of the Kingdom, born of the Spirit, redeemed by the blood of Jesus Christ. I walk in authority, living life without any apology because the power and authority has been given to me according to the Word of God in the book of Luke 9:1.

As I have come to pray today and to fellowship with my heavenly Father, I cover myself in the blood of Jesus Christ, and I put on the whole armor of God. I hereby come against every Prince of Persia that wants to hinder my prayer, I arrest you by the power in the blood of Jesus Christ, and I bind you and cast you down into the pit of hell.

I come against principalities and powers that wrestle with me and my prayers, I arrest you today by the power in the name of Jesus Christ, and I bind you and cast down into the pit of hell. I come against the rulers of the darkness of this world, against spiritual wickedness in high places, I arrest you all by the power in the name of Jesus Christ, and I bind you and cast you down into the pit of hell. I come against weakness and weariness, I arrest you today by the power in the name of Jesus Christ, and I bind you and cast you out of my life. I come against wondering

spirit and distractions, I arrest you today by the power in the name of Jesus Christ, and I bind you and cast you out of my life.

Today I receive the anointing to pray and get results, my prayers cannot be hindered nor delayed because Jesus is my Lord, I will pray today and get the desired results, I decree open heavens upon my prayers. I baptize myself in the fire of the Holy Ghost; therefore I have become too hot for the enemy to handle. My prayers today will attract divine intervention to every situation in my life; signs and wonders will follow my prayers today, testimonies will follow my prayers today and the name of God alone will be glorified, in Jesus name. Amen!

PRAYER POINTS:

1. O God my Father, thank you for being my God, my Father and my friend.
2. O God my Father, thank you for the privilege to know you and the power of the resurrection of Jesus Christ.
3. O God my Father, thank you for always being there for me and with me.
4. O God my Father, thank you for the great and mighty things that you are doing in my life.
5. O God my Father, thank you for your provision and protection over me and my household.
6. O God my Father, thank you for always answering my prayers.
7. I confess my sins before you today and I ask you to forgive me on the basis of your mercy, in the name of Jesus Christ.

8. Wash me clean today O Lord by the blood of Jesus Christ.
9. I cover myself and my household with the blood of Jesus Christ.
10. My prayers today will not go in vain; my prayers will produce the desired results in the name of Jesus Christ.

11. O God my Father, in the time of famine supply all my needs in the name of Jesus Christ.
12. O God my Father, even in the time of drought, my harvest shall continue, in the name of Jesus Christ.
13. As a child of the kingdom, I decree today that the famine of the land will not affect me, in the name of Jesus Christ.
14. As a child of the kingdom, I decree today that the famine of the land will not affect my crops/business, in the name of Jesus Christ.
15. As a child of the kingdom, I decree today that the famine of the land will not affect my family, in the name of Jesus Christ.
16. As a child of the kingdom, I decree today that the famine of the land will not affect my finances, in the name of Jesus Christ.
17. As a child of the kingdom, I decree today that the famine of the land will not affect my income, in the name of Jesus Christ.
18. As a child of the kingdom, I decree today that the famine of the land will not affect anything that concerns me, in the name of Jesus Christ.
19. No matter how terrible the famine in the land, I will not go down to Egypt, in the name of Jesus Christ.

20. No matter how terrible the famine in the land, I will not do anything against the will of God, in the name of Jesus Christ.
21. As a child of the Living God, in the time of famine, I will not lack any good thing in the name of Jesus Christ.
22. As a child of the Living God, in the time of famine, I will eat in abundance in the name of Jesus Christ.
23. As a child of the Living God, in the time of famine, I will have more than enough in every area, in the name of Jesus Christ.
24. As a child of the Living God, in the time of famine, I will sow in the land and reap in hundreds and thousands folds, in the name of Jesus Christ.
25. As a child of the kingdom, in the time of famine I shall receive uncommon blessings from God, in the name of Jesus Christ.
26. As a child of the kingdom, in the time of famine I shall eat the fruits of my labor in the name of Jesus Christ.
27. As a child of the kingdom, today I decree that even in the time of famine, my land shall yield her increase, in the name of Jesus Christ.
28. As a child of the kingdom, today I decree that even in the time of famine, my crops shall yield her increase, in the name of Jesus Christ.
29. As a child of the kingdom, today I decree that even in the time of famine, my harvest shall be plenteous, in the name of Jesus Christ.
30. As a child of the Living God, today I decree that even in the time of drought, the former and the latter rain shall be released upon my field, in the name of Jesus Christ.

31. As a child of the kingdom, today I decree that even in the time of drought, the former and the latter rain shall be released upon my crops, in the name of Jesus Christ.
32. As a child of the kingdom, today I decree that even in the time of drought, the former and the latter rain shall be released upon my harvest, in the name of Jesus Christ.
33. As a child of the kingdom, today I decree that drought will not affect my harvest, in the name of Jesus Christ.
34. In the time of famine I will prosper, in the name of Jesus Christ.
35. In the time of famine my business will flourish, in the name of Jesus Christ.
36. In the time of famine I will experience increase in my harvest, in the name of Jesus Christ.
37. In the time of famine I will experience increase in my finances, in the names of Jesus Christ.
38. In the time of famine I will experience increase in every area of my business, in the name of Jesus Christ.
39. In the time of famine I will have many things to be thankful for, in the name of Jesus Christ.
40. When people are saying there is casting down, I will say there is lifting up, in the name of Jesus Christ.

GOD CAN DO ANYTHING

Passages To Read Before You Pray:
Romans 10:9, Isaiah 43:13, Isaiah 45:2-3, Genesis 49:25

I have come today to fellowship with my heavenly Father, and make my requests and needs known unto Him. I cannot be hindered nor delayed because I know who I am in the Lord. I am a child of the Kingdom, born of the Spirit, redeemed by the blood of Jesus Christ. I walk in authority, living life without any apology because the power and authority has been given to me according to the Word of God in the book of Luke 9:1.

As I have come to pray today and to fellowship with my heavenly Father, I cover myself in the blood of Jesus Christ, and I put on the whole armor of God. I hereby come against every Prince of Persia that wants to hinder my prayer, I arrest you by the power in the blood of Jesus Christ, and I bind you and cast you down into the pit of hell.

I come against principalities and powers that wrestle with me and my prayers, I arrest you today by the power in the name of Jesus Christ, and I bind you and cast down into the pit of hell. I come against the rulers of the darkness of this world, against spiritual wickedness in high places, I arrest you all by the power in the name of Jesus Christ, and I bind you and cast you down into the pit of hell. I come against weakness and weariness, I arrest you today by the power in the name of Jesus Christ, and I bind you and cast you out of my life. I come against wondering spirit and distractions, I arrest you today by the power in the name of Jesus Christ, and I bind you and cast you out of my life.

Today I receive the anointing to pray and get results, my prayers cannot be hindered nor delayed because Jesus is my Lord, I will pray today and get the desired results, I decree open heavens upon my prayers. I baptize myself in the fire of the Holy Ghost; therefore I have become too hot for the enemy to handle. My prayers today will attract divine intervention to every situation in my life; signs and wonders will follow my prayers today, testimonies will follow my prayers today and the name of God alone will be glorified, in Jesus name. Amen!

PRAYER POINTS:

1. O God my Father, thank you for being my God, my Father and my friend.
2. O God my Father, thank you for the privilege to know you and the power of the resurrection of Jesus Christ.
3. O God my Father, thank you for always being there for me and with me.
4. O God my Father, thank you for the great and mighty things that you are doing in my life.
5. O God my Father, thank you for your provision and protection over me and my household.
6. O God my Father, thank you for always answering my prayers.
7. I confess my sins before you today and I ask you to forgive me on the basis of your mercy, in the name of Jesus Christ.
8. Wash me clean today O Lord by the blood of Jesus Christ.
9. I cover myself and my household with the blood of Jesus Christ.

10. My prayers today will not go in vain; my prayers will produce the desired results in the name of Jesus Christ.
11. With my heart I believe and with mouth I confess that every day of my life will bring glory to God, in the name of Jesus Christ.
12. With my heart I believe and with my mouth I confess that I will live to fulfill my purpose in life, in the name of Jesus Christ.
13. With my heart I believe and with my mouth I confess that the season of crying in my life is over, in the name of Jesus Christ.
14. With my heart I believe and with my mouth I confess that today marks the beginning of the season of joy and laughter in my life, in the name of Jesus Christ.
15. With my heart I believe and with my mouth I confess that the curse of poverty upon my life is removed, in the name of Jesus Christ.
16. With my heart I believe and with my mouth I confess that the curse of stagnancy in my life is removed, in the name of Jesus Christ.
17. With my heart I believe and with my mouth I confess that the curse of barrenness in my life is removed, in the name of Jesus Christ.
18. With my heart I believe and with my mouth I confess that the curse of vain hard labor in my life is removed, in the name of Jesus Christ.
19. When you are ready to work no one can stop you, Father Lord, perform your miracle in my life today, in the name of Jesus Christ.

20. O God my Father, when you are ready to work no one can stop you, arise and take me to the next level, in the name of Jesus Christ.
21. O God my Father, when you are ready to work no one can hinder you, arise and move my life forward in the name of Jesus Christ.
22. O God my Father, when you are ready to work no one can ask you why, arise and do the impossible in every area of my life in the name of Jesus Christ.
23. O God my Father, when you are ready to work no one can ask you why, arise and demonstrate your power in my life, in the name of Jesus Christ.
24. O God my Father, when you are ready to work no one can ask you why, arise and demonstrate your power in my home, in the name of Jesus Christ.
25. O God my Father, when you are ready to work no one can ask you why, arise and demonstrate your power in my finances, in the name of Jesus Christ.
26. O God my Father, when you are ready to work no one can ask why, arise and demonstrate your power in marriage, in the name of Jesus Christ.
27. O God my Father, when you are ready to work no one can ask you why, arise and demonstrate your power in the lives of my children, in the name of Jesus Christ.
28. O God my Father, when you are ready to work no one can ask you why, arise and demonstrate your power in the life of my spouse, in the name of Jesus Christ.
29. O God my Father, when you are ready to work no one can stop you, arise and destroy my greatest challenge, in the name of Jesus Christ.

30. O God my Father, when you are ready to work no one can stop you, arise and destroy all obstacles in my way, in the name of Jesus Christ.
31. O God my Father, when you are ready to work no one can stop you, arise and destroy my greatest fear, in the name of Jesus Christ.
32. O God my Father, when you are ready to work no one can stop you, arise and destroy the walls of Jericho in my life, in the name of Jesus Christ.
33. O God my Father, when you are ready to work no one can stop you, arise and destroy any spirit or power trying to change your plan for my life, in the name of Jesus Christ.
34. I refuse to dance to the music playing for me by the enemy, in the name of Jesus Christ.
35. You can do anything O Lord, let all my doubts and unbelief be permanently removed today, in the name of Jesus Christ.
36. O God my Father, go before me and make the crooked places straight, in the name of Jesus Christ.
37. O God my Father, go before me and make all impossibilities possible for me, in the name of Jesus Christ.
38. O God my Father, go before me today and let my lost hope be restored, in the name of Jesus Christ.
39. O God my Father, go before me today and let my weak faith be strengthened, in the name of Jesus Christ.
40. O God my Father, go before me today and let every door shut against me by the enemy be opened by your fire, in the name of Jesus Christ.

41. O God my Father, go before me today and let signs and wonders begin to manifest in every area of my life, in the name of Jesus Christ.
42. O God my Father, go before me today, locate my stolen blessings and bring them back to me, in the name of Jesus Christ.
43. O God my Father, go before me today, locate my helpers and bring them to help me, in the name of Jesus Christ.
44. O God my Father, go before me today and let every closed road be opened unto me, in the name of Jesus Christ.
45. O God my Father, as a child of the kingdom, let the treasures of darkness be given unto me according to your word, in the name of Jesus Christ.
46. O God my Father, as a child of the kingdom, let the treasures of the Gentiles be given unto me according to your word, in the name of Jesus Christ.
47. O God my Father, as a child of the kingdom, let the blessings of heaven above be released upon me, in the name of Jesus Christ.
48. O God my Father, as a child of the kingdom, let the blessings from the deep beneath be released into my life, in the name of Jesus Christ.
49. O God my Father, as a child of the kingdom, let the blessings of the womb and of the breasts be released into my life according to your word, in the name of Jesus Christ.
50. O God my Father, as a child of the kingdom, let the hidden riches of secrets places be given unto me, in the name of Jesus Christ.

PRAYER TO FULFILL PURPOSE

Passages To Read Before You Pray:
Habakkuk 2:2-4, 1 Chronicles 12:32, 1 Kings 18:46, Psalms 86

I have come today to fellowship with my heavenly Father, and make my requests and needs known unto Him. I cannot be hindered nor delayed because I know who I am in the Lord. I am a child of the Kingdom, born of the Spirit, redeemed by the blood of Jesus Christ. I walk in authority, living life without any apology because the power and authority has been given to me according to the Word of God in the book of Luke 9:1.

As I have come to pray today and to fellowship with my heavenly Father, I cover myself in the blood of Jesus Christ, and I put on the whole armor of God. I hereby come against every Prince of Persia that wants to hinder my prayer, I arrest you by the power in the blood of Jesus Christ, and I bind you and cast you down into the pit of hell.

I come against principalities and powers that wrestle with me and my prayers, I arrest you today by the power in the name of Jesus Christ, and I bind you and cast down into the pit of hell. I come against the rulers of the darkness of this world, against spiritual wickedness in high places, I arrest you all by the power in the name of Jesus Christ, and I bind you and cast you down into the pit of hell. I come against weakness and weariness, I arrest you today by the power in the name of Jesus Christ, and I bind you and cast you out of my life. I come against wondering spirit and distractions, I arrest you today by the power in the name of Jesus Christ, and I bind you and cast you out of my life.

Today I receive the anointing to pray and get results, my prayers cannot be hindered nor delayed because Jesus is my Lord, I will pray today and get the desired results, I decree open heavens upon my prayers. I baptize myself in the fire of the Holy Ghost; therefore I have become too hot for the enemy to handle. My prayers today will attract divine intervention to every situation in my life; signs and wonders will follow my prayers today, testimonies will follow my prayers today and the name of God alone will be glorified, in Jesus name. Amen!

PRAYER POINTS:

1. O God my Father, thank you for being my God, my Father and my friend.
2. O God my Father, thank you for the privilege to know you and the power of the resurrection of Jesus Christ.
3. O God my Father, thank you for always being there for me and with me.
4. O God my Father, thank you for the great and mighty things that you are doing in my life.
5. O God my Father, thank you for your provision and protection over me and my household.
6. O God my Father, thank you for always answering my prayers.
7. I confess my sins before you today and I ask you to forgive me on the basis of your mercy, in the name of Jesus Christ.
8. Wash me clean today O Lord by the blood of Jesus Christ.
9. I cover myself and my household with the blood of Jesus Christ.

10. My prayers today will not go in vain; my prayers will produce the desired results in the name of Jesus Christ.
11. Anything in me forcing my life to go backwards no matter how much I try to move forward, Father, let it be removed and destroyed.
12. Anything around me causing my life to be stagnant no matter how much effort I put in, Father let it be destroyed by your fire.
13. Anyone around me influencing me to go backwards, I don't want you in my life any longer, Father, let there be a permanent separation.
14. Lord, help me to understand your timetable for my life.
15. I will not miscalculate the divine calendar of my success.
16. O God my Father, help me to discover the hidden treasures in my life that will make me great.
17. Every handwriting upon my life driving my helpers away, Father Lord, let it be erased by the blood of Jesus Christ.
18. O God my Father, let the anointing of the children of Issachar fall upon me today, so that I may understand time and season and not miss out my appointed time.
19. I receive the grace of God to be in the right place at the right time.
20. I refuse to be a pushover in the race of life, I will make positive impact in this generation.
21. I refuse to be a shadow in life; my presence on earth will be known, seen and felt.
22. Any power anywhere hired to decide what my destiny should be or look like, you are fired.
23. Any power anywhere hired to destroy my dream, you are fired.

24. Any power anywhere hired to make my life miserable, you are fired.
25. Any power anywhere hired to hinder my miracle, you are fired.
26. Every negative energy around me, disappear now, and be replaced with grace and mercy.
27. I receive the power to overtake and outrun those that are ahead of me in the race of life.
28. O God my Father, let my dreams and vision begin to speak that they that hear it may believe and run with it.

PRAYER FOR GOD TO MAKE A WAY WHEN ALL DOORS ARE SHUT AGAINST YOU

Passages To Read Before You Pray:
Deuteronomy 2:14-15, Hebrews 12:15, Colossians 2:14, Psalms 103, 105, 106

I have come today to fellowship with my heavenly Father, and make my requests and needs known unto Him. I cannot be hindered nor delayed because I know who I am in the Lord. I am a child of the Kingdom, born of the Spirit, redeemed by the blood of Jesus Christ. I walk in authority, living life without any apology because the power and authority has been given to me according to the Word of God in the book of Luke 9:1.

As I have come to pray today and to fellowship with my heavenly Father, I cover myself in the blood of Jesus Christ, and I put on the whole armor of God. I hereby come against every Prince of Persia that wants to hinder my prayer, I arrest you by the power in the blood of Jesus Christ, and I bind you and cast you down into the pit of hell.

I come against principalities and powers that wrestle with me and my prayers, I arrest you today by the power in the name of Jesus Christ, and I bind you and cast down into the pit of hell. I come against the rulers of the darkness of this world, against spiritual wickedness in high places, I arrest you all by the power in the name of Jesus Christ, and I bind you and cast you down into the pit of hell. I come against weakness and weariness, I arrest you today by the power in the name of Jesus Christ, and I bind you and cast you out of my life. I come against wondering

spirit and distractions, I arrest you today by the power in the name of Jesus Christ, and I bind you and cast you out of my life.

Today I receive the anointing to pray and get results, my prayers cannot be hindered nor delayed because Jesus is my Lord, I will pray today and get the desired results, I decree open heavens upon my prayers. I baptize myself in the fire of the Holy Ghost; therefore I have become too hot for the enemy to handle. My prayers today will attract divine intervention to every situation in my life; signs and wonders will follow my prayers today, testimonies will follow my prayers today and the name of God alone will be glorified, in Jesus name. Amen!

PRAYER POINTS:

1. O God my Father, thank you for being my God, my Father and my friend.
2. O God my Father, thank you for the privilege to know you and the power of the resurrection of Jesus Christ.
3. O God my Father, thank you for always being there for me and with me.
4. O God my Father, thank you for the great and mighty things that you are doing in my life.
5. O God my Father, thank you for your provision and protection over me and my household.
6. O God my Father, thank you for always answering my prayers.
7. I confess my sins before you today and I ask you to forgive me on the basis of your mercy, in the name of Jesus Christ.

8. Wash me clean today O Lord by the blood of Jesus Christ.
9. I cover myself and my household with the blood of Jesus Christ.
10. My prayers today will not go in vain; my prayers will produce the desired results in the name of Jesus Christ.
11. Anything in my life making me a target of satanic attacks, be destroyed by the fire of God.
12. Anything in my life making me a target of spiritual bullies, be destroyed by the fire of God.
13. Every handwriting contrary to the will and the purpose of God for me, be erased by the blood of Jesus Christ.
14. Evil handwriting upon my life attracting hatred and failure, be erased by the blood of Jesus.
15. Every mark of rejection upon my life causing me to be rejected wherever I go, be removed now by the blood of Jesus Christ.
16. O God my Father, make a way for me out of this wilderness of trouble that I find myself.
17. O God my Father, for how long will I wander in this wilderness of disappointment, arise and make a way for me out of this wilderness.
18. Any power anywhere trying to turn the journey of ten days to ten years for me, you will not prosper and you will not escape the judgment of God.
19. O God my Father, for how long will I suffer before I get to my promise land, arise O Lord and expedite my progress.
20. O God my Father, let the spirit and the anointing of Caleb rest upon me, the boldness to possess my possessions.

21. I refuse to be afraid of the giants, I receive the power to possess my possessions.
22. O God my Father, send your fire to the root of my problems and let it be destroyed from the root.
23. O God my Father, let the root of bitterness in my life be destroyed by your fire.
24. O God my Father, send your fire to the root of frustration in my life and let it be destroyed by your fire.
25. I refuse to be frustrated.
26. In your presence O Lord, my case will not be impossible.

PRAYER TO REMOVE EVIL LOADS OF INFIRMITY

Passages To Read Before You Pray:
Luke 13:10-17, Matthew 11:28-30, Isaiah 53, Psalms 6, 88

I have come today to fellowship with my heavenly Father, and make my requests and needs known unto Him. I cannot be hindered nor delayed because I know who I am in the Lord. I am a child of the Kingdom, born of the Spirit, redeemed by the blood of Jesus Christ. I walk in authority, living life without any apology because the power and authority has been given to me according to the Word of God in the book of Luke 9:1.

As I have come to pray today and to fellowship with my heavenly Father, I cover myself in the blood of Jesus Christ, and I put on the whole armor of God. I hereby come against every Prince of Persia that wants to hinder my prayer, I arrest you by the power in the blood of Jesus Christ, and I bind you and cast you down into the pit of hell.

I come against principalities and powers that wrestle with me and my prayers, I arrest you today by the power in the name of Jesus Christ, and I bind you and cast down into the pit of hell. I come against the rulers of the darkness of this world, against spiritual wickedness in high places, I arrest you all by the power in the name of Jesus Christ, and I bind you and cast you down into the pit of hell. I come against weakness and weariness, I arrest you today by the power in the name of Jesus Christ, and I bind you and cast you out of my life. I come against wondering

spirit and distractions, I arrest you today by the power in the name of Jesus Christ, and I bind you and cast you out of my life.

Today I receive the anointing to pray and get results, my prayers cannot be hindered nor delayed because Jesus is my Lord, I will pray today and get the desired results, I decree open heavens upon my prayers. I baptize myself in the fire of the Holy Ghost; therefore I have become too hot for the enemy to handle. My prayers today will attract divine intervention to every situation in my life; signs and wonders will follow my prayers today, testimonies will follow my prayers today and the name of God alone will be glorified, in Jesus name. Amen!

PRAYER POINTS:

1. O God my Father, thank you for being my God, my Father and my friend.
2. O God my Father, thank you for the privilege to know you and the power of the resurrection of Jesus Christ.
3. O God my Father, thank you for always being there for me and with me.
4. O God my Father, thank you for the great and mighty things that you are doing in my life.
5. O God my Father, thank you for your provision and protection over me and my household.
6. O God my Father, thank you for always answering my prayers.
7. I confess my sins before you today and I ask you to forgive me on the basis of your mercy, in the name of Jesus Christ.

8. Wash me clean today O Lord by the blood of Jesus Christ.
9. I cover myself and my household with the blood of Jesus Christ.
10. My prayers today will not go in vain; my prayers will produce the desired results in the name of Jesus Christ.
11. Every evil load upon my life causing me to bend such that I cannot lift up my head, be removed completely in the name of Jesus Christ.
12. Satanic burden upon my life, be lifted now.
13. Evil load upon my life making it difficult for me to move forward, be destroyed by fire.
14. Evil load upon my life that is slowing down my progress, be destroyed by fire.
15. Today I am set free from any form of satanic bondage, in the name of Jesus.
16. Today I am set free from any form of infirmity, in the name of Jesus Christ.
17. Today O Lord, let my deliverance be made perfect.
18. O God my Father, let every yoke of the enemy upon my life be totally destroyed, in the name of Jesus Christ.
19. O God my Father, let the owner of the evil load carry it now in the name of Jesus Christ.
20. Any power anywhere boasting against me, be disgraced in the name of Jesus Christ.
21. O God my Father, here I am, let every heavy load upon my shoulders be removed today.
22. O God my Father, the struggle of life is too much for me, let me find rest in you in the name of Jesus Christ.
23. Today O Lord, take me to the green pasture beside the still waters where I can find rest for my soul.

24. O God my Father, this burden of life is too heavy, take it from me and give me peace.
25. O God my Father, I am ready to take your easy yoke and light burden, take my problems and stubborn situations away in the name of Jesus Christ.
26. O God my Father, give me boldness to confront and overcome any situation that comes my way in the name of Jesus Christ.
27. No matter what the enemy throws at me, I will come out victorious in the name of Jesus Christ.
28. O God my Father, let my greatest fear turn to a great testimony in the name of Jesus Christ.
29. O God my Father, in the middle of every disappointment in my life let there be divine appointment, in the name of Jesus Christ.
30. Today I receive the grace to recognize the doors of opportunities that are divinely opened unto me; I will not miss these opportunities in the name of Jesus Christ.

PRAYER TO EXPERIENCE A BETTER DAY

Passages To Read Before You Pray:
John 11:33-34, Habakkuk 1:5, Isaiah 43:19

I have come today to fellowship with my heavenly Father, and make my requests and needs known unto Him. I cannot be hindered nor delayed because I know who I am in the Lord. I am a child of the Kingdom, born of the Spirit, redeemed by the blood of Jesus Christ. I walk in authority, living life without any apology because the power and authority has been given to me according to the Word of God in the book of Luke 9:1.

As I have come to pray today and to fellowship with my heavenly Father, I cover myself in the blood of Jesus Christ, and I put on the whole armor of God. I hereby come against every Prince of Persia that wants to hinder my prayer, I arrest you by the power in the blood of Jesus Christ, and I bind you and cast you down into the pit of hell.

I come against principalities and powers that wrestle with me and my prayers, I arrest you today by the power in the name of Jesus Christ, and I bind you and cast down into the pit of hell. I come against the rulers of the darkness of this world, against spiritual wickedness in high places, I arrest you all by the power in the name of Jesus Christ, and I bind you and cast you down into the pit of hell. I come against weakness and weariness, I arrest you today by the power in the name of Jesus Christ, and I bind you and cast you out of my life. I come against wondering spirit and distractions, I arrest you today by the power in the name of Jesus Christ, and I bind you and cast you out of my life.

Today I receive the anointing to pray and get results, my prayers cannot be hindered nor delayed because Jesus is my Lord, I will pray today and get the desired results, I decree open heavens upon my prayers. I baptize myself in the fire of the Holy Ghost; therefore I have become too hot for the enemy to handle. My prayers today will attract divine intervention to every situation in my life; signs and wonders will follow my prayers today, testimonies will follow my prayers today and the name of God alone will be glorified, in Jesus name. Amen!

PRAYER POINTS:

1. O God my Father, thank you for being my God, my Father and my friend.
2. O God my Father, thank you for the privilege to know you and the power of the resurrection of Jesus Christ.
3. O God my Father, thank you for always being there for me and with me.
4. O God my Father, thank you for the great and mighty things that you are doing in my life.
5. O God my Father, thank you for your provision and protection over me and my household.
6. O God my Father, thank you for always answering my prayers.
7. I confess my sins before you today and I ask you to forgive me on the basis of your mercy, in the name of Jesus Christ.
8. Wash me clean today O Lord by the blood of Jesus Christ.
9. I cover myself and my household with the blood of Jesus Christ.

10. My prayers today will not go in vain; my prayers will produce the desired results in the name of Jesus Christ.
11. You destiny changers where have you taken my destiny, I command you to release my destiny now.
12. Any power anywhere attacking my finances, where have you taken my money, I command you to release my money now.
13. Any power anywhere attacking my helpers, where have you sent my helpers, I command you to release my helpers now.
14. O God my Father, let my stolen blessings begin to cause trouble in the camp of the enemy.
15. O God my Father, let my stolen blessings begin to cause confusion in the camp of my enemy.
16. O God arise and trouble those that trouble me.
17. O God arise and trouble those that trouble my family.
18. O God my Father, let the remaining months of this year be better than the last nine months.
19. O God my Father, this year is running out, give me the grace to fulfill purpose before this year comes to an end.
20. O God my Father, remember your promises and fulfill them before the end of this year.
21. O God my Father, let your grace rescue me from hardship and struggles, I have had enough.
22. O God my Father, let your power rescue me from the pit of hopelessness, arise and set me free.
23. Any evil covering that will not let my helpers see me, be destroyed now by fire.
24. Satanic embargo holding me back in life, be destroyed by fire.

PRAYER FOR PURIFICATION

Passages To Read Before You Pray:
Mark 9:25-26, Job 22:27-28, Psalms 15, 19, 24

I have come today to fellowship with my heavenly Father, and make my requests and needs known unto Him. I cannot be hindered nor delayed because I know who I am in the Lord. I am a child of the Kingdom, born of the Spirit, redeemed by the blood of Jesus Christ. I walk in authority, living life without any apology because the power and authority has been given to me according to the Word of God in the book of Luke 9:1.

As I have come to pray today and to fellowship with my heavenly Father, I cover myself in the blood of Jesus Christ, and I put on the whole armor of God. I hereby come against every Prince of Persia that wants to hinder my prayer, I arrest you by the power in the blood of Jesus Christ, and I bind you and cast you down into the pit of hell.

I come against principalities and powers that wrestle with me and my prayers, I arrest you today by the power in the name of Jesus Christ, and I bind you and cast down into the pit of hell. I come against the rulers of the darkness of this world, against spiritual wickedness in high places, I arrest you all by the power in the name of Jesus Christ, and I bind you and cast you down into the pit of hell. I come against weakness and weariness, I arrest you today by the power in the name of Jesus Christ, and I bind you and cast you out of my life. I come against wondering spirit and distractions, I arrest you today by the power in the name of Jesus Christ, and I bind you and cast you out of my life.

Today I receive the anointing to pray and get results, my prayers cannot be hindered nor delayed because Jesus is my Lord, I will pray today and get the desired results, I decree open heavens upon my prayers. I baptize myself in the fire of the Holy Ghost; therefore I have become too hot for the enemy to handle. My prayers today will attract divine intervention to every situation in my life; signs and wonders will follow my prayers today, testimonies will follow my prayers today and the name of God alone will be glorified, in Jesus name. Amen!

PRAYER POINTS:

1. O God my Father, thank you for being my God, my Father and my friend.
2. O God my Father, thank you for the privilege to know you and the power of the resurrection of Jesus Christ.
3. O God my Father, thank you for always being there for me and with me.
4. O God my Father, thank you for the great and mighty things that you are doing in my life.
5. O God my Father, thank you for your provision and protection over me and my household.
6. O God my Father, thank you for always answering my prayers.
7. I confess my sins before you today and I ask you to forgive me on the basis of your mercy, in the name of Jesus Christ.
8. Wash me clean today O Lord by the blood of Jesus Christ.
9. I cover myself and my household with the blood of Jesus Christ.

10. My prayers today will not go in vain; my prayers will produce the desired results in the name of Jesus Christ.
11. You spirit of spiritual laziness, I command you to get out of my life and never come back in the name of Jesus Christ.
12. You spirit of spiritual slumber, I command you to get out of my life and never come back in the name of Jesus Christ.
13. You spirit of rebellion, I command you to get out of my life and never come back, in the name of Jesus Christ.
14. You spirit of anger, I command you to get out of my life and never come back in the name of Jesus Christ.
15. You spirit of pride, I command you to get out of my life and never come back, in the name of Jesus Christ.
16. You spirit of spiritual adultery, I command you to get out of my life and never come back, in the name of Jesus Christ.
17. You spirit of ignorance, I command you to get out of my life and never come back, in the name of Jesus Christ.
18. You spirit of hatred, I command you to get out of my life and never come back, in the name of Jesus Christ.
19. You spirit of selfishness, I command you to get out of my life and never come back, in the name of Jesus Christ.
20. You spirit of self-righteousness, I command you to get out of my life and never come back, in the name of Jesus Christ.
21. You spirit of greediness, I command you to get out of my life and never come back, in the name of Jesus Christ.

22. You spirit of jealousy, I command you to get out of my life and never come back, in the name of Jesus Christ.
23. You spirit of impurity, I command you to get out of my life and never come back, in the name of Jesus Christ.
24. You spirit of addiction, I command you to get out of my life and never come back, in the name of Jesus Christ.
25. You spirit of sexual immorality, I command you to get out of my life and never come back, in the name of Jesus Christ.
26. You spirit of unbelief, I command you to get out of my life and never come back, in the name of Jesus Christ.
27. You spirit of doubt, I command you to get out of my life and never come back, in the name of Jesus Christ.
28. You lying spirit, I command you to get out of life and never come back, in the name of Jesus Christ.
29. You spirit of division, I command you to get out of my life and never come back, in the name of Jesus Christ.
30. You spirit of sinful desire, I command you to get out of my life and never come back, in the name of Jesus Christ.
31. You spirit of idolatry, I command you to get out of my life and never come back, in the name of Jesus Christ.
32. You spirit of confusion, I command you to get out of my life and never come back, in the name of Jesus Christ.
33. You spirit of fear, I command you to get out of my life and never come back, in the name of Jesus Christ.
34. You spirit of disobedience, I command you to get out of my life and never come back, in the name of Jesus Christ.
35. You spirit of spiritual blindness, I command you to get out of my life and never come back, in the name of Jesus Christ.

36. You spirit of prayerlessness, I command you to get out of my life and never come back, in the name of Jesus Christ.
37. You spirit of spiritual deafness, I command you to get out of my life and never come back, in the name of Jesus Christ.
38. You spirit of spiritual dumbness, I command you to get out of my life and never come back, in the name of Jesus Christ.
39. You spirit of cowardness, I command you to get out of my life and never come back, in the name of Jesus Christ.
40. You spirit of self-justification, I command you to get out of my life and never come back, in the name of Jesus Christ.
41. You manipulating spirit, I command you to get out of my life and never come back, in the name of Jesus Christ.
42. You spirit of deception, I command you to get out of my life and never come back, in the name of Jesus Christ.
43. You spirit of lawlessness, I command you to get out of my life and never come back, in the name of Jesus Christ.
44. You spirit of self-exaltation, I command you to get out of my life and never come back, in the name of Jesus Christ.
45. You sprit of stubbornness, I command you to get out of my life and never come back, in the name of Jesus Christ.
46. You spirit of spiritual slavery, I command you to get out of my life and never come back, in the name of Jesus Christ.

47. You spirit of lust, I command you to get out of my life and never come back, in the name of Jesus Christ.
48. You spirit of false doctrine, I command you to get out of my life and never come back, in the name of Jesus Christ.
49. You spirit of malice, I command you to get out of my life and never come back, in the name of Jesus Christ.
50. You spirit hopelessness, I command you to get out of my life and never come back, in the name of Jesus Christ.
51. You spirit of bitterness, I command you to get out of my life and never come back, in the name of Jesus Christ.
52. You spirit of evil speaking, I command you to get out of my life and never come back, I n the name of Jesus Christ.
53. You spirit of impatience, I command you to get out of my life and never come back, in the name of Jesus Christ.
54. You spirit self-condemnation, I command you to get out of my life and never come back, in the name of Jesus Christ.
55. You spirit of worldliness, I command you to get out of my life and never come back, in the name of Jesus Christ.
56. You spirit of indecision, I command you to get out of my life and never come back, in the name of Jesus Christ.
57. You spirit of double-mindedness, I command you to get out of my life and never come back, in the name of Jesus Christ.
58. You spirit of false profession, I command you to get out of my life and never come back, in the name of Jesus Christ.

59. You spirit of inconsistency, I command you to get out of my life and never come back, in the name of Jesus Christ.
60. You spirit of spiritual instability, I command you to get out of my life and never come back, in the name of Jesus Christ.

DELIVERANCE FROM ADDICTION

Passages To Read Before You Pray:
Romans 12:1-3, Psalms 30, 25, 42, 79, 80

I have come today to fellowship with my heavenly Father, and make my requests and needs known unto Him. I cannot be hindered nor delayed because I know who I am in the Lord. I am a child of the Kingdom, born of the Spirit, redeemed by the blood of Jesus Christ. I walk in authority, living life without any apology because the power and authority has been given to me according to the Word of God in the book of Luke 9:1.

As I have come to pray today and to fellowship with my heavenly Father, I cover myself in the blood of Jesus Christ, and I put on the whole armor of God. I hereby come against every Prince of Persia that wants to hinder my prayer, I arrest you by the power in the blood of Jesus Christ, and I bind you and cast you down into the pit of hell.

I come against principalities and powers that wrestle with me and my prayers, I arrest you today by the power in the name of Jesus Christ, and I bind you and cast down into the pit of hell. I come against the rulers of the darkness of this world, against spiritual wickedness in high places, I arrest you all by the power in the name of Jesus Christ, and I bind you and cast you down into the pit of hell. I come against weakness and weariness, I arrest you today by the power in the name of Jesus Christ, and I bind you and cast you out of my life. I come against wondering spirit and distractions, I arrest you today by the power in the name of Jesus Christ, and I bind you and cast you out of my life.

Today I receive the anointing to pray and get results, my prayers cannot be hindered nor delayed because Jesus is my Lord, I will pray today and get the desired results, I decree open heavens upon my prayers. I baptize myself in the fire of the Holy Ghost; therefore I have become too hot for the enemy to handle. My prayers today will attract divine intervention to every situation in my life; signs and wonders will follow my prayers today, testimonies will follow my prayers today and the name of God alone will be glorified, in Jesus name. Amen!

PRAYER POINTS:

1. O God my Father, thank you for being my God, my Father and my friend.
2. O God my Father, thank you for the privilege to know you and the power of the resurrection of Jesus Christ.
3. O God my Father, thank you for always being there for me and with me.
4. O God my Father, thank you for the great and mighty things that you are doing in my life.
5. O God my Father, thank you for your provision and protection over me and my household.
6. O God my Father, thank you for always answering my prayers.
7. I confess my sins before you today and I ask you to forgive me on the basis of your mercy, in the name of Jesus Christ.
8. Wash me clean today O Lord by the blood of Jesus Christ.
9. I cover myself and my household with the blood of Jesus Christ.

10. My prayers today will not go in vain; my prayers will produce the desired results in the name of Jesus Christ.
11. O God my Father, let my prayers attract divine intervention, in the name of Jesus Christ.
12. O God my Father, arise and deliver me from any form of addiction, in the name of Jesus Christ.
13. Today O Lord, arise and deliver .... from crack cocaine addiction, in the name of Jesus Christ.
14. Jesus Christ of Nazareth, set .... free today from this bondage in the name of Jesus Christ.
15. Today O Lord, arise and deliver .... from heroin addiction, in the name of Jesus Christ.
16. Jesus Christ of Nazareth, set .... free today from this bondage in the name of Jesus Christ.
17. Today O Lord, arise and deliver .... from sex addiction, in the name of Jesus Christ.
18. Jesus Christ of Nazareth, set .... free today from this bondage, in the name of Jesus Christ.
19. Jesus Christ of Nazareth, arise and deliver .... from food addiction, in the name of Jesus Christ.
20. Jesus Christ of Nazareth, set .... free today from this bondage, in the name of Jesus Christ.

WHEN YOUR SITUATION NEEDS URGENT ATTENTION

Passages To Read Before You Pray:
Psalms 30, 70, 68, 55, 18, 42, 86

I have come today to fellowship with my heavenly Father, and make my requests and needs known unto Him. I cannot be hindered nor delayed because I know who I am in the Lord. I am a child of the Kingdom, born of the Spirit, redeemed by the blood of Jesus Christ. I walk in authority, living life without any apology because the power and authority has been given to me according to the Word of God in the book of Luke 9:1.

As I have come to pray today and to fellowship with my heavenly Father, I cover myself in the blood of Jesus Christ, and I put on the whole armor of God. I hereby come against every Prince of Persia that wants to hinder my prayer, I arrest you by the power in the blood of Jesus Christ, and I bind you and cast you down into the pit of hell.

I come against principalities and powers that wrestle with me and my prayers, I arrest you today by the power in the name of Jesus Christ, and I bind you and cast down into the pit of hell. I come against the rulers of the darkness of this world, against spiritual wickedness in high places, I arrest you all by the power in the name of Jesus Christ, and I bind you and cast you down into the pit of hell. I come against weakness and weariness, I arrest you today by the power in the name of Jesus Christ, and I bind you and cast you out of my life. I come against wondering

spirit and distractions, I arrest you today by the power in the name of Jesus Christ, and I bind you and cast you out of my life.

Today I receive the anointing to pray and get results, my prayers cannot be hindered nor delayed because Jesus is my Lord, I will pray today and get the desired results, I decree open heavens upon my prayers. I baptize myself in the fire of the Holy Ghost; therefore I have become too hot for the enemy to handle. My prayers today will attract divine intervention to every situation in my life; signs and wonders will follow my prayers today, testimonies will follow my prayers today and the name of God alone will be glorified, in Jesus name. Amen!

PRAYER POINTS:

1. O God my Father, thank you for being my God, my Father and my friend.
2. O God my Father, thank you for the privilege to know you and the power of the resurrection of Jesus Christ.
3. O God my Father, thank you for always being there for me and with me.
4. O God my Father, thank you for the great and mighty things that you are doing in my life.
5. O God my Father, thank you for your provision and protection over me and my household.
6. O God my Father, thank you for always answering my prayers.
7. I confess my sins before you today and I ask you to forgive me on the basis of your mercy, in the name of Jesus Christ.

8. Wash me clean today O Lord by the blood of Jesus Christ.
9. I cover myself and my household with the blood of Jesus Christ.
10. My prayers today will not go in vain; my prayers will produce the desired results in the name of Jesus Christ.

11. O God my Father, arise and attend to my case, my case is urgent.
12. I refuse to go through this year without any tangible achievement, in the name of Jesus Christ.
13. O God my Father, arise today and turn my situation around for success, in the name of Jesus Christ.
14. O God my Father, arise today and turn my situation around for great achievements, in the name of Jesus Christ.
15. O God my Father, you promised to do great things in my life this year, arise now and fulfill your promise in the name of Jesus Christ.
16. O God my Father, you promised to make me the head, why am I still in this situation, arise now and fulfill your promise in the name of Jesus Christ.
17. O God my Father, you promised that I will be above only and not be beneath, why am I still operating below, arise now and fulfill your promise.
18. O God my Father, you promised to shake the heaven and the earth in order to bless me, I don't understand what's going on now, arise today and fulfill your promise in the name of Jesus Christ.
19. O God my Father, you told me that the battle is not mine but yours, why am I still fighting one battle after the other, arise today and fulfill your promise.

20. O God my Father, arise today and locate my helpers and command them to help me in the name of Jesus Christ.
21. O God my Father, arise today, locate my wandering blessings and redirect my blessings to me in the name of Jesus Christ.
22. As from today O Lord, let every remaining day of this year bring me success in the name of Jesus Christ.
23. As from today O Lord, let every remaining hour and minute of this year bring me promotion in every area in the name of Jesus Christ.
24. Today I receive the anointing of ease to breakthrough before the end of this year in the name of Jesus Christ.
25. Today I receive anointing of ease to have great achievements before the end of this year in the name of Jesus Christ.
26. Today I receive anointing and power to overcome obstacles in my way, in the name of Jesus Christ.
27. No matter the situation, I will make it before the end of this year in the name of Jesus Christ.
28. O God my Father, arise and make my dream a reality before the end of this year in the name of Jesus Christ.
29. O God my Father, for how long will I wait and expect, arise and answer my prayers today in the name of Jesus Christ.
30. O God my Father, for how long will I wait and expect, arise and bless me today in the name of Jesus Christ.
31. O God my Father, for how long will I wait and expect, arise and connect me with the people that will help me in the name of Jesus Christ.
32. O God m y Father, for how long will I wait and expect, arise and show me what to do next in my life, in the name of Jesus Christ.

33. O God my Father, I know this is not your plan for me, arise and fulfill your plan concerning my life, in the name of Jesus Christ.
34. O God my Father, for how long will I wait and expect, arise and take me to the next level in the name of Jesus Christ.
35. O God my Father, for how long will you allow the enemy to frustrate and terrorize me, arise today and fight my battle in the name of Jesus Christ.
36. O God my Father, I want to tell a better story about my life, arise today and change my story for the better in the name of Jesus Christ.

PRAYER FOR THE STORM VICTIMS
Psalms 46, 23, 91, 79

I have come today to fellowship with my heavenly Father, and make my requests and needs known unto Him. I cannot be hindered nor delayed because I know who I am in the Lord. I am a child of the Kingdom, born of the Spirit, redeemed by the blood of Jesus Christ. I walk in authority, living life without any apology because the power and authority has been given to me according to the Word of God in the book of Luke 9:1.

As I have come to pray today and to fellowship with my heavenly Father, I cover myself in the blood of Jesus Christ, and I put on the whole armor of God. I hereby come against every Prince of Persia that wants to hinder my prayer, I arrest you by the power in the blood of Jesus Christ, and I bind you and cast you down into the pit of hell.

I come against principalities and powers that wrestle with me and my prayers, I arrest you today by the power in the name of Jesus Christ, and I bind you and cast down into the pit of hell. I come against the rulers of the darkness of this world, against spiritual wickedness in high places, I arrest you all by the power in the name of Jesus Christ, and I bind you and cast you down into the pit of hell. I come against weakness and weariness, I arrest you today by the power in the name of Jesus Christ, and I bind you and cast you out of my life. I come against wondering spirit and distractions, I arrest you today by the power in the name of Jesus Christ, and I bind you and cast you out of my life.

Today I receive the anointing to pray and get results, my prayers cannot be hindered nor delayed because Jesus is my Lord, I will pray today and get the desired results, I decree open heavens upon my prayers. I baptize myself in the fire of the Holy Ghost; therefore I have become too hot for the enemy to handle. My prayers today will attract divine intervention to every situation in my life; signs and wonders will follow my prayers today, testimonies will follow my prayers today and the name of God alone will be glorified, in Jesus name. Amen!

PRAYER POINTS:

1. O God my Father, thank you for being my God, my Father and my friend.
2. O God my Father, thank you for the privilege to know you and the power of the resurrection of Jesus Christ.
3. O God my Father, thank you for always being there for me and with me.
4. O God my Father, thank you for the great and mighty things that you are doing in my life.
5. O God my Father, thank you for your provision and protection over me and my household.
6. O God my Father, thank you for always answering my prayers.
7. I confess my sins before you today and I ask you to forgive me on the basis of your mercy, in the name of Jesus Christ.
8. Wash me clean today O Lord by the blood of Jesus Christ.
9. I cover myself and my household with the blood of Jesus Christ.
10. My prayers today will not go in vain; my prayers will produce the desired results in the name of Jesus Christ.

11. O God my Father, you are the present help in trouble, send divine help for the victims of this hurricane.
12. O God my Father, fill the hearts of the victims with your peace that surpasses all understanding.
13. O God my Father, speak peace be still into the lives of those that have lost everything in this storm.
14. O God my Father, arise today and restore the life of those that have lost one thing or the other in this disaster.
15. O God my Father, grant your people strength and courage to go through this tough times.
16. O God my Father, let the Holy Spirit comfort those that have lost their loved ones in this storm.
17. O God my Father, give your people strength and courage to rise and rebuild their lives.
18. O God my Father, arise and let your light shine in the path of your people, that they may see clearly in this dark moment of their lives.
19. O God my Father, let there be divine intervention in this situation and give hope to the hopeless.
20. O God my Father, let restoration begin now and let the people know that you are the present help in the time of storms.
21. O God my Father, send help today that the people that have been displaced may find a place of rest.
22. O God my Father, let your love fill our heart even in the time of trouble.
23. O God my Father, keep everyone safe and provide for their immediate needs.
24. O God my Father, let the blast of your nostril drive this flood back into the ocean that people may get back to rebuilding their lives.

25. O God my Father, let there be quick recovery in the lives of the victims of this horrible storm.
26. O God my Father, send help now and let the system be resorted that people may get back to their lives.
27. O God my Father, let businesses be restored so that people may get back to their lives.
28. O God my Father, let those that have lost their homes receive help from heaven above, and immediate intervention from insurance companies.
29. O God my Father, make a way for your people out of this wilderness of frustration and confusion.
30. O God my Father, let the Holy Spirit constantly minister peace and joy to the lives of the victims of this hurricane.

TOTAL DELIVERANCE FROM EGYPTIAN BONDAGE

Passages To Read Before You Pray:
Exodus 3:7-10, 14:13-18, John 11:44, Psalms 35, 18, 69

I have come today to fellowship with my heavenly Father, and make my requests and needs known unto Him. I cannot be hindered nor delayed because I know who I am in the Lord. I am a child of the Kingdom, born of the Spirit, redeemed by the blood of Jesus Christ. I walk in authority, living life without any apology because the power and authority has been given to me according to the Word of God in the book of Luke 9:1.

As I have come to pray today and to fellowship with my heavenly Father, I cover myself in the blood of Jesus Christ, and I put on the whole armor of God. I hereby come against every Prince of Persia that wants to hinder my prayer, I arrest you by the power in the blood of Jesus Christ, and I bind you and cast you down into the pit of hell.

I come against principalities and powers that wrestle with me and my prayers, I arrest you today by the power in the name of Jesus Christ, and I bind you and cast down into the pit of hell. I come against the rulers of the darkness of this world, against spiritual wickedness in high places, I arrest you all by the power in the name of Jesus Christ, and I bind you and cast you down into the pit of hell. I come against weakness and weariness, I arrest you today by the power in the name of Jesus Christ, and I bind you and cast you out of my life. I come against wondering

spirit and distractions, I arrest you today by the power in the name of Jesus Christ, and I bind you and cast you out of my life.

Today I receive the anointing to pray and get results, my prayers cannot be hindered nor delayed because Jesus is my Lord, I will pray today and get the desired results, I decree open heavens upon my prayers. I baptize myself in the fire of the Holy Ghost; therefore I have become too hot for the enemy to handle. My prayers today will attract divine intervention to every situation in my life; signs and wonders will follow my prayers today, testimonies will follow my prayers today and the name of God alone will be glorified, in Jesus name. Amen!

PRAYER POINTS:

1. O God my Father, thank you for being my God, my Father and my friend.
2. O God my Father, thank you for the privilege to know you and the power of the resurrection of Jesus Christ.
3. O God my Father, thank you for always being there for me and with me.
4. O God my Father, thank you for the great and mighty things that you are doing in my life.
5. O God my Father, thank you for your provision and protection over me and my household.
6. O God my Father, thank you for always answering my prayers.
7. I confess my sins before you today and I ask you to forgive me on the basis of your mercy, in the name of Jesus Christ.

8. Wash me clean today O Lord by the blood of Jesus Christ.
9. I cover myself and my household with the blood of Jesus Christ.
10. My prayers today will not go in vain; my prayers will produce the desired results in the name of Jesus Christ.
11. Today O Lord, reveal yourself unto me the way I have never seen you before in the name of Jesus Christ.
12. Today O Lord, demonstrate your power in every area of my life, in the name of Jesus Christ.
13. O God my Father, send my Moses today to deliver me from any form of slavery, in the name of Jesus Christ.
14. O God my Father send my Moses today to deliver me from any form of bondage in the name of Jesus Christ.
15. O God my Father, send my Moses today to deliver me from any form of captivity, in the name of Jesus Christ.
16. O God my Father, send my Moses today to deliver me from any form of affliction, in the name of Jesus Christ.
17. Affliction will not happen the second time in my life in the name of Jesus Christ.
18. O God my Father, send my Moses today to deliver me from the hands of the taskmasters, in the name of Jesus Christ.
19. O God my Father, send my Moses today to deliver me from the hands of the oppressors, in the name of Jesus Christ.
20. Hear my cry today O Lord, and deliver me from sorrow.
21. Hear my cry today O Lord, and deliver me from hopelessness, in the name of Jesus Christ.

22. Hear my cry today O Lord, and deliver me from every long time problem manifesting in life, in the name of Jesus Christ.
23. O God my Father, bring me out of every stubborn situation by your power in the name of Jesus Christ.
24. You power of the grave contending with my glory, loose me and let me go, in the name of Jesus Christ.
25. You power of failure that is holding my life back, loose me and let me go, in the name of Jesus Christ.
26. You spirit of stagnancy that refuses to let me move forward, loose me and let me go in the name of Jesus Christ.
27. You spirit of unbelief that is robbing me of my blessings, loose me and let me go in the name of Jesus Christ.
28. All inherited curses manifesting in my life, your time is up, loose me and let me go in the name of Jesus Christ.
29. Every curse of financial embarrassment manifesting in my life, loose me and let me go in the name of Jesus Christ.
30. You spirit of confusion assigned against me, loose me and let me go in the name of Jesus Christ.
31. You spirit of retrogression assigned to make my life go backward, loose me and let me go in the name of Jesus Christ.
32. You spirit of infirmity assigned to torment me, loose me and let me go in the name of Jesus Christ.
33. You spirit of poverty manifesting in my life, loose me and let me go in the name of Jesus Christ.
34. You spirit of loneliness assigned against me, loose me and let me go in the name of Jesus Christ.

35. I believe with all my heart, that the problems that I see in my life today, I shall see them no more, in the name of Jesus Christ.
36. I believe with all my heart, failure that is manifesting in my life today, I shall see it no more in the name of Jesus Christ.
37. I believe it with all my heart, stagnancy that is manifesting in my life today, I shall see it no more for in the name of Jesus Christ.
38. I believe with all my heart, failure that is manifesting in my life today, I shall see it no more I the name of Jesus Christ.
39. I believe with all my heart, financial embarrassment that is manifesting in my life today, I shall see it no more in the name of Jesus Christ.
40. I believe with all my heart, barrenness that is manifesting in my life today, I shall see it no more in the name of Jesus Christ.
41. I believe with all my heart, the oppressors that are oppressing me today, I shall see them no more in the name of Jesus Christ.
42. I believe with all my heart, household wickedness that is troubling me today, I shall see it no more in the name of Jesus Christ.
43. I believe with all my heart, satanic embargo that is placed on my life today, I shall see it no more in the name of Jesus Christ.
44. I believe with all my heart, every burden upon my shoulder today, I shall see it no more in the name of Jesus Christ.
45. I believe with all my heart, every yoke upon my neck today, I shall see it no more in the name of Jesus Christ.

46. Every power assigned to make my life miserable, I shall see it no more in the name of Jesus Christ.
47. Every power assigned to hinder my prayers, I shall see it no more in the name of Jesus Christ.
48. Every power assigned to hinder my miracle; I shall see it no more in the name of Jesus Christ.
49. Every power assigned to block my breakthrough, I shall see it no more in the name of Jesus Christ.
50. Every power assigned to kill my dreams, I shall it no more in the name of Jesus Christ.
51. Every power assigned to torment me, I shall see it no more in the name of Jesus Christ.
52. Every power that is working against my success, I shall see it no more in the name of Jesus Christ.
53. Every power that is working against my prosperity, I shall see it no more in the name of Jesus Christ.
54. Every power that is attacking my marriage, I shall see no more in the name of Jesus Christ.
55. Every power assigned to rob me of my joy, I shall see it no more in the name of Jesus Christ.

UPON MOUNT ZION SHALL BE DELIVERANCE

Passages To Read Before You Pray:
Obadiah 1:17, Isaiah 10:27, Jeremiah 1:8-19, Psalms 69

I have come today to fellowship with my heavenly Father, and make my requests and needs known unto Him. I cannot be hindered nor delayed because I know who I am in the Lord. I am a child of the Kingdom, born of the Spirit, redeemed by the blood of Jesus Christ. I walk in authority, living life without any apology because the power and authority has been given to me according to the Word of God in the book of Luke 9:1.

As I have come to pray today and to fellowship with my heavenly Father, I cover myself in the blood of Jesus Christ, and I put on the whole armor of God. I hereby come against every Prince of Persia that wants to hinder my prayer, I arrest you by the power in the blood of Jesus Christ, and I bind you and cast you down into the pit of hell.

I come against principalities and powers that wrestle with me and my prayers, I arrest you today by the power in the name of Jesus Christ, and I bind you and cast down into the pit of hell. I come against the rulers of the darkness of this world, against spiritual wickedness in high places, I arrest you all by the power in the name of Jesus Christ, and I bind you and cast you down into the pit of hell. I come against weakness and weariness, I arrest you today by the power in the name of Jesus Christ, and I bind you and cast you out of my life. I come against wondering

spirit and distractions, I arrest you today by the power in the name of Jesus Christ, and I bind you and cast you out of my life.

Today I receive the anointing to pray and get results, my prayers cannot be hindered nor delayed because Jesus is my Lord, I will pray today and get the desired results, I decree open heavens upon my prayers. I baptize myself in the fire of the Holy Ghost; therefore I have become too hot for the enemy to handle. My prayers today will attract divine intervention to every situation in my life; signs and wonders will follow my prayers today, testimonies will follow my prayers today and the name of God alone will be glorified, in Jesus name. Amen!

PRAYER POINTS:

1. O God my Father, thank you for being my God, my Father and my friend.
2. O God my Father, thank you for the privilege to know you and the power of the resurrection of Jesus Christ.
3. O God my Father, thank you for always being there for me and with me.
4. O God my Father, thank you for the great and mighty things that you are doing in my life.
5. O God my Father, thank you for your provision and protection over me and my household.
6. O God my Father, thank you for always answering my prayers.
7. I confess my sins before you today and I ask you to forgive me on the basis of your mercy, in the name of Jesus Christ.

8. Wash me clean today O Lord by the blood of Jesus Christ.
9. I cover myself and my household with the blood of Jesus Christ.
10. My prayers today will not go in vain; my prayers will produce the desired results in the name of Jesus Christ.
11. Today O Lord, I have come to mount Zion, I receive power to possess my possession.
12. Today O Lord, I have come to mount Zion, I receive power to possess the gates of my enemies.
13. Today O Lord, I have come to mount Zion, I receive power to possess the goodness of this land.
14. Today O Lord, I have come to mount Zion, deliver me by your power from any form of captivity.
15. Today O Lord, I have come to mount Zion, deliver me by your power from ancestral curses.
16. Today O Lord, I have come to mount Zion, deliver me by your power from my long time problems.
17. Today O Lord, I have come to mount Zion, deliver me by your power from every shameful situation that I find myself in.
18. Today O Lord, I have come to mount Zion, deliver me by your power from anything holding my life back.
19. Today O Lord, I have come to mount Zion, deliver me by your mercy from self-inflicted poverty.
20. Today O Lord, I have come to mount Zion, deliver me by your power from any sin that will hinder me from making heaven.

PRAYER AGAINST EVIL AGENDA

Passages To Read Before You Pray:
Jeremiah 29:11, Psalms 35, 109, 59, 69, Isaiah 41:10-13

I have come today to fellowship with my heavenly Father, and make my requests and needs known unto Him. I cannot be hindered nor delayed because I know who I am in the Lord. I am a child of the Kingdom, born of the Spirit, redeemed by the blood of Jesus Christ. I walk in authority, living life without any apology because the power and authority has been given to me according to the Word of God in the book of Luke 9:1.

As I have come to pray today and to fellowship with my heavenly Father, I cover myself in the blood of Jesus Christ, and I put on the whole armor of God. I hereby come against every Prince of Persia that wants to hinder my prayer, I arrest you by the power in the blood of Jesus Christ, and I bind you and cast you down into the pit of hell.

I come against principalities and powers that wrestle with me and my prayers, I arrest you today by the power in the name of Jesus Christ, and I bind you and cast down into the pit of hell. I come against the rulers of the darkness of this world, against spiritual wickedness in high places, I arrest you all by the power in the name of Jesus Christ, and I bind you and cast you down into the pit of hell. I come against weakness and weariness, I arrest you today by the power in the name of Jesus Christ, and I bind you and cast you out of my life. I come against wondering spirit and distractions, I arrest you today by the power in the name of Jesus Christ, and I bind you and cast you out of my life.

Today I receive the anointing to pray and get results, my prayers cannot be hindered nor delayed because Jesus is my Lord, I will pray today and get the desired results, I decree open heavens upon my prayers. I baptize myself in the fire of the Holy Ghost; therefore I have become too hot for the enemy to handle. My prayers today will attract divine intervention to every situation in my life; signs and wonders will follow my prayers today, testimonies will follow my prayers today and the name of God alone will be glorified, in Jesus name. Amen!

PRAYER POINTS:

1. O God my Father, thank you for being my God, my Father and my friend.
2. O God my Father, thank you for the privilege to know you and the power of the resurrection of Jesus Christ.
3. O God my Father, thank you for always being there for me and with me.
4. O God my Father, thank you for the great and mighty things that you are doing in my life.
5. O God my Father, thank you for your provision and protection over me and my household.
6. O God my Father, thank you for always answering my prayers.
7. I confess my sins before you today and I ask you to forgive me on the basis of your mercy, in the name of Jesus Christ.
8. Wash me clean today O Lord by the blood of Jesus Christ.
9. I cover myself and my household with the blood of Jesus Christ.

10. My prayers today will not go in vain; my prayers will produce the desired results in the name of Jesus Christ.
11. Today O Lord, lead me to those who will bless me.
12. In this month O Lord, let my favor frustrate the plan of the enemy.
13. O God my Father, let the garden of my life yield super abundance.
14. Every desert spirit, loose your hold upon my life.
15. Holy Spirit of God, plug my life into divine prosperity.
16. Today I break every cycle of financial turbulence.
17. I break the control of every spirit of poverty over my life.
18. O God my Father, advertise your breakthroughs in my life.
19. O God my Father, make me a reference point of divine blessings.
20. I reject the lie of the devil, it is not over for me, this is just the beginning of great and mighty things that the Lord will do in my life.
21. I reject the lie of the devil, it is not over for me, this is the month of success in every area of my life.
22. I reject the lie of the devil, I cannot and I will not lose this battle, I receive victory over every battle in my life.
23. I reject the lie of the devil, this month will bring me joy and fulfillment.
24. I reject the lie of the devil, this is the beginning of my greatness.
25. I reject the lie of the devil, it is not over for me, I receive power to overcome every unpleasant situation in my life.
26. No matter the efforts of the enemy, I will not give up because the Lord is on my side.

27. Today O Lord, let the grace to recover everything that I have lost this year be given unto me.
28. Every minute of this month will cooperate with the plan of God for my life.
29. Today I receive miracles that will make me to forget all my past disappointments.
30. This month I shall have great success that will make me forget my past failures.
31. Today O Lord, arise and deliver me from the end of the year satanic agenda.
32. Today O Lord, arise and protect me from all evil in this month.
33. I cover myself and my household in the blood of Jesus Christ.
34. The good works that you have begun in my life since the beginning of this year, O God my Father, perfect it this month.
35. This month shall be the month of my great harvest.

DELIVERANCE FROM UNREPENTANT ENEMIES

Passages To Read Before You Pray:
Isaiah 50:7-9, Isaiah 41:10-13, Jeremiah 1:8-9, 19, Psalms 3, 35, 109

I have come today to fellowship with my heavenly Father, and make my requests and needs known unto Him. I cannot be hindered nor delayed because I know who I am in the Lord. I am a child of the Kingdom, born of the Spirit, redeemed by the blood of Jesus Christ. I walk in authority, living life without any apology because the power and authority has been given to me according to the Word of God in the book of Luke 9:1.

As I have come to pray today and to fellowship with my heavenly Father, I cover myself in the blood of Jesus Christ, and I put on the whole armor of God. I hereby come against every Prince of Persia that wants to hinder my prayers, I arrest you by the power in the blood of Jesus Christ, I bind you and cast you down into the pit of hell.

I come against principalities and powers that wrestle with me and my prayers, I arrest you today by the power in the name of Jesus Christ, I bind you and cast down into the pit of hell. I come against the rulers of the darkness of this world, against spiritual wickedness in high places, I arrest you all by the power in the name of Jesus Christ, I bind you and cast you down into the pit of hell. I come against weakness and weariness, I arrest you today by the power in the name of Jesus Christ, I bind you and cast you out of my life. I come against wondering spirit and distractions, I arrest you today by the power in the name of Jesus Christ, I bind you and cast you out of my life.

Today I receive the anointing to pray and get results, my prayers cannot be hindered nor delayed because Jesus is my Lord, I will pray today and get the desired results, I decree open heavens upon my prayers. I baptize myself in the fire of the Holy Ghost, so I have become too hot for the enemy to handle. My prayers today will attract divine intervention to every situation in my life; signs and wonders will follow my prayers today, testimonies will follow my prayer today and the name of God alone will be glorified, in Jesus name. Amen!

PRAYER POINTS:

1. O God my Father, thank you for being my God, my Father and my friend.
2. O God my Father, thank for the privilege to know you and the power of the resurrection of Jesus Christ.
3. O God my Father, thank you for always being there for me and with me.
4. O God my Father, thank you for the great and mighty things that you are doing in my life.
5. O God my Father, thank you for your provision and protection over me and my household.
6. O God my Father, thank you for always answering my prayers.
7. I confess my sins before you today and I ask you to forgive me on the basis of your mercy, in the name of Jesus Christ.

8. Wash me clean today O Lord by the blood of Jesus Christ.
9. I cover myself and my household with the blood of Jesus Christ.
10. My prayers today will not be in vain; my prayers will produce the desired results in the name of Jesus Christ.
11. By the power in the name of Jesus Christ, I cancel every arrangement of the enemy to keep me permanently in bondage.
12. By the power in the name of Jesus Christ, I cancel every arrangement of the enemy to keep me permanently stagnant, in the name of Jesus Christ.
13. By the power in the name of Jesus Christ, I cancel every arrangement of the enemy to make me a complete failure in the name of Jesus Christ.
14. By the power in the name of Jesus Christ, I cancel every arrangement of the enemy to make me completely blind to the truth of the knowledge of God, in the name of Jesus Christ.
15. O God my Father, arise and destroy them that want to destroy me, in the name of Jesus Christ.
16. O God my Father, arise and judge them that are accusing me day and night, in the name of Jesus Christ.
17. O God my Father, arise and fight them that fight against me in the name of Jesus Christ.
18. O God my Father, arise and dethrone them that want to dethrone me, in the name of Jesus Christ.
19. O God my Father, arise and disgrace them that want to disgrace me, in the name of Jesus Christ.

20. O God my Father, arise and disgrace them that want to push me out of the way to my promise land, in the name of Jesus Christ.
21. O God my Father, arise and disgrace whomever that is going around trying to destroy my name, in the name of Jesus Christ.
22. By the power in the name of Jesus Christ, I condemn every mouth speaking evil against me, in the name of Jesus Christ.
23. O God my Father, arise and destroy them that want to force me out of this race of life, in the name of Jesus Christ.
24. O God my Father, arise and frustrate them that want to frustrate me, in the name of Jesus Christ.
25. O God my Father, arise and condemn them that want to condemn me, in the name of Jesus Christ.
26. Any power anywhere hired to put me to shame, be destroyed today by the fire of God in the name of Jesus Christ.
27. Any power anywhere hired to bring me down, be destroyed by the fire of God, in the name of Jesus Christ.
28. Anybody anywhere issuing curses against me day and night, I command your curses to return back to you today by the power in the blood of Jesus Christ.
29. All the curses issued against me by anyone, return back to your sender now by the power in the blood of Jesus Christ.
30. Anybody anywhere assigned to spy on me; you will not survive the wrath of God that comes upon you today, in the name of Jesus Christ.

31. Anybody anywhere assigned to bring me down, you will not survive the wrath of God that comes upon you today, in the name of Jesus Christ.
32. Anybody anywhere assigned to confuse me; you will not survive the wrath of God that comes upon you today, in the name of Jesus Christ.
33. Any power anywhere hired to take my life; you will not survive the wrath of God that comes upon you today, in the name of Jesus Christ.
34. Anybody anywhere assigned to plant the seed of poverty into my life; you will not survive the wrath of God that comes upon you today, in the name of Jesus Christ.
35. Anybody anywhere assigned to make my future a complete struggle; you will not survive the wrath of God that comes upon you today, in the name of Jesus Christ.
36. Anybody anywhere that refuses to repent on my case, but keeps troubling me day and night, your time is up, today I withdraw your right to live, in the name of Jesus Christ.
37. Anybody anywhere that refuses to repent on my case, but keeps attacking my finances day and night, your time is up; today I withdraw your right to live, in the name of Jesus Christ.
38. Anybody anywhere that refuses to repent on my case, but keeps making my life miserable day and night, your time is up; today I withdraw your right to live, in the name of Jesus Christ.
39. Anybody anywhere that refuses to repent on my case, but keeps firing arrows of failure into my life day and night, your time is up; today I withdraw your right to live, in the name of Jesus Christ.

40. Anybody anywhere that refuses to repent on my case, but keeps firing arrows of satanic delay into my life day and night, your time is up; today I withdraw your right to live, in the name of Jesus Christ.
41. Anybody anywhere that refuses to repent on my case, but is determined to destroy my life, your time is up; today I withdraw your right to live, in the name of Jesus Christ.
42. Anybody anywhere that refuses to repent on my case, but is determined to destroy my marriage, your time is up; today I withdraw your right to live, in the name of Jesus Christ.
43. Anybody anywhere that refuses to repent on my case, but is determined to make me suffer, your time is up; today I withdraw your right to live, in the name of Jesus Christ.
44. Anybody anywhere that refuses to repent on my case, but is determined to make my life a living hell, your time is up; today I withdraw your right to live, in the name of Jesus Christ.
45. Anybody anywhere that refuses to repent on my case, but is determined to change the plan of God for my life, your time is up; today I withdraw your right to live, in the name of Jesus Christ.
46. Anybody anywhere that refuses to repent on my case, but is determined to make my life a permanent struggle, your time is up; today I withdraw your right to live, in the name of Jesus Christ.
47. Evil powers that pursed my parents and are now pursuing me; be destroyed today by the fire of God, in the name of Jesus Christ.

48. Evil powers that pursued my landlord and are now pursuing me; be destroyed today by the fire of God, in the name of Jesus Christ.
49. Evil powers that pursued the previous owners of my house and are now pursuing me; be destroyed today by the fire of God, in the name of Jesus Christ.
50. Evil powers that pursued the previous owners of my car and are now pursuing me; be destroyed today by the fire of God, in the name of Jesus Christ.
51. Evil powers that are pursuing my bosses at work and are now pursuing me; be destroyed today by the fire of God, in the name of Jesus Christ.
52. Evil powers that pursued my predecessors and are now pursuing me; be destroyed by the fire of God, in the name of Jesus Christ.
53. Every meeting organized to demote me, result in my promotion in the name of Jesus Christ.
54. Every meeting organized to rob me of joy, result in my celebration in the name of Jesus Christ.
55. Every meeting organized to hinder my prayer, result in my breakthrough in the name of Jesus Christ.
56. By the power in the name of Jesus Christ, I refuse to fall into trouble that my enemies have programmed for me in the name of Jesus Christ.
57. By the power in the name of Jesus Christ, I refuse to fall into the pit that my enemies have dug for me, in the name of Jesus Christ.
58. I refuse to dance to the tune playing by the enemies for my downfall in the name of Jesus Christ.
59. I refuse to follow the roadmap of the enemy, in the name of Jesus Christ.

60. Anybody anywhere going from place to place to destroy my life; destroy yourself today, in the name of Jesus Christ.

PRAYER OF DELIVERANCE FROM WITCHCRAFT ATTACKS

Passages To Read Before You Pray:
Exodus 22:18, Galatians 3:13, Isaiah 49:24-26, Isaiah 50:7-9, Psalms 3, 9, 35, 55, 69.

I have come today to fellowship with my heavenly Father, and make my requests and needs known unto Him. I cannot be hindered nor delayed because I know who I am in the Lord. I am a child of the Kingdom, born of the Spirit, redeemed by the blood of Jesus Christ. I walk in authority, living life without any apology because the power and authority has been given to me according to the Word of God in the book of Luke 9:1.

As I have come to pray today and to fellowship with my heavenly Father, I cover myself in the blood of Jesus Christ, and I put on the whole armor of God. I hereby come against every Prince of Persia that wants to hinder my prayer, I arrest you by the power in the blood of Jesus Christ, I bind you and cast you down into the pit of hell.

I come against principalities and powers that wrestle with me and my prayers, I arrest you today by the power in the name of Jesus Christ, I bind you and cast you down into the pit of hell. I come against the rulers of the darkness of this world, against spiritual wickedness in high places, I arrest you all by the power in the name of Jesus Christ, I bind you and cast you down into the pit of hell. I come against weakness and weariness, I arrest you today by the power in the name of Jesus Christ, I bind you and cast you out of my life. I come against wondering spirit and distractions, I arrest you today by the power in the name of Jesus Christ, I bind you and cast you out of my life.

Today I receive the anointing to pray and get results, my prayers cannot be hindered nor delayed because Jesus is my Lord, I will pray today and get the desired results, I decree open heavens upon my prayers. I baptize myself in the fire of the Holy Ghost, so I have become too hot for the enemy to handle. My prayers today will attract divine intervention to every situation in my life; signs and wonders will follow my prayers today, testimonies will follow my prayers today and the name of God alone will be glorified, in Jesus name. Amen!

PRAYER POINTS:

1. O God my Father, thank you for being my God, my Father and my friend.
2. O God my Father, thank for the privilege to know you and the power of the resurrection of Jesus Christ.
3. O God my Father, thank you for always being there for me and with me.
4. O God my Father, thank you for the great and mighty things that you are doing in my life.
5. O God my Father, thank you for your provision and protection over me and my household.
6. O God my Father, thank you for always answering my prayers.
7. I confess my sins before you today and I ask you to forgive me on the basis of your mercy, in the name of Jesus Christ.

8. Wash me clean today O Lord by the blood of Jesus Christ.
9. I cover myself and my household with the blood of Jesus Christ.
10. My prayers today will not be in vain; my prayers will produce the desired results in the name of Jesus Christ.
11. O God my Father, let every decision of the enemy against me be overturned in the name of Jesus Christ.
12. O God my Father, arise and re-arrange my life to fit into your divine plan, in the name of Jesus Christ.
13. O God my Father, arise and re-arrange my life to show forth your glory, in the name of Jesus Christ.
14. O God my Father, arise and re-arrange my life to fit into your divine progress set for me, in the name of Jesus Christ.
15. O God my Father, arise and re-arrange my life to fit into your divine favor set for me, in the name of Jesus Christ.
16. O God my Father, arise and re-arrange my life to receive miracles, in the name of Jesus Christ.
17. O God arise, re-arrange my life and prepare me for great achievements this month in the name of Jesus Christ.
18. By the power in the name of Jesus Christ, I receive divine strength to pursue, overtake and recover my stolen blessings.
19. By the power in the name of Jesus Christ, I receive divine strength to pursue, overtake and recover my stolen miracles.
20. By the power in the name of Jesus Christ, I receive divine strength to pursue, overtake and recover my prosperity from the hands of the household wickedness.
21. By the power in the name of Jesus Christ, I receive divine strength to pursue, overtake and recover my

breakthroughs from the hands of principalities and powers.

22. Every curse of "thou shall not excel" issued against me, break today by the power in the blood of Jesus Christ.
23. Every curse of "thou shall not make it" issued against me, break today by the power in the blood of Jesus Christ.
24. Every curse of "thou shall not prosper" issued against me, break today by the power in the blood of Jesus Christ.
25. Every curse of "thou shall not live long" issued against me, break today by the power in the blood of Jesus Christ.
26. Every curse of "thou shall not progress" issued against me, break today by the power in the blood of Jesus Christ.
27. Every curse of "thou shall not eat the fruits of thy labor" issued against me, break today by the power in the blood of Jesus Christ.
28. Every curse of "thou shall not rejoice" issued against me, break today by the power in the blood of Jesus Christ.
29. Every curse of "hard labor less blessing" issued against me, break today by the power in the blood of Jesus Christ.
30. Every curse of "failure at the point of breakthrough" issued against me, break by the power in the blood of Jesus Christ.
31. O God my Father, arise and cancel every evil pronouncement against my life, in the name of Jesus Christ.

32. O God my Father, arise and cancel every evil pronouncement against my future, in the name of Jesus Christ.
33. O God my Father, arise and cancel every evil pronouncement against my finances, in the name of Jesus Christ.
34. O God my Father, arise and cancel every evil pronouncement against my family, in the name of Jesus Christ.
35. O God my Father, arise and cancel every evil pronouncement against the works of my hands, in the name of Jesus Christ.
36. The negative history of my family trying to destroy my life, you will not succeed, in the name of Jesus Christ.
37. The negative history of my family that has been hindering my blessings, be replaced today with uncommon favor, in the name of Jesus Christ.
38. The negative history of my family that has been keeping my helpers away, be replaced today with uncommon favor, in the name of Jesus Christ.
39. The negative history of my family that has been making it difficult for me to excel, be replaced today with uncommon success, in the name of Jesus Christ.
40. O God my Father, do something in my life today that will rewrite my family history, in the name of Jesus Christ.
41. Voice of darkness crying against me; be silenced forever in the name of Jesus Christ.
42. Voice of witchcraft crying against me; be silenced forever in the name of Jesus Christ.
43. Voice of household wickedness crying against me; be silenced forever in the name of Jesus Christ.

44. Any evil meeting holding anywhere against me, scatter by the fire of God, in the name of Jesus Christ.
45. Any witchcraft meeting holding anywhere against me, scatter by the fire of God, in the name of Jesus Christ.
46. Demonic agents holding meetings to destroy me, arise today and begin to destroy yourselves; in the name of Jesus Christ.
47. Demonic agents holding meetings to attack my finances, arise today and begin to destroy yourselves; in the name of Jesus Christ.
48. Demonic agents holding meetings to make my life miserable, arise today and begin to destroy yourselves; in the name of Jesus Christ.
49. Demonic agents holding meetings to delay my miracles, arise today and begin to destroy yourselves; in the name of Jesus Christ.
50. Demonic agents holding meetings to hinder my prayers, arise today and begin to destroy yourselves; in the name of Jesus Christ.
51. Demonic agents holding meetings to attack my family, arise today and begin to destroy yourselves; in the name of Jesus Christ.
52. Demonic agents holding meetings to attack my marriage, arise today and begin to destroy yourselves; in the name of Jesus Christ.
53. Demonic agents holding meetings to change my destiny, arise today and begin to destroy yourselves; in the name of Jesus Christ.
54. Demonic agents holding meetings to destroy my future, arise today and begin to destroy yourselves; in the name of Jesus Christ.

55. Demonic agents holding meetings to change the plan of God for my life, arise today and begin to destroy yourselves; in the name of Jesus Christ.
56. Any power anywhere standing against my financial freedom; be destroyed today by thunder and the wild wind of God, in the name of Jesus Christ.
57. Any power anywhere standing against my breakthrough; be destroyed today by thunder and the wild wind of God, in the name of Jesus Christ.
58. Any power anywhere standing against my promotion; be destroyed today by thunder and the wild wind of God, in the name of Jesus Christ.
59. Any power anywhere standing against my open heavens; be destroyed today thunder and the wild wind of God, in the name of Jesus Christ.
60. Any power anywhere standing against my progress; be destroyed today by thunder and the wild wind of God in the name of Jesus Christ.
61. My blessings, what are you doing in the camp of the enemy; come out now by the fire of God.
62. My greatness, what are you doing in the camp of the enemy; come out now by the fire of God.
63. My financial freedom, what are you doing in the camp of the enemy; come out now by the fire of God.
64. My answered prayers, what are you doing in the camp of the enemy; come out now by the fire of God.
65. My miracles, what are you doing in the camp of the enemy; come out now by the fire of God.
66. My breakthroughs, what are doing in the camp of the enemy; come out now by the fire of God.
67. My promotion, what are you doing in the camp of the enemy; come out now by the fire of God.

68. My joy, what are you doing in the camp of the enemy; come out now by the fire of God.
69. My testimonies, what are you doing in the camp of the enemy; come out now by the fire of God.
70. Solution to my problems, what are you doing in the camp of the enemy; come out now by the fire of God.
71. My fulfilled promises of God, what are you doing in the camp of the enemy; come out now by the fire of God.
72. My divine fruitfulness, what are you doing in the camp of the enemy; come out now by the fire of God.
73. My healing, what are you doing in the camp of the enemy; come out now by the fire of God.
74. My prosperity, what are you doing in the camp of the enemy; come out now by the fire of God.
75. Anything in my life that witchcraft agents have turned upside-down; be reversed by the fire of God, in the name of Jesus Christ.
76. Anything in my home that witchcraft agents have turned upside-down; be reversed by the fire of God, in the name of Jesus Christ.
77. Anything in my marriage that witchcraft agents have turned upside-down; be reversed by the fire of God, in the name of Jesus Christ.
78. Anything in my business that witchcraft agents have turned upside-down; be reversed by the fire of God, in the name of Jesus Christ.
79. Anything in my ministry that witchcraft agents have turned upside-down; be reversed by the fire of God, in the name of Jesus Christ.
80. Anything in my church that witchcraft agents have turned upside-down; be reversed by the fire of God, in the name of Jesus Christ.

81. Anything in my neighborhood that witchcraft agents have turned upside-down; be reversed by the fire of God, in the name of Jesus Christ.
82. By the power in the blood of Jesus Christ, I withdraw my money from the witchcraft bank account, in the name of Jesus Christ.
83. By the power in the blood of Jesus Christ, I stop the direct deposit of my income into the witchcraft bank account, in the name of Jesus Christ.
84. By the power in the blood of Jesus Christ, I stop the direct deposit of my income into the household wickedness bank account, in the name of Jesus Christ.
85. By the power in the name of Jesus Christ, I stop the direct deposit of my income into the hands of the devourer, in the name of Jesus Christ.

AVENGE ME OF MY ENEMIES

Passages To Read Before You Pray:
Luke 18:1-7, Exodus 22:18, Daniel 6:1-24, Psalms 94, 35, 3, 109, 83, 55, 69.

I have come today to fellowship with my heavenly Father, and make my requests and needs known unto Him. I cannot be hindered nor delayed because I know who I am in the Lord. I am a child of the Kingdom, born of the Spirit, redeemed by the blood of Jesus Christ. I walk in authority, living life without any apology because the power and authority has been given to me according to the Word of God in the book of Luke 9:1.

As I have come to pray today and to fellowship with my heavenly Father, I cover myself in the blood of Jesus Christ, and I put on the whole armor of God. I hereby come against every Prince of Persia that wants to hinder my prayer, I arrest you by the power in the blood of Jesus Christ, and I bind you and cast you down into the pit of hell.

I come against principalities and powers that wrestle with me and my prayers, I arrest you today by the power in the name of Jesus Christ, and I bind you and cast down into the pit of hell. I come against the rulers of the darkness of this world, against spiritual wickedness in high places, I arrest you all by the power in the name of Jesus Christ, and I bind you and cast you down into the pit of hell. I come against weakness and weariness, I arrest you today by the power in the name of Jesus Christ, and I bind you and cast you out of my life. I come against wondering

spirit and distractions, I arrest you today by the power in the name of Jesus Christ, and I bind you and cast you out of my life.

Today I receive the anointing to pray and get results, my prayers cannot be hindered nor delayed because Jesus is my Lord, I will pray today and get the desired results, I decree open heavens upon my prayers. I baptize myself in the fire of the Holy Ghost; therefore I have become too hot for the enemy to handle. My prayers today will attract divine intervention to every situation in my life; signs and wonders will follow my prayers today, testimonies will follow my prayers today and the name of God alone will be glorified, in Jesus name. Amen!

PRAYER POINTS:

1. O God my Father, thank you for being my God, my Father and my friend.
2. O God my Father, thank you for the privilege to know you and the power of the resurrection of Jesus Christ.
3. O God my Father, thank you for always being there for me and with me.
4. O God my Father, thank you for the great and mighty things that you are doing in my life.
5. O God my Father, thank you for your provision and protection over me and my household.
6. O God my Father, thank you for always answering my prayers.
7. I confess my sins before you today and I ask you to forgive me on the basis of your mercy, in the name of Jesus Christ.

8. Wash me clean today O Lord by the blood of Jesus Christ.
9. I cover myself and my household with the blood of Jesus Christ.
10. My prayers today will not go in vain; my prayers will produce the desired results in the name of Jesus Christ.
11. O God the righteous Judge, I present my case before you today, avenge me of my enemies, in the name of Jesus Christ.
12. O God the righteous Judge, I am in your courtroom now, avenge me of my adversaries, in the name of Jesus Christ.
13. My stubborn enemies, I drag you to the court of the Almighty, the judgment is served and today you are sentenced to death, in the name of Jesus Christ.
14. My household wickedness, I drag you to the court of the Almighty, the judgment is served and today you are sentenced to death. (Psalms 9:6, Psalms 58:3-8, Isaiah 48:22, Isaiah 57:21.)
15. My neighborhood wickedness, I drag you to the court of the Almighty, the judgment is served and today you are sentenced to death.
16. Domestic witchcraft, I drag you to the court of the Almighty, the judgment is served and today you are sentenced to death.- (Exodus 22:18)
17. Enemies of my progress, I drag you to the court of the Almighty, the judgment is served and today you are sentenced to death.
18. Enemies of my joy, I drag you to the court of the Almighty, the judgment is served and today you are sentenced to death.

19. Enemies of my promotion, I drag you to the court of the Almighty, the judgment is served and today you are sentenced to death.
20. Enemies of my advancement, I drag you to the court of the Almighty, the judgment is served and today you are sentenced to death.
21. Environmental wickedness, I drag you to the court of the Almighty, the judgment is served and today you are sentenced to death.
22. Agent of failure assigned against me, I drag you to the court of the Almighty, the judgment is served and today you are sentenced to death.
23. Spirit of stagnancy assigned against me, I drag you to the court of the Almighty, the judgment is served and today you are sentenced to death.
24. Any power anywhere that wants me to die young, I drag you to the court of the Almighty, the judgment is served and today you are sentenced to death.
25. Any power anywhere that wants me to labor in vain, I drag you to the court of the Almighty, the judgment is served and today you are sentenced to death.
26. Anybody anywhere that knows the secret of my life and is using it to destroy me, I drag you to the court of the Almighty, the judgment is served and today you are sentenced to death.
27. Anybody anywhere trying to destroy my destiny, I drag you to the court of the Almighty, the judgment is served and today you are sentenced to death.
28. Anybody anywhere trying to change my destiny, I drag you to the court of the Almighty, the judgment is served and today you are sentenced to death.

29. Anybody anywhere trying to stop what God is doing in my life, I drag you to the court of the Almighty, the judgment is served and today you are sentenced to death.
30. Anybody anywhere trying to cover my star from shining, I drag to court of the Almighty, the judgment is served and today you are sentenced to death.
31. Anybody anywhere scattering what I'm gathering, I drag you to the court of the Almighty, the judgment is served and today you are sentenced to death.
32. Anybody anywhere attacking my finances, I drag you to the court of the Almighty, the judgment is served and today you are sentenced to death.
33. Anybody anywhere trying to stop my harvest, I drag you to the court of the Almighty, the judgment I served and today you are sentenced to death.
34. Anybody anywhere attacking my peace, I drag you to the court of the Almighty, the judgment is served and today you are sentenced to death.
35. Anybody anywhere disturbing my quiet enjoyment, I drag you to the court of the Almighty, the judgment is served and today you are sentenced to death.
36. Anybody anywhere forcing my life to go backward, I drag you to the court of the Almighty, the judgment is served and today you are sentenced to death.
37. Anybody anywhere blocking my breakthroughs, I drag you to the court of the Almighty, the judgment is served and today you are sentenced to death.
38. Anybody anywhere delaying my promotion, I drag you to the court of the Almighty, the judgment is served and today you are sentenced to death.
39. Anybody anywhere neutralizing my miracles before I receive them, I drag you to the court of the Almighty,

the judgment is served and today you are sentenced to death.
40. Anybody anywhere that wants me to die barren, I drag you to the court of the Almighty, the judgment is served and today you are sentenced to death.
41. Anybody anywhere that wants my business to remain unproductive, I drag you to the court of the Almighty, the judgment is served and you are sentenced to death.
42. Anybody anywhere attacking me with sickness and diseases, I drag you to the court of the Almighty, the judgment is served and today you are sentenced to death.
43. Anybody anywhere that wants me to labor but have nothing to show for it, I drag you to the court of the Almighty, the judgment is served and today you are sentenced to death.
44. Anybody anywhere attacking my home, I drag you to the court of the Almighty, the judgment is served and to day you are sentenced to death.
45. Anybody anywhere attacking my marriage, I drag you to the court of the Almighty, the judgment is served and today you are sentenced to death.
46. Anybody anywhere causing confusion in my marriage, I drag you to the court of the Almighty, the judgment is served and to day you are sentenced to death.
47. Anybody anywhere attacking my children, I drag you to the court of the Almighty, the judgment is served and today you are sentenced to death.
48. Any power anywhere assigned to kill my dream, I drag you to the court of the Almighty, the judgment is served and today you are sentenced to death.

49. Any power anywhere assigned to hinder my prayers, I drag you to the court of the Almighty, the judgment is served and today you are sentenced to death.
50. Any power anywhere assigned to delay my progress, I drag you to the court of the Almighty, the judgment is served and today you are sentenced to death.
51. Any power anywhere assigned to stop my progress, I drag you to the court of the Almighty, the judgment is served and today you are sentenced to death.
52. Any power anywhere assigned to delay my miracles, I drag you to the court of the Almighty, the judgment is served and today you are sentenced to death.
53. Any power anywhere assigned to destroy the works of my hands, I drag to the court of the Almighty, the judgment is served and to day you are sentenced to death.
54. Any power anywhere assigned to shut the door of blessing against me, I drag you to the court of the Almighty, the judgment is served and today you are sentenced to death.
55. Any power anywhere assigned to shut the door of opportunity against me, I drag you to the court of the Almighty, the judgment is served and today you are sentenced to death.
56. Any power anywhere driving my helpers away from me, I drag you to the court of the Almighty, the judgment is served and today you are sentenced to death.
57. Any power anywhere assigned to put me to shame, I drag you to the court of the Almighty, the judgment is served and today you are sentenced to death.

58. Agent of poverty assigned against me, I drag you to the court of the Almighty, the judgment is served and today you are sentenced to death.
59. Any power anywhere assigned to make my life miserable, I drag you to the court of the Almighty, the judgment is served and today you are sentenced to death.
60. Any power anywhere assigned to prolong my suffering, I drag you to the court of the Almighty, the judgment is served and today you are sentenced to death.
61. Any power anywhere assigned to keep me in bondage, I drag you to the court of the Almighty, the judgment is served and today you are sentenced to death.

PRAYER TO BREAK YOKES AND CURSES

Passages To Read Before You Pray:
Isaiah 10:27, 1 John 3:8, Galatians 3:13, Psalms 55, 106, 9

I have come today to fellowship with my heavenly Father, and make my requests and needs known unto Him. I cannot be hindered nor delayed because I know who I am in the Lord. I am a child of the Kingdom, born of the Spirit, redeemed by the blood of Jesus Christ. I walk in authority, living life without any apology because the power and authority has been given to me according to the Word of God in the book of Luke 9:1.

As I have come to pray today and to fellowship with my heavenly Father, I cover myself in the blood of Jesus Christ, and I put on the whole armor of God. I hereby come against every Prince of Persia that wants to hinder my prayer, I arrest you by the power in the blood of Jesus Christ, and I bind you and cast you down into the pit of hell.

I come against principalities and powers that wrestle with me and my prayers, I arrest you today by the power in the name of Jesus Christ, and I bind you and cast down into the pit of hell. I come against the rulers of the darkness of this world, against spiritual wickedness in high places, I arrest you all by the power in the name of Jesus Christ, and I bind you and cast you down into the pit of hell. I come against weakness and weariness, I arrest you today by the power in the name of Jesus Christ, and I bind you and cast you out of my life. I come against wondering spirit and distractions, I arrest you today by the power in the name of Jesus Christ, and I bind you and cast you out of my life.

Today I receive the anointing to pray and get results, my prayers cannot be hindered nor delayed because Jesus is my Lord, I will pray today and get the desired results, I decree open heavens upon my prayers. I baptize myself in the fire of the Holy Ghost; therefore I have become too hot for the enemy to handle. My prayers today will attract divine intervention to every situation in my life; signs and wonders will follow my prayers today, testimonies will follow my prayers today and the name of God alone will be glorified, in Jesus name. Amen!

PRAYER POINTS:

1. O God my Father, thank you for being my God, my Father and my friend.
2. O God my Father, thank you for the privilege to know you and the power of the resurrection of Jesus Christ.
3. O God my Father, thank you for always being there for me and with me.
4. O God my Father, thank you for the great and mighty things that you are doing in my life.
5. O God my Father, thank you for your provision and protection over me and my household.
6. O God my Father, thank you for always answering my prayers.
7. I confess my sins before you today and I ask you to forgive me on the basis of your mercy, in the name of Jesus Christ.
8. Wash me clean today O Lord by the blood of Jesus Christ.
9. I cover myself and my household with the blood of Jesus Christ.

10. My prayers today will not go in vain; my prayers will produce the desired results in the name of Jesus Christ.
11. O God my Father, let the anointing be released today and break every yoke of failure upon my life.
12. O God my Father, let the anointing be released today and break every yoke of stagnancy upon my life.
13. O God my Father, let the anointing be released today and destroy every work of the enemy in my life.
14. O God my Father, let the anointing be released today and destroy every seed of sickness in my body.
15. O God my Father, let the anointing be released today and destroy the curse of almost there upon my life.
16. O God my Father, let the anointing be released today and destroy the curse of failure at the point of breakthrough upon my life.
17. O God my Father, let the anointing be released today and destroy the curse of failure at the edge of miracle upon my life.
18. Every yoke upon my life that makes me to struggle but have nothing to show for it, be destroyed today because of the anointing.
19. Every yoke upon my life that makes me to fail where everybody else passes, be destroyed today because of the anointing.
20. Every yoke upon my life that makes me see no reason to dream for great things, be destroyed today because of the anointing.
21. Every yoke upon my life causing me to live a second class life, be destroyed today because of the anointing.
22. I am a child of the Kingdom, I deserve to be the best, I will be the best and enjoy the best in every area of my life.

23. Every yoke upon my life producing the fruit of frustration in every area of my life, be destroyed today because of the anointing.
24. Every yoke of poverty upon my life, enough is enough, be destroyed today because of the anointing.
25. Every curse upon my life that is producing failure, your time is up, break by the power in the name of Jesus Christ.
26. Cycle of tears manifesting in my life, break now by the power in the name of Jesus Christ. (Rev. 21:4)
27. Cycle of shame manifesting in my life, break now by the power in the name of Jesus Christ. (Isa. 54:4)
28. Cycle of pain manifesting in my life, break now by the power in the name of Jesus Christ. (Rev. 21:4)
29. Cycle of marital disappointment in my life, break now by the power in the name of Jesus Christ.
30. Cycle of loneliness in my life, break now by the power in the name of Jesus Christ. (Isa. 54:6-8)
31. Cycle of failure in my life, break now by the power in the name of Jesus Christ.
32. Curse of rejection upon my life, causing me to be rejected wherever I go, your time is up, break right now by the power in the name of Jesus Christ. (Isa. 54:6-8)
33. Curse of non-achievement upon my life, enough is enough, break right now by the power in the name of Jesus Christ.
34. Every curse upon me forcing my life to remain in the bottom no matter how much I try to get to the top, enough is enough, break right now by the power in the name of Jesus Christ.
35. Every curse upon me forcing my life to go round in circles no matter how much I try to move forward,

enough is enough, break right now by the power in the name of Jesus Christ.

36. Every curse upon me forcing my life to go backward no matter how hard I try to move forward, enough is enough, break right now by the power in the name of Jesus Christ.

37. Every curse upon me forcing my life to be stagnated no matter how hard I try to move forward, enough is enough, break right now by the power in the name of Jesus Christ.

38. Every curse upon my life making it impossible for me to breakthrough no matter how hard I try, enough is enough, break right now by the power in the name of Jesus Christ.

39. Every curse upon my life making my life unstable, enough is enough, break right now by the power in the name of Jesus Christ.

40. Every curse upon my life making it hard for me to find help wherever I turn, enough is enough, break right now by the power in the name of Jesus Christ.

PRAYER TO OVERCOME OBSTACLES IN YOUR WAY

Passages To Read Before You Pray:
Exodus 14:1-14, Isaiah 45:2-3, Psalms 46, 10, 118

I have come today to fellowship with my heavenly Father, and make my requests and needs known unto Him. I cannot be hindered nor delayed because I know who I am in the Lord. I am a child of the Kingdom, born of the Spirit, redeemed by the blood of Jesus Christ. I walk in authority, living life without any apology because the power and authority has been given to me according to the Word of God in the book of Luke 9:1.

As I have come to pray today and to fellowship with my heavenly Father, I cover myself in the blood of Jesus Christ, and I put on the whole armor of God. I hereby come against every Prince of Persia that wants to hinder my prayer, I arrest you by the power in the blood of Jesus Christ, and I bind you and cast you down into the pit of hell.

I come against principalities and powers that wrestle with me and my prayers, I arrest you today by the power in the name of Jesus Christ, and I bind you and cast down into the pit of hell. I come against the rulers of the darkness of this world, against spiritual wickedness in high places, I arrest you all by the power in the name of Jesus Christ, and I bind you and cast you down into the pit of hell. I come against weakness and weariness, I arrest you today by the power in the name of Jesus Christ, and I bind you and cast you out of my life. I come against wondering

spirit and distractions, I arrest you today by the power in the name of Jesus Christ, and I bind you and cast you out of my life.

Today I receive the anointing to pray and get results, my prayers cannot be hindered nor delayed because Jesus is my Lord, I will pray today and get the desired results, I decree open heavens upon my prayers. I baptize myself in the fire of the Holy Ghost; therefore I have become too hot for the enemy to handle. My prayers today will attract divine intervention to every situation in my life; signs and wonders will follow my prayers today, testimonies will follow my prayers today and the name of God alone will be glorified, in Jesus name. Amen!

PRAYER POINTS:

1. O God my Father, thank you for being my God, my Father and my friend.
2. O God my Father, thank you for the privilege to know you and the power of the resurrection of Jesus Christ.
3. O God my Father, thank you for always being there for me and with me.
4. O God my Father, thank you for the great and mighty things that you are doing in my life.
5. O God my Father, thank you for your provision and protection over me and my household.
6. O God my Father, thank you for always answering my prayers.
7. I confess my sins before you today and I ask you to forgive me on the basis of your mercy, in the name of Jesus Christ.

8. Wash me clean today O Lord by the blood of Jesus Christ.
9. I cover myself and my household with the blood of Jesus Christ.
10. My prayers today will not go in vain; my prayers will produce the desired results in the name of Jesus Christ.
11. By the power in the name of Jesus Christ, I command Red Sea on my way to give way right now, I am crossing over.
12. By the power in the name of Jesus Christ, I command every Red Sea that wants to keep me in the Egyptian bondage, to dry up.
13. By the power in the name of Jesus Christ, I command every Red Sea that wants me to die in Egypt to give way now.
14. By the power in the name of Jesus Christ, I command the Red Sea on my way to swallow my stubborn pursuers.
15. O God my Father, send the east wind today and divide the Red Sea on my way so that I may cross over to my promise land.
16. O ye Red Sea on the way to my promise land, I command you to cooperate with the divine agenda for my life.
17. O ye Red Sea on the way to my promise land, you cannot stop me I am a child of the King, give way now.
18. O ye Red Sea on the way to my promise land, you cannot hinder me I am a child of the King, give way now.
19. O ye Red Sea on the way to my promise land, you cannot delay me I am a child of the King, give way now.

20. Any power anywhere expecting me to die in the wilderness of hopelessness, you will not escape the judgment of God. (Ex. 14:3)
21. Any power anywhere expecting me to die in the wilderness of problem, you will not escape the judgment of God.
22. Any power anywhere expecting me to die in the wilderness of poverty, you will not escape the judgment of God.
23. Any power anywhere expecting me to die in the wilderness of suffering, you will not escape the judgment of God.
24. Any power anywhere expecting me to die in the wilderness of confusion, you will not escape the judgment of God.
25. Any power anywhere expecting me to die in the wilderness of ignorance, you will not escape the judgment of God.
26. Any power anywhere expecting me to die in the wilderness of sadness and bitterness, you will not escape the judgment of God.
27. Any power anywhere expecting me to die in the wilderness of lack, you will not escape the judgment of God.
28. Any power anywhere pursuing me in order to enslave me, fall today, you and your army in the order of Pharaoh. (Ex. 14:5-9)
29. Any power anywhere pursuing me in order to destroy the works of my hand, fall today, you and your army in the order of Pharaoh.

30. Household wickedness pursuing me in order to hinder the plan of God for my life, you will not escape the judgment of God.
31. Anybody anywhere pursuing me in order to stop what God is doing in my life, be disappointed today because you cannot stop God.
32. Anybody anywhere pursuing me in order to fulfill his desire upon my life, I command you to fail, my case is different.
33. O God my Father, when I am confused and don't know what to do, let there be divine intervention in every area of my life.
34. O God my Father, when all hope is lost and my faith is weak, arise and carry me in your arm.
35. O God my Father, when I am weak and don't have the strength to pray, let your grace be sufficient for me.
36. O God my Father, when all roads are closed and darkness covers my way, let your light shine and make a way where there seems to be no way.
37. O God my Father, deliver me today from the hands of the Pharaoh that wants to keep me in bondage.
38. No matter the situation around me, I will not die in Egypt.
39. Arise O Lord and sign my release form today, I am getting out of this bondage.
40. Arise O Lord and sign my release form today, I am getting out of this stubborn situation.
41. Arise O Lord and sign my release form today, I am getting out of this hopeless situation.
42. Arise O Lord and sign my release form today, I am getting out of this problem.

43. Arise O Lord and sign my release form today, I am getting out of this financial mess.
44. Arise O Lord and sign my release form today, I am getting out of this shameful situation.
45. Arise O Lord and sign my release form today, I am getting out of this wilderness.
46. As I lift up my voice in prayer today, let my stubborn situation tremble and bow at the name of Jesus Christ. (James 2:19)(Philippians 2:9-11)
47. As I lift up my voice in prayer today, let my stubborn enemy tremble and bow at the name of Jesus Christ.
48. As I lift up my voice in prayer today, let my household wickedness tremble and bow at the name of Jesus Christ.
49. As I lift up my voice in prayer today, let the power assigned to hinder my prayers tremble and bow at the name of Jesus Christ.
50. As I lift up my voice in prayer today, let the power assigned to stop my breakthrough tremble and bow at the name of Jesus Christ.
51. As I lift up my voice in prayer today, let the power assigned to delay my promotion tremble and bow at the name of Jesus Christ.
52. As I lift up my voice in prayer today, let the power assigned to attack my joy tremble and bow at the name of Jesus Christ.
53. As I lift up my voice in prayer today, let the power assigned to my marriage tremble and bow at the name of Jesus Christ.
54. As I lift up my voice in prayer today, let the power assigned to attack my finances tremble and bow at the name of Jesus Christ.

55. As I lift up my voice in prayer today, let the power of sickness in my life tremble and bow at the name of Jesus Christ.
56. As I lift up my voice in prayer today, let the power of poverty in my life tremble and bow at the name of Jesus Christ.
57. Today O Lord, let every mountain of problem in my life disappear.
58. Today O Lord, let every ocean of problem in my life disappear.
59. Today O Lord, let every wilderness of problem in my life disappear.
60. Today O Lord, let every cloud of problem over my life clear away.

PRAYER TO TAKE YOUR LIFE BACK

Passages To Read Before You Pray:
Matthew 11:12, Psalms 3, 9, 18, 35, 68, 70, 109

I have come today to fellowship with my heavenly Father, and make my requests and needs known unto Him. I cannot be hindered nor delayed because I know who I am in the Lord. I am a child of the Kingdom, born of the Spirit, redeemed by the blood of Jesus Christ. I walk in authority, living life without any apology because the power and authority has been given to me according to the Word of God in the book of Luke 9:1.

As I have come to pray today and to fellowship with my heavenly Father, I cover myself in the blood of Jesus Christ, and I put on the whole armor of God. I hereby come against every Prince of Persia that wants to hinder my prayer, I arrest you by the power in the blood of Jesus Christ, and I bind you and cast you down into the pit of hell.

I come against principalities and powers that wrestle with me and my prayers, I arrest you today by the power in the name of Jesus Christ, and I bind you and cast down into the pit of hell. I come against the rulers of the darkness of this world, against spiritual wickedness in high places, I arrest you all by the power in the name of Jesus Christ, and I bind you and cast you down into the pit of hell. I come against weakness and weariness, I arrest you today by the power in the name of Jesus Christ, and I bind you and cast you out of my life. I come against wondering

spirit and distractions, I arrest you today by the power in the name of Jesus Christ, and I bind you and cast you out of my life.

Today I receive the anointing to pray and get results, my prayers cannot be hindered nor delayed because Jesus is my Lord, I will pray today and get the desired results, I decree open heavens upon my prayers. I baptize myself in the fire of the Holy Ghost; therefore I have become too hot for the enemy to handle. My prayers today will attract divine intervention to every situation in my life; signs and wonders will follow my prayers today, testimonies will follow my prayers today and the name of God alone will be glorified, in Jesus name. Amen!

PRAYER POINTS:

1. O God my Father, thank you for being my God, my Father and my friend.
2. O God my Father, thank you for the privilege to know you and the power of the resurrection of Jesus Christ.
3. O God my Father, thank you for always being there for me and with me.
4. O God my Father, thank you for the great and mighty things that you are doing in my life.
5. O God my Father, thank you for your provision and protection over me and my household.
6. O God my Father, thank you for always answering my prayers.
7. I confess my sins before you today and I ask you to forgive me on the basis of your mercy, in the name of Jesus Christ.

8. Wash me clean today O Lord by the blood of Jesus Christ.
9. I cover myself and my household with the blood of Jesus Christ.
10. My prayers today will not go in vain; my prayers will produce the desired results in the name of Jesus Christ.

11. Today O Lord, I take my life back by force, from the hands of every power that wants to keep me in bondage.
12. Today O Lord, I take my life back from the hands of the household wickedness.
13. Today O Lord, I take my life back by force from the hands of the power of poverty.
14. Today O Lord, I take my life back by force from the hands of the power that wants me to die poor.
15. Today O Lord, I take my life back by force from the hands of the power that wants me to struggle and never make it.
16. Today O Lord, I take my life back by force from the hands that want me to die alone.
17. Today O Lord, I take my life back by force from the hands of the evil controller that is controlling my life.
18. Today O Lord, I take my life back by force from the hands of evil manipulators, manipulating me in any way.
19. Today O Lord, I take my life back by force from the hands of the power that's refueling my problems.
20. Today O Lord, I take my life back by force from the hands of the power that's turning my helpers against me.
21. Today O Lord, I take my life back by force from the hands of the power that wants to destroy my life.
22. Today O Lord, I take my life back by force from the hands of the power that wants to destroy my future.

23. Today O Lord, I take my life back by force from the hands of the Pharaoh terrorizing me day and night.
24. Today O Lord, I take my life back by force from the hands of the power that wants to make my life a living hell.
25. Today O Lord, I take my life back by force from the hands of the power that vows that I will never make it in life no matter how much I try.
26. Today O Lord, I take my life back by force from the bondage of fear.
27. Today O Lord, I take my life back by force from the fear of failure.
28. All the blessings stolen away from me, I take it back by force.
29. My breakthroughs taken away from me, today I take it back by force.
30. My miracle that has been hindered by the enemy, today I take it back by force.
31. Promotion that has been eluding me all this time, today I take it by force.
32. Financial prosperity that I have been waiting for me but I am yet to receive, today I take it by force.
33. Open heavens that I have been expecting to manifest in my life but have yet to happen, I take it by force.
34. Business opportunities that I have been praying for but have yet to manifest, today I take it by force.
35. O God my Father, I have been praying for a long time for victory over the attack of the enemy, today I take it by force.
36. The good job and stable employment that I have been praying for which has yet to manifest, today O Lord, I take it by force.

37. The nice house that I have been praying for which has yet to manifest, today I take it by force.
38. Success in every area that I have been praying for but have yet to manifest, today O Lord, I take it by force.
39. My blessing that has fallen into wrong hands, today I take it back by force.
40. My promotion that has been given to another person, today I take it back by force.
41. My miracles that have been hindered by the enemy, today I take it back by force.
42. Answers to my prayers that have been delayed by the Prince of Persia, today I take it back by force.
43. My breakthroughs that have fallen into wrong hands, today I take it back by force.
44. Good things that I have lost because of ignorance, today I take it back by force.
45. Good things that I have lost because of sin, I repent today and I take it back by force.
46. The promise of God for me in 2012 that is yet to be fulfilled, today I take it by force.
47. Good things that the enemy says can never happen in my life, today O Lord, it take it by force.
48. The breakthrough that everyone around me believes I can never achieve in life, today O Lord, I take it by force.
49. The position that everyone around me believes I can never get it in life, today O Lord, I take it by force.
50. The situation that everyone around me believes I can never overcome, today O Lord, I overcome this situation by force.

51. The pit of hopelessness that everyone around me believes I can never get out of, today O Lord, I am getting out by force.
52. The wilderness of trouble that everyone around me believes I can never get out of, today O Lord, I am getting out by force.
53. The stubborn situation that everyone me believes I can never overcome, today O Lord, I overcome this situation by force.
54. Today O Lord. I take my life back by force from the hands of the power that wants to kill my dreams.
55. Today O Lord, I take my life back by force from the hands of the power that wants to destroy my destiny.
56. Today O Lord, I take my life back from the hands of the power that is using my life for an experiment.
57. Today O Lord, I take my life back by force from the hands of the power of darkness that is using my life to get promotion.
58. Today O Lord, I take my life back by force from the hands of the power that is prolonging my journey to my promise land.
59. Today O Lord, I take my life back by force from the foundational curse affecting my bloodline.
60. Today O Lord, I take my life back by force from the generational curse affecting my bloodline.
61. Today O Lord, I take my life back by force from the curse of failure that is affecting my progress in life.
62. Today O Lord, I take my life back by force from the curse of failure that is affecting my desired success.
63. Today O Lord, I take my life back by force from the curse of poverty that is affecting the works of my hands.

64. Today O Lord, I take my life back by force from the curse of poverty that is destroying my harvest.
65. Today O Lord, I take my life back by force from the hands of the power assigned to increase my pain.
66. Today O Lord, I take my life back by force from the hands of the power assigned to make my life miserable.
67. Today O Lord, I take my life back by force from the hands of the power assigned to make success impossible for me.
68. Today O Lord, I take my life back by force from the hands of the power assigned to make it impossible for me to breakthrough in life.
69. Today O Lord, I take my life back by force from the hands of the power assigned to frustrate me.
70. Today O Lord, I take my life back by force from the hands of the wicked. Let the wickedness of the wicked fall upon their own heads.

POWER FOR DELIVERANCE

Passages To Read Before You Pray:
Philippians 2:7-11, Acts 4:12, Romans 10:13, Acts 2:21, Psalms 29, 19, 44, 70, 86.

I have come today to fellowship with my heavenly Father, and make my requests and needs known unto Him. I cannot be hindered nor delayed because I know who I am in the Lord. I am a child of the Kingdom, born of the Spirit, redeemed by the blood of Jesus Christ. I walk in authority, living life without any apology because the power and authority has been given to me according to the Word of God in the book of Luke 9:1.

As I have come to pray today and to fellowship with my heavenly Father, I cover myself in the blood of Jesus Christ, and I put on the whole armor of God. I hereby come against every Prince of Persia that wants to hinder my prayer, I arrest you by the power in the blood of Jesus Christ, and I bind you and cast you down into the pit of hell.

I come against principalities and powers that wrestle with me and my prayers, I arrest you today by the power in the name of Jesus Christ, and I bind you and cast down into the pit of hell. I come against the rulers of the darkness of this world, against spiritual wickedness in high places, I arrest you all by the power in the name of Jesus Christ, and I bind you and cast you down into the pit of hell. I come against weakness and weariness, I arrest you today by the power in the name of Jesus Christ, and I bind you and cast you out of my life. I come against wondering

spirit and distractions, I arrest you today by the power in the name of Jesus Christ, and I bind you and cast you out of my life.

Today I receive the anointing to pray and get results, my prayers cannot be hindered nor delayed because Jesus is my Lord, I will pray today and get the desired results, I decree open heavens upon my prayers. I baptize myself in the fire of the Holy Ghost; therefore I have become too hot for the enemy to handle. My prayers today will attract divine intervention to every situation in my life; signs and wonders will follow my prayers today, testimonies will follow my prayers today and the name of God alone will be glorified, in Jesus name. Amen!

PRAYER POINTS:

1. O God my Father, thank you for being my God, my Father and my friend.
2. O God my Father, thank you for the privilege to know you and the power of the resurrection of Jesus Christ.
3. O God my Father, thank you for always being there for me and with me.
4. O God my Father, thank you for the great and mighty things that you are doing in my life.
5. O God my Father, thank you for your provision and protection over me and my household.
6. O God my Father, thank you for always answering my prayers.
7. I confess my sins before you today and I ask you to forgive me on the basis of your mercy, in the name of Jesus Christ.

8. Wash me clean today O Lord by the blood of Jesus Christ.
9. I cover myself and my household with the blood of Jesus Christ.
10. My prayers today will not go in vain; my prayers will produce the desired results in the name of Jesus Christ.
11. Today O Lord, I refuse to pray in vain, my prayers will produce the desired results.
12. No matter the situation around me, prayer will work for me.
13. I cover myself and my household in the precious blood of Jesus Christ.
14. Today I receive the anointing to pray my way to breakthroughs.
15. Today O Lord, let my prayers attract divine intervention into every area of my life.
16. I command every stubborn situation in my life to bow at the name of Jesus Christ.
17. I command every problem in my life to receive solution at the mention of the name of Jesus Christ.
18. I command my trouble to disappear at the mention of the name of Jesus Christ.
19. I command every long time problem in my life to vanish at the mention of the name of Jesus Christ.
20. I command my frustration to go away forever at the mention of the name of Jesus Christ.
21. I command every work of the devil in my life to be destroyed at the mention of the name of Jesus Christ.
22. I command my household wickedness to surrender at the mention of the name of Jesus Christ.

23. I command every witchcraft working on my case to loose their power at the mention of the name of Jesus Christ.
24. I command principalities and powers working on my case to enter into everlasting captivity at the mention of the name of Jesus Christ.
25. I command poverty in my life to disappear at the mention of the name of Jesus Christ.
26. I command my ridicule to turn to miracle at the mention of the name of Jesus Christ.
27. I command my miracles to appear at the mention of the name of Jesus Christ.
28. I command my breakthroughs to manifest at the mention of the name of Jesus Christ.
29. I command my open heavens to manifest at the mention of the name of Jesus Christ.
30. I command every evil mark upon my life to completely disappear at the mention of the name of Jesus Christ.
31. I command evil loads upon me to be removed at the mention of the name of Jesus Christ.
32. I command every burden upon my life to be destroyed at the mention of the name of Jesus Christ.
33. I command every yoke upon my life to be destroyed at the mention of the name of Jesus Christ.
34. I command every poison that I have consumed in my dream to be neutralized today at the mention of the name of Jesus Christ.
35. I command every satanic arrow fired at me to return to sender today at the mention of the name of Jesus Christ.
36. I command every evil pronouncement upon my life to be nullified at the mention of the name of Jesus Christ.

37. I command every curse upon my life to be broken at the mention of the name of Jesus Christ
38. I command divine healing to take place in my body now, at the mention of name of Jesus Christ.
39. I command my double promotion to manifest now, at the mention of the name of Jesus Christ.
40. I command doors of opportunity to open unto me now, at the mention of the name of Jesus Christ.
41. I command my prosperity to appear now, at the mention of the name of Jesus Christ.
42. I command failure to turn to success in my life now, at the mention of the name of Jesus Christ.
43. I command every seed of sickness in my life to disappear now, at the mention of the name of Jesus Christ.
44. I command every mountain of disappointment on my way to be destroyed today at the mention of the name of Jesus Christ.
45. I command deliverance from inherited sickness to take place in my life now, at the mention of the name of Jesus Christ.
46. I command deliverance from ancestral poverty to take place in my life now, at the mention of the name of Jesus Christ.
47. I command deliverance from foundational problems to take place in my life now, at the mention of the name of Jesus Christ.
48. I command deliverance from satanic bondage to take place in my life now, at the mention of the name of Jesus Christ.

49. I command deliverance from the spirit of rags to take place in my life now, at the mention of the name of Jesus Christ.
50. I command deliverance from the spirit of delay to take place now in my life, at the mention of the name of Jesus Christ.
51. I command deliverance from the spirit of barrenness to take place in my life now, at the mention of the name of Jesus Christ.
52. I command deliverance from the spirit of almost there to take place in my life now, at the mention of the name of Jesus Christ.
53. I command financial freedom to begin to manifest in my life now, at the mention of the name of Jesus Christ.
54. As I call upon the name of Jesus Christ, people will arise from every corner of the world to help me.
55. As I call upon the name of Jesus Christ, people will arise from every corner of the world to show me favor.
56. I command my challenges to turn to testimonies at the mention of the name of Jesus Christ.
57. As I call upon the name of Jesus Christ, my situation will turn around for the better.
58. O God my Father, let the rain of abundance be released upon my life at the mention of the name of Jesus Christ.
59. As I call upon the name of Jesus Christ, my mouth will be filled with laughter.
60. As I call upon the name of Jesus Christ, every road closed against me shall be opened by the fire of God.
61. As I call upon the name of Jesus Christ, money will begin to work for me.
62. Let there be serious trouble in the camp of my enemy as I call upon the name of Jesus Christ.

63. Let there be life claiming accidents in the camp of the wicked as I call upon the name of Jesus Christ.
64. Let the thunder of God destroy the camp of my household wickedness as I call upon the name of Jesus Christ.
65. Let the mighty hands of God return the wickedness of the wicked upon their own heads as I call upon the name of Jesus Christ.
66. Let my stubborn pursuers fall and never rise again as I call upon the name of Jesus Christ.
67. Let every evil network working against me be scattered and never regroup again as I call upon the name of Jesus Christ.
68. Today I claim victory in every area of my life as I call upon the name of Jesus Christ.
69. I command loneliness in my life to disappear as I call upon the name of Jesus Christ.
70. Let the glory of The Lord descend upon my life as I call upon the name of Jesus Christ.

PRAY BY THE POWER IN JESUS NAME

Passages To Read Before You Pray:
John 14:12-14, Isaiah 10:27, Philippians 2:5-11, Psalms 19, 22

I have come today to fellowship with my heavenly Father, and make my requests and needs known unto Him. I cannot be hindered nor delayed because I know who I am in the Lord. I am a child of the Kingdom, born of the Spirit, redeemed by the blood of Jesus Christ. I walk in authority, living life without any apology because the power and authority has been given to me according to the Word of God in the book of Luke 9:1.

As I have come to pray today and to fellowship with my heavenly Father, I cover myself in the blood of Jesus Christ, and I put on the whole armor of God. I hereby come against every Prince of Persia that wants to hinder my prayer, I arrest you by the power in the blood of Jesus Christ, and I bind you and cast you down into the pit of hell.

I come against principalities and powers that wrestle with me and my prayers, I arrest you today by the power in the name of Jesus Christ, and I bind you and cast down into the pit of hell. I come against the rulers of the darkness of this world, against spiritual wickedness in high places, I arrest you all by the power in the name of Jesus Christ, and I bind you and cast you down into the pit of hell. I come against weakness and weariness, I arrest you today by the power in the name of Jesus Christ, and I bind you and cast you out of my life. I come against wondering spirit and distractions, I arrest you today by the power in the name of Jesus Christ, and I bind you and cast you out of my life.

Today I receive the anointing to pray and get results, my prayers cannot be hindered nor delayed because Jesus is my Lord, I will pray today and get the desired results, I decree open heavens upon my prayers. I baptize myself in the fire of the Holy Ghost; therefore I have become too hot for the enemy to handle. My prayers today will attract divine intervention to every situation in my life; signs and wonders will follow my prayers today, testimonies will follow my prayers today and the name of God alone will be glorified, in Jesus name. Amen!

PRAYER POINTS:

1. O God my Father, thank you for being my God, my Father and my friend.
2. O God my Father, thank you for the privilege to know you and the power of the resurrection of Jesus Christ.
3. O God my Father, thank you for always being there for me and with me.
4. O God my Father, thank you for the great and mighty things that you are doing in my life.
5. O God my Father, thank you for your provision and protection over me and my household.
6. O God my Father, thank you for always answering my prayers.
7. I confess my sins before you today and I ask you to forgive me on the basis of your mercy, in the name of Jesus Christ.
8. Wash me clean today O Lord by the blood of Jesus Christ.
9. I cover myself and my household with the blood of Jesus Christ.

10. My prayers today will not go in vain; my prayers will produce the desired results in the name of Jesus Christ.
11. O God my Father, let anything in my life that can hinder my prayers be removed today in the name of Jesus Christ.
12. I am tired of living a stagnant life, according to your Word O Lord, I ask in the name of Jesus Christ, let my life move forward by your power.
13. I don't want to continue my life like this, I ask in the name of Jesus Christ, let there be a positive change in every area of my life.
14. I am tired of being a follower all my life, I ask in the name of Jesus Christ, let the anointing and wisdom of a leader rest upon me today.
15. For how long will I suffer like a criminal, I ask in the name of Jesus Christ, let there be divine intervention in every area of my life.
16. I am tired of failing over and over again, I ask in the name of Jesus Christ, let the anointing for success be released upon me today.
17. I am tired of living a hopeless life, I ask in the name of Jesus Christ, let new things begin to manifest in my life that everyone around may see your works in my life.
18. I am tired of eating left over miracles, I ask in the name of Jesus Christ, let something miraculous begin to happen in my life now.
19. I am tired of eating left over blessings, I ask in the name of Jesus Christ, let the blessings of heaven and earth be released into my life today.

20. I am tired of living in the valley, I ask in the name of Jesus Christ, transport me today to the mountain top by your power.
21. I am tired of being in the circle of the poor, I ask in the name of Jesus Christ, let your riches and wealth be released into my life.
22. I am tired of living at the bottom of the ladder, I ask in the name of Jesus Christ, catapult me to the top.
23. O God my Father, for how long will I suffer like this, I ask in the name of Jesus Christ, let there be divine intervention in my life.
24. O God my Father, for how long will I be in this situation, I ask in the name of Jesus Christ, let my situation receive solution today.
25. O God my Father, for how long will you allow the enemy to mock me? I ask in the name of Jesus Christ, give me reasons to laugh.
26. O God my Father, this pain is too much for me, I ask in the name of Jesus Christ, let my pain be taken away and give me peace and joy everlasting.
27. O God my Father, I don't like my financial situation, I hereby ask in the name of Jesus Christ, grant me financial breakthroughs.
28. O God my Father, this battle is too much for and you know I can't fight, I hereby ask in the name of Jesus Christ, arise and fight for me in every area of my life.
29. I am tired of this loneliness, I ask in the name of Jesus Christ, surround me with good and faithful people.
30. I am tired of seeing my life go backward, I ask in the name of Jesus Christ, let there be progress in every area of my life.

31. For how long will the enemy boast over my life, I ask in the name of Jesus Christ, let my enemies be silenced permanently.
32. O God my Father, when would it be my turn to testify, I ask in the name of Jesus Christ, let my testimonies begin now.
33. O God my Father, when will you show people around me that you are my God, I ask in the name of Jesus Christ, demonstrate your power in every area of my life.
34. O God my Father, this burden upon my life is too heavy for me, I ask in the name of Jesus Christ, let this burden be taken away from me.
35. Every burden of sin upon my life, I ask in the name of Jesus Christ, be destroyed by the fire of God.
36. Every ancestral burden upon my life, I ask in the name of Jesus Christ, be destroyed now by the fire of God.
37. Every burden that I inherited through marriage, I ask in the name of Jesus Christ, be destroyed now by the fire of God.
38. Every burden that I inherited through my business relationships, I ask in the name of Jesus Christ, be destroyed now by the fire of God.
39. Every burden that I inherit through friendships, I ask in the name of Jesus Christ, be destroyed now by the fire of God.
40. Every evil load placed on my shoulder by the enemy, I ask in the name of Jesus Christ, be destroyed now by the fire of God.
41. Every yoke of debt on my neck, I ask in the name of Jesus Christ, be destroyed now by the fire of God.

42. Every yoke upon my life slowing down my progress, I ask in the name of Jesus Christ, be destroyed now by the fire of God.
43. Every yoke of infirmity upon my life, I ask in the name of Jesus Christ, be destroyed now by the fire of God.
44. Every yoke of infirmity upon my spouse, I ask in the name of Jesus Christ, be destroyed now by the fire of God.
45. Every yoke of infirmity upon my children, I ask in the name of Jesus Christ, be destroyed now by the fire of God.
46. Every yoke of failure upon my life, I ask in the name of Jesus Christ, be destroyed in the name of Jesus Christ.
47. Every yoke of failure upon my spouse, I ask in the name of Jesus Christ, be destroyed by the fire of God.
48. Every yoke of failure upon my children, I ask in the name of Jesus Christ, be destroyed by the fire of God.

MY LIFE IS BUILT UPON THE ROCK

Passages To Read Before You Pray:
Matthew 16:13-20, Matthew 7:24-27, Hebrews 4:12, Psalms 29, 24, 3, 125, 30, 55, 86

I have come today to fellowship with my heavenly Father, and make my requests and needs known unto Him. I cannot be hindered nor delayed because I know who I am in the Lord. I am a child of the Kingdom, born of the Spirit, redeemed by the blood of Jesus Christ. I walk in authority, living life without any apology because the power and authority has been given to me according to the Word of God in the book of Luke 9:1.

As I have come to pray today and to fellowship with my heavenly Father, I cover myself in the blood of Jesus Christ, and I put on the whole armor of God. I hereby come against every Prince of Persia that wants to hinder my prayer, I arrest you by the power in the blood of Jesus Christ, and I bind you and cast you down into the pit of hell.

I come against principalities and powers that wrestle with me and my prayers, I arrest you today by the power in the name of Jesus Christ, and I bind you and cast down into the pit of hell. I come against the rulers of the darkness of this world, against spiritual wickedness in high places, I arrest you all by the power in the name of Jesus Christ, and I bind you and cast you down into the pit of hell. I come against weakness and weariness, I arrest you today by the power in the name of Jesus Christ, and I bind you and cast you out of my life. I come against wondering

spirit and distractions, I arrest you today by the power in the name of Jesus Christ, and I bind you and cast you out of my life.

Today I receive the anointing to pray and get results, my prayers cannot be hindered nor delayed because Jesus is my Lord, I will pray today and get the desired results, I decree open heavens upon my prayers. I baptize myself in the fire of the Holy Ghost; therefore I have become too hot for the enemy to handle. My prayers today will attract divine intervention to every situation in my life; signs and wonders will follow my prayers today, testimonies will follow my prayers today and the name of God alone will be glorified, in Jesus name. Amen!

PRAYER POINTS:

1. O God my Father, thank you for being my God, my Father and my friend.
2. O God my Father, thank you for the privilege to know you and the power of the resurrection of Jesus Christ.
3. O God my Father, thank you for always being there for me and with me.
4. O God my Father, thank you for the great and mighty things that you are doing in my life.
5. O God my Father, thank you for your provision and protection over me and my household.
6. O God my Father, thank you for always answering my prayers.
7. I confess my sins before you today and I ask you to forgive me on the basis of your mercy, in the name of Jesus Christ.

8. Wash me clean today O Lord by the blood of Jesus Christ.
9. I cover myself and my household with the blood of Jesus Christ.
10. My prayers today will not go in vain; my prayers will produce the desired results in the name of Jesus Christ.
11. In this month and in everyday of my life, prayer will work for me.
12. O God my Father, let the power of your word bring transformation into every area of my life.
13. O God my Father, let the power of your word bring transformation into the life of my spouse.
14. O God my Father, let the power of your word bring transformation into the life of my children.
15. O God my Father, let the power of your word bring transformation into my home.
16. O God my Father, let the power of your word bring transformation into my marriage.
17. O God my Father, let the power of your word bring transformation into my spiritual life.
18. Today O Lord, I hereby build my life upon the rock, the gates of hell will not prevail against me.
19. Today O Lord, my finances is hereby built upon the rock, the gates of hell will not prevail against it.
20. Today O Lord, my home is hereby built upon the rock, the gates of hell will not prevail against it.
21. Today O Lord, my family is hereby built upon the rock, the gates of hell will not prevail against it.
22. Today O Lord, my business is hereby built upon the rock, the gates of hell will not prevail against it.

23. Today O Lord, my future is hereby built upon the rock, the gates of hell will not prevail against it.
24. Today O Lord, my dream is hereby built upon the rock, the gates of hell will not prevail against it.
25. Today O Lord, I hereby build my success upon the rock, the gates of hell will not prevail against it.
26. With all authority I command today, lift up your head you gate of failure, I am ready to go.
27. With all authority I command today, lift up your head you gate of frustration, I am ready to rejoice.
28. With all authority I command today, lift up your head you gate of disappointment, I am ready to be appointed for greatness.
29. With all authority I command today, lift up your head you gate of disappointment, I am ready to be appointed for greater achievement.
30. With all authority I command today, lift up your head you gate of financial failure, I am ready to walk in prosperity.
31. With all authority I command today, lift up your head you gate of stagnancy, I am ready to move forward.
32. With all authority I command today, lift up your head you gate of satanic delay, I am ready to achieve great things.
33. With all authority I command today, lift up your head you gate of loneliness, my helpers shall locate me today.
34. With all authority I command today, lift up your head you gate of poverty, that I may enjoy super-abundance that is coming my way.
35. With all authority I command today, lift up your head you gate of rejection because my time of acceptance has come.

36. O God my Father, arise and destroy the everlasting door of infirmity erected against me.
37. O God my Father, arise and destroy the everlasting door of ridicule erected against me.
38. O God my Father, arise and destroy the everlasting door of slow progress erected against me.
39. O God my Father, arise and destroy the everlasting door of failure erected against me.
40. O God my Father, arise and destroy the everlasting door of failure erected against my household.
41. O God my Father, arise and destroy the everlasting door of financial embarrassment erected against me.
42. Today I decree that my life shall flourish like a tree planted by the riverside.
43. Today I decree that my spouse shall flourish like a tree planted by the riverside.
44. Today I decree that my children shall prosper like a tree planted by the riverside.
45. Today I decree that my business shall flourish like a tree planted by the riverside.
46. Today I decree that my finances shall flourish like a tree planted by the riverside.
47. Today I decree that whatsoever I do shall flourish like a tree planted by the riverside.
48. Today I decree that my ministry shall flourish like a tree planted by the riverside.
49. Today I decree that every work of my hands shall flourish like a tree planted by the riverside.
50. Satanic violence set up against me, be scattered by the fire of God.
51. Satanic violence set up against my family, be scattered by the fire of God.

52. Satanic violence set up against God's plan for me, be scattered by the fire of God.
53. Satanic violence set up against my joy, be scattered by the fire of God.
54. Satanic violence set up against my dreams, be scattered by the fire of God.
55. Satanic violence set up to rob me of my blessing, be scattered by the fire of God.
56. Satanic violence set up against my marriage, be scattered by the fire of God.
57. Satanic violence set up to hinder my prayers, be scattered by the fire of God.
58. Satanic violence set up to delay my miracles, be scattered by the fire of God.
59. Satanic violence set up to stop the move of God in my life, be scattered by the fire of God.
60. Satanic violence set up to make my life miserable, be scattered by the fire of God.
61. Satanic violence set up to put my life on hold, be scattered by the fire of God.
62. Satanic violence set up to enslave me, be scattered by the fire of God.
63. Satanic violence set up to keep me in bondage, be scattered by the fire of God.
64. O God my Father, arise and stop them that want to stop me.
65. Today O Lord, bless me with many blessings.
66. Today O Lord, bless my family with blessings, of heaven, of the deep, of the breast and of the womb.
67. Today O Lord, bless the works of my hands and let it prosper.
68. O God my Father, show case your power in my life.

69. O God my Father, thank you for answering my prayers.

NEW THINGS THAT THE ENEMY CANNOT STOP

Passages To Read Before You Pray:
2 Kings 2:1-15, Isaiah 43:18-19, Mark 10:46-52, Isaiah 40:29-31

I have come today to fellowship with my heavenly Father, and make my requests and needs known unto Him. I cannot be hindered nor delayed because I know who I am in the Lord. I am a child of the Kingdom, born of the Spirit, redeemed by the blood of Jesus Christ. I walk in authority, living life without any apology because the power and authority has been given to me according to the Word of God in the book of Luke 9:1.

As I have come to pray today and to fellowship with my heavenly Father, I cover myself in the blood of Jesus Christ, and I put on the whole armor of God. I hereby come against every Prince of Persia that wants to hinder my prayer, I arrest you by the power in the blood of Jesus Christ, and I bind you and cast you down into the pit of hell.

I come against principalities and powers that wrestle with me and my prayers, I arrest you today by the power in the name of Jesus Christ, and I bind you and cast down into the pit of hell. I come against the rulers of the darkness of this world, against spiritual wickedness in high places, I arrest you all by the power in the name of Jesus Christ, and I bind you and cast you down into the pit of hell. I come against weakness and weariness, I arrest you today by the power in the name of Jesus Christ, and I bind you and cast you out of my life. I come against wondering

spirit and distractions, I arrest you today by the power in the name of Jesus Christ, and I bind you and cast you out of my life.

Today I receive the anointing to pray and get results, my prayers cannot be hindered nor delayed because Jesus is my Lord, I will pray today and get the desired results, I decree open heavens upon my prayers. I baptize myself in the fire of the Holy Ghost; therefore I have become too hot for the enemy to handle. My prayers today will attract divine intervention to every situation in my life; signs and wonders will follow my prayers today, testimonies will follow my prayers today and the name of God alone will be glorified, in Jesus name. Amen!

PRAYER POINTS:

1. O God my Father, thank you for being my God, my Father and my friend.
2. O God my Father, thank you for the privilege to know you and the power of the resurrection of Jesus Christ.
3. O God my Father, thank you for always being there for me and with me.
4. O God my Father, thank you for the great and mighty things that you are doing in my life.
5. O God my Father, thank you for your provision and protection over me and my household.
6. O God my Father, thank you for always answering my prayers.
7. I confess my sins before you today and I ask you to forgive me on the basis of your mercy, in the name of Jesus Christ.

8. Wash me clean today O Lord by the blood of Jesus Christ.
9. I cover myself and my household with the blood of Jesus Christ.
10. My prayers today will not go in vain; my prayers will produce the desired results in the name of Jesus Christ.
11. I receive the power and anointing to mount up with wings as eagles.
12. Any power anywhere that wants to stop me this month, be destroy by the fire of God.
13. Any power that wants to stand in my way this month, be destroyed by fire.
14. Any power that wants to hinder my miracles, be destroyed by fire.
15. Today I receive double portion of the anointing.
16. Today I receive double portion of success.
17. Today I receive double portion of breakthroughs.
18. O God my Father, new things that the enemy cannot stop, let it begin to manifest in my life.
19. O God my Father, new things that the enemy cannot stop, let it begin to manifest in my home.
20. O God my Father, new things that the enemy cannot stop, let it begin to manifest in my finances.
21. O God my Father, new things that the enemy cannot stop, let it begin to manifest in the life of my spouse.
22. O God my Father, new things that the enemy cannot stop, let it begin to manifest in the life of my children.
23. O God my Father, new things that the enemy cannot stop, let it begin to manifest in my marriage.
24. O God my Father, new things that the enemy cannot stop, let it begin to manifest in my business.

25. O God my Father, new things that the enemy cannot stop, let it begin to manifest in my ministry.
26. O God my Father, new things that the enemy cannot stop, let it begin to manifest in my spiritual life.
27. O God my Father, do something new in my life today that will put my enemy to shame.
28. O God my Father, do something new in my life today that will make me forget my shameful past.
29. O God my Father, do something new in my life today that will make me forget my painful past.
30. O God my Father, do something new in my life today that will make me forget my sorrowful past.
31. O God my Father, do something new in my life today that will fill my mouth with laughter.
32. Miracles that the enemy cannot stop, Father Lord, do it in my life today.
33. Breakthroughs that the enemy cannot stop, Father Lord, do it in my life today.
34. Undeniable success that the enemy cannot stop, I receive it today.
35. Uncommon open heaven that the enemy cannot stop, I receive it today.
36. Unusual progress that the enemy cannot stop, I receive it today.
37. Uncommon increase that the enemy cannot stop, I receive it today.
38. Financial breakthrough that the enemy cannot stop, I receive it today.
39. Financial freedom that the enemy cannot stop, I receive it today.
40. Double promotion that the enemy cannot stop, I receive it today.

41. Spiritual blessings that the enemy cannot stop, I receive it today.
42. Financial blessings that the enemy cannot stop, I receive it today.
43. Material blessings that the enemy cannot stop, I receive it today.
44. Uncommon favor that the enemy cannot stop, I receive it today.
45. Divine connection that the enemy cannot stop, let it happen now in my life.
46. Divine arrangement that the enemy cannot stop, let it begin to happen now in my life.
47. Divine turn-around that the enemy cannot stop, let it begin to happen now in my life.
48. Divine provision that the enemy cannot stop, I receive it today.
49. Greater achievement that the enemy cannot stop, I receive it today.
50. Divine healing that the enemy cannot stop, I receive it today.
51. Divine restoration that the enemy cannot stop, do it in my life today.
52. Uncommon harvest that the enemy cannot stop, I receive it today.
53. Divine helpers that the enemy cannot stop, locate me now.
54. Divine opportunity that the enemy cannot stop, I receive it today.
55. Spirit of excellence that the enemy cannot stop, I receive it today.
56. Miracles that will silence those that want to mock me, do it in my life today O Lord.

57. Transformation that will silence those that are laughing at me, do it in my life today O Lord.
58. Great success that will covert my ridicule to miracles, do it in my life today O Lord.
59. I know it beyond any doubt that I will testify before the end of this month.
60. Miracles that will make me to sing a new song, do it in my life today O Lord.

FATHER, STOP THEM THAT WANT TO STOP ME

Passages To Read Before You Pray:
2 Kings 2:1-15, Isaiah 43:18-19, Mark 10:46-52, Isaiah 40:29-31, Numbers 22:1-41,

I have come today to fellowship with my heavenly Father, and make my requests and needs known unto Him. I cannot be hindered nor delayed because I know who I am in the Lord. I am a child of the Kingdom, born of the Spirit, redeemed by the blood of Jesus Christ. I walk in authority, living life without any apology because the power and authority has been given to me according to the Word of God in the book of Luke 9:1.

As I have come to pray today and to fellowship with my heavenly Father, I cover myself in the blood of Jesus Christ, and I put on the whole armor of God. I hereby come against every Prince of Persia that wants to hinder my prayer, I arrest you by the power in the blood of Jesus Christ, and I bind you and cast you down into the pit of hell.

I come against principalities and powers that wrestle with me and my prayers, I arrest you today by the power in the name of Jesus Christ, and I bind you and cast down into the pit of hell. I come against the rulers of the darkness of this world, against spiritual wickedness in high places, I arrest you all by the power in the name of Jesus Christ, and I bind you and cast you down into the pit of hell. I come against weakness and weariness, I arrest you today by the power in the name of Jesus Christ, and I bind you and cast you out of my life. I come against wondering

spirit and distractions, I arrest you today by the power in the name of Jesus Christ, and I bind you and cast you out of my life.

Today I receive the anointing to pray and get results, my prayers cannot be hindered nor delayed because Jesus is my Lord, I will pray today and get the desired results, I decree open heavens upon my prayers. I baptize myself in the fire of the Holy Ghost; therefore I have become too hot for the enemy to handle. My prayers today will attract divine intervention to every situation in my life; signs and wonders will follow my prayers today, testimonies will follow my prayers today and the name of God alone will be glorified, in Jesus name. Amen!

PRAYER POINTS:

1. O God my Father, thank you for being my God, my Father and my friend.
2. O God my Father, thank you for the privilege to know you and the power of the resurrection of Jesus Christ.
3. O God my Father, thank you for always being there for me and with me.
4. O God my Father, thank you for the great and mighty things that you are doing in my life.
5. O God my Father, thank you for your provision and protection over me and my household.
6. O God my Father, thank you for always answering my prayers.
7. I confess my sins before you today and I ask you to forgive me on the basis of your mercy, in the name of Jesus Christ.

8. Wash me clean today O Lord by the blood of Jesus Christ.
9. I cover myself and my household with the blood of Jesus Christ.
10. My prayers today will not go in vain; my prayers will produce the desired results in the name of Jesus Christ.
11. O God my Father, arise and stop any power that wants to stop me, in the name of Jesus Christ.
12. O God my Father, arise and stop anybody that wants to stop my progress, in the name of Jesus Christ.
13. O God my Father, arise and stop household wickedness that wants to stop me, in the name of Jesus Christ.
14. O God my Father, arise and stop the evil power of my father's house that wants to stop me, in the name of Jesus Christ.
15. O God my Father, arise and stop the evil power of mother's house that wants to stop me, in the name of Jesus Christ.
16. O God my Father, arise and stop every conspiracy of the enemy planned to stop me, in the name of Jesus Christ.
17. O God my Father, arise and stop every agent of darkness assigned to stop me, in the name of Jesus Christ.
18. O God my Father, arise and stop every agent of darkness assigned to stop my progress, in the name of Jesus Christ.
19. O God my Father, arise and stop every agent of darkness assigned to stop my advancement, in the name of Jesus Christ.
20. O God my Father, arise and stop every agent of darkness assigned to stop the move of God in my life, in the name of Jesus Christ.

21. O God my Father, arise and stop every agent of darkness assigned to stop my financial freedom, in the name of Jesus Christ.
22. O God my Father, arise and stop every agent of darkness assigned to stop my prosperity, in the name of Jesus Christ.
23. Anybody anywhere assigned to stop me from moving forward, Father, stop them by your fire, in the name of Jesus Christ.
24. Anybody anywhere assigned to stop me from achieving my goals, Father, stop them today by your fire in the name of Jesus Christ.
25. Anybody anywhere assigned to stop me from entering my promise land, Father, stop them today by your fire in the name of Jesus Christ.
26. Anybody anywhere assigned to stop me from fulfilling my dreams, Father, stop them today by your fire in the name of Jesus Christ.
27. Anybody anywhere assigned to stop me from being what I was born to be, Father, stop them today by your fire in the name of Jesus Christ.
28. Anybody anywhere assigned to stop my prayers, Father, stop them today by your fire in the name of Jesus Christ.
29. Anybody anywhere assigned to stop my promotion, Father, stop them today by your fire in the name of Jesus Christ.
30. Anybody anywhere assigned to stop me from getting to the top, Father, stop them today by your fire in the name of Jesus Christ.
31. Jesus is on my side, I cannot be stopped.
32. Jesus is on my side, no matter the situation, I will not be moved.

33. I am moving forward by the power in the blood of Jesus Christ.
34. Any power anywhere that wants to stand in my way, let the fire of God destroy them, in the name of Jesus Christ.
35. Any stubborn mountain standing on my way to my promise land, be destroyed today by the fire of God in the name of Jesus Christ.
36. Satan, you cannot stop me, I have the mark of The Lord Jesus Christ on my body, in the name of Jesus Christ.
37. Household wickedness, you cannot stop me, I have the mark of The Lord Jesus Christ on my body, in the name of Jesus Christ.
38. Principalities and powers, you cannot stop me, I have the mark of The Lord Jesus Christ on my body, in the name of Jesus Christ.
39. Spiritual wickedness cannot stop me, I have the mark of the Jesus Christ on my body, in the name of Jesus Christ.
40. Territorial powers cannot stop me, I have the mark of The Lord Jesus Christ on my body, in the name of Jesus Christ.
41. Power of witchcraft cannot stop me, I have the mark of The Lord Jesus Christ on my body, in the name of Jesus Christ.
42. Unfriendly friends cannot stop me, I have the mark of The Lord Jesus Christ on my body, in the name of Jesus Christ.
43. Rulers of darkness cannot stop me, I have the mark of The Lord Jesus Christ on my body, in the name of Jesus Christ.
44. Because Jesus Christ is my Lord, I am unstoppable, in the name of Jesus Christ.

45. Because Jesus Christ is my Lord, I will not be moved.
46. Because Jesus Christ is my Lord, I will see the goodness of The Lord in the land of the living, in the name of Jesus Christ.
47. Because Jesus died on the cross and resurrected, no power can stop my joy, in the name of Jesus Christ.
48. Because Jesus died on the cross and resurrected, no power can delay my miracles, in the name of Jesus Christ.
49. Because Jesus died on the cross and resurrected, no power can hinder my prayers, in the name of Jesus Christ.
50. Because Jesus died on the cross and resurrected, no power can hinder my blessings, in the name of Jesus Christ.
51. Because Jesus died on the cross and resurrected, no power will be able to stand before me, in the name of Jesus Christ.
52. Because Jesus died on the cross and resurrected, no power can steal from me this year, in the name of Jesus Christ.
53. Because Jesus died on the cross and resurrected, no power can hinder my promotion, in the name of Jesus Christ.
54. Because Jesus died on the cross and resurrected, nobody can change God's plan for my life, in the name of Jesus Christ.
55. Because Jesus died on the cross and resurrected, this year I will make it to the finish line, in the name of Jesus Christ.
56. No matter how rough the journey, this year I will make it to the finish line, in the name of Jesus Christ.

57. No matter how tough the situation, this year I will make it to the finish line, in the name of Jesus Christ.
58. O God my Father, arise and stop anybody that wants to stop my helpers from helping me, in the name of Jesus Christ.
59. Any power anywhere that wants to delay my testimonies, O God my Father, arise and stop them by your fire in the name of Jesus Christ.
60. Any power anywhere that wants to stop the demonstration of God's power in my life, Father, arise and stop them by your fire in the name of Jesus Christ.
61. Any power anywhere that wants to stop the manifestation of the glory of God in my life, arise O Lord and stop them by your fire in the name of Jesus Christ.
62. Any power anywhere that wants to stop what God is doing in my life, arise O Lord and stop them by your fire, in the name of Jesus Christ.
63. Any power anywhere that wants to stop what God is doing in my home, arise O Lord and stop them by force in the name of Jesus Christ.
64. Any power anywhere that wants to stop what God is doing in my marriage, arise O Lord and stop them by force in the name of Jesus Christ.
65. Any power anywhere that wants to stop what God is doing in the life of my spouse, arise O Lord and stop them by your fire in the name of Jesus Christ.
66. Any power anywhere that wants to stop what God is doing in the life of my children, arise O Lord and stop them by your fire in the name of Jesus Christ.

67. Any power anywhere that wants to stop what God is doing in my ministry, arise O Lord and stop them by your fire, in the name of Jesus Christ.
68. Any power anywhere hired to stop my advancement, be destroyed by fire.
69. Any power anywhere hired to stop my miracles, be destroyed by fire.
70. Any power anywhere hired to stop my progress, be destroyed by fire.
71. Any power anywhere hired to stop me from moving forward, be destroyed by fire.
72. Any power anywhere hired to attack my finances, be disgraced in the name of Jesus Christ.
73. Any power anywhere hired to attack my family, be disgraced in the name of Jesus Christ.
74. Any power anywhere hired to attack the source of my joy, be disgraced in the name of Jesus Christ.
75. Any power anywhere hired to neutralize my testimony, be disappointed in the name of Jesus Christ.
76. The Lord Jesus Christ is my Rock, I will not be put to shame in the name of Jesus Christ.
77. The Lord Jesus Christ is my refuge, I will not be afraid in the name of Jesus Christ.
78. Because The Lord Jesus is with me, no one can be against me in the name of Jesus Christ.
79. I cover myself in the blood of Jesus Christ and I put on the whole armor of God, in every area of life I am unstoppable.
80. Today O Lord, let every power assigned or hired to stop me be put to an open shame, in the name of Jesus Christ.
81. If Herod couldn't stop Jesus Christ when He was born, I cannot be stopped in the name of Jesus Christ.

82. If Herod couldn't stop Jesus Christ when He was born, my progress cannot be stopped in the name of Jesus Christ.
83. If Herod couldn't stop Jesus Christ when He was born, my advancement cannot be stopped in the name of Jesus Christ.
84. If Herod couldn't stop Jesus Christ when He was born, my miracles will not be hijacked, in the name of Jesus Christ.
85. If Herod couldn't stop Jesus Christ when He was born, my blessings will not be hijacked, in the name of Jesus Christ.
86. If Herod couldn't stop Jesus Christ when He was born, my testimonies will not be stolen away, in the name of Jesus Christ.
87. If the grave couldn't stop Jesus Christ from resurrecting, let my buried blessings be released now, in the name of Jesus Christ.
88. If the grave couldn't stop Jesus Christ from resurrecting, let my stolen blessings turn to me now, in the name of Jesus Christ.
89. If the grave couldn't stop Jesus Christ from resurrecting, my promotion will not be given to another, in the name of Jesus Christ.
90. If the grave couldn't stop Jesus Christ from resurrecting, my financial freedom will not be hijacked in the name of Jesus Christ.

PRAYER FOR DIVINE REPOSITIONING

Passages To Read Before You Pray:
Proverbs 3:26, 1 John 5:14-15, 2 Timothy 1:7, Psalms 71:5, 126,
Philippians 4:13, James 1:5-8, Job 42:10-12

I have come today to fellowship with my heavenly Father, and make my requests and needs known unto Him. I cannot be hindered nor delayed because I know who I am in the Lord. I am a child of the Kingdom, born of the Spirit, redeemed by the blood of Jesus Christ. I walk in authority, living life without any apology because the power and authority has been given to me according to the Word of God in the book of Luke 9:1.

As I have come to pray today and to fellowship with my heavenly Father, I cover myself in the blood of Jesus Christ, and I put on the whole armor of God. I hereby come against every Prince of Persia that wants to hinder my prayer, I arrest you by the power in the blood of Jesus Christ, and I bind you and cast you down into the pit of hell.

I come against principalities and powers that wrestle with me and my prayers, I arrest you today by the power in the name of Jesus Christ, and I bind you and cast down into the pit of hell. I come against the rulers of the darkness of this world, against spiritual wickedness in high places, I arrest you all by the power in the name of Jesus Christ, and I bind you and cast you down into the pit of hell. I come against weakness and weariness, I arrest you today by the power in the name of Jesus Christ, and I bind you and cast you out of my life. I come against wondering

spirit and distractions, I arrest you today by the power in the name of Jesus Christ, and I bind you and cast you out of my life.

Today I receive the anointing to pray and get results, my prayers cannot be hindered nor delayed because Jesus is my Lord, I will pray today and get the desired results, I decree open heavens upon my prayers. I baptize myself in the fire of the Holy Ghost; therefore I have become too hot for the enemy to handle. My prayers today will attract divine intervention to every situation in my life; signs and wonders will follow my prayers today, testimonies will follow my prayers today and the name of God alone will be glorified, in Jesus name. Amen!

PRAYER POINTS:

1. O God my Father, thank you for being my God, my Father and my friend.
2. O God my Father, thank you for the privilege to know you and the power of the resurrection of Jesus Christ.
3. O God my Father, thank you for always being there for me and with me.
4. O God my Father, thank you for the great and mighty things that you are doing in my life.
5. O God my Father, thank you for your provision and protection over me and my household.
6. O God my Father, thank you for always answering my prayers.
7. I confess my sins before you today and I ask you to forgive me on the basis of your mercy, in the name of Jesus Christ.

8. Wash me clean today O Lord by the blood of Jesus Christ.
9. I cover myself and my household with the blood of Jesus Christ.
10. My prayers today will not go in vain; my prayers will produce the desired results in the name of Jesus Christ.
11. O God my Father, let my confidence in you be restored, so that I will not miss my blessings in the name of Jesus Christ.
12. O God my Father, let my confidence in myself be restored, so that I will be able to achieve great things in life, in the name of Jesus Christ.
13. I believe I can do all things because my strength comes from the Lord, in the name of Jesus Christ.
14. Any situation in my life making me to doubt what God will do in me and through me, receive solution now in the name of Jesus Christ.
15. O God my Father, demonstrate your power and set me up for a dramatic comeback, in the name of Jesus Christ.
16. O God my Father, demonstrate your power and set my finances up for a dramatic comeback, in the name of Jesus Christ.
17. O God my Father, demonstrate your power and set my health up for a dramatic comeback, in the name of Jesus Christ.
18. O God my Father, demonstrate your power and set my marriage up for a dramatic comeback, in the name of Jesus Christ.
19. O God my Father, demonstrate your power and set my business up for a dramatic comeback, in the name of Jesus Christ.

20. O God my Father, demonstrate your power and set my relationship up for a dramatic comeback, in the name of Jesus Christ.
21. O God my Father, demonstrate your power and set my joy up for a dramatic comeback, in the. Name of Jesus Christ.
22. Today I regain my confidence in the Lord, in the name of Jesus Christ.
23. Today I regain confidence in the plan of God for my life, in the name of Jesus Christ.
24. Today I regain confidence in myself, in the name of Jesus Christ.
25. Today I regain confidence in the Word of God, in the name of Jesus Christ.
26. Today I regain confidence in the anointing of God upon my life, in the name of Jesus Christ.
27. Today I regain confidence in the power of God that is within me, in the name of Jesus Christ.
28. Today I regain confidence in what God is doing in my life, in the name of Jesus Christ.
29. By the authority in the name of Jesus Christ, I reposition myself for a dramatic comeback, in the name of Jesus Christ.
30. By the authority in the name of Jesus Christ, I reposition myself for the supernatural, in the name of Jesus Christ.
31. By the authority in the name of Jesus Christ, I reposition myself for complete victory over all battles of life, in the name of Jesus Christ.
32. By the authority in the name of Jesus Christ, I reposition myself for uncommon breakthrough, in the name of Jesus Christ.

33. By the authority in the name of Jesus Christ, I reposition myself for uncommon greatness, in the name of Jesus Christ.
34. By the authority in the name of Jesus Christ, I reposition myself for a total deliverance, in the name of Jesus Christ.
35. By the authority in the name of Jesus Christ, I reposition myself for double promotion, in the name of Jesus Christ.
36. By the authority in the name of Jesus Christ, I reposition myself for financial breakthrough, in the name of Jesus Christ.
37. O God my Father, position me today to the appointed location, in the name of Jesus Christ.
38. O God my Father, restore me to a better situation than before, in the name of Jesus Christ.
39. O God my Father, restore my finances to a better situation than before, in the name of Jesus Christ.
40. O God my Father, restore my marriage to a better situation than before, in the name of Jesus Christ.
41. O God my Father, restore my health to a better situation than before, in the name of Jesus Christ.
42. O God my Father, restore my relationship with my loved ones to a better situation than before, in the name of Jesus Christ.
43. O God my Father, restore my relationship with you to a better situation than before, in the name of Jesus Christ.
44. O God my Father, restore my business to a better situation than before, in the name of Jesus Christ.
45. I am so confident and I know that God is taking me to a greater height before the end of this month, in the name of Jesus Christ.

46. I am so confident and I know that I will have my breakthroughs before the end of this month, in the name of Jesus Christ.
47. I am so confident and I know that I will have my testimonies before the end of this month, in the name of Jesus Christ.
48. I am so confident and I know that God will do great and mighty things in my life before the end of this month, in the name of Jesus Christ.
49. I am so confident and I know that my promotion will come before the end of this month, in the name of Jesus Christ.
50. I am so confident and I know that I will sing a new song before the end of this month, in the name of Jesus Christ.
51. I am so confident and I know that I will dance a new dance before the end of this month, in the names of Jesus Christ.
52. I am so confident and I know that I will laugh a new laugh before the end of this month, in the name of Jesus Christ.
53. I am so confident and I know that I will tell a new and better story before the end of this month, in the name of Jesus Christ.
54. I am so confident and I know that prayer will work for me, in the name of Jesus Christ.
55. I am so confident and I know that the Word of God will work for me, in the name of Jesus Christ.
56. I am so confident and I know that the anointing will break and destroy my yokes, in the name of Jesus Christ.
57. I am so confident and I know that the power of God can and will deliver me from every bondage, in the name of Jesus Christ.

58. I am so confident and I know that the Lord will fight my battles, in the name of Jesus Christ.
59. I am so confident and I know that the wall of Jericho in my life will fall today, in the name of Jesus Christ.
60. I am so confident and I know that my Goliath will die today, he will not live another day in the name of Jesus Christ.
61. I am so confident and I know that solution is coming my way, in the name of Jesus Christ.
62. I am coming out of my problems in a better condition than before, in the name of Jesus Christ.
63. I am coming out of my financial problems in a better condition than before, in the name of Jesus Christ.
64. In every situation and problem of my life, the time of my recovery begins now in the name of Jesus Christ.

PRAYER TO ENTER THE SOLUTION ROOM

Passages To Read Before You Pray:
Jeremiah 32:27, Luke 1:37, Matthew 11:28-30, Isaiah 10:27,
Isaiah 41:10-13, Psalms 44, 18, 9, 105, 107, 103, 55

I have come today to fellowship with my heavenly Father, and make my requests and needs known unto Him. I cannot be hindered nor delayed because I know who I am in the Lord. I am a child of the Kingdom, born of the Spirit, redeemed by the blood of Jesus Christ. I walk in authority, living life without any apology because the power and authority has been given to me according to the Word of God in the book of Luke 9:1.

As I have come to pray today and to fellowship with my heavenly Father, I cover myself in the blood of Jesus Christ, and I put on the whole armor of God. I hereby come against every Prince of Persia that wants to hinder my prayer, I arrest you by the power in the blood of Jesus Christ, and I bind you and cast you down into the pit of hell.

I come against principalities and powers that wrestle with me and my prayers, I arrest you today by the power in the name of Jesus Christ, and I bind you and cast down into the pit of hell. I come against the rulers of the darkness of this world, against spiritual wickedness in high places, I arrest you all by the power in the name of Jesus Christ, and I bind you and cast you down into the pit of hell. I come against weakness and weariness, I arrest you today by the power in the name of Jesus Christ, and I

bind you and cast you out of my life. I come against wondering spirit and distractions, I arrest you today by the power in the name of Jesus Christ, and I bind you and cast you out of my life.

Today I receive the anointing to pray and get results, my prayers cannot be hindered nor delayed because Jesus is my Lord, I will pray today and get the desired results, I decree open heavens upon my prayers. I baptize myself in the fire of the Holy Ghost; therefore I have become too hot for the enemy to handle. My prayers today will attract divine intervention to every situation in my life; signs and wonders will follow my prayers today, testimonies will follow my prayers today and the name of God alone will be glorified, in Jesus name. Amen!

PRAYER POINTS:

1. O God my Father, thank you for being my God, my Father and my friend.
2. O God my Father, thank you for the privilege to know you and the power of the resurrection of Jesus Christ.
3. O God my Father, thank you for always being there for me and with me.
4. O God my Father, thank you for the great and mighty things that you are doing in my life.
5. O God my Father, thank you for your provision and protection over me and my household.
6. O God my Father, thank you for always answering my prayers.
7. I confess my sins before you today and I ask you to forgive me on the basis of your mercy, in the name of Jesus Christ.

8. Wash me clean today O Lord by the blood of Jesus Christ.
9. I cover myself and my household with the blood of Jesus Christ.
10. My prayers today will not go in vain; my prayers will produce the desired results in the name of Jesus Christ.
11. Every stubborn situation in my life, I take you to the solution room today where my God reigns supreme, and I will never see you again.
12. Every unpleasant situation in my life, I take you to the solution room today, and I will never see you again.
13. Spirit of fear that wants to enslave me, I take you to the solution room today, and I will never see you again.
14. Spirit of fear that is attacking my faith, I take you to the solution room today, and I will never see you again.
15. Spirit of fear that is robbing me of my blessings, I take you to the solution room today, and I will never see you again.
16. Spirit of fear terrorizing me day and night, I take you to the solution room today, and I will never see you again.
17. Spirit of fear that wants to take away my confidence in the Lord, I take you to the solution room today, and I will never see you again.
18. Spirit of fear that is attacking my mind, enough is enough, I take you to the solution room today, and I will never see you again.
19. Spirit of fear trying to make me a stranger in my own home, enough is enough, I take you to the solution room today, and I will never see you again.

20. Spirit of fear that is trying to make my place of work a living hell for me, I take you to the solution room today, and I will never see you again.
21. Spirit of fear that is making me to feel insecure, enough is enough, I take you to the solution room today, and I will never see you again.
22. Heavy load of problems upon my head, I carry you to the solution room today, and I will never see you again.
23. Impossibilities in every area of my life, I take you to the solution room today, and I will never see you again.
24. Impossibilities manifesting in my home, I take you to the solution room today, and I will never see you again.
25. Impossibilities manifesting in my business, I take you to the solution room today, and I will never see you again.
26. Impossibilities on my way to the top, I take you to the solution room today, and I will never see you again.
27. Impossibilities affecting my finances, I take you to the solution room today, and I will never see you again.
28. Any power anywhere trying to make my success impossible, I take you to the solution room today, and I will never see you again.
29. Any power anywhere trying to make my breakthroughs impossible, I take you to the solution room today, and I will never see you again.
30. Any power anywhere trying to my happiness impossible, I take you to the solution room today, and I will never see you again.
31. Self-inflicted problems trying to make my promotion impossible, I take you to the solution room today, and I will never see you again.

32. Self-inflicted problems trying to make my progress impossible, I take you to the solution room today, and I will never see you again.
33. Self-inflicted problems trying to make my deliverance impossible, I take you to the solution room today, and I will never see you again.
34. Self-inflicted problems trying to make my breakthroughs impossible, I take you to the solution room today, and I will never see you again.
35. Self-inflicted problems trying to make my prosperity impossible, I take you to the solution room today, and I will never see you again.
36. Every chain of impossibility around my situation, I command you to break now.
37. Every chain of impossibility around my problem, I command you to break now.
38. Every physical and spiritual challenge in my life, I take you to the solution room today, and I will never see you again.
39. Evil weight upon my life that will not allow me to move forward, I carry to the solution room today, and I will never see you again.
40. Anything in my life causing problems whenever I want to do good, I take you to the solution room today, and I will never see you again.
41. Anything in my life causing problems whenever I want to move forward, I take you to the solution room today, and I will never see you again.
42. Anything in my life causing me to lose my temper in front of my helpers, I take you to the solution room today, and I will never see you again.

43. Anything in my life causing me to lose control when I'm supposed to make progress, I take you to the solution room today, and I will never see you again.
44. Anything in my life causing me to lose jobs over and over again, I take you to the solution room today, and I will never see you again.
45. Anything in my life causing me to make the wrong decisions over and over again, I take you to the solution room today, and I will never see you again.
46. Anything in my life attracting evil to me, I take you to the solution room today, and I will never see you again.
47. Anything in my life scattering what I am gathering, I take you to the solution today, and I will never see you again.
48. Anything in my life causing me to be financially irresponsible, I take you to the solution room today, and I will never see you again.
49. Anything in my life causing me to drive my helpers away, I take you to the solution room today, and I will never see you again.
50. Anything in my life causing me to be unfaithful to God and man, I take you to the solution room today, and I will never see you again.
51. Anything in my life causing me to be unfruitful in every area, I take you to the solution room today, and I will never see you again.
52. Anything in my life limiting my progress, I take you to the solution room today, and I will never see you again.
53. Anything in my life limiting my spiritual growth, I take you to the solution room today, and I will never see you again.

54. Anything in my life limiting the level of my harvest, I take you to the solution room today, and I will never see you again.
55. Anything in my life causing me to be physically barren, I take you to the solution room today, and I will never see you again.
56. Anything in my life causing me to be spiritually barren, I take you to the solution room today, and I will never see you again.
57. Anything in my life causing to be financially barren, I take you to the solution room today, and I will never see you again.
58. Anything in my life attracting any form of barrenness, I take you to the solution room today, and I will never see you again.
59. Anything in my life opening the door for the devourer to destroy my finances, I take you to the solution room today, and I will never see you again.
60. Anything in my life attracting any form of sickness into my body, I take you to the solution room today, and I will never see you again.
61. You spirit of disobedience that wants to control my children, I take you to the solution room today, and I will never see you again.
62. You spirit of the street that wants to control my children, I take you to the solution room today, and I will never see you again.
63. You spirit of home destruction assigned against my marriage, I take you to the solution room today, and I will never see you again.

64. You spirit of home destruction causing problems in my home, I take you to the solution room today, and I will never see you again.
65. You spirit of home destruction escalating unnecessary arguments in my marriage, I take you to the solution room today, and I will never see you again.
66. You spirit of home destruction causing misunderstanding in marriage, I take you to the solution room today, and I will never see you again.
67. You spirit of home destruction creating lack of trust in marriage, I take you to the solution room today, and I will never see you again.
68. You spirit of home destruction causing my spouse to do the unthinkable, I take you to the solution room today, and I will never see you again.
69. You spirit of home destruction causing me to make bad decisions in my relationship, I take you to the solution room today, and I will never see you again.
70. You spirit of home destruction causing separation in my relationship, I take you to the solution room today, and I will never see you again.
71. Every curse of failure affecting my life, I take you to the solution room today, and I will never see you again.
72. Every curse of failure affecting my academics, I take you to the solution room today, and I will never see you again.
73. Every curse of failure affecting my business, I take you to the solution room today, and I will never see you again.
74. Every curse of failure affecting my job, I take you to the solution room today, and I will never see you again.

75. Every curse of failure affecting my family, I take you to the solution room today, and I will never see you again.
76. Every problem of almost there making my life go around in circles, I take you to the solution room today, and I will never see you again.
77. Every problem of almost there that allows me to smell promotion but never get it, I take you to the solution room today, and I will never see you again.
78. Every problem of almost there that allows me see my breakthroughs but never get it, I take you to the solution room today, and I will never see you again.
79. Every problem of almost there that allows me to dream of success that never comes to fulfillment, I take you to the solution room today, and I will never see you again.
80. Every problem of almost there that allows me to compete but never make it to the end of the race, I take you to the solution room today, and I will never see you again.
81. Every problem of almost there that allows me to do business but never make profit, I take you to the solution room today, and I will never see you again.
82. Every problem of almost there that allows me to get married but never have children, I take you to the solution room today, and I will never see you again.
83. Every problem of almost there that allows me to sow but never reap, I take you to the solution room today, and I will never see you again.
84. Any problem in my life causing me to lose interest in praying, I take you to the solution room today, and I will never see you again.

85. Any problem in my life causing me to lose interest in holiness, I take you to the solution room today, and I will never see you again.
86. Any problem in my life causing me to lose faith in God, I take you to the solution room today, and I will never see you again.
87. Any problem in my life causing me to lose interest in success, I take you to the solution room today, and I will never see you again.
88. Any problem in my life causing me to lose interest in God's promises, I take you to the solution room today, and I will never see you again.
89. Any problem in my life causing to lose interest in what will benefit me, I take you to the solution room today, and I will never see you again.
90. Any problem in my life causing me to lose interest in what will benefit my family, I take you to the solution room today, and I will never see you again.
91. Any problem in my life causing me to lose interest in how my future turns out, I take you to the solution room today, and I will never see you again.
92. Anything in my life causing delay to my prayers, I take you to the solution room today, and I will never see you again.
93. Any problem in my life causing me to lose hope, I take you to the solution room today, and I will never see you again.
94. Every satanic chain used to tie me down, I take you to the solution room today, and I will never see you again.
95. Any power anywhere forcing me to act against the will of God, I take you to the solution room today, and I will never see you again.

96. Any power anywhere destroying my blessings before I receive them, I take you to the solution room today, and I will never see you again.
97. Any power anywhere assigned to make me a loser, I take you to the solution room today, and I will never see you again.
98. You spirit of confusion causing me to make bad decisions, I take you to the solution room today, and I will never see you again.
99. Every mouth speaking evil against me, I take you to the solution room today, and I will never see you again.
100. Every mouth speaking failure into my business, I take you to the solution room today, and I will never see you again.
101. Every mouth speaking failure into my academics, I take you to the solution room today, and I will never see you again.
102. Every mouth speaking evil against my family, I take you to the solution room today, and I will never see you again.
103. Every mouth speaking evil against my spouse, I take you to the solution room today, and I will never see you again.
104. Every mouth speaking evil against my children, I take you to the solution room today, and I will never see you again.
105. Every mouth speaking evil against my marriage, I take you to the solution room today, and I will never see you again.
106. Every evil network working against me, I take you to the solution room today, and I will never see you again.

107. Anything anywhere causing my life to be stagnant, I take you to the solution room today, and I will never see you again.
108. Anything anywhere causing my life to go backward, I take you to the solution room today, and I will never see you again.
109. Any power anywhere turning my life to a battleground, I take you to the solution room today, and I will never see you again.
110. Every shameful situation in my life, I take you to the solution room today, and I will never see you again.
111. Every work of the enemy manifesting in my life, I take you to the solution room today, and I will never see you again.
112. Every sign of poverty manifesting in my life, I take you to the solution room today, and I will never see you again.
113. Anything anywhere assigned to destroy my dreams, I take you to the solution room today, and I will never see you again.

PRAYER TO OVERCOME FEAR

Passages To Read Before You Pray:
2 Timothy 1:7, Psalms 27, 118, 56, 23, 46

I have come today to fellowship with my heavenly Father, and make my requests and needs known unto Him. I cannot be hindered nor delayed because I know who I am in the Lord. I am a child of the Kingdom, born of the Spirit, redeemed by the blood of Jesus Christ. I walk in authority, living life without any apology because the power and authority has been given to me according to the Word of God in the book of Luke 9:1.

As I have come to pray today and to fellowship with my heavenly Father, I cover myself in the blood of Jesus Christ, and I put on the whole armor of God. I hereby come against every Prince of Persia that wants to hinder my prayer, I arrest you by the power in the blood of Jesus Christ, and I bind you and cast you down into the pit of hell.

I come against principalities and powers that wrestle with me and my prayers, I arrest you today by the power in the name of Jesus Christ, and I bind you and cast down into the pit of hell. I come against the rulers of the darkness of this world, against spiritual wickedness in high places, I arrest you all by the power in the name of Jesus Christ, and I bind you and cast you down into the pit of hell. I come against weakness and weariness, I arrest you today by the power in the name of Jesus Christ, and I bind you and cast you out of my life. I come against wondering spirit and distractions, I arrest you today by the power in the name of Jesus Christ, and I bind you and cast you out of my life.

Today I receive the anointing to pray and get results, my prayers cannot be hindered nor delayed because Jesus is my Lord, I will pray today and get the desired results, I decree open heavens upon my prayers. I baptize myself in the fire of the Holy Ghost; therefore I have become too hot for the enemy to handle. My prayers today will attract divine intervention to every situation in my life; signs and wonders will follow my prayers today, testimonies will follow my prayers today and the name of God alone will be glorified, in Jesus name. Amen!

PRAYER POINTS:

1. O God my Father, thank you for being my God, my Father and my friend.
2. O God my Father, thank you for the privilege to know you and the power of the resurrection of Jesus Christ.
3. O God my Father, thank you for always being there for me and with me.
4. O God my Father, thank you for the great and mighty things that you are doing in my life.
5. O God my Father, thank you for your provision and protection over me and my household.
6. O God my Father, thank you for always answering my prayers.
7. I confess my sins before you today and I ask you to forgive me on the basis of your mercy, in the name of Jesus Christ.
8. Wash me clean today O Lord by the blood of Jesus Christ.
9. I cover myself and my household with the blood of Jesus Christ.

10. My prayers today will not go in vain; my prayers will produce the desired results in the name of Jesus Christ.

11. Spirit of fear, you cannot hinder my blessings this year, there is no room for you in my life, park your things and get out of my life now.

12. Spirit of fear, you cannot hinder my miracles this year, there is no room for you in my life, park your things and get out of my life now.

13. Spirit of fear, you cannot hinder my progress this year, there is no room for you in my life, park your things and get out of my life now.

14. Spirit of fear, you cannot hinder my prayers this year, there is no room for you in my life, park your things and get out of my life.

15. Spirit of fear, you cannot stop what God is doing in my life, park your things and get out of my life now.

16. Spirit of fear, you have tormented me long enough, there is no room for you in my life anymore, park your things and get out of my life now.

17. Spirit of fear, you can no longer keep me in bondage, I have seen the light, park your things and get out of my life now.

18. Spirit of fear, you can no longer inflict me with sickness, now I know the truth, park your things and get out of my life now.

19. Spirit of fear, I am no longer your slave, I am not afraid anymore, park your things and get out of my life now.

20. The Lord is my light and my salvation, I am not afraid no matter the situation around me.

21. Though I walk through the valley of the shadow of death, I will fear no evil because the Lord is with me.

22. I am not afraid, what man can do to me, because the Lord is with me, I am more than a conqueror.
23. God has not given me the spirit of fear, fear you are a stranger in my life, park your things and get out of my life now.
24. Spirit of fear, you cannot rob me of my financial freedom, park your things and get out of my life now.
25. Spirit of fear, you cannot rob me of my joy, park your things and get out of my life now.
26. Spirit of fear, you cannot stop me from moving forward, park your things and get out of my life now.
27. O God my Father, you promised to do great things, let it begin to manifest in my life.
28. O God my Father, you promised to do great things, let it begin to manifest in my home.
29. O God my Father, you promised to do great things, let it begin to manifest in my marriage.
30. O God my Father, you promised to do great things, let it begin to manifest in the life of my spouse.
31. O God my Father, you promised to do great things, let it begin to manifest in the life of my children.
32. O God my Father, you promised to do great things, let it begin to manifest in my business.
33. O God my Father, you promise to do great things, let it manifest in my finances.
34. O God my Father, you promised to do great things, let it begin to manifest in every area of my interest.
35. O God my Father, you promised to do great things, let it begin to manifest in my ministry.
36. O God my Father, you promised to do great things, let it begin to manifest in everything that I do.

PRAYER FOR RAIN OF BLESSING

Passages To Read Before You Pray:
Joel 2:21-26, Psalms 27, 23, 19, 42, 29, 86, 78.

I have come today to fellowship with my heavenly Father, and make my requests and needs known unto Him. I cannot be hindered nor delayed because I know who I am in the Lord. I am a child of the Kingdom, born of the Spirit, redeemed by the blood of Jesus Christ. I walk in authority, living life without any apology because the power and authority has been given to me according to the Word of God in the book of Luke 9:1.

As I have come to pray today and to fellowship with my heavenly Father, I cover myself in the blood of Jesus Christ, and I put on the whole armor of God. I hereby come against every Prince of Persia that wants to hinder my prayer, I arrest you by the power in the blood of Jesus Christ, and I bind you and cast you down into the pit of hell.

I come against principalities and powers that wrestle with me and my prayers, I arrest you today by the power in the name of Jesus Christ, and I bind you and cast down into the pit of hell. I come against the rulers of the darkness of this world, against spiritual wickedness in high places, I arrest you all by the power in the name of Jesus Christ, and I bind you and cast you down into the pit of hell. I come against weakness and weariness, I arrest you today by the power in the name of Jesus Christ, and I bind you and cast you out of my life. I come against wondering spirit and distractions, I arrest you today by the power in the name of Jesus Christ, and I bind you and cast you out of my life.

Today I receive the anointing to pray and get results, my prayers cannot be hindered nor delayed because Jesus is my Lord, I will pray today and get the desired results, I decree open heavens upon my prayers. I baptize myself in the fire of the Holy Ghost; therefore I have become too hot for the enemy to handle. My prayers today will attract divine intervention to every situation in my life; signs and wonders will follow my prayers today, testimonies will follow my prayers today and the name of God alone will be glorified, in Jesus name. Amen!

PRAYER POINTS:

1. O God my Father, thank you for being my God, my Father and my friend.
2. O God my Father, thank you for the privilege to know you and the power of the resurrection of Jesus Christ.
3. O God my Father, thank you for always being there for me and with me.
4. O God my Father, thank you for the great and mighty things that you are doing in my life.
5. O God my Father, thank you for your provision and protection over me and my household.
6. O God my Father, thank you for always answering my prayers.
7. I confess my sins before you today and I ask you to forgive me on the basis of your mercy, in the name of Jesus Christ.
8. Wash me clean today O Lord by the blood of Jesus Christ.
9. I cover myself and my household with the blood of Jesus Christ.

10. My prayers today will not go in vain; my prayers will produce the desired results in the name of Jesus Christ.
11. Let there be open heavens O Lord, and let it rain upon my life, the former rain and the latter rain.
12. Let there be open heavens O Lord, and let it rain upon my family, the former rain and the latter rain.
13. Let there be open heavens O Lord, and let it rain upon my field, the former rain and the latter rain.
14. Let there be open heavens O Lord, and let it rain upon my seeds, the former rain and the latter rain.
15. Let there be open heavens O Lord, and let it rain upon every desert area of my life, the former rain and the latter rain.
16. Let there be open heavens O Lord, and let it rain upon all my efforts, the former rain and the latter rain.
17. Let there be open heavens O Lord, and let it rain upon my business, the former rain and the latter rain.
18. Let there be open heavens O Lord, and let it rain upon my finances, the former rain and he latter rain.
19. O God my Father, let it rain upon my field that I may have a great harvest year.
20. O God my Father, let it rain upon my seeds that my seeds may bring forth good harvest this year.
21. O God my Father, let it rain upon every desert area of my life that my desert may turn to a fertile land.
22. Let there be open heavens and let the rain of abundance be released upon me today.
23. Let there be open heavens and let the rain of abundance be released upon my home today.
24. Let there be open heavens and let the rain of abundance be released upon my family today.

25. Let there be open heavens and let the rain of prosperity be released upon me today.
26. Let there be open heavens and let the rain of prosperity be released upon the works of my hands today.
27. Let there be open heavens and let the rain of prosperity be released upon my household today.
28. Let there be open heavens and let the rain of prosperity be released into my finances today.
29. Let there be open heavens and let the rain of prosperity be released into my business today.
30. Let there be open heavens and let the rain of prosperity be released into the source of my income today.
31. Let there be open heavens and let the rain of prosperity be released upon my helpers today.
32. Let there be open heavens and let the rain of increase be released upon me today.
33. Let there be open heavens and let the rain of increase be released upon my family today.
34. Let there be open heavens and let the rain of increase be released upon my home today.
35. Let there be open heavens and let the rain of increase be released upon my finances today.
36. I have had enough financial drought in life, Father Lord, let it rain.
37. I have had enough marital drought in life, Father Lord, let it rain.
38. Today O Lord, let the peace of God that surpasses all understanding rain upon my life.
39. Today O Lord, let joy everlasting that no one can take away rain upon my life.
40. Today O Lord, let victory over every situation of life rain upon me now.

41. Today I decree, this is my season to give birth to good things.
42. Today I decree, this is my season to bring forth harvest.
43. Today I decree, this is the season that my life will be fruitful in every area.
44. Today I decree, this is the season that my land will yield its strength.
45. This year I will live in abundance.
46. This year I will eat in plenty.
47. This year I will lend to nations and not borrow.
48. This year I will lead and not follow.
49. This year I will be the head and not the tail.
50. This year I will be above only and not be beneath.
51. This year I am blessed beyond any curse.
52. This year The Lord will satisfy me with good things.
53. From the beginning to the end of this year. I will have reasons to celebrate.
54. From the beginning to the end of this year, I will have reasons to bless the name of The Lord.
55. From the beginning to the end of this year, I will have reasons to testify to the goodness of The Lord.
56. From the beginning to the end of this year, I will receive favor from God and man.
57. From the beginning to the end of this year, favor of God will speak on my behalf in the presence of those that will come across my path.
58. From the beginning to the end of this year, favor of God will speak on my behalf in the presence of those that will help me.
59. From the beginning to the end of this year, favor of God will speak on my behalf in the presence of those that will decide on my fate.

60. From the beginning to the end of this year, favor of God will speak on my behalf in the presence of those that will contribute to my success.
61. From the beginning to the end of this year, favor of God will speak on my behalf in the presence of those that will lead me to my promise land.
62. From the beginning to the end of this year, surely goodness and mercy shall follow me.
63. From the beginning to the end of this year, the grace of God will be sufficient for me.
64. From the beginning to the end of this year, I will always have cause to bless the Lord.

I AM DELIVERED

Passages To Read Before You Pray:
Isaiah 49:24-25, Jeremiah 1:8-19, Psalms 35, 9, 18, 59, 69, 70

I have come today to fellowship with my heavenly Father, and make my requests and needs known unto Him. I cannot be hindered nor delayed because I know who I am in the Lord. I am a child of the Kingdom, born of the Spirit, redeemed by the blood of Jesus Christ. I walk in authority, living life without any apology because the power and authority has been given to me according to the Word of God in the book of Luke 9:1.

As I have come to pray today and to fellowship with my heavenly Father, I cover myself in the blood of Jesus Christ, and I put on the whole armor of God. I hereby come against every Prince of Persia that wants to hinder my prayer, I arrest you by the power in the blood of Jesus Christ, and I bind you and cast you down into the pit of hell.

I come against principalities and powers that wrestle with me and my prayers, I arrest you today by the power in the name of Jesus Christ, and I bind you and cast down into the pit of hell. I come against the rulers of the darkness of this world, against spiritual wickedness in high places, I arrest you all by the power in the name of Jesus Christ, and I bind you and cast you down into the pit of hell. I come against weakness and weariness, I arrest you today by the power in the name of Jesus Christ, and I bind you and cast you out of my life. I come against wondering spirit and distractions, I arrest you today by the power in the name of Jesus Christ, and I bind you and cast you out of my life.

Today I receive the anointing to pray and get results, my prayers cannot be hindered nor delayed because Jesus is my Lord, I will pray today and get the desired results, I decree open heavens upon my prayers. I baptize myself in the fire of the Holy Ghost; therefore I have become too hot for the enemy to handle. My prayers today will attract divine intervention to every situation in my life; signs and wonders will follow my prayers today, testimonies will follow my prayers today and the name of God alone will be glorified, in Jesus name. Amen!

PRAYER POINTS:

1. O God my Father, thank you for being my God, my Father and my friend.
2. O God my Father, thank you for the privilege to know you and the power of the resurrection of Jesus Christ.
3. O God my Father, thank you for always being there for me and with me.
4. O God my Father, thank you for the great and mighty things that you are doing in my life.
5. O God my Father, thank you for your provision and protection over me and my household.
6. O God my Father, thank you for always answering my prayers.
7. I confess my sins before you today and I ask you to forgive me on the basis of your mercy, in the name of Jesus Christ.
8. Wash me clean today O Lord by the blood of Jesus Christ.
9. I cover myself and my household with the blood of Jesus Christ.

10. My prayers today will not go in vain; my prayers will produce the desired results in the name of Jesus Christ.

11. Holy Spirit of God, have you way in my life today, in the name of Jesus Christ.
12. O God my Father, let the power of the Holy Spirit rest upon me today, and empower me to pray and get results, in the name of Jesus Christ.
13. By the power in the blood of Jesus Christ, I disconnect myself from any ancestral pipeline of failure, in the name of Jesus Christ.
14. By the power in the blood of Jesus Christ, I disconnect myself from any ancestral pipeline of poverty, in the name of Jesus Christ.
15. By the power in the blood of Jesus Christ, I disconnect myself from any ancestral pipeline of infirmity, in the name of Jesus Christ.
16. By the power in the blood of Jesus Christ, I disconnect myself from any problem flowing in my bloodline, in the name of Jesus Christ.
17. By the power in the blood of Jesus Christ, I disconnect myself from any curse flowing in my bloodline, in the name of Jesus Christ.
18. By the power in the blood of Jesus Christ, I disconnect myself from every inherited evil yoke, in the name of Jesus Christ.
19. By the power in the blood of Jesus Christ, I disconnect myself from every evil attachment to my family name, in the name of Jesus Christ.
20. By the power in the blood of Jesus Christ, I disconnect myself from every evil attachment to my personal name, in the name of Jesus Christ.

21. By the power in the blood of Jesus Christ, I disconnect myself from ancient evil pronouncements affecting my family line, in the name of Jesus Christ.
22. By the power in the blood of Jesus Christ, I disconnect myself from the idol of my father's house, in the name of Jesus Christ.
23. By the power in the name of Jesus Christ, I disconnect myself today from every unfriendly friend holding me back from moving forward, in the name of Jesus Christ.
24. By the power in the blood of Jesus Christ, I disconnect myself from every relationship designed to destroy my life, in the name of Jesus Christ.
25. By the power in the blood of Jesus Christ, I disconnect myself from every evil association, in the name of Jesus Christ.
26. I release myself from every conscious and unconscious bondage of poverty, in the name of Jesus Christ.
27. I release myself from every conscious and unconscious bondage of infirmity, in the name of Jesus Christ.
28. I release myself from any form of captivity, in the name of Jesus Christ.
29. I release myself today from any form of backwardness, I am ready to move in the name of Jesus Christ.
30. I release myself today from the bondage of household wickedness, in the name of Jesus Christ.
31. I release myself today from the bondage of household witchcraft in the name of Jesus Christ.
32. I release myself today from the hands of the Pharaoh of my father's house, in the name of Jesus Christ.
33. I release myself today from the hands of the Jezebel of my father's house, in the name of Jesus Christ.

34. I release myself today from the hands of the Jezebel of my mother's house, in the name of Jesus Christ.
35. I release myself today from the hands of the Jezebel of my in-laws house, in the name of Jesus Christ.
36. I release myself today from the hands of the Goliath that wants to kill my David, in the name of Jesus Christ.
37. I release myself today from the prison of the household wickedness, in the name of Jesus Christ.
38. I release myself today from the hands of principalities and powers wrestling with me, in the name of Jesus Christ.
39. I release myself today from the hands of principalities and powers wrestling with my destiny, in the name of Jesus Christ.
40. I release myself today from the hands of principalities and powers fighting against my future, in the name of Jesus Christ.
41. I release myself today from the hands of principalities and powers fighting against my finances, in the name of Jesus Christ.
42. I release myself today from the hands of spiritual wickedness fighting against me, in the name of Jesus Christ.
43. I release my family today from the hands of territorial powers fighting against my family, in the name of Jesus Christ.
44. I break myself loose from every inherited bondage, in the name of Jesus Christ.
45. I break myself loose from any form of captivity, in the name of Jesus Christ.
46. I break myself loose from the prison of the devil, in the name of Jesus Christ.

47. I break myself loose from the bondage of ancestral sickness, in the name of Jesus Christ.
48. I break myself loose from every chain and shackle used to tie me down, in the name of Jesus Christ.
49. I break myself loose from any form of satanic arrest, in the name of Jesus Christ.
50. I break myself loose from any form of oppression, in the name of Jesus Christ.
51. I break myself loose from the spirit of depression, in the name of Jesus Christ.
52. I break myself loose from any form of evil possession, in the name of Jesus Christ.
53. By the power in the blood of Jesus Christ, I am delivered today from the hands of evil taskmasters, in the name of Jesus Christ.
54. By the power in the blood of Jesus Christ, I am delivered today from the hands of the Jezebel of my father's house, in the name of Jesus Christ.
55. By the power in the blood of Jesus Christ, I am delivered today from the hands of the power that wants to destroy my life, in the name of Jesus Christ.
56. By the power in the blood of Jesus Christ, I am delivered today from the hands of the power that wants to kill my dreams, in the name of Jesus Christ.
57. By the power in the blood of Jesus Christ, I am delivered today from the hands of the power of witchcraft of my father's house, in the name of Jesus Christ.
58. By the power in the blood of Jesus Christ, I am delivered today from the hands of the power that wants to waste my life, in the name of Jesus Christ.

59. By the power in the blood of Jesus Christ, I am delivered today from any form of sickness and infirmity, in the name of Jesus Christ.
60. By the power in the blood of Jesus Christ, I am delivered today from the hands of the power that wants to keep me in bondage, in the name of Jesus Christ.
61. By the power in the blood of Jesus Christ, I am delivered today from stagnancy, in the name of Jesus Christ.
62. By the power in the blood of Jesus Christ, I am delivered today from any form of demotion, in the name of Jesus Christ.
63. By the power in the blood of Jesus Christ, I am delivered today from any form of financial embarrassment, in the name of Jesus Christ.
64. By the power in the blood of Jesus Christ, I am delivered today from shame, in the name of Jesus Christ.
65. By the power in the blood of Jesus Christ, I am delivered today from repeated disappointment, in the name of Jesus Christ.
66. By the power in the blood of Jesus Christ, I am delivered today from the spirit of non-achievement, in the name of Jesus Christ.
67. By the power in the blood of Jesus Christ, I am delivered today from any form of barrenness, In the name of Jesus Christ.
68. By the power in the blood of Jesus Christ, I am delivered today from loneliness, in the name of Jesus Christ.
69. By the power in the blood of Jesus Christ, I am delivered today from collective captivity, in the name of Jesus Christ.

70. By the power in the blood of Jesus Christ, I am delivered today from failure at the edge miracle, in the name of Jesus Christ.
71. By the power in the blood of Jesus Christ, I am delivered today from the spirit of almost there, in the name of Jesus Christ.
72. By the power in the blood of Jesus Christ, I am delivered today from any form of addiction, in the name of Jesus Christ.
73. By the power in the blood of Jesus Christ, I am delivered today from every satanic attack, in the name of Jesus Christ.
74. By the power in the blood of Jesus Christ, I am delivered today from marital failure, in the name of Jesus Christ.
75. By the power in the blood of Jesus Christ, I am delivered today from any form of business failure, in the name of Jesus Christ.

PRAYER TO KNOW THE PLAN OF GOD

Passages To Read Before You Pray:
Jeremiah 29:10-14; 33:14; Psalm 40; Psalm 42; Psalm 89; Isaiah 60; Isaiah 61

I have come today to fellowship with my heavenly Father, and make my requests and needs known unto Him. I cannot be hindered nor delayed because I know who I am in the Lord. I am a child of the Kingdom, born of the Spirit, redeemed by the blood of Jesus Christ. I walk in authority, living life without any apology because the power and authority has been given to me according to the Word of God in the book of Luke 9:1.

As I have come to pray today and to fellowship with my heavenly Father, I cover myself in the blood of Jesus Christ, and I put on the whole armor of God. I hereby come against every Prince of Persia that wants to hinder my prayer, I arrest you by the power in the blood of Jesus Christ, and I bind you and cast you down into the pit of hell.

I come against principalities and powers that wrestle with me and my prayers, I arrest you today by the power in the name of Jesus Christ, and I bind you and cast down into the pit of hell. I come against the rulers of the darkness of this world, against spiritual wickedness in high places, I arrest you all by the power in the name of Jesus Christ, and I bind you and cast you down into the pit of hell. I come against weakness and weariness, I arrest you today by the power in the name of Jesus Christ, and I bind you and cast you out of my life. I come against wondering

spirit and distractions, I arrest you today by the power in the name of Jesus Christ, and I bind you and cast you out of my life.

Today I receive the anointing to pray and get results, my prayers cannot be hindered nor delayed because Jesus is my Lord, I will pray today and get the desired results, I decree open heavens upon my prayers. I baptize myself in the fire of the Holy Ghost; therefore I have become too hot for the enemy to handle. My prayers today will attract divine intervention to every situation in my life; signs and wonders will follow my prayers today, testimonies will follow my prayers today and the name of God alone will be glorified, in Jesus name. Amen!

PRAYER POINTS:

1. O God my Father, thank you for being my God, my Father and my friend.
2. O God my Father, thank you for the privilege to know you and the power of the resurrection of Jesus Christ.
3. O God my Father, thank you for always being there for me and with me.
4. O God my Father, thank you for the great and mighty things that you are doing in my life.
5. O God my Father, thank you for your provision and protection over me and my household.
6. O God my Father, thank you for always answering my prayers.
7. I confess my sins before you today and I ask you to forgive me on the basis of your mercy, in the name of Jesus Christ.

8. Wash me clean today O Lord by the blood of Jesus Christ.
9. I cover myself and my household with the blood of Jesus Christ.
10. My prayers today will not go in vain; my prayers will produce the desired results in the name of Jesus Christ.

11. O God my Father, show me your plan for my life so that I may work in agreement with it and not against it, in the name of Jesus Christ.
12. O God my Father, let me know your plan for my spouse so that we may work in agreement with it and not against it, in the name of Jesus Christ.
13. O God my Father, let me know your plans for my children so that we may work in agreement with it and not against it, in the name of Jesus Christ.
14. O God my Father, let me know your plan concerning my future, so that I may work in agreement with it and not against it, in the name of Jesus Christ.
15. O God my Father, let me know your plan concerning my business or career, so that I will not waste my time and efforts, in the name of Jesus Christ.
16. O God my Father, let me know your plan concerning every decision I will make in life, so that I will not do anything against your will, in the name of Jesus Christ.
17. Today O Lord, I submit my will to you; let your will alone be done in every area of my life, in the name of Jesus Christ.
18. O God my Father, show me the next step I need to take in life so that I will not work against your plan for my life, in the name of Jesus Christ.

19. O God my Father, let your plan for my life prevail against the plan of the enemy, in the name of Jesus Christ.
20. I know your thoughts towards me are of peace and not of evil, let it come to physical manifestation in the name of Jesus Christ.
21. O God my Father, I know you plan to take me to a higher ground; sin will not hinder your plan for me, in the name of Jesus Christ.
22. O God my Father, I know you plan to bless me beyond expectation, works of the flesh will not hinder your plan for me, in the name of Jesus Christ.
23. O God my Father, I know you plan to take me to a higher level of grace; ignorance will not hinder your plan for me, in the name of Jesus Christ.
24. O God my Father, I know you plan to promote me according to your Word, pride will not hinder your plan for me, in the name of Jesus Christ.
25. O God my Father, show me what you want me to do in life in the name of Jesus Christ.
26. O God my Father, show me where you want me to be in life in the name of Jesus Christ.
27. O God my Father, grant me the grace to consult you before I make any plan in life, in the name of Jesus Christ.
28. I hereby cancel any plan of the wicked against my life, in the name of Jesus Christ. - Exodus 15:9
29. I cancel every plan of the household wickedness against my marriage, in the name of Jesus Christ.
30. I cancel every plan of the enemy against my children, in the name of Jesus Christ.

31. I cancel every plan of the enemy against my destiny, in the name of Jesus Christ.
32. I cancel every plan of the wicked against my future, in the name of Jesus Christ.
33. I cancel every plan of the wicked against my finances, in the name of Jesus Christ.
34. Every plan of the enemy to pollute my joy, be terminated in the name of Jesus Christ.
35. Every plan of the enemy to hinder my progress, be terminated in the name of Jesus Christ.
36. Every plan of the enemy to delay my miracles, be terminated in the name of Jesus Christ.
37. I will not work against the plan of God for my life no matter the distraction, in the name of Jesus Christ.
38. I will not work against the plan of God for my life no matter the efforts of the enemy, in the name of Jesus Christ.
39. O God my Father, let your plan for my life be crystal clear unto me that I will have no reason to doubt it, in the name of Jesus Christ.
40. O God my Father, let your plan for my life be crystal clear to me, that I may follow it as a road map, in the name of Jesus Christ.
41. O God my Father, let your will alone be done in every area of my life, in the name of Jesus Christ.
42. My plan will not hinder the plan of God for my life, in the name of Jesus Christ.
43. O God my Father, help me to see beyond the natural, so that I may follow your plan for my life, in the name of Jesus Christ.

44. O God my Father, help me to see beyond the ordinary, so that I may see where you are taking me, in the name of Jesus Christ.
45. O God my Father, help me to see beyond my present situation, so that I may see your glory in the name of Jesus Christ.
46. O God my Father, help me to see beyond the frustration that the enemy sent my way, in the name of Jesus Christ.
47. O God my Father, help me to see beyond the agenda of the wicked, so that I may see your grace and mercy, in the name of Jesus Christ.
48. No matter the activity of the enemy, I will not fall out of the plan of God, in the name of Jesus Christ.
49. O God my Father, let your willpower bring to manifestation all your plans for my life, in the name of Jesus Christ.
50. O God my Father, let your willpower bring to manifestation all your plans concerning my future in the name of Jesus Christ.
51. O God my Father, let your willpower bring to manifestation all your plans concerning my finances in the name of Jesus Christ.
52. O God my Father, let your willpower bring to manifestation all your plans concerning my business or career in the name of Jesus Christ.
53. Today I decree that testimonies, miracles, signs and wonders will follow my prayers, in the name of Jesus Christ.

PRAYER WHEN YOU DESIRE THE BEST

Passages To Read Before You Pray:
Psalms 37, 29, 19, 16, 42, 86, 56, Isaiah 60:1-22, Jeremiah 32:17-19, 27

I have come today to fellowship with my heavenly Father, and make my requests and needs known unto Him. I cannot be hindered nor delayed because I know who I am in the Lord. I am a child of the Kingdom, born of the Spirit, redeemed by the blood of Jesus Christ. I walk in authority, living life without any apology because the power and authority has been given to me according to the Word of God in the book of Luke 9:1.

As I have come to pray today and to fellowship with my heavenly Father, I cover myself in the blood of Jesus Christ, and I put on the whole armor of God. I hereby come against every Prince of Persia that wants to hinder my prayer, I arrest you by the power in the blood of Jesus Christ, and I bind you and cast you down into the pit of hell.

I come against principalities and powers that wrestle with me and my prayers, I arrest you today by the power in the name of Jesus Christ, and I bind you and cast down into the pit of hell. I come against the rulers of the darkness of this world, against spiritual wickedness in high places, I arrest you all by the power in the name of Jesus Christ, and I bind you and cast you down into the pit of hell. I come against weakness and weariness, I arrest you today by the power in the name of Jesus Christ, and I bind you and cast you out of my life. I come against wondering

spirit and distractions, I arrest you today by the power in the name of Jesus Christ, and I bind you and cast you out of my life.

Today I receive the anointing to pray and get results, my prayers cannot be hindered nor delayed because Jesus is my Lord, I will pray today and get the desired results, I decree open heavens upon my prayers. I baptize myself in the fire of the Holy Ghost; therefore I have become too hot for the enemy to handle. My prayers today will attract divine intervention to every situation in my life; signs and wonders will follow my prayers today, testimonies will follow my prayers today and the name of God alone will be glorified, in Jesus name. Amen!

PRAYER POINTS:

1. O God my Father, thank you for being my God, my Father and my friend.
2. O God my Father, thank you for the privilege to know you and the power of the resurrection of Jesus Christ.
3. O God my Father, thank you for always being there for me and with me.
4. O God my Father, thank you for the great and mighty things that you are doing in my life.
5. O God my Father, thank you for your provision and protection over me and my household.
6. O God my Father, thank you for always answering my prayers.
7. I confess my sins before you today and I ask you to forgive me on the basis of your mercy, in the name of Jesus Christ.

8. Wash me clean today O Lord by the blood of Jesus Christ.
9. I cover myself and my household with the blood of Jesus Christ.
10. My prayers today will not go in vain; my prayers will produce the desired results in the name of Jesus Christ.

11. O God my Father, I desire the best things in life, let my heart desire be granted today.
12. O God my Father, I desire breakthroughs in life, let my heart desire be granted unto me today.
13. O God my Father, I desire miracles in every area of my life, let my heart desire be granted unto me today.
14. O God my Father, I desire uncommon blessings in my life, let my heart desire be granted unto me today.
15. O God my Father, I desire uncommon blessings in my home, let my desire be granted unto me today.
16. O God my Father, I desire uncommon blessings in my finances, let my heart desire be granted unto me today.
17. O God my Father, I desire uncommon blessings in my business, let my heart desire be granted unto me today.
18. O God my Father, I desire uncommon blessings to come upon my marriage, let my heart desire be granted unto me today.
19. O God my Father, I desire uncommon blessings to come upon the works of my hands, let my heart desire be granted unto me today.
20. O God my Father, I desire uncommon blessings to come upon my family, let my heart desire be granted unto me today.
21. O God my Father, I desire to have good things, let my heart desire be granted unto me today.

22. O God my Father, I desire to have beautiful things, let my heart desire be granted unto me today.
23. O God my Father, I desire to have a beautiful house, let my heart desire be granted unto me today.
24. O God my Father, I desire to drive a beautiful car that is paid for, let my heart desire be granted unto me today.
25. O God my Father, I desire to live a debt free life, let my heart desire be granted unto me today.
26. O God my Father, I desire to live a comfortable life, let my heart desire be granted unto me today.
27. O God my Father, I desire to live a meaningful life, let my heart desire be granted unto me today.
28. O God my Father, I desire that your glory manifest in every area of my life, let my heart desire be granted unto me today.
29. O God my Father, I desire that your glory manifest in my home, let my heart desire be granted unto me today.
30. O God my Father, I desire that your glory manifest upon my marriage, let my heart desire be granted unto me today.
31. O God my Father, I desire that your glory manifest in the life of my spouse, let my heart desire be granted unto me today.
32. O God my Father, I desire that your glory manifest in life of my children, let my heart desire be granted unto me today.
33. O God my Father, I desire that your glory manifest in the life of my parents, let my heart desire be granted unto me today.
34. O God my Father, I desire that your glory manifest upon my finances, let my heart desire be granted today.

35. O God my Father, I desire that your glory manifest upon every work of my hands, let my heart desire be granted unto me today.
36. O God my Father, I desire that your glory manifest upon my business, let my heart desire be granted unto me today.
37. O God my Father, I desire that your glory manifest upon my ministry, let my heart desire be granted unto me today.
38. O God my Father, because you are a rich God, I desire to be rich, let my heart desire be granted unto me today.
39. O God my Father, I desire that the riches of the Gentiles be transferred to me, let my heart desire be granted unto me today.
40. O God my Father, I desire to be a wealthy man/woman in life, let my heart desire be granted unto me today.
41. O God my Father, I desire that the wealth of the Gentiles be transferred to me, let my heart desire be granted unto me today.
42. O God my Father, in my father's house I desire to be the head and not the tail, let my heart desire be granted unto me today.
43. O God my Father, in my mother's house I desire to be the head and not the tail. Let my heart desire be granted unto me today.
44. O God my Father, among my siblings I desire to be the head and not the tail, let my heart desire be granted unto me today.
45. O God my Father, among my friends I desire to be the head and not the tail, let my heart desire be granted unto me today.

46. O God my Father, in my neighborhood I desire to be the head and not the tail, let my heart desire be granted unto me today.
47. O God my Father, among my co-workers I desire to be the head and not the tail, let my heart desire be granted unto me today.
48. O God my Father, among my business partners I desire to be the head and not the tail, let my heart desire be granted unto me today.
49. O God my Father, in my in-laws house I desire to be the head and not the tail, let my heart desire be granted unto today.
50. O God my Father, among my contemporaries I desire to be the head and not the tail, let my heart desire be granted unto me today.
51. O God my Father, I desire to be the best in everything that I do, let my heart desire be granted unto me today.
52. O God my Father, I desire to be the best in my academics, let my heart desire be granted unto me today.
53. O God my Father, I desire to be the best among my friends, let my heart desire be granted unto me today.
54. O God my Father, I desire to be the best above my competitors, let my heart desire be granted unto me today.
55. O God my Father, I desire to be the best no matter the activity of the enemy, let my heart desire be granted unto me today.
56. O God my Father, I desire to be the best no matter the situation around me, let my heart desire be granted unto me today.

57. O God my Father, I desire that the power of the enemy will not be able to stop me, no matter how much they try.
58. O God my Father, I desire that the power of the enemy will not be able to stop me from moving forward, let my heart desire be granted unto me today.
59. O God my Father, I desire that the power of the enemy will not be able to stop what God is doing in my life.
60. O God my Father, I desire to have divine connections with the people you have prepared to help me, let the desires of my heart be granted unto me today.
61. O God my Father, I desire that my spouse will be the best in everything he/she does in the name of Jesus Christ.
62. O God my Father, I desire that my spouse will be above only and not be beneath in the name of Jesus Christ.
63. O God my Father, I desire that my spouse will be the head and not the tail in his/her father's house in the name of Jesus Christ.
64. O God my Father, I desire that my spouse will be the head and not the tail in his/her mother's house in the n are of Jesus Christ.
65. O God my Father, I desire that my spouse will be the head and not the tail among his/her siblings in the name of Jesus Christ.
66. O God my Father, I desire that my spouse will be the head and not the tail among his/her friends in the name of Jesus Christ.
67. O God my Father, I desire that my spouse will be the head and not the tail among his/her business partners in the name of Jesus Christ.

68. O God my Father, I desire that my spouse will be the head and not the tail among his/her co-workers in the name of Jesus Christ.
69. O God my Father, I desire that my spouse will be the head and not the tail above his/her contemporaries in the name of Jesus Christ.
70. O God my Father, I desire that my spouse's life will reflect your glory in every area in the name of Jesus Christ.
71. O God my Father, I desire that my spouse will live a godly life in the name of Jesus Christ.
72. O God my Father, I desire that my spouse will be the best he/she can ever be in the name of Jesus Christ.
73. O God my Father, I desire that my children will be the best in every area of their lives in the name of Jesus Christ.
74. O God my Father, I desire that my children will be for signs and wonders, in the name of Jesus Christ.
75. O God my Father, I desire that my children be like olive plants round about my table, in the name of Jesus Christ.
76. O God my Father, I desire that my children shall be taught of The Lord, in the name of Jesus Christ.
77. O God my Father, I desire that great shall be the peace of my children, in the name of Jesus Christ.
78. O God my Father, I desire that my children's lives reflect your glory in the name of Jesus Christ.
79. O God my Father, I desire that my children shall be filled with an excellent spirit in the name of Jesus Christ.
80. O God my Father, I desire that my children shall be filled with divine knowledge from heaven above, in the name of Jesus Christ.

IMPOSSIBILITY IS OVER

Passages To Read Before You Pray:
Luke 1:37, Mark 9:23, Matthew 17:20, Psalms 44, 103, 106

I have come today to fellowship with my heavenly Father, and make my requests and needs known unto Him. I cannot be hindered nor delayed because I know who I am in the Lord. I am a child of the Kingdom, born of the Spirit, redeemed by the blood of Jesus Christ. I walk in authority, living life without any apology because the power and authority has been given to me according to the Word of God in the book of Luke 9:1.

As I have come to pray today and to fellowship with my heavenly Father, I cover myself in the blood of Jesus Christ, and I put on the whole armor of God. I hereby come against every Prince of Persia that wants to hinder my prayer, I arrest you by the power in the blood of Jesus Christ, and I bind you and cast you down into the pit of hell.

I come against principalities and powers that wrestle with me and my prayers, I arrest you today by the power in the name of Jesus Christ, and I bind you and cast down into the pit of hell. I come against the rulers of the darkness of this world, against spiritual wickedness in high places, I arrest you all by the power in the name of Jesus Christ, and I bind you and cast you down into the pit of hell. I come against weakness and weariness, I arrest you today by the power in the name of Jesus Christ, and I bind you and cast you out of my life. I come against wondering spirit and distractions, I arrest you today by the power in the name of Jesus Christ, and I bind you and cast you out of my life.

Today I receive the anointing to pray and get results, my prayers cannot be hindered nor delayed because Jesus is my Lord, I will pray today and get the desired results, I decree open heavens upon my prayers. I baptize myself in the fire of the Holy Ghost; therefore I have become too hot for the enemy to handle. My prayers today will attract divine intervention to every situation in my life; signs and wonders will follow my prayers today, testimonies will follow my prayers today and the name of God alone will be glorified, in Jesus name. Amen!

PRAYER POINTS:

1. O God my Father, thank you for being my God, my Father and my friend.
2. O God my Father, thank you for the privilege to know you and the power of the resurrection of Jesus Christ.
3. O God my Father, thank you for always being there for me and with me.
4. O God my Father, thank you for the great and mighty things that you are doing in my life.
5. O God my Father, thank you for your provision and protection over me and my household.
6. O God my Father, thank you for always answering my prayers.
7. I confess my sins before you today and I ask you to forgive me on the basis of your mercy, in the name of Jesus Christ.
8. Wash me clean today O Lord by the blood of Jesus Christ.
9. I cover myself and my household with the blood of Jesus Christ.

10. My prayers today will not go in vain; my prayers will produce the desired results in the name of Jesus Christ.
11. Today I declare that in every area of my life, nothing shall be impossible.
12. Today I declare that concerning my business, nothing shall be impossible for me.
13. Today I declare that concerning the works of my hands, nothing shall be impossible for me.
14. Today I declare that concerning my finances, nothing shall be impossible for me.
15. In my marriage O Lord, nothing shall be impossible.
16. In my home O Lord, nothing shall be impossible.
17. My dream is bigger than me, but because I believe nothing shall be impossible for me.
18. My goals are greater than the expectations of my enemy, but because I believe nothing shall be impossible for me.
19. I have set goals to be great in life, because I believe nothing shall be impossible for me.
20. Every mountain of impossibility confronting my life, be thou removed now in the name of Jesus Christ.
21. Mountain of impossibility confronting my progress in life, be thou removed now in the name of Jesus Christ.
22. Mountain of impossibility confronting my success in life, be thou removed in the name of Jesus Christ.
23. Mountain of impossibility confronting my efforts, be thou removed in t he name of Jesus Christ.
24. Mountain of impossibility planning to follow me into the new year, be thou removed now in the name of Jesus Christ.

25. Mountain of impossibility confronting my children's academics, be thou removed now in the name of Jesus Christ.
26. Mountain of impossibility confronting my ministry, be thou removed now in the name of Jesus Christ.
27. Mountain of impossibility confronting my source of income, be thou removed now in the name of Jesus Christ.
28. Mountain of impossibility confronting my helpers, be thou removed now in the name of Jesus Christ.
29. Mountain of impossibility standing in my way to the promise land, be thou removed now in the name of Jesus Christ.
30. Mountain of impossibility standing in my way to breakthrough, be thou removed now in the name of Jesus Christ.
31. Mountain of impossibility blocking my open heavens, be thou removed now in the name of Jesus Christ.
32. Mountain of impossibility that is making life hard for me, be thou removed now in the name of Jesus Christ.
33. Mountain of impossibility standing between me and my helpers, be thou removed now in the name of Jesus Christ.
34. Mountain of impossibility making it impossible for me to be happy, be thou removed now in the name of Jesus Christ.
35. Mountain of impossibility making it impossible for me to be fruitful, be thou removed now in the name of Jesus Christ.
36. Mountain of impossibility making it impossible for me to be where God has prepared for me, be thou removed now in the name of Jesus Christ.

37. Mountain of impossibility making it impossible for me to recognize my moment, be thou removed now in the name of Jesus Christ.
38. Mountain of impossibility making it impossible for me to move forward, be thou removed now in the name of Jesus Christ.
39. Mountain of impossibility making it impossible for me to ascend to the throne prepared for me, be thou removed now in the name of Jesus Christ.
40. Mountain of impossibility making it impossible for me to cross my Red Sea, be thou removed now in the name of Jesus Christ.
41. Mountain of impossibility making it impossible for me to overcome sin, be thou removed now in the name of Jesus Christ.
42. Mountain of impossibility making it impossible for me to overcome the works of the flesh, be thou removed now in the name of Jesus Christ.
43. Mountain of impossibility making it impossible for me to live a holy life, be thou removed now in the name of Jesus Christ.
44. Mountain of impossibility making it impossible for me to know the will of God for my life, be thou removed now in the name of Jesus Christ.
45. Mountain of impossibility making it impossible for me to receive my miracles, be thou removed now in the name of Jesus Christ.
46. Mountain of impossibility making it impossible for me to receive my breakthroughs, be thou removed now in the name of Jesus Christ.

47. Mountain of impossibility making it impossible for me to receive my financial freedom, be thou removed now in the name of Jesus Christ.
48. Mountain of impossibility making it impossible for me to receive total deliverance, be thou removed in the name of Jesus Christ.
49. Mountain of impossibility making it impossible for me to experience open heavens, be thou removed now in the name of Jesus Christ.

PRAYER TO OPEN A NEW CHAPTER IN YOUR LIFE

Passages To Read Before You Pray:
Genesis 41:1-14, Esther 6:1-14, Isaiah 43:18-19, Psalms 19, 24, 30, 42, 86

I have come today to fellowship with my heavenly Father, and make my requests and needs known unto Him. I cannot be hindered nor delayed because I know who I am in the Lord. I am a child of the Kingdom, born of the Spirit, redeemed by the blood of Jesus Christ. I walk in authority, living life without any apology because the power and authority has been given to me according to the Word of God in the book of Luke 9:1.

As I have come to pray today and to fellowship with my heavenly Father, I cover myself in the blood of Jesus Christ, and I put on the whole armor of God. I hereby come against every Prince of Persia that wants to hinder my prayer, I arrest you by the power in the blood of Jesus Christ, and I bind you and cast you down into the pit of hell.

I come against principalities and powers that wrestle with me and my prayers, I arrest you today by the power in the name of Jesus Christ, and I bind you and cast down into the pit of hell. I come against the rulers of the darkness of this world, against spiritual wickedness in high places, I arrest you all by the power in the name of Jesus Christ, and I bind you and cast you down into the pit of hell. I come against weakness and weariness, I arrest you today by the power in the name of Jesus Christ, and I bind you and cast you out of my life. I come against wondering

spirit and distractions, I arrest you today by the power in the name of Jesus Christ, and I bind you and cast you out of my life.

Today I receive the anointing to pray and get results, my prayers cannot be hindered nor delayed because Jesus is my Lord, I will pray today and get the desired results, I decree open heavens upon my prayers. I baptize myself in the fire of the Holy Ghost; therefore I have become too hot for the enemy to handle. My prayers today will attract divine intervention to every situation in my life; signs and wonders will follow my prayers today, testimonies will follow my prayers today and the name of God alone will be glorified, in Jesus name. Amen!

PRAYER POINTS:

1. O God my Father, thank you for being my God, my Father and my friend.
2. O God my Father, thank you for the privilege to know you and the power of the resurrection of Jesus Christ.
3. O God my Father, thank you for always being there for me and with me.
4. O God my Father, thank you for the great and mighty things that you are doing in my life.
5. O God my Father, thank you for your provision and protection over me and my household.
6. O God my Father, thank you for always answering my prayers.
7. I confess my sins before you today and I ask you to forgive me on the basis of your mercy, in the name of Jesus Christ.

8. Wash me clean today O Lord by the blood of Jesus Christ.
9. I cover myself and my household with the blood of Jesus Christ.
10. My prayers today will not go in vain; my prayers will produce the desired results in the name of Jesus Christ.
11. No matter the situation, prayer will work for me in the name of Jesus Christ.
12. O God my Father, open a new chapter in my life, give me a fresh start in the name of Jesus Christ.
13. O God my Father, let my helpers have problems that only me can solve, in the name of Jesus Christ.
14. O God my Father, let my helpers get on the road that will lead them to me, in the name of Jesus Christ.
15. O God my Father, let my helpers from every corner of the world relocate to locate me, in the name of Jesus Christ.
16. O God my Father, let my helpers find themselves in a situation that will connect them to me, in the name of Jesus Christ.
17. My helpers will not sleep nor rest until he or she helps me in the name of Jesus Christ.
18. Today O Lord, let the book of remembrance be opened concerning my life in the name of Jesus Christ.
19. Today O Lord, let the book of remembrance be opened concerning my family in the name of Jesus Christ.
20. Today O Lord, let the book of remembrance be opened concerning my destiny, in the name of Jesus Christ.
21. Today O Lord, let the book of remembrance of promotion be opened concerning my life in the name of Jesus Christ.

22. Today O Lord, let the book of remembrance of breakthroughs be opened concerning my life in the name of Jesus Christ.
23. Today O Lord, let the book of remembrance of miracles be opened concerning my life now in the name of Jesus Christ.
24. Today O Lord, let the book of remembrance of financial breakthroughs be opened concerning my life now in the name of Jesus Christ.
25. Today O Lord, let the book of remembrance of divine connection be opened concerning my life in the name of Jesus Christ.
26. Today O Lord, let the book of remembrance of double promotion be opened concerning my life now in the name of Jesus Christ.
27. O God my Father, trouble my helpers with sleepless night until they remember to help me in the name of Jesus Christ.
28. O God my Father, let every situation and circumstance remind my helper of his assignment to help me in the name of Jesus Christ.
29. Holy Spirit of God, remind my helpers today to rise and help me in every area, in the name of Jesus Christ.
30. In my life today O Lord, open a new chapter of joy in the name of Jesus Christ.
31. In my life today O Lord, open a new chapter of celebration in the name of Jesus Christ.
32. In my life today O Lord, open a new chapter of testimonies in the name of Jesus Christ.
33. In my life today O Lord, open a new chapter of elevation in the name of Jesus Christ.

34. In my life today O Lord, open a new chapter of unstoppable progress in the name of Jesus Christ.
35. In my life today O Lord, open a new chapter of uncommon favor in the name of Jesus Christ.
36. In my life today O Lord, open a new chapter of unusual breakthroughs in the name of Jesus Christ.
37. In my life today O Lord, open a new chapter of double promotion in the name of Jesus Christ.
38. In my life today O Lord, open a new chapter of divine connection in the name of Jesus Christ.
39. In my life today O Lord, open a new chapter of the manifestation of your glory in the name of Jesus Christ.
40. In my life today O Lord, open a new chapter of financial freedom in the name of Jesus Christ.
41. In my life today O Lord, open a new chapter of divine turn around in the name of Jesus Christ.
42. In my life today O Lord, open a new chapter written to launch me into greatness, in the name of Jesus Christ.
43. In my life today O Lord, open a new chapter written to launch me into my promise land, in the name of Jesus Christ.
44. In my life today O Lord, open a new chapter written for the fulfillment of my dreams, in the name of Jesus Christ.
45. In my life today O Lord, open a new chapter written for my coronation in the name of Jesus Christ.
46. In my life today O Lord, open a new chapter of riches and wealth in the name of Jesus Christ.
47. In my life today O Lord, open a new chapter of divine appointment in the name of Jesus Christ.

48. In my life today O Lord, open a new chapter written to position me for breakthroughs in the name of Jesus Christ.
49. In my life today O Lord, open a new chapter written to position me for a positive change in the name of Jesus Christ.
50. In my life today O Lord, open a new chapter written to position me for great achievements in the name of Jesus Christ.
51. In my life today O Lord, open a new chapter written for me to sing a new song, in the name of Jesus Christ.
52. In my life today O Lord, open a new chapter written for me to dance a new dance, in the name of Jesus Christ.
53. In my life today O Lord, open a new chapter written for me to laugh a new laugh, in the name of Jesus Christ.
54. In my life today O Lord, open a new chapter written to showcase your power, in the name of Jesus Christ.
55. In my life today O Lord, open a new chapter written to convert impossibilities to possibilities in the name of Jesus Christ.
56. In my life today O Lord, open a new chapter written to give me a new story to tell in the name of Jesus Christ.
57. In my life today O Lord, open a new chapter written for me to experience victory in every area, in the name of Jesus Christ.
58. In my life today O Lord, open a new chapter written for me to experience peace that surpasses all understanding, in the name of Jesus Christ.
59. In my life today O Lord, open a new chapter written for me to experience total deliverance, in the name of Jesus Christ.

60. In my life today O Lord, open a new chapter written for me to forget my shame and reproach, in the name of Jesus Christ.
61. In my life today O Lord, open a new chapter of divine direction in the name of Jesus Christ.
62. In my life today O Lord, open a new chapter written to cause my heavens to open, in the name of Jesus Christ.
63. In my life today O Lord, open a new chapter written to cause the former rain and latter rain to fall upon me, in the name of Jesus Christ.
64. In my life today O Lord, open a new chapter of unstoppable advancement in the name of Jesus Christ.

PRAYER TO STOP EVIL ACCESS TO YOUR LIFE

Passages To Read Before You Pray:
Luke 4:30-36, 1 Samuel 17:26, Psalms 46, 94, 9, 109, 59

I have come today to fellowship with my heavenly Father, and make my requests and needs known unto Him. I cannot be hindered nor delayed because I know who I am in the Lord. I am a child of the Kingdom, born of the Spirit, redeemed by the blood of Jesus Christ. I walk in authority, living life without any apology because the power and authority has been given to me according to the Word of God in the book of Luke 9:1.

As I have come to pray today and to fellowship with my heavenly Father, I cover myself in the blood of Jesus Christ, and I put on the whole armor of God. I hereby come against every Prince of Persia that wants to hinder my prayer, I arrest you by the power in the blood of Jesus Christ, and I bind you and cast you down into the pit of hell.

I come against principalities and powers that wrestle with me and my prayers, I arrest you today by the power in the name of Jesus Christ, and I bind you and cast down into the pit of hell. I come against the rulers of the darkness of this world, against spiritual wickedness in high places, I arrest you all by the power in the name of Jesus Christ, and I bind you and cast you down into the pit of hell. I come against weakness and weariness, I arrest you today by the power in the name of Jesus Christ, and I bind you and cast you out of my life. I come against wondering

spirit and distractions, I arrest you today by the power in the name of Jesus Christ, and I bind you and cast you out of my life.

Today I receive the anointing to pray and get results, my prayers cannot be hindered nor delayed because Jesus is my Lord, I will pray today and get the desired results, I decree open heavens upon my prayers. I baptize myself in the fire of the Holy Ghost; therefore I have become too hot for the enemy to handle. My prayers today will attract divine intervention to every situation in my life; signs and wonders will follow my prayers today, testimonies will follow my prayers today and the name of God alone will be glorified, in Jesus name. Amen!

PRAYER POINTS:

1. O God my Father, thank you for being my God, my Father and my friend.
2. O God my Father, thank you for the privilege to know you and the power of the resurrection of Jesus Christ.
3. O God my Father, thank you for always being there for me and with me.
4. O God my Father, thank you for the great and mighty things that you are doing in my life.
5. O God my Father, thank you for your provision and protection over me and my household.
6. O God my Father, thank you for always answering my prayers.
7. I confess my sins before you today and I ask you to forgive me on the basis of your mercy, in the name of Jesus Christ.

8. Wash me clean today O Lord by the blood of Jesus Christ.
9. I cover myself and my household with the blood of Jesus Christ.
10. My prayers today will not go in vain; my prayers will produce the desired results in the name of Jesus Christ.
11. Any power anywhere that has been tormenting me, you are no longer allowed to do so.
12. Any power anywhere making my life miserable, you are no longer allowed to do so.
13. Any power anywhere assigned to kill my dreams; you are no long allowed to do so.
14. Any power anywhere assigned to hindering my prayers, you are no longer allowed to do so.
15. Any power anywhere delaying my miracles, you are no longer allowed to do so.
16. Any power anywhere delaying my breakthroughs, you are no longer allowed to do so.
17. Any power anywhere that has been delaying my promotion, you are no longer allowed to do so.
18. Any power anywhere that has been delaying the manifestation of God's glory in my life, you are no longer allowed to do so.
19. Any power anywhere that has been delaying the demonstration of the power of God in my life, you are no longer allowed to do so.
20. Any power anywhere that has been delaying the fulfillment of the promise of God in my life, you are no longer allowed to do so.
21. Any power anywhere assigned to stop my progress, you are no longer allowed to do so.

22. Any power anywhere that has been delaying my testimonies, you are no longer allowed to do so.
23. Any power anywhere challenging the power of God in my life, you are no longer allowed to do so.
24. Every stubborn situation challenging the power of God in my life, you are no longer allowed to do so.
25. Every stubborn situation in my life making me live a hopeless life, you are no longer allowed to do so.
26. Every seed of sickness in my body, you are no longer allowed to dwell in my body, my body is the temple of the Holy Ghost.
27. You spirit of poverty manifesting in my life, you are no longer allowed, I cast you out by the authority in the name of Jesus Christ.
28. You spirit of poverty affecting my finances, you are no longer allowed, I bind you and cast you out of my finances now.
29. You spirit of poverty affecting my business, you are no longer allowed, I bind and cast you out of my business now.
30. You spirit of poverty affecting my family, you are no longer allowed, I bind and cast you out now.
31. You spirit of poverty causing me to live a second class life, you are no longer allowed in my life, I bind and cast you out now.
32. You mountain of impossibility blocking my way to success, you are no longer allowed to do so, be thou removed by the fire of God.
33. You mountain of impossibility blocking my breakthroughs, you are no longer allowed to do so, be thou removed by the fire of God.

34. You mountain of impossibility standing between me and my helpers, you are no longer allowed to do so, be thou removed now by the fire of God.
35. You mountain of impossibility trying to stop me from moving up, you are not allowed to do so, be thou removed now by the fire of God.
36. You mountain of impossibility blocking my open doors, be thou removed now by the fire of God.
37. You mountain of impossibility blocking my access to success, be thou removed now by the fire of God.
38. You mountain of impossibility blocking my access to uncommon favor, be thou removed now by the fire of God.
39. You mountain of impossibility blocking my access to business opportunities, be thou removed now by the fire of God.
40. You mountain of impossibility blocking my opportunity to meet my helpers, be thou removed now by the fire of God.
41. Any power anywhere turning my life to a battle field, you are no longer allowed to do so, my life is precious, loose your hold over my life.
42. Any power anywhere turning my sleep to a battle field, you are no longer allowed to do so, loose your hold over my life.
43. Any power anywhere turning my life to a punching bag, you are no longer allowed to do so, my life is precious, loose your hold over my life now.
44. Household wickedness tormenting me day and night, you are no longer allowed to do so.
45. Household wickedness postponing my breakthroughs, you are no longer allowed to do so.

46. Household wickedness postponing the day of my testimony, you are no longer allowed to do so, now is my time to testify.
47. Any power anywhere inflicting me with any kind of sickness, you are no longer allowed to do so, by Jesus stripes I am healed.
48. Any power anywhere inflicting me with any kinds of problems, you are no longer allowed to do so, today I am free indeed.
49. Any power anywhere renewing evil covenants over my life, you are no longer allowed to do so, today I break every evil covenant by the fire of God.
50. Any power anywhere closing my heavens of joy, you are no longer allowed to do so, the joy of the Lord shall be my strength.
51. Any power anywhere closing my heavens of abundance, you are no longer allowed to do so.
52. Any power anywhere that has been keeping me in bondage all these years, you are no longer allowed to do so, today I am free.
53. Any power anywhere that has been replacing my glory with shame, you are no longer allowed to do so, today my life will reflect the glory of God.
54. Any power anywhere that has been replacing my joy with tears, you are no longer allowed, today the Lord has wiped away my tears.
55. Any power anywhere that has been replacing my success with failure no matter how much I try, you are no longer allowed to do so, I will never fail again.
56. Failure in any area of my life, you are no longer allowed.
57. The work of the devil manifesting in my life, you are no longer allowed.

58. Delay in any area of my life, you are no longer allowed.
59. Infirmity of any form in my life, you are no longer allowed.
60. Stagnancy of any kind in my life, you are no longer allowed.
61. Backwardness of any kind in my life, you are no longer allowed.
62. Demotion of any form in my life, you are no longer allowed.
63. Barrenness of any kind in my life, you are no longer allowed.
64. Loneliness of any form in my life, you are no longer allowed.
65. Confusion of any form in my life, you are no longer allowed.
66. Insufficiency of any form in my life, you are no longer allowed.
67. Demonic attack of any form against me, you are no longer allowed.
68. Demonic activity of any form manifesting in my life, you are no longer allowed.
69. Sadness of any form in my life, you are no longer allowed.
70. Rejection of any form in my life, you are no longer allowed.
71. Low self-esteem in any form in my life, you are no longer allowed.
72. Depression of any form in my life, you are no longer allowed.
73. Oppression of any form in my life, you are no longer allowed.

74. Slavery of any form in my life, you are no longer allowed.
75. Collective captivity of any form in my life, you are no longer allowed.
76. The mouth and tongue speaking evil against me, you are no longer allowed to do so, today you are condemned.
77. The mouth and tongue speaking evil against my family, you are no longer allowed to do so, today you are condemned.
78. The mouth and tongue speaking evil against my finances, you are no longer allowed to do so, today you are condemned.
79. The mouth and tongue speaking evil against my spouse, you are no longer allowed to do so, today you are condemned.
80. The mouth and tongue speaking evil against my children, you are no longer allowed to do so, today you are condemned.
81. The mouth and tongue speaking evil against my parents, you are no longer allowed to do so, today you are condemned.
82. The mouth and tongue speaking evil against my destiny, you are no longer allowed to do so, today you are condemned.
83. The mouth and tongue planting evil seeds into my future, you are no longer allowed to do so, today you are condemned.
84. The mouth and tongue planting evil seeds into the future of my spouse, you are no longer allowed to do so, today you are condemned.

85. The mouth and tongue planting evil seeds into the future of my children, you are no longer allowed to do so, today you are condemned.
86. Any power anywhere using my weakness against me, you are no longer allowed to do so, the Lord shall be my strength.
87. You spirit of devourer attacking my finances, you are no longer allowed, my God will destroy you today.
88. Every satanic chain that has been holding me down, you are no longer allowed to do so, today I am free.
89. You spirit of fear that has been attacking my faith, you are no longer allowed because I know my God.
90. You prince of Persia that has been hindering my prayers, you are no longer allowed to do so, today there will be divine intervention in every area of my life.
91. Any power anywhere terrorizing me day and night, you are no longer allowed to do so.

PRAYER TO CLOSE EVIL CHAPTER IN YOUR LIFE

Passages To Read Before You Pray:
Exodus 14:13, Genesis 41:1-14, Psalms 3, 9, 18, 83, 30.

I have come today to fellowship with my heavenly Father, and make my requests and needs known unto Him. I cannot be hindered nor delayed because I know who I am in the Lord. I am a child of the Kingdom, born of the Spirit, redeemed by the blood of Jesus Christ. I walk in authority, living life without any apology because the power and authority has been given to me according to the Word of God in the book of Luke 9:1.

As I have come to pray today and to fellowship with my heavenly Father, I cover myself in the blood of Jesus Christ, and I put on the whole armor of God. I hereby come against every Prince of Persia that wants to hinder my prayer, I arrest you by the power in the blood of Jesus Christ, and I bind you and cast you down into the pit of hell.

I come against principalities and powers that wrestle with me and my prayers, I arrest you today by the power in the name of Jesus Christ, and I bind you and cast down into the pit of hell. I come against the rulers of the darkness of this world, against spiritual wickedness in high places, I arrest you all by the power in the name of Jesus Christ, and I bind you and cast you down into the pit of hell. I come against weakness and weariness, I arrest you today by the power in the name of Jesus Christ, and I bind you and cast you out of my life. I come against wondering

spirit and distractions, I arrest you today by the power in the name of Jesus Christ, and I bind you and cast you out of my life.

Today I receive the anointing to pray and get results, my prayers cannot be hindered nor delayed because Jesus is my Lord, I will pray today and get the desired results, I decree open heavens upon my prayers. I baptize myself in the fire of the Holy Ghost; therefore I have become too hot for the enemy to handle. My prayers today will attract divine intervention to every situation in my life; signs and wonders will follow my prayers today, testimonies will follow my prayers today and the name of God alone will be glorified, in Jesus name. Amen!

PRAYER POINTS:

1. O God my Father, thank you for being my God, my Father and my friend.
2. O God my Father, thank you for the privilege to know you and the power of the resurrection of Jesus Christ.
3. O God my Father, thank you for always being there for me and with me.
4. O God my Father, thank you for the great and mighty things that you are doing in my life.
5. O God my Father, thank you for your provision and protection over me and my household.
6. O God my Father, thank you for always answering my prayers.
7. I confess my sins before you today and I ask you to forgive me on the basis of your mercy, in the name of Jesus Christ.

8. Wash me clean today O Lord by the blood of Jesus Christ.
9. I cover myself and my household with the blood of Jesus Christ.
10. My prayers today will not go in vain; my prayers will produce the desired results in the name of Jesus Christ.

11. Today O Lord, I command the chapter of failure in my life to be permanently closed, in the name of Jesus Christ.
12. Today O Lord, I command the chapter of pain in my life to be permanently closed, in the name of Jesus Christ.
13. Today O Lord, I command the chapter of stagnancy in my life to be permanently closed, in the name of Jesus Christ.
14. Today O Lord, I command the chapter of almost there in my life to be permanently closed in the name of Jesus Christ.
15. Today O Lord, I command the chapter of backwardness in my life to be permanently closed in the name of Jesus Christ.
16. Today O Lord, I command the chapter of fruitless hard labor in my life to be permanently closed in the name of Jesus Christ.
17. Today O Lord, I command the chapter of poverty in my life to be permanently closed in the name of Jesus Christ.
18. Today O Lord, I command the chapter of disappointment in my life to be permanently closed in the name of Jesus Christ.

19. Today O Lord, I command the chapter of shame in my life to be permanently closed in the name of Jesus Christ.
20. Today O Lord, I command the chapter of satanic bondage in my life to be permanently closed in the name of Jesus Christ.
21. Today O Lord, I command the chapter of closed heaven in my life to be permanently closed in the name of Jesus Christ.
22. Today O Lord. I command the chapter of unanswered prayers in my life to be permanently closed in the name of Jesus Christ.
23. Today O Lord, I command the chapter of non-achievement in my life to be permanently closed in the name of Jesus Christ.
24. Today O Lord, I command the chapter of misfortune in my life to be permanently closed in the name of Jesus Christ.
25. Today O Lord, I command the chapter of ridicule in my life to be permanently closed in the name of Jesus Christ.
26. Today O Lord, I command the chapter of satanic attack in my life to be permanently closed in the name of Jesus Christ.
27. Today O Lord, I command the chapter of evil cycle in my life to be permanently closed in the name of Jesus Christ.
28. Today O Lord, I command the chapter of doubt and unbelief in my life to be permanently closed in the name of Jesus Christ.

29. Today O Lord, I command the chapter of demotion in my life to be permanently closed in the name of Jesus Christ.
30. Today O Lord, I command the chapter of unfavorable situation in my life to be closed permanently in the name of Jesus Christ.
31. Today O Lord, I command the chapter of problems in my life to be permanently closed in the name of Jesus Christ.
32. Today O Lord, I command the chapter of affliction in my life to be permanently closed in the name of Jesus Christ.
33. Today O Lord, I command the chapter of no breakthrough in my life to be permanently closed in the name of Jesus Christ.
34. Today O Lord. I command the chapter of failure at the edge of miracle in my life to be permanently closed in the name of Jesus Christ.
35. Today O Lord, I command the chapter of frustration in my life to be permanently closed in the name of Jesus Christ..

PRAYER TO DESTROY EVIL STRONGHOLDS

Passages To Read Before You Pray:
2 Corinthians 10:3-6, Psalms 83, 94, 109, 55, 140

I have come today to fellowship with my heavenly Father, and make my requests and needs known unto Him. I cannot be hindered nor delayed because I know who I am in the Lord. I am a child of the Kingdom, born of the Spirit, redeemed by the blood of Jesus Christ. I walk in authority, living life without any apology because the power and authority has been given to me according to the Word of God in the book of Luke 9:1.

As I have come to pray today and to fellowship with my heavenly Father, I cover myself in the blood of Jesus Christ, and I put on the whole armor of God. I hereby come against every Prince of Persia that wants to hinder my prayer, I arrest you by the power in the blood of Jesus Christ, and I bind you and cast you down into the pit of hell.

I come against principalities and powers that wrestle with me and my prayers, I arrest you today by the power in the name of Jesus Christ, and I bind you and cast down into the pit of hell. I come against the rulers of the darkness of this world, against spiritual wickedness in high places, I arrest you all by the power in the name of Jesus Christ, and I bind you and cast you down into the pit of hell. I come against weakness and weariness, I arrest you today by the power in the name of Jesus Christ, and I bind you and cast you out of my life. I come against wondering spirit and distractions, I arrest you today by the power in the name of Jesus Christ, and I bind you and cast you out of my life.

Today I receive the anointing to pray and get results, my prayers cannot be hindered nor delayed because Jesus is my Lord, I will pray today and get the desired results, I decree open heavens upon my prayers. I baptize myself in the fire of the Holy Ghost; therefore I have become too hot for the enemy to handle. My prayers today will attract divine intervention to every situation in my life; signs and wonders will follow my prayers today, testimonies will follow my prayers today and the name of God alone will be glorified, in Jesus name. Amen!

PRAYER POINTS:

1. O God my Father, thank you for being my God, my Father and my friend.
2. O God my Father, thank you for the privilege to know you and the power of the resurrection of Jesus Christ.
3. O God my Father, thank you for always being there for me and with me.
4. O God my Father, thank you for the great and mighty things that you are doing in my life.
5. O God my Father, thank you for your provision and protection over me and my household.
6. O God my Father, thank you for always answering my prayers.
7. I confess my sins before you today and I ask you to forgive me on the basis of your mercy, in the name of Jesus Christ.
8. Wash me clean today O Lord by the blood of Jesus Christ.
9. I cover myself and my household with the blood of Jesus Christ.

10. My prayers today will not go in vain; my prayers will produce the desired results in the name of Jesus Christ.

11. Every stronghold of confusion erected against me, I pull you down today, be destroyed by the fire of God.
12. Every stronghold of infirmity erected against me, I pull you down today, be destroyed by the fire of God.
13. Every stronghold of inherited sickness against me, I pull you down today, be destroyed by the fire of God.
14. Every stronghold of failure erected against me, I pull you down today, be destroyed by the fire of God.
15. Every stronghold of failure erected against my business in any form, I pull you down today, be destroyed by the fire of God.
16. Every stronghold of failure erected against my family, I pull you down today, be destroyed by the fire of God.
17. Every stronghold of failure erected against my efforts, I pull you down today, be destroyed by the fire of God.
18. Every stronghold of failure erected against the works of my hands, I pull you down today, be destroyed by the fire of God.
19. Every stronghold of poverty erected against me, I pull you down today, be destroyed by the fire of God.
20. Every stronghold of poverty erected against my finances, I pull you down today, be destroyed by the fire of God.
21. Every stronghold of failure erected against my ministry, I pull you down today, be destroyed y the fire of God.
22. Every stronghold of any form of addiction erected against me, I pull you down today, be destroyed by the fire of God.

23. Every stronghold of any form of addiction erected against my spouse, I pull you down today, be destroyed by the fire of God.
24. Every stronghold of any form addiction erected against my children, I pull you down today, be destroyed by the fire of God.
25. Today O Lord, in every area of my life, power must change hands.
26. Today O Lord, in every area of my life, there must be a turn around.
27. By the power in the name of Jesus Christ, I set myself loose from any form of captivity.
28. By the power in the name of Jesus Christ, I set myself loose from bondage of confusion.
29. By the power in the name of Jesus Christ, I set myself loose from the bondage of household wickedness.
30. By the power in the name of Jesus Christ, I set myself loose from the bondage of inherited failure.
31. By the power in the name of Jesus Christ, I set myself loose from the hands of evil controllers.
32. By the power in the name of Jesus Christ, I separate myself from every unfriendly friend.
33. By the power in the name of Jesus Christ, I separate myself from mixed multitude that has been affecting my life.
34. By the power in the name of Jesus Christ, I separate myself from mixed multitude that has been making my journey longer than expected.
35. By the power in the name of Jesus Christ, I separate myself from mixed multitude that has been affecting my success.

36. By the power in the name of Jesus Christ, I separate myself from the mixed multitude that has been negatively affecting my life decisions.
37. By the power in the name of Jesus Christ, I separate myself from the wrong crowd around me.
38. By the power in the name of Jesus Christ, I separate myself from the mixed multitude that have causing unexpected go slow to my progress.
39. By the power in the name of Jesus Christ, I separate myself from the mixed multitude that have been causing unexpected go slow in my journey to the promise land.
40. By the power in the name of Jesus Christ, I separate myself from the mixed multitude that been causing unexpected delay to my miracles.
41. By the power in the name of Jesus Christ, I separate myself from the mixed multitude that has been causing unexpected delay to my breakthroughs.
42. By the power in the name of Jesus Christ, I separate myself from the mixed multitude that has been causing unexpected delay to my blessings.
43. By the power in the name of Jesus Christ, I separate myself from the mixed multitude that has been causing unexpected delay to my financial freedom.
44. By the power in the name of Jesus Christ, I separate myself from the mixed multitude that has been causing unexpected delay to my open heavens.
45. By the power in the name of Jesus Christ, I separate myself from the mixed multitude that has been causing unexpected delay to my total deliverance.
46. Any power anywhere that has been holding me down since the beginning of this year, I command you now, loose me and let me go.

47. Any power anywhere that has been attacking my joy since the beginning of this year, loose me now and let me go.
48. Any power anywhere that has been attacking my marriage since the beginning of this year, loose me now and let me go.
49. Any power anywhere that has been attacking my home since the beginning of this year, loose me now and let me go.
50. Any power anywhere that has been attacking my health since the beginning of this year, loose me now and let me go.
51. Any power anywhere that has been attacking my finances since the beginning of this year, loose me now and let me go.
52. Any power anywhere hat has been attacking my peace since the beginning of this year, loose me now and let me go.
53. Any power anywhere that has been attacking my source of income since the beginning of this year, loose me now and let me go.
54. Any power anywhere that has been attacking my business since the beginning of this year, loose me now and let me go.
55. Any power anywhere that has been attacking my spiritual life since the beginning of this year, loose me now and let me go.
56. Any power anywhere that has been attacking my faith in God since the beginning of this year, loose me and let me go.

57. Any power anywhere that has been attacking my confidence in The Lord since the beginning of this year, loose me now and let me go.
58. Any power anywhere that has been challenging the power of God in my life since the beginning of this year, loose me now and let me go.
59. Any power anywhere that has been delaying my prayers since the beginning of this year, loose me now and let me go.
60. Any power anywhere that has been delaying my miracles since the beginning of this year, loose me now and let me go.
61. Any power anywhere assigned to frustrate me, your time is up, loose me now and let me go.
62. Any power anywhere assigned to make my life miserable, your time is up, loose me now and let me go.
63. Any power anywhere assigned to stop me from moving forward, your time is up, loose me now and let me go.
64. Any power anywhere assigned to stop my progress, your time is up, loose me now and let me go.
65. Any power anywhere assigned to stop my promotion, your secret is out, loose me now and let me go.
66. Any power anywhere forcing me to go against the will of God, loose me now and let me go.

PRAYER FOR LAST MINUTE MIRACLE

Passages To Read Before You Pray:
2 Kings 6:24-33, 2 Kings 7:1-20, Psalms 44, 56, 59, 86, 89

I have come today to fellowship with my heavenly Father, and make my requests and needs known unto Him. I cannot be hindered nor delayed because I know who I am in the Lord. I am a child of the Kingdom, born of the Spirit, redeemed by the blood of Jesus Christ. I walk in authority, living life without any apology because the power and authority has been given to me according to the Word of God in the book of Luke 9:1.

As I have come to pray today and to fellowship with my heavenly Father, I cover myself in the blood of Jesus Christ, and I put on the whole armor of God. I hereby come against every Prince of Persia that wants to hinder my prayer, I arrest you by the power in the blood of Jesus Christ, and I bind you and cast you down into the pit of hell.

I come against principalities and powers that wrestle with me and my prayers, I arrest you today by the power in the name of Jesus Christ, and I bind you and cast down into the pit of hell. I come against the rulers of the darkness of this world, against spiritual wickedness in high places, I arrest you all by the power in the name of Jesus Christ, and I bind you and cast you down into the pit of hell. I come against weakness and weariness, I arrest you today by the power in the name of Jesus Christ, and I bind you and cast you out of my life. I come against wondering spirit and distractions, I arrest you today by the power in the name of Jesus Christ, and I bind you and cast you out of my life.

Today I receive the anointing to pray and get results, my prayers cannot be hindered nor delayed because Jesus is my Lord, I will pray today and get the desired results, I decree open heavens upon my prayers. I baptize myself in the fire of the Holy Ghost; therefore I have become too hot for the enemy to handle. My prayers today will attract divine intervention to every situation in my life; signs and wonders will follow my prayers today, testimonies will follow my prayers today and the name of God alone will be glorified, in Jesus name. Amen!

PRAYER POINTS:

1. O God my Father, thank you for being my God, my Father and my friend.
2. O God my Father, thank you for the privilege to know you and the power of the resurrection of Jesus Christ.
3. O God my Father, thank you for always being there for me and with me.
4. O God my Father, thank you for the great and mighty things that you are doing in my life.
5. O God my Father, thank you for your provision and protection over me and my household.
6. O God my Father, thank you for always answering my prayers.
7. I confess my sins before you today and I ask you to forgive me on the basis of your mercy, in the name of Jesus Christ.
8. Wash me clean today O Lord by the blood of Jesus Christ.
9. I cover myself and my household with the blood of Jesus Christ.

10. My prayers today will not go in vain; my prayers will produce the desired results in the name of Jesus Christ.
11. Today O Lord, I claim last minute blessings, it is not over yet.
12. Today O Lord, I claim last minute solution to my situation, it is not over yet.
13. Today O Lord, I claim last minute open heavens, it is not over yet.
14. Today O Lord, I claim last minute breakthroughs, it is not over yet.
15. Today O Lord, I claim last minute promotion, it is not over yet.
16. Today O Lord, I claim last minute turn around, it is not over yet.
17. Today O Lord, I claim last minute intervention in every area of my life, it is not over yet.
18. Today O Lord, I claim last minute victory over every situation, it is not over yet.
19. Today O Lord, I claim last minute financial freedom, it is not over yet.
20. Today O Lord, I claim last minute opportunities, it is not over yet.
21. Today O Lord, I claim last minute restoration in every area of my life, it is not over yet.
22. Today O Lord, I claim last minute open doors, it is not over yet.
23. Today O Lord, I claim last minute approval in every area that I have been rejected, it is not over yet.
24. Before this year comes to an end, I shall laugh last.
25. In every area that I have been cast down, in the last days of this year I shall be lifted up.

26. Today O Lord, I claim last minute double promotion, it is not over yet.
27. It is not over yet, my helpers shall locate me before the end of this year.
28. It is not over yet, I shall experience the fullness of joy before the end of this year.
29. It is not over yet, I am getting out of this bondage before the end of this year.
30. Today O Lord, I claim last minute deliverance from the bondage of poverty, it is not over yet.
31. Today O Lord, I claim last minute deliverance from the bondage of stagnancy, it is not over yet.
32. Today O Lord, I claim last minute deliverance from the bondage of almost there, it is not over yet.
33. Today O Lord, I claim last minute deliverance from the bondage of Egypt, it is not over yet.
34. Today O Lord, I claim last minute deliverance from the hands of the Pharaoh that refuse to let me go.
35. Today O Lord, I claim last minute deliverance from the hands of the Goliath that is threatening to destroy me.
36. Today O Lord, I claim last minute deliverance from the bondage of household wickedness.
37. Today O Lord, I claim last minute deliverance from the power of backwardness.
38. Today O Lord, I claim last minute deliverance from the curse of failure.
39. Today O Lord, I claim last minute deliverance from any form of infirmity.
40. Today O Lord, I claim last minute deliverance from any form of satanic attack upon my life.
41. Today O Lord, I claim last minute deliverance from any form of satanic attack against my marriage.

42. Today O Lord, I claim last minute deliverance from any form of satanic attack against my children.
43. Today O Lord, I claim last minute deliverance from any form of satanic attack against my spouse.
44. Today O Lord, I claim last minute deliverance from any form of satanic attack against my finances.
45. Today O Lord, I claim last minute deliverance from any form of satanic attack against my source of income.
46. Today O Lord, I claim last minute deliverance from any form of satanic attack against my health.
47. Today O Lord, I claim last minute deliverance from any form of satanic attack against my destiny.
48. Today O Lord, I claim last minute deliverance from any form of satanic attack against my future.
49. Today O Lord, I claim last minute deliverance from any form of satanic attack against my children's future.
50. Today O Lord, I claim last minute deliverance from any form of satanic attack against the source of my joy.
51. Today O Lord, I claim last minute deliverance from any form of satanic attack against God's plan for my life.
52. Today O Lord, I claim last minute deliverance from ancestral curse of poverty.
53. Today O Lord, I claim last minute deliverance from ancestral curse of emptiness.
54. Today O Lord, I claim last minute deliverance from ancestral curse of loneliness.
55. Today O Lord, I claim last minute deliverance from ancestral curse of barrenness.
56. Today O Lord, I claim last minute deliverance from ancestral curse of vain labor.
57. Today O Lord, I claim last minute miracles, it is not over yet.

58. Today O Lord, I claim last minute testimonies, it is not over yet.
59. Today O Lord, I claim last minute double portion of the anointing, it is not over yet.
60. Today O Lord, I claim last minute double portion of miracles, it is not over yet.
61. The remaining days of this year shall bring me joy.
62. The remaining days of this year shall bring me laughter.
63. In the remaining days of this year, I shall have reasons to celebrate.
64. In the remaining days of this year, I will sing a new song.
65. In the remaining days of this year, I will dance a new dance.
66. In the remaining days of this year, I will experience the demonstration of the power of God.
67. In the remaining days of this year, I will experience transformation in every area of my life.
68. In the remaining days of this year, I will experience turn around in my situations.
69. In the remaining days of this year, I will experience uncommon favor.
70. In the remaining days of this year, I will experience divine touch of God in every area of my life.

PRAYER TO REJECT EVIL MANIFESTATION

Passages To Read Before You Pray:
1 Kings 3:16-28, Matthew 13:24-30, 1 John 3:8, Psalms 18, 59, 69, 55, 140

I have come today to fellowship with my heavenly Father, and make my requests and needs known unto Him. I cannot be hindered nor delayed because I know who I am in the Lord. I am a child of the Kingdom, born of the Spirit, redeemed by the blood of Jesus Christ. I walk in authority, living life without any apology because the power and authority has been given to me according to the Word of God in the book of Luke 9:1.

As I have come to pray today and to fellowship with my heavenly Father, I cover myself in the blood of Jesus Christ, and I put on the whole armor of God. I hereby come against every Prince of Persia that wants to hinder my prayer, I arrest you by the power in the blood of Jesus Christ, and I bind you and cast you down into the pit of hell.

I come against principalities and powers that wrestle with me and my prayers, I arrest you today by the power in the name of Jesus Christ, and I bind you and cast down into the pit of hell. I come against the rulers of the darkness of this world, against spiritual wickedness in high places, I arrest you all by the power in the name of Jesus Christ, and I bind you and cast you down into the pit of hell. I come against weakness and weariness, I arrest you today by the power in the name of Jesus Christ, and I bind you and cast you out of my life. I come against wondering

spirit and distractions, I arrest you today by the power in the name of Jesus Christ, and I bind you and cast you out of my life.

Today I receive the anointing to pray and get results, my prayers cannot be hindered nor delayed because Jesus is my Lord, I will pray today and get the desired results, I decree open heavens upon my prayers. I baptize myself in the fire of the Holy Ghost; therefore I have become too hot for the enemy to handle. My prayers today will attract divine intervention to every situation in my life; signs and wonders will follow my prayers today, testimonies will follow my prayers today and the name of God alone will be glorified, in Jesus name. Amen!

PRAYER POINTS:

1. O God my Father, thank you for being my God, my Father and my friend.
2. O God my Father, thank you for the privilege to know you and the power of the resurrection of Jesus Christ.
3. O God my Father, thank you for always being there for me and with me.
4. O God my Father, thank you for the great and mighty things that you are doing in my life.
5. O God my Father, thank you for your provision and protection over me and my household.
6. O God my Father, thank you for always answering my prayers.
7. I confess my sins before you today and I ask you to forgive me on the basis of your mercy, in the name of Jesus Christ.

8. Wash me clean today O Lord by the blood of Jesus Christ.
9. I cover myself and my household with the blood of Jesus Christ.
10. My prayers today will not go in vain; my prayers will produce the desired results in the name of Jesus Christ.

11. Today O Lord, perfect the good works that you have begun in my life in the name of Jesus Christ.
12. O God my Father, this is day of completion, let my prayers bring forth testimonies in the name of Jesus Christ.
13. O God my Father, this is the day of completion, let miracles manifest in my life as a result of my prayers in the name of Jesus Christ.
14. O God my Father, let signs and wonders follow my prayers in the name of Jesus Christ.
15. Any power anywhere trying to exchange my glory, you will not escape the judgment of God in the name of Jesus Christ.
16. Any power anywhere trying to exchange my miracles, you will not escape the judgment of God in the name of Jesus Christ.
17. Any power anywhere trying to exchange my testimony, you will not escape the judgment of God in the name of Jesus Christ.
18. Any power anywhere trying to exchange the plan of God for my life, you will not escape the judgment of God in the name of Jesus Christ.
19. Any power anywhere trying to reprogram my life, you will not escape the judgment of God in the name of Jesus Christ.

20. Any power anywhere trying to redesign my life, you will not escape the judgment of God in the name of Jesus Christ.
21. Any power anywhere trying to keep me in bondage, you will not escape the judgment of God in the name of Jesus Christ.
22. I receive the grace of God to wake out of spiritual sleep that causes me to lose my blessings, in the name of Jesus Christ.
23. I receive the grace of God to wake out of spiritual sleep that causes me to lose my miracles in the name of Jesus Christ.
24. I receive the grace of God to wake out of spiritual sleep that causes me to lose my harvest in the name of Jesus Christ.
25. I receive the grace of God to wake out of spiritual sleep that allows my enemy to sow evil seeds into my life in the name of Jesus Christ.
26. I receive the grace of God to wake out of spiritual sleep that allows my enemy to rob me of my miracles in the name of Jesus Christ.
27. I receive the grace of God to wake out of spiritual sleep that allows my enemy to reprogram my life in the name of Jesus Christ.
28. O God my Father, when I look into my life I see something that is not mine, failure is not mine, let it be removed now by your fire in the name of Jesus Christ.
29. O God my Father, when I look into my life I see something that is not mine, rejection is not mine, let it be removed now by your fire in the name of Jesus Christ.
30. O God my Father, when I look into my life I see something that is not mine, loneliness is not mine, let it

be removed now by your fire in the name of Jesus Christ.
31. O God my Father, when I look into my life I see something that is not mine, stagnation is not mine, let it be removed now by your fire in the name of Jesus Christ.
32. O God my Father, when I look into my life I see something that is not mine, barrenness is not mine, let it be removed now by your fire in the name of Jesus Christ.
33. O God my Father, when I look into my life I see something that is not mine, backwardness is not mine, let it be removed by your fire in the name of Jesus Christ.
34. O God my Father. When I look into my life I see something that is not mine, demotion is not mine, let it be removed now by your fire in the name of Jesus Christ.
35. O God my Father, when I look into my life I see something that is n it mine, poverty is not mine, let it be removed now by your fire in the name of Jesus Christ.
36. O God my Father, when I look into my life I see something that is not mine, satanic delay is not mine, let it be removed now by your fire in the name of Jesus Christ.
37. O God my Father, when I look into my life I see something that is not mine, fruitless effort is not mine, let it be removed now in the name of Jesus Christ.
38. O God my Father, when I look into my life I see something that is not mine, marital failure is not mine, let it be removed now by your fire in the name of Jesus Christ.

39. O God my Father, when I look into my life I see something that is not mine, sickness is not mine, let it be removed now by your fire in the name of Jesus Christ.
40. O God my Father, when I look into my life I see something that is not mine, financial failure is not mine, let it be removed now by your fire in the name of Jesus Christ.
41. O God my Father, closed heaven is not mine, let it be removed now by your fire in the name of Jesus Christ.
42. O God my Father, fruitless hard labor is not mine, let it be removed now by your fire in the name of Jesus Christ.
43. O God my Father, sadness is not mine, let it be removed now by your fire in the name of Jesus Christ.
44. O God my Father, shame is not mine, let it be removed now by your fire in the name of Jesus Christ.
45. O God my Father, ridicule is not mine, let it be removed now by your fire in the name of Jesus Christ.
46. O God my Father, reproach is not mine, let it be removed by your fire in the name of Jesus Christ.
47. O God my Father, bad luck is not mine, let it be removed now by your fire in the name of Jesus Christ.
48. O God my Father, unemployment is not mine, let it be removed now by your fire in the name of Jesus Christ.
49. O God my Father, pain is not mine, let it be removed now by your fire in the name of Jesus Christ.
50. O God my Father, financial embarrassment is not mine, let it removed now by your fire in the name of Jesus Christ.
51. O God my Father, living below standard is not mine, let it be removed now by your fire in the name of Jesus Christ.

52. O God my Father, life of mediocrity is not mine, let it be removed now by your fire in the name of Jesus Christ.
53. O God my Father, lack of achievement is not mine; let it be removed now by your fire in the name of Jesus Christ.

PRAYER TO EXPERIENCE GREAT THINGS

Passages To Read Before You Pray:
Proverbs 18:21, Job 22:28, Joel 2:21-27, Psalms 106

I have come today to fellowship with my heavenly Father, and make my requests and needs known unto Him. I cannot be hindered nor delayed because I know who I am in the Lord. I am a child of the Kingdom, born of the Spirit, redeemed by the blood of Jesus Christ. I walk in authority, living life without any apology because the power and authority has been given to me according to the Word of God in the book of Luke 9:1.

As I have come to pray today and to fellowship with my heavenly Father, I cover myself in the blood of Jesus Christ, and I put on the whole armor of God. I hereby come against every Prince of Persia that wants to hinder my prayer, I arrest you by the power in the blood of Jesus Christ, and I bind you and cast you down into the pit of hell.

I come against principalities and powers that wrestle with me and my prayers, I arrest you today by the power in the name of Jesus Christ, and I bind you and cast down into the pit of hell. I come against the rulers of the darkness of this world, against spiritual wickedness in high places, I arrest you all by the power in the name of Jesus Christ, and I bind you and cast you down into the pit of hell. I come against weakness and weariness, I arrest you today by the power in the name of Jesus Christ, and I bind you and cast you out of my life. I come against wondering spirit and distractions, I arrest you today by the power in the name of Jesus Christ, and I bind you and cast you out of my life.

Today I receive the anointing to pray and get results, my prayers cannot be hindered nor delayed because Jesus is my Lord, I will pray today and get the desired results, I decree open heavens upon my prayers. I baptize myself in the fire of the Holy Ghost; therefore I have become too hot for the enemy to handle. My prayers today will attract divine intervention to every situation in my life; signs and wonders will follow my prayers today, testimonies will follow my prayers today and the name of God alone will be glorified, in Jesus name. Amen!

PRAYER POINTS:

1. O God my Father, thank you for being my God, my Father and my friend.
2. O God my Father, thank you for the privilege to know you and the power of the resurrection of Jesus Christ.
3. O God my Father, thank you for always being there for me and with me.
4. O God my Father, thank you for the great and mighty things that you are doing in my life.
5. O God my Father, thank you for your provision and protection over me and my household.
6. O God my Father, thank you for always answering my prayers.
7. I confess my sins before you today and I ask you to forgive me on the basis of your mercy, in the name of Jesus Christ.
8. Wash me clean today O Lord by the blood of Jesus Christ.
9. I cover myself and my household with the blood of Jesus Christ.

10. My prayers today will not go in vain; my prayers will produce the desired results in the name of Jesus Christ.
11. No matter what is going on presently in my life, before the end of this year, I will experience success.
12. No matter what is going on presently in my life, before the end of this year I will experience victory.
13. No matter what is going on in my life right now, before the end of this year, I will experience financial freedom.
14. No matter what is going on in my life right now, before the end of this year, I will experience joy to the fullest.
15. I will experience abundance.
16. Today I command all my lost blessings to come back to me
17. I command my lost opportunities to come back to me
18. I command my lost miracles to come back to me.
19. O God my Father, dispatch your angels to locate my helpers today, and let them come back to me.
20. No matter what is going on in my life right now, from this moment, I will experience uncommon favor.
21. No matter what is going on right now in my life, from this moment, I will experience unusual breakthroughs.
22. No matter what is going on in my life right now, from this moment, I will experience the mighty move of God.
23. No matter what is going in my life right now, from this moment, I will experience a great turn around in every area of my life.
24. No matter what the doctors are saying concerning my health, from this moment, I will experience divine healing in every area of my body.

LET MY BLESSINGS COME TO ME

Passages To Read Before You Pray:
Genesis 49:25-26, Genesis 12:1-3, Deuteronomy 16:15, Isaiah 60:1-22, Psalms 78, 115, 42.

I have come today to fellowship with my heavenly Father, and make my requests and needs known unto Him. I cannot be hindered nor delayed because I know who I am in the Lord. I am a child of the Kingdom, born of the Spirit, redeemed by the blood of Jesus Christ. I walk in authority, living life without any apology because the power and authority has been given to me according to the Word of God in the book of Luke 9:1.

As I have come to pray today and to fellowship with my heavenly Father, I cover myself in the blood of Jesus Christ, and I put on the whole armor of God. I hereby come against every Prince of Persia that wants to hinder my prayer, I arrest you by the power in the blood of Jesus Christ, and I bind you and cast you down into the pit of hell.

I come against principalities and powers that wrestle with me and my prayers, I arrest you today by the power in the name of Jesus Christ, and I bind you and cast down into the pit of hell. I come against the rulers of the darkness of this world, against spiritual wickedness in high places, I arrest you all by the power in the name of Jesus Christ, and I bind you and cast you down into the pit of hell. I come against weakness and weariness, I arrest you today by the power in the name of Jesus Christ, and I bind you and cast you out of my life. I come against wondering

spirit and distractions, I arrest you today by the power in the name of Jesus Christ, and I bind you and cast you out of my life.

Today I receive the anointing to pray and get results, my prayers cannot be hindered nor delayed because Jesus is my Lord, I will pray today and get the desired results, I decree open heavens upon my prayers. I baptize myself in the fire of the Holy Ghost; therefore I have become too hot for the enemy to handle. My prayers today will attract divine intervention to every situation in my life; signs and wonders will follow my prayers today, testimonies will follow my prayers today and the name of God alone will be glorified, in Jesus name. Amen!

PRAYER POINTS:

1. O God my Father, thank you for being my God, my Father and my friend.
2. O God my Father, thank you for the privilege to know you and the power of the resurrection of Jesus Christ.
3. O God my Father, thank you for always being there for me and with me.
4. O God my Father, thank you for the great and mighty things that you are doing in my life.
5. O God my Father, thank you for your provision and protection over me and my household.
6. O God my Father, thank you for always answering my prayers.
7. I confess my sins before you today and I ask you to forgive me on the basis of your mercy, in the name of Jesus Christ.

8. Wash me clean today O Lord by the blood of Jesus Christ.
9. I cover myself and my household with the blood of Jesus Christ.
10. My prayers today will not go in vain; my prayers will produce the desired results in the name of Jesus Christ.

11. My blessings for this year that I am yet to receive, come to me now by the power in the name of Jesus Christ.
12. O God my Father, I refuse to let go of the blessing that you have prepared for me.
13. O God my Father, let the blessings of heaven above be released unto me according to your Word.
14. O God my Father, let the blessings of the deep beneath be released unto me now according to your Word.
15. O God my Father, let the blessings of the womb be released unto me now according to your Word.
16. O God my Father, let the blessings of the breast be released unto me now according to your Word.
17. Today O Lord, I claim the covenant of Abraham by faith, let the blessings of this covenant manifest in life from today.
18. Today O Lord, I claim the covenant of Abraham by faith, let the joy of this covenant manifest in my life from today.
19. Today O Lord, I claim the covenant of Abraham by faith, let the prosperity that follows this covenant manifest in my life from today.
20. Today O Lord. I claim the covenant of Abraham by faith, let the abundance that follows this covenant manifest in my life from today.

21. Today O Lord, I claim the covenant of Abraham by faith, let the Shekinah glory upon this covenant rest upon me today.
22. My blessings in the wrong hands, I command you to come to me now by the fire of God.
23. My breakthroughs in the wrong hands, I command you to come to me now by the fire of God.
24. My promotion in the wrong hands, I command you to come to me now by the fire of God.
25. My miracles that have fallen into the wrong hands, I command you to come to me now by the fire of God.
26. My financial breakthrough that is going in the wrong direction, I command you to turn around and come to me now by the fire of God.
27. My rain of blessing that is falling on a strange land, I command you to locate me now by the fire of God.
28. The former and the latter rain of blessing, be released upon me now.
29. My blessings in the hands of the wicked, be released unto me now by the fire of God.
30. My blessings in the hands of the enemy, be released unto me now by the fire of God.
31. My blessings in the hands of unfriendly friends, be released unto me now by the fire of God.
32. My blessings in the hands of jealous friends, be released unto me now by the fire of God.
33. My blessings in the hands of household wickedness, be released unto me now by the fire of God.
34. My blessings in the hands of those who want me to be poor, be released unto me now by the fire of God.
35. My blessings in the hands of those who want to stop it at all cost, be released unto now by the fire of God.

36. My blessings in the hands of those who want to hinder it, be released unto me now by the fire of God.
37. My blessings in the hands of those who want me to suffer, be released unto me now by the fire of God.
38. My blessings in the hands of those that don't know it's value, be released unto me now by the fire of God.
39. All my blessings, wherever you are, find your way to locate me now.
40. My breakthroughs, wherever you are, find your way to locate me now.
41. My miracles, wherever you are, find your way to locate me now.
42. My success, wherever you are, find your way to locate me now.
43. My divine helpers, wherever you are, find your way to locate me now.
44. Today O Lord, I claim all my stolen blessings back by force.
45. Today O Lord, I claim all my stolen miracles back by force.
46. Bless me today O Lord, with a blessing that has no sorrow in it.
47. O God my Father, let the abundance of your blessing be released upon me.
48. O God my Father, let the abundance of your blessing be released upon my family.
49. O God my Father, let the abundance of your blessing be released upon the works of my hands.
50. O God my Father, let the abundance of your blessing be released upon my business.
51. O God my Father, let the abundance of your blessing be released upon my spouse.

52. O God my Father, let the abundance of your blessing be released upon my children.
53. O God my Father, let the abundance of your blessing be released upon my finances.
54. O God my Father, let my stolen blessings begin to cause trouble in the camp of my enemy until they return it back to me.
55. O God my Father, let my stolen breakthroughs begin to cause trouble in the camp of my enemy until they return it back to me.
56. O God my Father, let your blessings be multiplied upon my life.
57. O God my Father, bless me when I go out and when I come in.
58. O God my Father, let everyone around me blessed because of me.
59. O God my Father, let my family be blessed because of me.
60. O God my Father, let my true friends be blessed because of me.
61. O God my Father, let my spouse be blessed because of me.
62. O God my Father, let my children be blessed because of me.
63. O God my Father, let all my neighbors be blessed I live in the neighborhood.
64. O God my Father, let my coworkers be blessed because they work with me.
65. O God my Father, let this city be blessed because I live here.
66. As from today, anything I touch shall be blessed.

67. As from today, anyone that crosses my path shall be blessed.
68. The works of my hands are blessed.
69. The fruit of my womb / loins is blessed.
70. The source of my income is blessed.
71. My business is blessed.
72. My future is blessed.
73. The future of my spouse is blessed.
74. The future of my children is blessed.
75. My ministry is blessed.
76. O God my Father, let my church be blessed because I fellowship there.
77. O God my Father, let my church members be blessed because of me.
78. I shall be a blessing to this generation and generations to come.
79. I shall be blessed enough to leave an inheritance for me children and their children.
80. I shall be blessed enough to be a blessing to everyone around me.
81. I shall be blessed enough that anyone that comes to me crying shall leave happy and smiling.
82. I shall be blessed enough that anyone that comes to me hopeless shall leave hopeful and blessed.
83. I shall be blessed enough that anyone that comes to me with nothing shall leave with abundance.
84. I shall be blessed enough that anyone that comes to me hungry shall go back satisfied.
85. I shall be blessed enough who has lost everything that comes to me shall go back restored.
86. I shall be blessed enough that anyone who comes to me for help will not go back disappointed.

87. I shall be blessed enough to be a source of inspiration to others.
88. I shall be blessed enough to be a beacon of hope in the life of the rejects.
89. O God my Father, let your blessings upon my life be a tool to bring unbelievers to the kingdom.
90. Today, I receive the blessings of God that make rich and add no sorrow to it.
91. As from today O Lord, let everyone around me call me the blessed of The Lord.

PRAYER TO POSSESS YOUR THRONE

Passages To Read Before You Pray:
Revelation 5:10, 1 Peter 2:9, Genesis 37:5-11, Daniel 6:1-28,
Exodus 3:7-10, Psalms 3, 30, 68, 79, 80

I have come today to fellowship with my heavenly Father, and make my requests and needs known unto Him. I cannot be hindered nor delayed because I know who I am in the Lord. I am a child of the Kingdom, born of the Spirit, redeemed by the blood of Jesus Christ. I walk in authority, living life without any apology because the power and authority has been given to me according to the Word of God in the book of Luke 9:1.

As I have come to pray today and to fellowship with my heavenly Father, I cover myself in the blood of Jesus Christ, and I put on the whole armor of God. I hereby come against every Prince of Persia that wants to hinder my prayer, I arrest you by the power in the blood of Jesus Christ, and I bind you and cast you down into the pit of hell.

I come against principalities and powers that wrestle with me and my prayers, I arrest you today by the power in the name of Jesus Christ, and I bind you and cast down into the pit of hell. I come against the rulers of the darkness of this world, against spiritual wickedness in high places, I arrest you all by the power in the name of Jesus Christ, and I bind you and cast you down into the pit of hell. I come against weakness and weariness, I arrest you today by the power in the name of Jesus Christ, and I bind you and cast you out of my life. I come against wondering

spirit and distractions, I arrest you today by the power in the name of Jesus Christ, and I bind you and cast you out of my life.

Today I receive the anointing to pray and get results, my prayers cannot be hindered nor delayed because Jesus is my Lord, I will pray today and get the desired results, I decree open heavens upon my prayers. I baptize myself in the fire of the Holy Ghost; therefore I have become too hot for the enemy to handle. My prayers today will attract divine intervention to every situation in my life; signs and wonders will follow my prayers today, testimonies will follow my prayers today and the name of God alone will be glorified, in Jesus name. Amen!

PRAYER POINTS:

1. O God my Father, thank you for being my God, my Father and my friend.
2. O God my Father, thank you for the privilege to know you and the power of the resurrection of Jesus Christ.
3. O God my Father, thank you for always being there for me and with me.
4. O God my Father, thank you for the great and mighty things that you are doing in my life.
5. O God my Father, thank you for your provision and protection over me and my household.
6. O God my Father, thank you for always answering my prayers.
7. I confess my sins before you today and I ask you to forgive me on the basis of your mercy, in the name of Jesus Christ.

8. Wash me clean today O Lord by the blood of Jesus Christ.
9. I cover myself and my household with the blood of Jesus Christ.
10. My prayers today will not go in vain; my prayers will produce the desired results in the name of Jesus Christ.
11. Whatever needs to happen that will lead me to the throne, let it begin to happen now. (Gen. 37:18-20)
12. O God my Father, let my household wickedness planning to sell me into slavery ignorantly cooperate with your plan for my life.
13. O God my Father, transfer me today by your power to the land you have prepare for me to rule and reign as king.
14. O God my Father, rescue today me from the hands of my household wickedness that want to kill my dreams.
15. O God my Father, separate me today from the people that are not part of your plan for my life.
16. O God my Father, deliver me today from any form of slavery.
17. O God my Father, I don't belong in this situation, deliver me today by your power.
18. I have served my time in slavery, O God arise and deliver me today.
19. Let my cry come to your presence today O Lord, send my Moses to rescue me from the bondage of Egypt.
20. I refuse to get used to my bondage.
21. Today O Lord, make a way for me out of this dungeon of poverty.
22. Today O Lord, make a way for me out of this dungeon of hopelessness.

23. Today O Lord, make a way for me out of this dungeon and let every satanic animal assigned against me be destroyed by your fire.
24. Today O Lord, make a way for me out of this dungeon and let every assigned agent sent to destroy my dreams be destroyed by your power.
25. Today O Lord, make a way for me out of this dungeon and let every unfriendly friend working against be put to an open shame.
26. Today O Lord, make a way for me out of this dungeon, I desire to possess my throne.
27. O God my Father, grant me unusual favor in the sight of God and man.
28. Today O Lord, let my taskmaster go the extra mile to help me.
29. O God my Father, let there be confusion in the camp of my enemies that will lead to my deliverance.
30. O God my Father, let there be confusion in the camp of my enemies that will accelerate my journey to the throne.
31. O God my Father, let there be confusion in the camp of my enemies that will lead to the fulfillment of your promises in my life.
32. I shall receive favor in the sight of man and woman.
33. Today I shall receive favor from the sight of old and young.
34. Today I shall receive favor in the sight of the people that I know and people that I don't know.
35. Today O Lord, crown me with your favor and clothe me with your goodness.
36. Today O Lord, let your favor go before me to speak on my behalf.

37. By the power in the name of Jesus Christ, today I possess my possessions.
38. By the power in the name of Jesus Christ, today I possess my throne.
39. By the power in the name of Jesus Christ, today I possess my financial freedom.
40. Today by the power in the name of Jesus Christ, I possess all that belong to me.
41. Today by the power in the name of Jesus Christ, I possess my freedom from any form of bondage.
42. Today is the day, I am getting out of this bondage.
43. Today is the day, I am getting off this stubborn situation.
44. Today is the day, I claim my throne by force.
45. Today is the day, I claim my promotion by force.
46. Today is the day, I claim my healing by force.
47. Today is the day, I claim my prosperity by force.
48. Today is the day, I claim my breakthroughs by force.
49. Today is the day, I claim my joy by force.
50. As from today O Lord, let every decision made anywhere work to my favor.
51. O God my Father, give me the wisdom needed to ascend to my throne.
52. O God my Father, give me knowledge and understanding needed to ascend to my throne.
53. Anybody anywhere vowing that I will not make it to my promise land, you will witness my testimonies.
54. Anybody anywhere vowing that I will not be crowned, you will witness my coronation.
55. Anybody anywhere that wants me to die in bondage, you will perish with Pharaoh in the Red Sea.
56. Anybody anywhere that refuse to let me go, I command you to loose your hold upon my life now.

57. Anybody anywhere seducing me in order to rob me of my glory, you will not escape the judgment of God.
58. Anybody anywhere that wants me to die in Potiphar's house, you will witness my coronation.
59. Anybody anywhere that wants me to remain a local champion, you will witness my coronation.
60. Today I have come to claim my crown by force.
61. Today I have come to claim my throne by force.
62. Today I have come to my authority and power by force.
63. Today I have come to claim my rights as the child of the King of kings.
64. Today I have come to claim my rights as the child of the Kingdom.
65. I refuse to lose my throne to another man.
66. I refuse to lose my throne to the enemy.
67. Everyone around me shall witness my coronation and rejoice with me.
68. Any power anywhere that wants me to lose my crown, you will not escape the judgment of God.
69. Any power anywhere that wants me to lose my throne, you will not escape the judgment of God.
70. Any power anywhere that wants to take away my rights, you will not escape the judgment of God.
71. Any power anywhere doing everything to stop my coronation, you will live to witness it.
72. Every conspiracy to take away my crown, scatter by the fire of God.
73. Every conspiracy to take away my throne, scatter by the fire of God.
74. Every conspiracy to stop me from moving up in life, scatter by the fire of God.

75. Every conspiracy to use the authority and power of the land against me, scatter by the fire of God.
76. Every satanic gang up against me, scatter by the fire of God.
77. Every evil collaboration working against me, scatter by the fire of God.
78. Whether my enemies like it or not, I possess my throne today.
79. Whether my enemies like it or not, I possess my crown today.
80. Whether my enemies like it or not, today I possess what belong to me.
81. Today I receive grace and power of God to ascend to the throne prepared for me.
82. Anybody anywhere presently occupying my throne, I dethrone you today.
83. Anybody anywhere presently wearing my crown, today I take my crown back by force.
84. Anybody anywhere presently occupying my promise land, I relocate you today by force.
85. Anybody anywhere presently occupying my position of authority, I remove you today by force.
86. Anybody anywhere presently occupying my position of promotion, I remove you today by force.

DIVINE RELOCATION

Passages To Read Before You Pray:
Isaiah 40:28-31, Exodus 3:7-8, 2 Kings 2:19-22, Psalms 29, 46, 103

I have come today to fellowship with my heavenly Father, and make my requests and needs known unto Him. I cannot be hindered nor delayed because I know who I am in the Lord. I am a child of the Kingdom, born of the Spirit, redeemed by the blood of Jesus Christ. I walk in authority, living life without any apology because the power and authority has been given to me according to the Word of God in the book of Luke 9:1.

As I have come to pray today and to fellowship with my heavenly Father, I cover myself in the blood of Jesus Christ, and I put on the whole armor of God. I hereby come against every Prince of Persia that wants to hinder my prayer, I arrest you by the power in the blood of Jesus Christ, and I bind you and cast you down into the pit of hell.

I come against principalities and powers that wrestle with me and my prayers, I arrest you today by the power in the name of Jesus Christ, and I bind you and cast down into the pit of hell. I come against the rulers of the darkness of this world, against spiritual wickedness in high places, I arrest you all by the power in the name of Jesus Christ, and I bind you and cast you down into the pit of hell. I come against weakness and weariness, I arrest you today by the power in the name of Jesus Christ, and I bind you and cast you out of my life. I come against wondering

spirit and distractions, I arrest you today by the power in the name of Jesus Christ, and I bind you and cast you out of my life.

Today I receive the anointing to pray and get results, my prayers cannot be hindered nor delayed because Jesus is my Lord, I will pray today and get the desired results, I decree open heavens upon my prayers. I baptize myself in the fire of the Holy Ghost; therefore I have become too hot for the enemy to handle. My prayers today will attract divine intervention to every situation in my life; signs and wonders will follow my prayers today, testimonies will follow my prayers today and the name of God alone will be glorified, in Jesus name. Amen!

PRAYER POINTS:

1. O God my Father, thank you for being my God, my Father and my friend.
2. O God my Father, thank you for the privilege to know you and the power of the resurrection of Jesus Christ.
3. O God my Father, thank you for always being there for me and with me.
4. O God my Father, thank you for the great and mighty things that you are doing in my life.
5. O God my Father, thank you for your provision and protection over me and my household.
6. O God my Father, thank you for always answering my prayers.
7. I confess my sins before you today and I ask you to forgive me on the basis of your mercy, in the name of Jesus Christ.

8. Wash me clean today O Lord by the blood of Jesus Christ.
9. I cover myself and my household with the blood of Jesus Christ.
10. My prayers today will not go in vain; my prayers will produce the desired results in the name of Jesus Christ.
11. No matter the situation around me, prayer will work for me.
12. I cover myself and my household in the blood of Jesus Christ.
13. Today O Lord, let there be divine intervention in every area of my life.
14. Today O Lord, arise in your power, fight my battle and give me the victory.
15. My prayers today shall cause signs and wonders to happen in my life.
16. My prayers today shall bring testimonies.
17. Miracles will happen in my life today before the end of this prayer session.
18. Deliverance will take place in my life today before the end of this prayer.
19. Today I relocate by the power of God, from Egypt to Canaan.
20. Today I relocate by the power of God from slavery to my promise land.
21. Today I relocate by the power of God from poverty close to riches avenue.
22. Today I relocate by the power of God from the valley to the mountain top.
23. Today I relocate by the power of God from failure drive to success-boulevard.

24. Today I relocate by the power of God from where I am to where you want me to be.
25. Today I relocate by the power of God from the land of bondage to a land flowing with milk and honey.
26. Today I relocate by the power of God from a desert land to a fertile land flowing with milk and honey.
27. O God my Father, heal my life from the foundation as Elisha did in the city of Jericho.
28. O God my Father, heal my marriage from the foundation as Elisha did in the city of Jericho.
29. Today O Lord, break every curse upon my life from the foundation.
30. Today I nullify every evil pronouncement release upon my life.
31. O God my Father, there is power in your voice, speak solution to my situation today.
32. O God my Father, there is power in your voice, speak breakthrough to every mediocrity of my life.
33. O God my Father, there is power in your voice, speak riches and wealth to my life and let poverty disappear.
34. O God my Father, there is power in your voice, speak healing into my body and let every seed of sickness disappear.
35. O God my Father, there is deliverance in your voice, speak deliverance into my life and let every chain holding me down break into unrepairable pieces.
36. O God my Father, there is deliverance in your voice, speak deliverance into my life and rescue me from the pit of hopelessness.
37. O God my Father, there is deliverance in your voice, speak deliverance into my life and rescue me from the bondage of witchcraft.

38. O God my Father, there is deliverance in your voice, speak deliverance into my life and rescue me from the bondage of household wickedness.
39. O God my Father, there is deliverance in your voice, speak deliverance into my life and break every ancestral curse upon my life.
40. O God my Father, there is deliverance in your voice, speak deliverance into my life and let obstacles in my way be destroyed.
41. O God my Father, there is deliverance in your voice, speak deliverance into my life and let every roadblock in my way be destroyed.
42. O God my Father, there is deliverance in your voice, speak deliverance into my life and let impossibilities be possible for me.
43. O God my Father, there is power in your voice, let the power in your voice drive away my fear.
44. O God my Father, let the power in your voice take away my shame.
45. Today O Lord, deliver me by your power from any form of affliction.
46. Today O Lord, deliver me by your power from any form of oppression.
47. Today O Lord, deliver me by your power from any stage of depression.
48. Today O Lord, deliver me by your power from the hands my taskmaster.
49. Today O Lord, deliver me by your power from the hands of my household pharaoh.

PRAYER TO CALM THE STORM OF LIFE

Passages To Read Before You Pray:
Mark 4:35-41, Psalms 29, 44, 114, 103

I have come today to fellowship with my heavenly Father, and make my requests and needs known unto Him. I cannot be hindered nor delayed because I know who I am in the Lord. I am a child of the Kingdom, born of the Spirit, redeemed by the blood of Jesus Christ. I walk in authority, living life without any apology because the power and authority has been given to me according to the Word of God in the book of Luke 9:1.

As I have come to pray today and to fellowship with my heavenly Father, I cover myself in the blood of Jesus Christ, and I put on the whole armor of God. I hereby come against every Prince of Persia that wants to hinder my prayer, I arrest you by the power in the blood of Jesus Christ, and I bind you and cast you down into the pit of hell.

I come against principalities and powers that wrestle with me and my prayers, I arrest you today by the power in the name of Jesus Christ, and I bind you and cast down into the pit of hell. I come against the rulers of the darkness of this world, against spiritual wickedness in high places, I arrest you all by the power in the name of Jesus Christ, and I bind you and cast you down into the pit of hell. I come against weakness and weariness, I arrest you today by the power in the name of Jesus Christ, and I bind you and cast you out of my life. I come against wondering spirit and distractions, I arrest you today by the power in the name of Jesus Christ, and I bind you and cast you out of my life.

Today I receive the anointing to pray and get results, my prayers cannot be hindered nor delayed because Jesus is my Lord, I will pray today and get the desired results, I decree open heavens upon my prayers. I baptize myself in the fire of the Holy Ghost; therefore I have become too hot for the enemy to handle. My prayers today will attract divine intervention to every situation in my life; signs and wonders will follow my prayers today, testimonies will follow my prayers today and the name of God alone will be glorified, in Jesus name. Amen!

PRAYER POINTS:

1. O God my Father, thank you for being my God, my Father and my friend.
2. O God my Father, thank you for the privilege to know you and the power of the resurrection of Jesus Christ.
3. O God my Father, thank you for always being there for me and with me.
4. O God my Father, thank you for the great and mighty things that you are doing in my life.
5. O God my Father, thank you for your provision and protection over me and my household.
6. O God my Father, thank you for always answering my prayers.
7. I confess my sins before you today and I ask you to forgive me on the basis of your mercy, in the name of Jesus Christ.
8. Wash me clean today O Lord by the blood of Jesus Christ.
9. I cover myself and my household with the blood of Jesus Christ.

10. My prayers today will not go in vain; my prayers will produce the desired results in the name of Jesus Christ.
11. By the power in the name of Jesus, I am crossing over to my promise land.
12. By the power in the name of Jesus, I am crossing over the Red Sea of my life.
13. Today I command the Red Sea of my life to give way for me to cross over.
14. Today O Lord, let the blast of your nostril make a way for me in the Red Sea, that I may cross over.
15. Every Pharaoh that wants to hold me back, I command you to perish in the Red Sea.
16. Egyptian army that wants to stop me at all cost, I command you to perish in the Red Sea.
17. Every Red Sea situation in my life, hear the voice of God tonight and give way for me to cross over.
18. I refuse to stay in Egypt, I am moving forward to my promise land.
19. By the power in the name of Jesus, today I am crossing over river Jordan into my promise land.
20. Today O Lord, let your angels that bear the Ark of God step into river Jordan to make a way for me.
21. You river Jordan of my life, I command you to be driven back by the power in the name of Jesus Christ.
22. No matter the plan of the enemy, I am crossing over today.
23. No matter the activity of the wicked, I am crossing over today.
24. No matter the situation or circumstance, I am crossing over today.

25. Arise O Lord and rebuke every storm that wants to destroy my life.
26. O Lord arise and rebuke every storm that wants to hinder what you are doing in my life.
27. Every satanic storm that wants to drown me in the ocean of life, I rebuke you today.
28. Every satanic storm sent to scatter what I have gathered, I rebuke you today in the name of Jesus Christ.
29. Every satanic storm sent to trouble my life, I rebuke you today in the name of Jesus Christ.
30. Every satanic storm sent to frustrate my life, I rebuke you today in the name of Jesus Christ.
31. Every satanic storm sent to delay my progress, I rebuke you today in the name of Jesus Christ.
32. Every satanic storm sent to hinder my prayers, I rebuke you today in the name of Jesus Christ.
33. Every satanic storm sent to stop my progress, I rebuke you today in the name of Jesus Christ.
34. Every satanic storm sent to challenge my faith in God, I rebuke you today in the name of Jesus Christ.
35. Every satanic storm sent to confuse me when I am ready to make important decisions, I rebuke you today in the name of Jesus Christ.
36. Every satanic storm sent to make my God a liar, I rebuke you today in the name of Jesus Christ.
37. Arise O Lord and rebuke the evil wind that is working against me.
38. Arise O Lord and rebuke the evil wind that is working against my family.
39. Arise O Lord and rebuke the evil wind that is working against my spouse.

40. Arise O Lord and rebuke the evil wind that is working against my children.
41. Arise O Lord and rebuke the evil wind that is working against my finances.
42. Arise O Lord and rebuke the evil wind that is working against my joy.
43. Arise O Lord and rebuke the evil wind that is working against my success.
44. Arise O Lord and rebuke the evil wind that is working against your plan for my life.
45. Arise O Lord and rebuke the evil wind that is working against my destiny.
46. I speak peace be still to every storm of my life.
47. I speak peace be still to every contrary wind working against me.
48. I speak peace be still to every storm confronting my marriage.
49. I speak peace be still to every turbulent situation in my life.
50. I speak peace be still to every unpleasant situation in my life.
51. I command every storm of my life to hear the voice of the Living God and vanish.
52. I command every storm confronting my family to hear the voice of The Lord and vanish.
53. I command every storm confronting my finances to hear the voice of The Lord and vanish.
54. I command every strong wind sent by the enemy to hear the voice of The Lord and vanish.
55. O God my Father, let your power swallow every satanic storm sent against me.

56. O God my Father, let your power swallow every contrary wind sent to scatter what I have gathered.
57. O God my Father, let every contrary wind sent to destroy me bring positive change into every area of my life.
58. Arise today O Lord and rearrange my life for a complete turnaround.
59. Arise today O Lord and rearrange my life for a total deliverance.
60. Arise today O Lord and rearrange my life for uncommon breakthroughs.
61. Arise today O Lord and rearrange my life for double promotion.
62. Arise today O Lord and rearrange my life for uncommon favor.
63. Arise today O Lord and rearrange my life for undeniable success.
64. Arise today O Lord and rearrange my life for unusual progress.
65. Arise today O Lord and rearrange my life for unbelievable miracles.
66. Arise today O Lord and rearrange my life for financial breakthroughs.
67. Arise today O Lord and rearrange my life for the fulfillment of your promises.
68. Arise today O Lord and rearrange my life for favorable surprises.
69. Arise today O Lord and take my life to the next level that you have prepared for me.
70. Arise today O Lord and showcase your power in my life.

FOR GOD NOTHING IS IMPOSSIBLE

Passages To Read Before You Pray:
Matthew 19:26, Luke 1:37, Psalms 44, 46, 103, 105, 107

I have come today to fellowship with my heavenly Father, and make my requests and needs known unto Him. I cannot be hindered nor delayed because I know who I am in the Lord. I am a child of the Kingdom, born of the Spirit, redeemed by the blood of Jesus Christ. I walk in authority, living life without any apology because the power and authority has been given to me according to the Word of God in the book of Luke 9:1.

As I have come to pray today and to fellowship with my heavenly Father, I cover myself in the blood of Jesus Christ, and I put on the whole armor of God. I hereby come against every Prince of Persia that wants to hinder my prayer, I arrest you by the power in the blood of Jesus Christ, and I bind you and cast you down into the pit of hell.

I come against principalities and powers that wrestle with me and my prayers, I arrest you today by the power in the name of Jesus Christ, and I bind you and cast down into the pit of hell. I come against the rulers of the darkness of this world, against spiritual wickedness in high places, I arrest you all by the power in the name of Jesus Christ, and I bind you and cast you down into the pit of hell. I come against weakness and weariness, I arrest you today by the power in the name of Jesus Christ, and I bind you and cast you out of my life. I come against wondering spirit and distractions, I arrest you today by the power in the name of Jesus Christ, and I bind you and cast you out of my life.

Today I receive the anointing to pray and get results, my prayers cannot be hindered nor delayed because Jesus is my Lord, I will pray today and get the desired results, I decree open heavens upon my prayers. I baptize myself in the fire of the Holy Ghost; therefore I have become too hot for the enemy to handle. My prayers today will attract divine intervention to every situation in my life; signs and wonders will follow my prayers today, testimonies will follow my prayers today and the name of God alone will be glorified, in Jesus name. Amen!

PRAYER POINTS:

1. O God my Father, thank you for being my God, my Father and my friend.
2. O God my Father, thank you for the privilege to know you and the power of the resurrection of Jesus Christ.
3. O God my Father, thank you for always being there for me and with me.
4. O God my Father, thank you for the great and mighty things that you are doing in my life.
5. O God my Father, thank you for your provision and protection over me and my household.
6. O God my Father, thank you for always answering my prayers.
7. I confess my sins before you today and I ask you to forgive me on the basis of your mercy, in the name of Jesus Christ.
8. Wash me clean today O Lord by the blood of Jesus Christ.
9. I cover myself and my household with the blood of Jesus Christ.

10. My prayers today will not go in vain; my prayers will produce the desired results in the name of Jesus Christ.
11. O God my Father, as you did unto Hannah, hear my cry today and change my story.
12. O God my Father, as you did unto Hannah, let there be a miracle in my life that will silence my enemies.
13. O God my Father, the problem that has been tormenting me year after year must come to an end today.
14. O God my Father, the problem that has been causing me to cry must come to an end today.
15. O God my Father, that ridiculous situation in my life must come to an end today.
16. Today O Lord, let my problems push me into solution.
17. Today O Lord, let my enemies force me to seek your face.
18. Today O Lord, let my affliction turn to celebration.
19. O God my Father, let the point of ridicule in my life become the source of miracle.
20. O God my Father, do something special in my life today that will bring me back to testify in your presence.
21. With you O Lord nothing is impossible, let my situation become a testimony.
22. With you O Lord nothing is impossible, showcase your power in my life today.
23. With you O Lord nothing is impossible, let new things begin to manifest in my life now.
24. With you O Lord nothing is impossible, deliver me today from this hopeless situation.
25. With you O Lord nothing is impossible, deliver me today from collective captivity.

26. With you O Lord nothing is impossible, let my greatest fear turn to joy and testimony.
27. With you O Lord nothing is impossible, let my cry turn to laughter.
28. With you O Lord nothing is impossible, let my failure turn to success.
29. With you O Lord nothing is impossible, let every delay in my way disappear at the mention of the name of Jesus Christ.
30. With you O Lord nothing is impossible, let solution to my stubborn situations come sooner than expected.
31. With you O Lord nothing is impossible, let my miracles come sooner than expected.
32. With you O Lord nothing is impossible, let my breakthroughs come sooner than expected.
33. With you O Lord nothing is impossible, let my deliverance come sooner than expected.
34. With you O Lord nothing is impossible, let every chain that ties me down break that I may live a fulfilling life.
35. With you O Lord nothing is impossible, let there be restoration in every area of my life.

PRAYER FOR UNCOMMON BREAKTHROUGH

Passages To Read Before You Pray:
Habakkuk 1:5, Joel 2:21-27, Psalms 19, 29, 30, 75, 78

I have come today to fellowship with my heavenly Father, and make my requests and needs known unto Him. I cannot be hindered nor delayed because I know who I am in the Lord. I am a child of the Kingdom, born of the Spirit, redeemed by the blood of Jesus Christ. I walk in authority, living life without any apology because the power and authority has been given to me according to the Word of God in the book of Luke 9:1.

As I have come to pray today and to fellowship with my heavenly Father, I cover myself in the blood of Jesus Christ, and I put on the whole armor of God. I hereby come against every Prince of Persia that wants to hinder my prayer, I arrest you by the power in the blood of Jesus Christ, and I bind you and cast you down into the pit of hell.

I come against principalities and powers that wrestle with me and my prayers, I arrest you today by the power in the name of Jesus Christ, and I bind you and cast down into the pit of hell. I come against the rulers of the darkness of this world, against spiritual wickedness in high places, I arrest you all by the power in the name of Jesus Christ, and I bind you and cast you down into the pit of hell. I come against weakness and weariness, I arrest you today by the power in the name of Jesus Christ, and I bind you and cast you out of my life. I come against wondering

spirit and distractions, I arrest you today by the power in the name of Jesus Christ, and I bind you and cast you out of my life.

Today I receive the anointing to pray and get results, my prayers cannot be hindered nor delayed because Jesus is my Lord, I will pray today and get the desired results, I decree open heavens upon my prayers. I baptize myself in the fire of the Holy Ghost; therefore I have become too hot for the enemy to handle. My prayers today will attract divine intervention to every situation in my life; signs and wonders will follow my prayers today, testimonies will follow my prayers today and the name of God alone will be glorified, in Jesus name. Amen!

PRAYER POINTS:

1. O God my Father, thank you for being my God, my Father and my friend.
2. O God my Father, thank you for the privilege to know you and the power of the resurrection of Jesus Christ.
3. O God my Father, thank you for always being there for me and with me.
4. O God my Father, thank you for the great and mighty things that you are doing in my life.
5. O God my Father, thank you for your provision and protection over me and my household.
6. O God my Father, thank you for always answering my prayers.
7. I confess my sins before you today and I ask you to forgive me on the basis of your mercy, in the name of Jesus Christ.

8. Wash me clean today O Lord by the blood of Jesus Christ.
9. I cover myself and my household with the blood of Jesus Christ.
10. My prayers today will not go in vain; my prayers will produce the desired results in the name of Jesus Christ.

11. Father, guide and direct me to rectify any problems I have with my business.
12. Every strongman of my father's House, die, in the name of Jesus
13. Let the backbone of the stubborn pursuer and strongman break, in the name of Jesus.
14. I clear my goods from the warehouse of the strongman, in the name of Jesus.
15. I bind every strongman delegated to hinder my progress, in the name of Jesus.
16. I bind the strongman behind my spiritual blindness and deafness and paralyze his operations in my life, in the name of Jesus.
17. Every inherited covenant affecting my life, break and release me, in the name of Jesus
18. Any covenant prospering in my family, be broken by the blood of Jesus.
19. Let my stubborn enemy wake up with confusion, in the name of Jesus.
20. I scatter any wicked meeting designed against my destiny, scatter, in the name of Jesus.
21. Any serpent assigned to swallow my destiny, die, in the name of Jesus.
22. I receive uncommon wisdom to excel, in the name of Jesus

23. Every gang-up against my peace, scatter, in the name of Jesus
24. Every program of failure against my destiny, scatter, in the name of Jesus.
25. Lord, grant me unquestionable victory, in the name of Jesus.
26. My Father, accelerate my speed and close the gap between where I am and where I should be, in the name of Jesus.
27. Every power assigned to put off my light, receive confusion, in the name of Jesus.
28. All destiny robbers, bow, in the name of Jesus.
29. Every evil eye monitoring my destiny, go blind by fire, in the name of Jesus.
30. Every curse or covenant bearing my name in the heavenlies, break, in the name of Jesus.
31. My Father, deliver me from the power of the lions, in the name of Jesus.
32. Every Python assigned to squeeze out my prayer life, die, in the name of Jesus.
33. All foxes assigned to destroy my life, be destroyed, in the name of Jesus.
34. My Father, let me dip my feet in your oil, in the name of Jesus.
35. My Father, let my teeth be white with milk, in the name of Jesus.
36. My Father, wash my steps with butter, in the name of Jesus.
37. I break all curses of premature death, in the name of Jesus.
38. O God, recover every dart from my liver, in the name of Jesus.

39. Any sickness assigned to eat my flesh, die, in the name of Jesus.
40. Every tumor and any evil growth, melt away by the power in the blood of Jesus.
41. Any infection in my body, receive the fire of God and burn to ashes, in the name of Jesus.
42. I rebuke all Foxes against my prosperity, in the name of Jesus.
43. O God, surround my life with songs of deliverance, in the name of Jesus.
44. O Lord, let your angels ascend and descend upon my life, in the name of Jesus.
45. I loose my neck from satanic bands in the name of Jesus.
46. Make haste oh Lord, deliver me in the name of Jesus.
47. Every germ of sickness that touches my body, die, in the name of Jesus.
48. O Lord, give me a sound heart, in the name of Jesus.
49. Power of evil pain, die in the name of Jesus.

NEVER AGAIN

Passages To Read Before You Pray:
Exodus 13:1-14, Psalms 18, 3, 9, 109, 35

I have come today to fellowship with my heavenly Father, and make my requests and needs known unto Him. I cannot be hindered nor delayed because I know who I am in the Lord. I am a child of the Kingdom, born of the Spirit, redeemed by the blood of Jesus Christ. I walk in authority, living life without any apology because the power and authority has been given to me according to the Word of God in the book of Luke 9:1.

As I have come to pray today and to fellowship with my heavenly Father, I cover myself in the blood of Jesus Christ, and I put on the whole armor of God. I hereby come against every Prince of Persia that wants to hinder my prayer, I arrest you by the power in the blood of Jesus Christ, and I bind you and cast you down into the pit of hell.

I come against principalities and powers that wrestle with me and my prayers, I arrest you today by the power in the name of Jesus Christ, and I bind you and cast down into the pit of hell. I come against the rulers of the darkness of this world, against spiritual wickedness in high places, I arrest you all by the power in the name of Jesus Christ, and I bind you and cast you down into the pit of hell. I come against weakness and weariness, I arrest you today by the power in the name of Jesus Christ, and I bind you and cast you out of my life. I come against wondering spirit and distractions, I arrest you today by the power in the name of Jesus Christ, and I bind you and cast you out of my life.

Today I receive the anointing to pray and get results, my prayers cannot be hindered nor delayed because Jesus is my Lord, I will pray today and get the desired results, I decree open heavens upon my prayers. I baptize myself in the fire of the Holy Ghost; therefore I have become too hot for the enemy to handle. My prayers today will attract divine intervention to every situation in my life; signs and wonders will follow my prayers today, testimonies will follow my prayers today and the name of God alone will be glorified, in Jesus name. Amen!

PRAYER POINTS:

1. O God my Father, thank you for being my God, my Father and my friend.
2. O God my Father, thank you for the privilege to know you and the power of the resurrection of Jesus Christ.
3. O God my Father, thank you for always being there for me and with me.
4. O God my Father, thank you for the great and mighty things that you are doing in my life.
5. O God my Father, thank you for your provision and protection over me and my household.
6. O God my Father, thank you for always answering my prayers.
7. I confess my sins before you today and I ask you to forgive me on the basis of your mercy, in the name of Jesus Christ.
8. Wash me clean today O Lord by the blood of Jesus Christ.
9. I cover myself and my household with the blood of Jesus Christ.

10. My prayers today will not go in vain; my prayers will produce the desired results in the name of Jesus Christ.
11. I declare never again, to any bad experience I have had in my life, you shall not repeat yourself, in the name of Jesus.
12. Repeated oppression, you are no longer allowed in the name of Jesus.
13. I re-write my family history by the authority in the name of Jesus.
14. Repeated Calamities, you are no longer allowed in the name of Jesus.
15. Affliction, hear the word of the Lord, never again will you rise in my life, in the name of Jesus.
16. Witchcraft manipulations I cry out against you, never again will you rise against me, in the name of Jesus.
17. Demonic powers assigned to use me as a foot mat, I cry out against you, never again, in the name of Jesus.
18. Power of almost there, I cry out against you, never again in the name of Jesus.
19. Spirit of bless and lose, I cry out against you, never again in the name of Jesus.
20. Any power anywhere closing my heavens, I cry against you, never again in the name of Jesus.
21. Frustrations and backwardness assigned against me, I cry against you, never again in the name of Jesus.
22. Access of darkness into my life, you are evicted today and never again will you enter into my life in the name of Jesus.
23. The lions of past problems roaring against me, I command you to be silenced forever, in the name of Jesus.
24. Shame and disfavor I cry out against you, never again in the name of Jesus.
25. Diminishing returns I cry out against you, never again in the name of Jesus.

26. Visitations of the merchants of death, you are no longer allowed in my life in the name of Jesus.
27. Satanic embarrassments I cry out against you, never again in the name of Jesus.
28. I decree today that everything begin to turn around for my favor, in the name of Jesus.

DELIVERANCE PRAYER AGAINST EVIL PATTERNS

Passages To Read Before You Pray:
Galatians 3:13-14, Psalms 114, 27, 121, 140

I have come today to fellowship with my heavenly Father, and make my requests and needs known unto Him. I cannot be hindered nor delayed because I know who I am in the Lord. I am a child of the Kingdom, born of the Spirit, redeemed by the blood of Jesus Christ. I walk in authority, living life without any apology because the power and authority has been given to me according to the Word of God in the book of Luke 9:1.

As I have come to pray today and to fellowship with my heavenly Father, I cover myself in the blood of Jesus Christ, and I put on the whole armor of God. I hereby come against every Prince of Persia that wants to hinder my prayer, I arrest you by the power in the blood of Jesus Christ, and I bind you and cast you down into the pit of hell.

I come against principalities and powers that wrestle with me and my prayers, I arrest you today by the power in the name of Jesus Christ, and I bind you and cast down into the pit of hell. I come against the rulers of the darkness of this world, against spiritual wickedness in high places, I arrest you all by the power in the name of Jesus Christ, and I bind you and cast you down into the pit of hell. I come against weakness and weariness, I arrest you today by the power in the name of Jesus Christ, and I

bind you and cast you out of my life. I come against wondering spirit and distractions, I arrest you today by the power in the name of Jesus Christ, and I bind you and cast you out of my life.

Today I receive the anointing to pray and get results, my prayers cannot be hindered nor delayed because Jesus is my Lord, I will pray today and get the desired results, I decree open heavens upon my prayers. I baptize myself in the fire of the Holy Ghost; therefore I have become too hot for the enemy to handle. My prayers today will attract divine intervention to every situation in my life; signs and wonders will follow my prayers today, testimonies will follow my prayers today and the name of God alone will be glorified, in Jesus name. Amen!

PRAYER POINTS:

1. O God my Father, thank you for being my God, my Father and my friend.
2. O God my Father, thank you for the privilege to know you and the power of the resurrection of Jesus Christ.
3. O God my Father, thank you for always being there for me and with me.
4. O God my Father, thank you for the great and mighty things that you are doing in my life.
5. O God my Father, thank you for your provision and protection over me and my household.
6. O God my Father, thank you for always answering my prayers.
7. I confess my sins before you today and I ask you to forgive me on the basis of your mercy, in the name of Jesus Christ.

8. Wash me clean today O Lord by the blood of Jesus Christ.
9. I cover myself and my household with the blood of Jesus Christ.
10. My prayers today will not go in vain; my prayers will produce the desired results in the name of Jesus Christ.

11. You evil pattern of Marital Failure in my life, I destroy you today, in the name of Jesus.
12. O God of success, my marital life must not fail, in the name of Jesus.
13. The failure that happened in the lives of my parents, will not happen in my life, in the name of Jesus.
14. Every plantation of witchcraft in my family, I command you to be destroyed with all your roots, in the name of Jesus.
15. Every pattern of household witchcraft in my family, I bury you today, in the name of Jesus.
16. O God arise, and let every witchcraft power release my destiny, in the name of Jesus.
17. Every stronghold of death and tragedy in my family, scatter by the fire of God, in the name of Jesus.
18. Every messenger of death operating in my family line, die in the name of Jesus.
19. Every garment of evil pattern against my divine goal, be destroyed by the fire of God, in the name of Jesus.
20. Every evil pattern of non-achievement in my family clear out now, in the name of Jesus.
21. Every giant of almost -there in my family, drop dead, in the name of Jesus.
22. You evil pattern of poverty, be destroyed by the fire of God, in the name of Jesus.

23. Every bacteria of poverty in my life, die in the name of Jesus.
24. O Lord, let my life attract prosperity, in the name of Jesus.
25. I command every pattern of Chronic disease in my life to cease, in the name of Jesus.
26. Every evil pattern of infirmity in my life, break in the name of Jesus.
27. I disconnect my life from all evil calendars in the name of Jesus.
28. Every river of sadness, dry up by fire, in the name of Jesus.
29. Crying shall not be my lot again, in the name of Jesus.
30. Every curse of disorder upon my family, be broken by fire, in the name of Jesus.
31. O Lord, manifest your glory in my family, in the name of Jesus.
32. Every pattern of failure in my root, be destroyed by the fire of God, in the name of Jesus.
33. I wash away every deposit of failure, in the name of Jesus.
34. Every evil pattern of marital failure in my life, break in the name of Jesus.
35. Every evil pattern of unstable husband/wife in my life, break in the name of Jesus.
36. I receive fire to destroy every sexual defilement in my life, in the name of Jesus.
37. You stronghold of sexual impurity in my body, I pull you down, in the name of Jesus.
38. I shake away every serpent of sexual immorality hiding in my life, in the name of Jesus.

39. Every wall of Jericho of adultery in my life, I pull you down, in the mighty name of Jesus.
40. Every satanic influence in my life, be quenched by fire, in the name of Jesus.
41. Every anointing of destructive anger in my blood, dry up by fire, in the name of Jesus.
42. O Lord, deliver me from the spirit of ancestral anger in the name of Jesus.
43. You the satanic strongman of anger assigned to push me to hell, die, in the name of Jesus.
44. Every evil pattern of Jezebel Spirit in my life, be destroyed by the fire of God, in the name of Jesus.
45. Every contract of evil pattern of Jezebel spirit in my family, be terminated, in the name of Jesus.
46. Every seed of depression in the salvation of my life, be destroyed by the fire of God, in the name of Jesus.
47. O God my father, send down your fire and turn me to fire, in the name of Jesus.
48. You the root cause of bad habits, together with your branches, be destroyed by the fire of God, in the name of Jesus.
49. Every ancestral spirit, responsible for bad habits in my life, be utterly destroyed, in the name of Jesus.
50. O Lord, strengthen me for holy living patterns in the name of Jesus.
51. O God, forgive me today, of every sin of unforgiveness in my family, in the name of Jesus.
52. God arise, and help me to recover all my blessings that I have lost as a result of evil patterns, in the name of Jesus.
53. I receive the power to overcome, in the name of Jesus.

54. O Lord, repair every damage done to my life by evil pattern of argumentative spirit, in the name of Jesus.
55. Every satanic attempt to downgrade my potential with argumentative spirit, be frustrated now, in the name of Jesus.
56. Every root of bitterness in my life, be destroyed by the fire of God, in the name of Jesus
57. Blood of Jesus Christ, purge every bitterness away from my life, in the name of Jesus.
58. Everything that bitterness has destroyed in my life, be restored by the resurrection power of God, in the name of Jesus.
59. Every curse and pattern of careless indifference, affecting my destiny, break by fire, in the name of Jesus.
60. The salt of my life shall not become sand, in the name of Jesus.
61. Every evil word spoken in my home town against my family, backfire, in the name of Jesus.
62. I shall reach my goal no matter what anybody says about me, in the name of Jesus.
63. Every power magnetizing me to the pattern of confusion, I bury you alive today, in the name of Jesus.
64. You pattern of confusion turning me back at the edge of breakthroughs, enough is enough, be destroyed by the fire of God, in the name of Jesus.
65. Every cycle of confusion operating in my life, break, in the name of Jesus.
66. Every lying tongue against me, roast by fire, in the name of Jesus.
67. Any evil lie planted in anybody's heart against me, be melted by fire, in the name of Jesus.

68. Any satanic agent that has ever lied against me, receive angelic slap; receive divine hammer and die, in the name of Jesus.
69. Every family fountain chasing away my helpers, dry up by fire, in the name of Jesus.
70. O Lord, pour your anointing of favor upon my life, in the name of Jesus.
71. Every power attacking my blessings day and night, be destroyed by the fire of God, in the name of Jesus.
72. O God arise and give me the anointing of the winners, in the name of Jesus.
73. Every hidden curse of evil pattern, riding upon the horses of my destiny, I pull you down by fire, in the name of Jesus.
74. Every re-arrangement of my destiny through the curse of evil pattern, be reversed by fire, in the name of Jesus.
75. I _____ (mention your name), shall begin to follow the divine pattern for my life from today, in the name of Jesus.
76. Every evil pattern of slavery in my family, be destroyed by the fire of God in the name of Jesus.
77. I refuse to work like an elephant and eat like an ant, in the name of Jesus.
78. O Lord, let all my problems become my promotions in the name of Jesus.
79. Every pattern of laziness and slavery in my foundation, break, in the name of Jesus.
80. Any evil pattern of laziness sponsoring fear and wastage in my life, break, in the name of Jesus.
81. My life, refuse to co-operate with the spirit of laziness, in the name of Jesus.

82. I break free and lose myself from the grip and control of family idol spirit in the name of Jesus.
83. Every problem in my life promoted by idol worship, be destroyed by the fire of God in the name of Jesus.
84. O Lord, deliver me from every evil pattern, emanating from evil family idol, in the name of Jesus.
85. Every arrow of mental disorder, fired into my brain, go back to your sender, in the name of Jesus.
86. Every evil computer system against my life in the demonic world, shatter to pieces, in the name of Jesus.
87. Any evil pot cooking my destiny, break by fire, in the name of Jesus.
88. Evil pattern of horrible dreams in my life, break by fire, in the name of Jesus.
89. Let every evil pattern of satanic discipline in my life be terminated, in the name of Jesus.

FOUNDATIONAL DELIVERANCE

Passages To Read Before You Pray:
Galatians 3:13-14, Colossians 1:12-15, 2 Kings 2:19-22, Psalms 11, 30, 59, 69, 70

I have come today to fellowship with my heavenly Father, and make my requests and needs known unto Him. I cannot be hindered nor delayed because I know who I am in the Lord. I am a child of the Kingdom, born of the Spirit, redeemed by the blood of Jesus Christ. I walk in authority, living life without any apology because the power and authority has been given to me according to the Word of God in the book of Luke 9:1.

As I have come to pray today and to fellowship with my heavenly Father, I cover myself in the blood of Jesus Christ, and I put on the whole armor of God. I hereby come against every Prince of Persia that wants to hinder my prayer, I arrest you by the power in the blood of Jesus Christ, and I bind you and cast you down into the pit of hell.

I come against principalities and powers that wrestle with me and my prayers, I arrest you today by the power in the name of Jesus Christ, and I bind you and cast down into the pit of hell. I come against the rulers of the darkness of this world, against spiritual wickedness in high places, I arrest you all by the power in the name of Jesus Christ, and I bind you and cast you down into the pit of hell. I come against weakness and weariness, I arrest you today by the power in the name of Jesus Christ, and I bind you and cast you out of my life. I come against wondering

spirit and distractions, I arrest you today by the power in the name of Jesus Christ, and I bind you and cast you out of my life.

Today I receive the anointing to pray and get results, my prayers cannot be hindered nor delayed because Jesus is my Lord, I will pray today and get the desired results, I decree open heavens upon my prayers. I baptize myself in the fire of the Holy Ghost; therefore I have become too hot for the enemy to handle. My prayers today will attract divine intervention to every situation in my life; signs and wonders will follow my prayers today, testimonies will follow my prayers today and the name of God alone will be glorified, in Jesus name. Amen!

PRAYER POINTS:

1. O God my Father, thank you for being my God, my Father and my friend.
2. O God my Father, thank you for the privilege to know you and the power of the resurrection of Jesus Christ.
3. O God my Father, thank you for always being there for me and with me.
4. O God my Father, thank you for the great and mighty things that you are doing in my life.
5. O God my Father, thank you for your provision and protection over me and my household.
6. O God my Father, thank you for always answering my prayers.
7. I confess my sins before you today and I ask you to forgive me on the basis of your mercy, in the name of Jesus Christ.

8. Wash me clean today O Lord by the blood of Jesus Christ.
9. I cover myself and my household with the blood of Jesus Christ.
10. My prayers today will not go in vain; my prayers will produce the desired results in the name of Jesus Christ.

11. Father Lord, let the foothold and the seat of the enemy be destroyed completely in my life, in the name of Jesus.
12. Let the blood of Jesus erase all the legal ground that the enemy has against my life, in the name of Jesus.
13. I close all the doors opened to the enemies in my life, in the name of Jesus.
14. Let all the concrete constructed by the enemy to stop the germination of the seed of my life be broken down completely, in the name of Jesus.
15. Every foundation constructed by the enemy in my life, be destroyed completely, in the name of Jesus.
16. I command all the words contrary to God's words spoken against me to fall dead to the ground and bear no fruit, in Jesus' name.
17. I bind the strongman in my life, and I clear my goods from his possession, in Jesus' name.
18. You strongman of body destruction, be bound, in the name of Jesus.
19. You strongman of mind destruction, be bound, in the name of Jesus.
20. You strongman of financial destruction, be bound, in Jesus' name.
21. Every battle waged against me by the kingdom of darkness, receive defeat, in Jesus' name.

22. Distributors of spiritual poison, swallow your poison, in Jesus' name.
23. All forces of Egypt in my life, rise up against yourselves, in Jesus' name.
24. Father Lord, let the joy of the enemy over my life be turned to sorrow, in the name of Jesus.
25. You demonic armies stationed against my life, receive the judgment of leprosy, in Jesus' name.
26. I command the evil power source in my place of birth to be destroyed completely, in the name of Jesus.
27. Every access to my life by the enemy, I block you, in the name of Jesus.
28. Every problem that came into my life by personal invitation, you are no longer allowed, I command you to get out of my life now, in the name of Jesus.
29. Any problem that has entered into my life through my parents, you are no longer allowed, I command you to get out of my life now, in Jesus' name.
30. Any problem that has entered into my life as a result of attack by satanic agents, you are no longer allowed, I command you to get out of my life now, in the name of Jesus.
31. All my trapped blessings, be released now, in the name of Jesus.
32. Bondage repairers, I bind you by the power in the name of Jesus.
33. Every locked up blessing, be released now by the fire of God, in the name of Jesus.
34. Every evil agreement fashioned against me, be destroyed now by the fire of God, in the name of Jesus.
35. I disallow the strengthening of any problem, in the name of Jesus Christ.

36. Let all evil thrones set up against me be destroyed completely, in the name of Jesus Christ.
37. You God of promotion, promote me beyond my wildest dream, in Jesus' name.
38. I fire back every arrow of witchcraft seven-fold, in the name of Jesus Christ.
39. Every satanic agent in my family who refuses to repent, I destroy your power, in the name of Jesus.
40. Shadow of death, flee away from me! Heavenly light, shine on me!! in Jesus' name.
41. I rebuke all the spirits against the soundness of my mind, in the name of Jesus.

PRAYER TO PURGE YOUR FOUNDATION

Passages To Read Before You Pray:
Galatians 3:13-14, Colossians 1:12-15, 2 Kings 2:19-22, Psalms 11, 30, 59, 69, 70

I have come today to fellowship with my heavenly Father, and make my requests and needs known unto Him. I cannot be hindered nor delayed because I know who I am in the Lord. I am a child of the Kingdom, born of the Spirit, redeemed by the blood of Jesus Christ. I walk in authority, living life without any apology because the power and authority has been given to me according to the Word of God in the book of Luke 9:1.

As I have come to pray today and to fellowship with my heavenly Father, I cover myself in the blood of Jesus Christ, and I put on the whole armor of God. I hereby come against every Prince of Persia that wants to hinder my prayer, I arrest you by the power in the blood of Jesus Christ, and I bind you and cast you down into the pit of hell.

I come against principalities and powers that wrestle with me and my prayers, I arrest you today by the power in the name of Jesus Christ, and I bind you and cast down into the pit of hell. I come against the rulers of the darkness of this world, against spiritual wickedness in high places, I arrest you all by the power in the name of Jesus Christ, and I bind you and cast you down into the pit of hell. I come against weakness and weariness, I arrest you today by the power in the name of Jesus Christ, and I bind you and cast you out of my life. I come against wondering

spirit and distractions, I arrest you today by the power in the name of Jesus Christ, and I bind you and cast you out of my life.

Today I receive the anointing to pray and get results, my prayers cannot be hindered nor delayed because Jesus is my Lord, I will pray today and get the desired results, I decree open heavens upon my prayers. I baptize myself in the fire of the Holy Ghost; therefore I have become too hot for the enemy to handle. My prayers today will attract divine intervention to every situation in my life; signs and wonders will follow my prayers today, testimonies will follow my prayers today and the name of God alone will be glorified, in Jesus name. Amen!

PRAYER POINTS:

1. O God my Father, thank you for being my God, my Father and my friend.
2. O God my Father, thank you for the privilege to know you and the power of the resurrection of Jesus Christ.
3. O God my Father, thank you for always being there for me and with me.
4. O God my Father, thank you for the great and mighty things that you are doing in my life.
5. O God my Father, thank you for your provision and protection over me and my household.
6. O God my Father, thank you for always answering my prayers.
7. I confess my sins before you today and I ask you to forgive me on the basis of your mercy, in the name of Jesus Christ.

8. Wash me clean today O Lord by the blood of Jesus Christ.
9. I cover myself and my household with the blood of Jesus Christ.
10. My prayers today will not go in vain; my prayers will produce the desired results in the name of Jesus Christ.
11. Every placenta witchcraft targeted against my destiny, what are you waiting for, die, in Jesus name.
12. Every caldron of darkness that is harassing my destiny, break, in the name of Jesus.
13. Every chain of darkness around my waist, break, in the name of Jesus. (Lay your hand on your belly-button)
14. Placenta witchcraft manipulating my destiny, die, in the name of Jesus.
15. Thou bank of satan, release my placenta, in the name of Jesus.
16. Every satanic transfer into my destiny through the placenta, I cut you off, in the name of Jesus.
17. Blood of Jesus, recover my placenta from the earth, in the name of Jesus.
18. Blood of Jesus, recover my destiny from the waters, in the name of Jesus.
19. Every placenta attachment to my place of birth, what are you waiting for, die, in the name of Jesus.
20. Thou eater of flesh and drinker of blood, vomit my placenta, in the name of Jesus.
21. Thou power of God, deliver me from placenta bondage, in the name of Jesus.
22. Every power using my placenta against me, what are you waiting for, die, in the name of Jesus.

23. Every covenant between any tree and my placenta, break, in the name of Jesus.
24. Every blessing that I have lost through placenta witchcraft, I possess you, in the name of Jesus.
25. Every cage of placenta manipulation, break, in the name of Jesus.
26. I release myself from any inherited bondage and limitations in the name of Jesus.
27. Lord, send Your axe of fire to the foundation of my life and destroy every evil plantation.
28. I release myself from the grip of any problem transferred into my life from the womb in Jesus name.
29. I break and loose myself from every inherited evil covenant in the name of Jesus.
30. I break and loose myself from every inherited evil curse in the name of Jesus.
31. I command all foundational strongmen attached to my life to be paralyzed in the name of Jesus.
32. Let the roots of family witchcraft be uprooted from the foundation of my life in the name of Jesus.
33. I release myself from any inherited bondage in the name of Jesus.
34. I release myself from the grip of any problem transferred into my life from the womb in the name of Jesus.
35. I break and loose myself from every inherited evil covenant in the name of Jesus.
36. I break and loose myself from every inherited evil curse in the name of Jesus.

37. I release myself from every inherited disease in the name of Jesus.
38. Let the blood of Jesus correct any inherited defect in my body in the name of Jesus.
39. I break any curse of rejection from the womb or illegitimacy that may be in my family back to ten generations on both sides of the family in the name of Jesus.
40. I break all the curses of deformity, infirmity and sickness in my family back to ten generations on both sides of my family in the name of Jesus.
41. I command the spirit of death and hell to loose its hold upon my life in the name of Jesus.
42. I break every demonic circle in my life, in the name of Jesus.
43. Lord, send your axe of fire to the foundation of my life and destroy every evil plantation.
44. Father, let the fire of the Holy Ghost enter into my blood stream and cleanse my system, in Jesus name.
45. I break every curse of automatic failure mechanism working in the name of Jesus.
46. I revoke every satanic decree issued against my promotion in the name of Jesus.
47. I silence every evil dog barking against my breakthroughs in the name of Jesus.
48. Every agent of disgrace, backwardness and shame, release me in the mighty name of Jesus.
49. Let every spiritual vulture delegated against me eat their own flesh in the name of Jesus.

50. Holy Spirit, transform me from weakness to strength in the name of Jesus.
51. I disgrace every evil wisdom working against my breakthroughs in the name of Jesus.
52. Lord, let me be extraordinary.
53. Holy Spirit, deposit Your wonders in my life in the name of Jesus.
54. Lord Jesus, set me ablaze with your Spirit.
55. Let divine earthquake shake down the foundation of every satanic prison in the name of Jesus.
56. I bind every evil spirit withholding good testimonies in my life in the name of Jesus.
57. Let every satanic river of backwardness dry up in the name of Jesus.
58. Holy Ghost, fulfill your purpose in me now in the name of Jesus.
59. O Lord, create within me a hunger and thirst for purity and holiness.
60. Holy Spirit, promote divine possibility in my life in the name of Jesus.

PRAYER TO BREAK ANCESTRAL EVIL HOLD

Passages To Read Before You Pray:
Isaiah 47, Nahum 3, Galatians 3:13-14, Colossians 1:12-15,
Psalms 11, 30, 59, 69, 70

I have come today to fellowship with my heavenly Father, and make my requests and needs known unto Him. I cannot be hindered nor delayed because I know who I am in the Lord. I am a child of the Kingdom, born of the Spirit, redeemed by the blood of Jesus Christ. I walk in authority, living life without any apology because the power and authority has been given to me according to the Word of God in the book of Luke 9:1.

As I have come to pray today and to fellowship with my heavenly Father, I cover myself in the blood of Jesus Christ, and I put on the whole armor of God. I hereby come against every Prince of Persia that wants to hinder my prayer, I arrest you by the power in the blood of Jesus Christ, and I bind you and cast you down into the pit of hell.

I come against principalities and powers that wrestle with me and my prayers, I arrest you today by the power in the name of Jesus Christ, and I bind you and cast down into the pit of hell. I come against the rulers of the darkness of this world, against spiritual wickedness in high places, I arrest you all by the power in the name of Jesus Christ, and I bind you and cast you down into the pit of hell. I come against weakness and weariness, I arrest you today by the power in the name of Jesus Christ, and I bind you and cast you out of my life. I come against wondering

spirit and distractions, I arrest you today by the power in the name of Jesus Christ, and I bind you and cast you out of my life.

Today I receive the anointing to pray and get results, my prayers cannot be hindered nor delayed because Jesus is my Lord, I will pray today and get the desired results, I decree open heavens upon my prayers. I baptize myself in the fire of the Holy Ghost; therefore I have become too hot for the enemy to handle. My prayers today will attract divine intervention to every situation in my life; signs and wonders will follow my prayers today, testimonies will follow my prayers today and the name of God alone will be glorified, in Jesus name. Amen!

PRAYER POINTS:

1. O God my Father, thank you for being my God, my Father and my friend.
2. O God my Father, thank you for the privilege to know you and the power of the resurrection of Jesus Christ.
3. O God my Father, thank you for always being there for me and with me.
4. O God my Father, thank you for the great and mighty things that you are doing in my life.
5. O God my Father, thank you for your provision and protection over me and my household.
6. O God my Father, thank you for always answering my prayers.
7. I confess my sins before you today and I ask you to forgive me on the basis of your mercy, in the name of Jesus Christ.

8. Wash me clean today O Lord by the blood of Jesus Christ.
9. I cover myself and my household with the blood of Jesus Christ.
10. My prayers today will not go in vain; my prayers will produce the desired results in the name of Jesus Christ.

11. Every covenant with water spirit be broken by the blood of Jesus Christ.
12. Every covenant with desert spirit be broken by the blood of Jesus Christ.
13. Every covenant with witchcraft spirits or powers, be broken by the blood of Jesus Christ.
14. Every covenant with spirits in evil sacred trees, be broken by the blood of Jesus Christ.
15. Every covenant with masquerade spirits, be broken by the blood of Jesus Christ.
16. Every covenant with evil family guardian spirits, be broken by the blood of Jesus Christ.
17. Every covenant with family gods, be broken by the blood of Jesus Christ.
18. Every covenant with family serpentine spirit, be broken by the blood of Jesus Christ.
19. Every covenant with inherited spirit husband/wife, be broken by the blood of Jesus Christ.
20. Every unconscious evil soul-tie and covenant with the spirits of my dead grandfather, grandmother, occult uncles, aunties, custodian of family gods/oracles/shrines, be broken by the blood of Jesus.

21. Every decision, vow or promise made by my forefathers contrary to my divine destiny, loose your hold by fire, in the name of Jesus.
22. Every legal ground that ancestral/guardian spirits have in my life, be destroyed by the blood of Jesus.
23. Every generational curse of God resulting from the sin of idolatry on my forefathers, loose your hold, in the name of Jesus.
24. Every ancestral evil altar prospering against me, be dashed against the Rock of Ages, in Jesus name.
25. Every hold of any sacrifice ever offered in my family or on my behalf, I break your power in my life, in the name of Jesus.
26. Any ancestral blood shed of animals, or human beings affecting me, loose your hold by the blood of Jesus.
27. Any curse placed on my ancestral line by anybody cheated, maltreated or at the point of death, break now, in Jesus' name.
28. Every evil ancestral river flowing down to my generation, I cut you off, in the name of Jesus.
29. Every evil ancestral habit and weakness of moral failures manifesting in my life, loose your grip and release me now, in Jesus' name.
30. Every rage and rampage of ancestral and family spirits resulting from my being born again, be quenched by the liquid fire of God, in the name of Jesus.
31. I recover every good thing stolen by ancestral evil spirits from my forefathers, my immediate family and myself, in Jesus' name.

32. Every ancestral embargo, be lifted; and let good things begin to break forth in my life and in my family, in the name of Jesus.
33. Any demonic incisions loose your hold over my life and be purged out of my foundation.
34. Any dream pollution loose your hold over my life and be purged out of my foundation.
35. Any demonic sacrifices loose your hold over my life and be purged out of my foundation.
36. Any demonic marriages loose your hold over my life and be purged out of my foundation.
37. Any wrong exposures to sex loose your hold over my life and be purged out of my foundation.
38. Any demonic incisions loose your hold over my life and be purged out of my foundation.
39. Any fellowships with family idols loose your hold over my life and be purged out of my foundation.
40. I command all the enemy of God in my life, husband/wife, family to carry their entire problems today, in Jesus name.
41. Lord, nullify the evil influence of family strongman upon my life in the name of Jesus.
42. Every stronghold of family strongman upon my spirit, soul and body, be shattered to pieces in the name of Jesus.
43. Let the wickedness of the family strongman be overturned in the mighty name of Jesus.
44. I arrest the spiritual soldiers of any family strongman watching over the affairs of my life in the name of Jesus.

45. Let the thunder of God strike the altar of any family strongman in the name of Jesus.
46. I cancel the evil dedication of my name to any evil family strongman in the name of Jesus.
47. I bring the Blood of Jesus over every evil claim from the family strongman over my life in the name of Jesus.
48. The gates of the ancestral demon working against my divine goal in life is broken by the power of Jesus in the name of Jesus.
49. I break the yoke of any family strongman upon my life in the name of Jesus.
50. Every foundation of family strongmen rooted in my dreams, visions and destiny, be uprooted in the name of Jesus.
51. The tree of family strongmen in my life, be cut down in the name of Jesus.
52. Destiny vultures, vomit my destiny in the name of Jesus.
53. Visions of my divine destiny, come upon my life, in Jesus name.
54. Every witchcraft servant riding on the horse of my destiny, come down now, in the name of Jesus.
55. Every family destiny cage, be destroyed by the fire of God, in Jesus name.
56. Every evil destiny pattern, be destroyed by the fire of God, in Jesus name.
57. Every spiritual bastard pursuing my destiny, die, in Jesus name.
58. Every job that will not move me forward, change by the fire of God, in Jesus name.

59. Every spiritual relative stealing from me, scatter now, in Jesus name.
60. Every curse issued against my destiny, backfire, in the name of Jesus.
61. Every witchcraft embargo on my finances, be destroyed by the fire of God,, in the name of Jesus.
62. Every witchcraft embargo on my career and business, be destroyed by the fire of God,, in the name of Jesus.
63. Every witchcraft embargo on my marriage, be destroyed by the fire of God,, in the name of Jesus.
64. I deliver my goods and my destiny from the hands of the evil strongmen in the name of Jesus.
65. I recover all my confiscated and stolen properties, in Jesus' name.
66. You devil take off your legs from my finances in the name of Jesus.
67. I bind every strongman holding my privileges and rights captive, in the name of Jesus.
68. I retrieve all properties from the satanic banks, in Jesus' name.
69. I possess all my possessions, in the name of Jesus.
70. Any power sitting on an evil mat against my prosperity, fall down and die in the name of Jesus.
71. Lord, restore seven-fold, everything that spiritual thieves have stolen from me.
72. I bind every spirit sitting on my possession, in the name of Jesus.
73. I command my money being caged by the enemy to be completely released in the name of Jesus.

74. Let my proposals be too hot for the enemy to sit upon, in the name of Jesus.
75. Let the riches of the Gentiles be transferred to me, in Jesus' name.
76. I recover my blessings from water, forest and satanic banks, in the name of Jesus.
77. O Lord, create new and profitable opportunities for me.
78. Every stolen and satanically transferred virtues, be restored, in the name of Jesus.
79. Every darkness planted in my foundation, scatter, in the name of Jesus.
80. Every foundational arrester, be arrested, in the name of Jesus.
81. Every serpent in my foundation, die, in the name of Jesus.
82. Every scorpion in my foundation, die, in the name of Jesus.
83. Let God arise and let all foundational witchcraft scatter, in the, name of Jesus.
84. Every seed of witchcraft in my foundation, be destroyed by the fire of God, in the name of Jesus.
85. Every foundational confusion, be destroyed by the fire of God, in the name of Jesus.
86. Every foundational familiar spirit, I bind you and cast you out, in the name of Jesus.
87. Every foundational marine power, bow, in the name of Jesus.
88. Every problem attached to my family name, be neutralized, in the name of Jesus.

89. Family idols, receive the consuming fire of God, in the name of Jesus.
90. I release myself from every ancestral demonic pollution in the name of Jesus.
91. I release myself from every demonic pollution emanating from my parents' religion in the name of Jesus.
92. I release myself from demonic pollution emanating from my past involvement in any demonic religion in the name of Jesus.
93. I break and loose myself from every idol and related association in the name of Jesus.

PRAYER FOR DIVINE RE-ARRANGEMENT

Passages To Read Before You Pray:
Genesis 17:1-22, Psalms 18, 109, 86, 35, 38, 61

I have come today to fellowship with my heavenly Father, and make my requests and needs known unto Him. I cannot be hindered nor delayed because I know who I am in the Lord. I am a child of the Kingdom, born of the Spirit, redeemed by the blood of Jesus Christ. I walk in authority, living life without any apology because the power and authority has been given to me according to the Word of God in the book of Luke 9:1.

As I have come to pray today and to fellowship with my heavenly Father, I cover myself in the blood of Jesus Christ, and I put on the whole armor of God. I hereby come against every Prince of Persia that wants to hinder my prayer, I arrest you by the power in the blood of Jesus Christ, and I bind you and cast you down into the pit of hell.

I come against principalities and powers that wrestle with me and my prayers, I arrest you today by the power in the name of Jesus Christ, and I bind you and cast down into the pit of hell. I come against the rulers of the darkness of this world, against spiritual wickedness in high places, I arrest you all by the power in the name of Jesus Christ, and I bind you and cast you down into the pit of hell. I come against weakness and weariness, I arrest you today by the power in the name of Jesus Christ, and I bind you and cast you out of my life. I come against wondering

spirit and distractions, I arrest you today by the power in the name of Jesus Christ, and I bind you and cast you out of my life.

Today I receive the anointing to pray and get results, my prayers cannot be hindered nor delayed because Jesus is my Lord, I will pray today and get the desired results, I decree open heavens upon my prayers. I baptize myself in the fire of the Holy Ghost; therefore I have become too hot for the enemy to handle. My prayers today will attract divine intervention to every situation in my life; signs and wonders will follow my prayers today, testimonies will follow my prayers today and the name of God alone will be glorified, in Jesus name. Amen!

PRAYER POINTS:

1. O God my Father, thank you for being my God, my Father and my friend.
2. O God my Father, thank you for the privilege to know you and the power of the resurrection of Jesus Christ.
3. O God my Father, thank you for always being there for me and with me.
4. O God my Father, thank you for the great and mighty things that you are doing in my life.
5. O God my Father, thank you for your provision and protection over me and my household.
6. O God my Father, thank you for always answering my prayers.
7. I confess my sins before you today and I ask you to forgive me on the basis of your mercy, in the name of Jesus Christ.

8. Wash me clean today O Lord by the blood of Jesus Christ.
9. I cover myself and my household with the blood of Jesus Christ.
10. My prayers today will not go in vain; my prayers will produce the desired results in the name of Jesus Christ.
11. Lord, rearrange my situation to glorify your name.
12. O Lord, re-arrange my situation to defeat and disgrace my enemies.
13. O Lord, speak deliverance to any bondage situation in my life.
14. Let the Pharaoh in my place of birth fall down and die, in the name of Jesus.
15. O Lord, make me attractive to prosperity.
16. O Lord, let your purpose for my life be fulfilled.
17. O Lord, let Your electric love flow into my life.
18. O Lord, wash and cleanse me from past wounds and scars.
19. O Lord, bring light into the shadows of my life.
20. O Lord, bring light into all the dark rooms in my soul.
21. O Lord, uproot the root cause of any chronic failures.
22. Let all good things burned alive come forth now, in the name of Jesus.
23. I cancel the effect of all former satanic benefits upon my life, in the name of Jesus.
24. I claim back any territory of my life handed over to Satan, in the name of Jesus.
25. Any witchcraft practiced under any water against my life, receive immediate judgment of fire, in Jesus name.

26. Every witchcraft power that has introduced spirit husband/wife or child into my dreams be roasted by fire, in the mighty name of Jesus.
27. Every agent of witchcraft power posing as my husband, wife or child in my dreams, be roasted by fire, in Jesus mighty name.
28. Every agent of witchcraft power physically attached to my marriage to frustrate it, fall down and perish now, in Jesus name.
29. Every agent of witchcraft power assigned to attack my finances through dream, fall down and perish, in Jesus mighty name.
30. Let the thunderbolts of God locate and destroy every witchcraft power covens where deliberations and decisions were ever fashioned against me, in Jesus name.
31. Any water spirit from my village, in my birth place, practicing witchcraft against me and my family, be amputated by the word of God, in Jesus name.
32. Any power of witchcraft holding any of my blessings in bondage, receive the fire of judgment of God and release them, in the name of Jesus.
33. I loose my mind and soul from the bondage of marine witches, in Jesus mighty name.
34. Any witchcraft power chain, binding my hands and feet from prospering, be broken and shattered to pieces, in the name of Jesus.
35. I reject every satanic re-arrangement of my destiny, in the name of Jesus.

36. I refuse to live below my divine standard, in Jesus' name.
37. Every evil power having negative awareness of my destiny, be impotent, in the name of Jesus.
38. I paralyze every destiny polluter, in the name of Jesus.
39. Every damage done to my destiny, be repaired now, in the name of Jesus.
40. The enemy will not convert my destiny to rags, in the name of Jesus.
41. O Lord, restore me to Your original design for my life.
42. I reject destiny-demoting names, in the name of Jesus.
43. Every internal warfare in my life, be quenched, in the name of Jesus.
44. Every internal thief, be exposed, in the name of Jesus.
45. God arise in your east wind and make my Pharaoh fall into the red sea, in the name of Jesus.
46. Every evil power struggling to restructure my destiny die, in the name of Jesus.
47. Umbrella of the Almighty God – cover my life, in the name of Jesus.
48. O God, arise and incubate me with wisdom and knowledge, in the name of Jesus.
49. Power to wait on the Lord fall upon me, in the name of Jesus.
50. Thou power of inherited failure die, in the name of Jesus.
51. I am unbeatable by the devil, in the name of Jesus.
52. I declare myself free from genetic demons, in the name of Jesus.

53. I declare myself free from national and continental curses, in the name of Jesus.
54. My enemies shall bow down to me, in the name of Jesus.
55. Every satanic agenda for my life be aborted, in the name of Jesus.
56. Let your deliverance hand be stretched out upon my life now, in the name of Jesus.
57. I annul every engagement with the spirit of death, in Jesus' name.
58. I rebuke every refuge of sickness, in the name of Jesus.
59. I destroy the grip and operation of sickness upon my life, in the name of Jesus.
60. Every knee of infirmity in my life, bow, in the name of Jesus.
61. Let all my negatives be converted to positives, in the name of Jesus.
62. I command death upon any sickness in any area of my life, in the name of Jesus.
63. I shall see my sickness no more, in the name of Jesus.
64. Let the whirlwind scatter every vessel of infirmity fashioned against my life, in the name of Jesus.
65. Every spirit hindering my perfect healing, fall down and die now, in the name of Jesus.
66. Let all death contractors begin to kill themselves, in Jesus' name.
67. Let every germ of infirmity in my body die, in the name of Jesus.
68. Let every agent of sickness working against my health disappear, in the name of Jesus.

69. Fountain of discomfort in my life, dry up now, in the name of Jesus.
70. Every dead organ in my body, receive life now, in Jesus' name.
71. Let my blood be transfused with the blood of Jesus to affect my perfect health, in the name of Jesus.
72. Every internal disorder, receive order, in the name of Jesus.
73. Every infirmity, come out with all your roots, in the name of Jesus.
74. I withdraw every conscious and unconscious cooperation with sickness, in the name of Jesus.
75. Let the whirlwind of the Lord blow every wind of infirmity away, in the name of Jesus.
76. I release my body from every curse of infirmity, in Jesus' name.

PRAYER AGAINST OPPRESSION AT WORKPLACE

Passages To Read Before You Pray:
Exodus 3:7-22, Genesis 11:1-9, Psalms 35, 3, 9

I have come today to fellowship with my heavenly Father, and make my requests and needs known unto Him. I cannot be hindered nor delayed because I know who I am in the Lord. I am a child of the Kingdom, born of the Spirit, redeemed by the blood of Jesus Christ. I walk in authority, living life without any apology because the power and authority has been given to me according to the Word of God in the book of Luke 9:1.

As I have come to pray today and to fellowship with my heavenly Father, I cover myself in the blood of Jesus Christ, and I put on the whole armor of God. I hereby come against every Prince of Persia that wants to hinder my prayer, I arrest you by the power in the blood of Jesus Christ, and I bind you and cast you down into the pit of hell.

I come against principalities and powers that wrestle with me and my prayers, I arrest you today by the power in the name of Jesus Christ, and I bind you and cast down into the pit of hell. I come against the rulers of the darkness of this world, against spiritual wickedness in high places, I arrest you all by the power in the name of Jesus Christ, and I bind you and cast you down into the pit of hell. I come against weakness and weariness, I arrest you today by the power in the name of Jesus Christ, and I bind you and cast you out of my life. I come against wondering

spirit and distractions, I arrest you today by the power in the name of Jesus Christ, and I bind you and cast you out of my life.

Today I receive the anointing to pray and get results, my prayers cannot be hindered nor delayed because Jesus is my Lord, I will pray today and get the desired results, I decree open heavens upon my prayers. I baptize myself in the fire of the Holy Ghost; therefore I have become too hot for the enemy to handle. My prayers today will attract divine intervention to every situation in my life; signs and wonders will follow my prayers today, testimonies will follow my prayers today and the name of God alone will be glorified, in Jesus name. Amen!

PRAYER POINTS:

1. O God my Father, thank you for being my God, my Father and my friend.
2. O God my Father, thank you for the privilege to know you and the power of the resurrection of Jesus Christ.
3. O God my Father, thank you for always being there for me and with me.
4. O God my Father, thank you for the great and mighty things that you are doing in my life.
5. O God my Father, thank you for your provision and protection over me and my household.
6. O God my Father, thank you for always answering my prayers.
7. I confess my sins before you today and I ask you to forgive me on the basis of your mercy, in the name of Jesus Christ.

8. Wash me clean today O Lord by the blood of Jesus Christ.
9. I cover myself and my household with the blood of Jesus Christ.
10. My prayers today will not go in vain; my prayers will produce the desired results in the name of Jesus Christ.
11. O God arise, visit my work place and carry out a shaking for my sake, in the name of Jesus Christ.
12. O God arise, visit my work place and trouble them that trouble me in the name of Jesus Christ.
13. O God arise, visit my work place and fight them that fight against me, in the name of Jesus Christ.
14. O God my Father, arise and let everyone in my work place know that I serve a Might God, in the name of Jesus Christ.
15. O God my Father, I have been groaning under the hand of the oppressors; arise O Lord and fight for me, in the name of Jesus Christ.
16. O God my Father, roar in your fierce anger and crush every unrepentant oppressor that troubles me, in the name of Jesus Christ.
17. I command the yoke of oppression to be broken and terminated by the blood of Jesus Christ.
18. I arrest and bind every oppressor that is opposed to my promotion, in the name of Jesus Christ.
19. I release the plague of Egypt against every unrepentant oppressor that is seating on my promotion, in the name of Jesus Christ.
20. O God my Father, cover me with your fire and turn me into fear and terror for all my troublers in my work place, in the name of Jesus Christ.

21. I neutralize and scatter every spell of oppression that is working against me, in the name of Jesus Christ.
22. By the power in the name of Jesus Christ, I arrest and bind the power of witchcraft working against me, in the name of Jesus Christ.
23. You wind of hatred blowing against me in my work place, enough is enough, I command you to seize forever in the name of Jesus Christ.
24. You evil conspirators conspiring against me in my work place, fall and never rise again in the name of Jesus Christ.
25. O God my Father, execute your judgment on my stubborn oppressor in the name of Jesus Christ.
26. I snatch my promotion from the hand of my enemies today, in the name of Jesus Christ.
27. I release the fire of God to destroy the presence of evil in my work place, in the name of Jesus Christ.
28. I charge the atmosphere in my work place by the blood of Jesus Christ.
29. I charge the atmosphere in my work place by the fire of the Holy Ghost.
30. I take my place by the power in the name of Jesus Christ.
31. I assume my position now in the name of Jesus Christ.
32. I take my portion now in the name of Jesus Christ.
33. I take my possessions today by the power in the name of Jesus Christ.
34. I command every power that is not of God in my work place to bow at the name of Jesus Christ.
35. Today I declare, let no man trouble me, because I have the mark of Jesus Christ upon me, in the name of Jesus Christ.

PRAYER FOR UNSTOPPABLE PROGRESS

Passages To Read Before You Pray:
Isaiah 45:1-3, Zechariah 4:7, Psalm 23, 19, 29, 42, 121

I have come today to fellowship with my heavenly Father, and make my requests and needs known unto Him. I cannot be hindered nor delayed because I know who I am in the Lord. I am a child of the Kingdom, born of the Spirit, redeemed by the blood of Jesus Christ. I walk in authority, living life without any apology because the power and authority has been given to me according to the Word of God in the book of Luke 9:1.

As I have come to pray today and to fellowship with my heavenly Father, I cover myself in the blood of Jesus Christ, and I put on the whole armor of God. I hereby come against every Prince of Persia that wants to hinder my prayer, I arrest you by the power in the blood of Jesus Christ, and I bind you and cast you down into the pit of hell.

I come against principalities and powers that wrestle with me and my prayers, I arrest you today by the power in the name of Jesus Christ, and I bind you and cast down into the pit of hell. I come against the rulers of the darkness of this world, against spiritual wickedness in high places, I arrest you all by the power in the name of Jesus Christ, and I bind you and cast you down into the pit of hell. I come against weakness and weariness, I arrest you today by the power in the name of Jesus Christ, and I bind you and cast you out of my life. I come against wondering spirit and distractions, I arrest you today by the power in the name of Jesus Christ, and I bind you and cast you out of my life.

Today I receive the anointing to pray and get results, my prayers cannot be hindered nor delayed because Jesus is my Lord, I will pray today and get the desired results, I decree open heavens upon my prayers. I baptize myself in the fire of the Holy Ghost; therefore I have become too hot for the enemy to handle. My prayers today will attract divine intervention to every situation in my life; signs and wonders will follow my prayers today, testimonies will follow my prayers today and the name of God alone will be glorified, in Jesus name. Amen!

PRAYER POINTS:

1. O God my Father, thank you for being my God, my Father and my friend.
2. O God my Father, thank you for the privilege to know you and the power of the resurrection of Jesus Christ.
3. O God my Father, thank you for always being there for me and with me.
4. O God my Father, thank you for the great and mighty things that you are doing in my life.
5. O God my Father, thank you for your provision and protection over me and my household.
6. O God my Father, thank you for always answering my prayers.
7. I confess my sins before you today and I ask you to forgive me on the basis of your mercy, in the name of Jesus Christ.
8. Wash me clean today O Lord by the blood of Jesus Christ.
9. I cover myself and my household with the blood of Jesus Christ.

10. My prayers today will not go in vain; my prayers will produce the desired results in the name of Jesus Christ.
11. Let frustration and disappointment, be the portion of every object fashioned against my life and family, in the name of Jesus.
12. Every ties to polluted objects and items between my life and family, break, in the name of Jesus.
13. Every unspoken curse against my life, break, in the name of Jesus.
14. Every curse pronounced inwardly against my destiny, break, in the name of Jesus.
15. You inward curses, militating against my virtues, break, in the name of Jesus.
16. Any power given the mandate to curse and hinder my progress, summersault and die, in the name of Jesus.
17. Let every spirit of Balaam hired to curse my progress, fall down and die, in the name of Jesus.
18. Every curse that I have brought into my life through ignorance and disobedience, break by fire, in the name of Jesus.
19. Every power magnetizing physical and spiritual curses to me, I raise the blood of Jesus against you and I challenge you by fire, in the name of Jesus.
20. Father, Lord, turn all my self-imposed curses to blessings, in the name of Jesus.
21. Every instrument, put in place to frustrate me become impotent, in the name of Jesus.
22. I reject every cycle of frustration, in the name of Jesus.
23. Every agent assigned to frustrate me, perish by fire, in the name of Jesus.

24. Every power tormenting me, die by the sword, in the name of Jesus.
25. I destroy the power of every satanic arrest in my life, in the name of Jesus.
26. All satanic-arresting agents, release me in the mighty name of our Lord Jesus Christ.
27. Everything that is representing me in the demonic world against my career, be destroyed by the fire of God, in the name of Jesus.
28. Spirit of the living God, quicken the whole of my being, in the name of Jesus.
29. O God my Father, smash me and renew my strength, in the name of Jesus.
30. Holy Spirit, open my eyes to see beyond the visible to the invisible, in the name of Jesus.
31. Today O Lord, ignite my career with your fire.
32. O Lord, liberate my spirit to follow the leading of the Holy Spirit.
33. Holy Spirit, teach me to pray through problems instead of praying about, in the name of Jesus.
34. O Lord, deliver me from the lies I tell myself.
35. Every evil spiritual padlock and evil chain hindering my success, be roasted, in the name of Jesus.
36. I rebuke every spirit of spiritual deafness and blindness in my life, in the name of Jesus.
37. O Lord, empower me to resist satan that he may flee.
38. I chose to believe the report of the Lord and no other, in the name of Jesus.
39. Lord, anoint my eyes and my ears that I may see and hear wondrous things from heaven.
40. O Lord, anoint me to pray without ceasing.

41. In the name of Jesus, I capture every power behind any career failure.
42. Holy Spirit, rain on me now, in the name of Jesus.
43. Holy Spirit, uncover my darkest secrets, in the name of Jesus.
44. You spirit of confusion, loose your hold over my life, in the name of Jesus.
45. In the power of the Holy Spirit, I defy satan's power upon my career, in the name of Jesus.
46. Let the water of life flush out every unwanted stranger in my life, in the name of Jesus.
47. You the enemies of my career, be paralyzed, in the name of Jesus.
48. O Lord, begin to clean away from my life all that does not reflect You.
49. Holy Spirit fire, ignite me to the glory of God, in the name of Jesus.
50. Oh Lord, let the anointing of the Holy Spirit break every yoke of backwardness in my life.
51. I frustrate every demonic arrest over my spirit-man, in the name of Jesus.
52. Let the blood of Jesus remove any unprogressive label from every aspect of my life, in Jesus' name.
53. Anti-breakthrough decrees, be revoked, in the name of Jesus.
54. Holy Ghost fire, destroy every satanic garments in my life, in the name of Jesus.
55. Begin to thank God

PRAYER TO OPEN THE BOOK OF REMEMBRANCE

Passages To Read Before You Pray:
Esther 3:1-15, Nehemiah 13:14-31, Psalms 23, 19, 30

I have come today to fellowship with my heavenly Father, and make my requests and needs known unto Him. I cannot be hindered nor delayed because I know who I am in the Lord. I am a child of the Kingdom, born of the Spirit, redeemed by the blood of Jesus Christ. I walk in authority, living life without any apology because the power and authority has been given to me according to the Word of God in the book of Luke 9:1.

As I have come to pray today and to fellowship with my heavenly Father, I cover myself in the blood of Jesus Christ, and I put on the whole armor of God. I hereby come against every Prince of Persia that wants to hinder my prayer, I arrest you by the power in the blood of Jesus Christ, and I bind you and cast you down into the pit of hell.

I come against principalities and powers that wrestle with me and my prayers, I arrest you today by the power in the name of Jesus Christ, and I bind you and cast down into the pit of hell. I come against the rulers of the darkness of this world, against spiritual wickedness in high places, I arrest you all by the power in the name of Jesus Christ, and I bind you and cast you down into the pit of hell. I come against weakness and weariness, I arrest you today by the power in the name of Jesus Christ, and I bind you and cast you out of my life. I come against wondering

spirit and distractions, I arrest you today by the power in the name of Jesus Christ, and I bind you and cast you out of my life.

Today I receive the anointing to pray and get results, my prayers cannot be hindered nor delayed because Jesus is my Lord, I will pray today and get the desired results, I decree open heavens upon my prayers. I baptize myself in the fire of the Holy Ghost; therefore I have become too hot for the enemy to handle. My prayers today will attract divine intervention to every situation in my life; signs and wonders will follow my prayers today, testimonies will follow my prayers today and the name of God alone will be glorified, in Jesus name. Amen!

PRAYER POINTS:

1. O God my Father, thank you for being my God, my Father and my friend.
2. O God my Father, thank you for the privilege to know you and the power of the resurrection of Jesus Christ.
3. O God my Father, thank you for always being there for me and with me.
4. O God my Father, thank you for the great and mighty things that you are doing in my life.
5. O God my Father, thank you for your provision and protection over me and my household.
6. O God my Father, thank you for always answering my prayers.
7. I confess my sins before you today and I ask you to forgive me on the basis of your mercy, in the name of Jesus Christ.

8. Wash me clean today O Lord by the blood of Jesus Christ.
9. I cover myself and my household with the blood of Jesus Christ.
10. My prayers today will not go in vain; my prayers will produce the desired results in the name of Jesus Christ.
11. O God arise and open your book of remembrance and locate me now, in the name of Jesus Christ.
12. O God arise and fast-forward my breakthroughs, in the name of Jesus.
13. Every power of my father's house that does not want me to lift my head, be destroyed by the fire of God, in the name of Jesus.
14. Every power of my mother's house, that does not want me to lift my head, be destroyed by the fire of God, in the name of Jesus.
15. Let my tears fill the bottle of the Lord's mercy, in the name of Jesus.
16. In the valley of forgetfulness that the enemy has put me, O God my Father, draw me out by your mercy, in the name of Jesus.
17. O book of remembrance, assigned for my uncommon breakthroughs, open now, in the name of Jesus.
18. O book of remembrance, assigned for my uncommon miracles, open now, in the name of Jesus.
19. O book of remembrance, assigned for my uncommon blessings, within twenty-four hours, open in the name of Jesus.
20. Every enemy that wants me to die, die in my place, in the name of Jesus.

21. My Father, remember me by your mercy, in the name of Jesus.
22. My book of honor, open today by the fire of God, in the name of Jesus.
23. Begin to thank the Lord for what He has done for you.

PRAYER FOR BUSINESS AND FINANCIAL PROSPERITY

Passages To Read Before You Pray:
Deuteronomy 28:1-14, 8:18; Proverbs 10:4, 22:29, 24:27, 27:23-27; Joshua 1:8; Ecclesiastes 5:19.

I have come today to fellowship with my heavenly Father, and make my requests and needs known unto Him. I cannot be hindered nor delayed because I know who I am in the Lord. I am a child of the Kingdom, born of the Spirit, redeemed by the blood of Jesus Christ. I walk in authority, living life without any apology because the power and authority has been given to me according to the Word of God in the book of Luke 9:1.

As I have come to pray today and to fellowship with my heavenly Father, I cover myself in the blood of Jesus Christ, and I put on the whole armor of God. I hereby come against every Prince of Persia that wants to hinder my prayer, I arrest you by the power in the blood of Jesus Christ, and I bind you and cast you down into the pit of hell.

I come against principalities and powers that wrestle with me and my prayers, I arrest you today by the power in the name of Jesus Christ, and I bind you and cast down into the pit of hell. I come against the rulers of the darkness of this world, against spiritual wickedness in high places, I arrest you all by the power in the name of Jesus Christ, and I bind you and cast you down into the pit of hell. I come against weakness and weariness, I arrest you today by the power in the name of Jesus Christ, and I

bind you and cast you out of my life. I come against wondering spirit and distractions, I arrest you today by the power in the name of Jesus Christ, and I bind you and cast you out of my life.

Today I receive the anointing to pray and get results, my prayers cannot be hindered nor delayed because Jesus is my Lord, I will pray today and get the desired results, I decree open heavens upon my prayers. I baptize myself in the fire of the Holy Ghost; therefore I have become too hot for the enemy to handle. My prayers today will attract divine intervention to every situation in my life; signs and wonders will follow my prayers today, testimonies will follow my prayers today and the name of God alone will be glorified, in Jesus name. Amen!

PRAYER POINTS:

1. O God my Father, thank you for being my God, my Father and my friend.
2. O God my Father, thank you for the privilege to know you and the power of the resurrection of Jesus Christ.
3. O God my Father, thank you for always being there for me and with me.
4. O God my Father, thank you for the great and mighty things that you are doing in my life.
5. O God my Father, thank you for your provision and protection over me and my household.
6. O God my Father, thank you for always answering my prayers.
7. I confess my sins before you today and I ask you to forgive me on the basis of your mercy, in the name of Jesus Christ.

8. Wash me clean today O Lord by the blood of Jesus Christ.
9. I cover myself and my household with the blood of Jesus Christ.
10. My prayers today will not go in vain; my prayers will produce the desired results in the name of Jesus Christ.
11. Lord, baptize me with the generous spirit of a cheerful giver who gives out of love and not out of compulsion.
12. The Lord will make me a pillar of support for the expansion of God's Kingdom in Jesus name.
13. All my past generosity will be remembered by God. Every impossible situation in my life will be turned around by God on the account of my past generosity in Jesus name.
14. I believe in miracles, I serve a God of miracles therefore; every chapter closed by men against me will be re-opened by God in my favor in Jesus name.
15. Just as the famine in the days of Joseph elevated him, help me Lord to see the opportunity that the current global financial crisis has creating for my prosperity in Jesus name.
16. O Lord endow me with the required mental skills to interpret every opportunity that comes my way correctly and take maximum advantage of them in Jesus name.
17. I receive grace to enjoy riches that will endure throughout my life time in Jesus name.
18. I receive total liberty from the embarrassing yoke of debt in Jesus name.
19. I receive total deliverance from the embarrassing stigma of knocking on doors and repeated phone calls begging for financial assistance in Jesus name.

20. I will enjoy the surplus of heaven to achieve my purpose and have leftovers in Jesus name.
21. Murmuring will not take the place of money in my life and money will not mess me up; all my bills will be supernaturally settled in Jesus name.
22. I refuse to be a burden on my neighbors, families and friends. I am a lender and not a borrower in Jesus name.
23. Whenever anyone needs my help my purse will not be empty. I will be readily available to meet their needs in Jesus name.
24. O Lord, deliver me from the slavery of evil appetite/habit that are killing my health and destiny in Jesus name.
25. O Lord, deliver my spouse from the slavery of evil appetite/habit that are killing my health and destiny in Jesus name.
26. O Lord, deliver my children from the slavery of evil appetite/habit that are killing my health and destiny in Jesus name.
27. The Lord will satisfy my mouth with good things. I shall have appetite and money to eat choice foods and accomplish great things in Jesus name.
28. I receive total deliverance from the curse of poverty and affliction that has ever plaque my family line. I will live to transfer prosperity to my posterity in Jesus name.
29. I shall not only be great in wealth but also have a great name in Jesus name.
30. Let your Spirit empower me O Lord, to attain, sustain and enjoy success in Jesus name.
31. My joy shall multiply at the end of this month; I shall therefore count blessings and not sorrows in Jesus name.

32. O Lord, deliver me from profitless labor and confused activities in Jesus name.
33. I shall not waste my seed. I will be divinely guided to plant my seed on fertile soil in Jesus name.
34. O Lord, let the resources required to fulfill my dream in the custody of my enemies relocate into the custody of my friends and helpers in Jesus name.
35. O Lord, let money forever remain my loyal messenger in Jesus name.
36. Both the help from above and abroad will combine and compete to settle my bills and fulfill my dreams this year in Jesus name.
37. From now on all my investments and labor since the beginning of my career and ministry will begin to yield their full profit in Jesus name.
38. In every tight situation, let my tithe provoke heavenly solution in Jesus name.
39. This week my past generosity will spring forth a pleasant surprise in Jesus name.
40. Throughout this year, none of my resources shall be wasted on medical bills or any form of profitless venture in Jesus name.
41. Satan will not receive the backing of heaven to wipe out my financial resources with evil erosion in Jesus name.
42. Whosoever looks up to me for help this year will not be disappointed. I shall have enough to satisfy my needs and plenty to give to others in need in Jesus name.
43. I receive deliverance from the bondage of doubt and fear that past failures and misfortune have introduced into my life in Jesus name.
44. I receive the required courage to step into the greatness God has ordained for me in Jesus name.

45. I submit to the leadership of God's Spirit and I receive the backing of heaven to breakthrough and succeed in all my undertakings in Jesus name.
46. I receive the favorable countenance of God, therefore Heaven will agree with all my steps of faith and God's will shall prosper in my hands.
47. I refuse to submit my courage to frustration. God will send me encouragement today; I will be energized to continue the race in Jesus name.
48. The sun is rising today announcing my season of success and fulfilling my purpose in Jesus name.
49. Those that believe in me and have invested in my dream, encouraging and supporting me will not be disappointed in Jesus name.
50. The Lord will allow something better to come out of every bad situation that baffles me in Jesus name.
51. Let the prophetic power that operated in the valley of dry bones re-unite me with my lost glory, in Jesus name.
52. Let the prophetic power that operated in the valley of dry bones re-unite me with my helper, in Jesus name.
53. Let the prophetic power that operated in the valley of dry bones re-unite me with my husband/wife, in Jesus name.
54. Let the prophetic power that operated in the valley of dry bones re-unite me with my children, in Jesus name.
55. Let the prophetic power that operated in the valley of dry bones re-unite me with my joy, in Jesus name.
56. Every carnal attitude of disobedience and demonic spirits that are promoting barrenness in my life are terminated today in Jesus name.
57. Those doubting my ability to succeed will soon become my subjects in Jesus name.

58. Those that refuse to lend unto me during my moment of struggling will soon begin to lean on me in Jesus name.
59. Those laughing at me today will soon laugh with me and regret their folly of looking down on me in Jesus name.
60. Those who gather to frustrate my vision will beg to be part of my celebration in Jesus name.
61. Every opposition I encounter today will soon form a chapter of my success story in Jesus name.
62. The Lord will release a measure of prosperity into my life that will swallow all my history of poverty in Jesus name.
63. The Lord will give me a new name and a new identity that will bury all the ugly stories associated with my background in Jesus name.
64. My new life in Christ has clothed me with a garment of righteousness; my past sinful life will no longer hurt or haunt me in Jesus name.
65. A similar grace that made Jabez more honorable than his brethren will distinguish me among my equals in Jesus name.
66. Today marks the beginning of my bouncing back. My spiritual life shall be restored and my lost glory shall be fully recovered.
67. I declare every department of my life under the control of Satan disconnected in Jesus name.
68. All the sinful habits that enslave me to Satan will henceforth irritate me in Jesus name.
69. In all the areas where men have failed me, let your mercy prevail for me in Jesus name.
70. In all the areas where money may disgrace me, let your mercy raise men of influence in my favor in Jesus name.

71. This week I will encounter God's mercy that will end all problems of money associated with my family in Jesus name.
72. Inadequate supply will not compel me to abandon God. Excess supply will not deceive me to disconnect from God in Jesus name.
73. I receive Christ's Spirit of endurance to endure the season of adversity and wait for the era of prosperity in Jesus name.
74. The present adversity will not last forever; my business will not sink with the ongoing economic meltdown. The Spirit of God will usher in a new era of prosperity in Jesus name.
75. God's covenant of exception as it was in the land of Goshen will work in my favor against the ongoing economic recession in Jesus name.
76. Whatever positive purpose, I pursue, I will possess because the Spirit of God will instruct my steps in the right direction in Jesus name.
77. I rebuke the spirit of bareness from my business; my business will be fruitful and profitable in Jesus name.
78. The Holy Spirit will be the invincible Chief Executive Officer of my business in Jesus name.
79. I will not suffer scarcity of ideas nor inadequate capital to take my business to the next level in Jesus name.
80. The Spirit of God will expose and expel every Achan (traitor) among my employees that has the tendency of ruining my business in Jesus name.
81. The Spirit of God will deliver me from making recruitment error that is capable of crippling my business in Jesus name.

82. The Spirit of excellence, commitment, loyalty and uprightness will compel all my employees to work for the progress of my company in Jesus name.
83. Evil intentions and machination of my competitors will fail in Jesus name.
84. Every weapon sponsored through family relations or friends to wreck my business will not succeed in Jesus name.
85. I pronounce unstoppable prosperity over every project of my company in Jesus name.
86. Because this business is founded in partnership with God, it will take root downward, develop into branches and bear fruits upward in Jesus name.
87. I command a miraculous and total recovery of all debts owed to my company in Jesus name.
88. All my long-forgotten proposals will begin to receive the attention of the right and relevant authority in Jesus name.
89. The favor of God will envelope my company, office and shop in Jesus name.
90. Both my company's identity and complimentary card will carry God's presence and attract favor of my prospective customers, clients and contracts in Jesus name.
91. I repeal every Local and International legislation that is not in favor of the prosperity of my business in Jesus name.
92. My business premises will not receive demonic visitation of armed robbers and dupes; law enforcement agents sponsored against me will not succeed at implicating me in Jesus name.

93. Partnership that will ruin my business will not receive my endorsement in Jesus name.
94. Agent of darkness on evil assignment against my business will receive God's judgment of blindness in Jesus name.
95. The economic policy of this nation will begin to favor the prosperity of my business in Jesus name.
96. The vision of the Government in power will not antagonize my business prosperity in Jesus name.
97. Anoint me Lord to breakthrough without bribery in Jesus name.
98. Holy Ghost fire will consume all satanic ropes and chains that are around my wrongly seized goods; heaven will secure their release this week in Jesus name.
99. I untie all my customers and clients that have been tied around the aprons of my competitors with demonic spell in Jesus name.
100. Every goods that have overstayed in my shop and are at the risk of expiration will bring in money and relocate to its end users (consumer) in Jesus name.
101. This month I will sign a contract which's profit will pay all my debts and leave me with surplus that will make me to have nothing to do with debt again in Jesus name.
102. This month, my business premises will relocate from a rented apartment to our own property in Jesus name.
103. Henceforth, I will not borrow to pay my staff again in Jesus name.
104. My business will be sufficient to pay my bills, pay my staff and surplus enough to contribute to community development in Jesus name.

105. I receive help from above to resurrect my collapsed business and expand and diversify my flourishing ones in Jesus name.
106. I will not lack creative ideas to satisfy my customers / clients in Jesus name.
107. All the customers that I have pursued in the past without success will begin to beg to do business with me in Jesus name.
108. The current economic meltdown will not fold up my business in Jesus name.
109. The winnowing power of God's Spirit will blow away the spirit of waste and agents of waste from my business in Jesus name.
110. God's wind of wonder will deposit wealth into my business in Jesus name.
111. The Spirit of God will guide my business decisions; my capital shall not be tied down in unprofitable goods in Jesus name.
112. Products that have lost market value, and customers taste and appetite will not be grounded in my shop in Jesus name.
113. The Spirit of God will resist me from being manipulated by fraudsters to sign away all that I have labored for in Jesus name.
114. I shall not be manipulated by greed and covetousness to disobey heavenly warnings through dream and prophecy in Jesus name.
115. None of my business trips will record armed robbery attack or accident in Jesus name.
116. The supreme council of heaven will repeal, reverse, and amend every decree, policy, legislation that

is contrary to all my noble business vision in Jesus name.

SPECIAL PRAYER FOR THE MONTH OF JANUARY

Passages To Read Before You Pray:
Isaiah 43:19, Habakkuk 1:5, Joel 2:21-27, Psalms 19, 29, 42

"I enter this year with thanksgiving in my heart. I enter this year with Praise; I say this is the year that my Lord has made, I will rejoice for He has made me glad": O God of new beginnings and wonderful surprises, I thank you for the gift of a New Year. I declare this year a time of grace and joy for me and my family, a year to grow in faith and love, a year to renew my commitment and my fellowship with God. This is a year of blessing for me, a year of a new wine in a new bottle, a year to renew my efforts at my work and get good increase, a year that my barn shall be full of harvest and my land flowing with milk and honey. Lord Jesus, walk with me every-day, every-week, every-month, every-hour, every-minute and every-second of this year, in the name of Jesus. The light of Jesus Christ will shine upon me and through me, in all areas of my life. In my weakness this year, the Lord shall be my strength, in the name of Jesus. Above all things; I will always remember this year and all my days that I am a pilgrim on this earth and heaven is my eternal home: I have started this year in peace by the Power of the Most High God, and I will end this year in peace in the name of Jesus.

PRAYER POINTS:

1. Lord I thank you for the victory over the past year and your joy and mercy to enter into this New Year, be glorified in the name of Jesus.
2. O God my Father, thank you for being my God, my Father and my friend.
3. O God my Father, thank you for the privilege to know you and the power of the resurrection of Jesus Christ.
4. O God my Father, thank you for always being there for me and with me.
5. O God my Father, thank you for the great and mighty things that you are doing in my life.
6. O God my Father, thank you for your provision and protection over me and my household.
7. O God my Father, thank you for always answering my prayers.
8. I confess my sins before you today and I ask you to forgive me on the basis of your mercy, in the name of Jesus Christ.
9. Wash me clean today O Lord by the blood of Jesus Christ.
10. I cover myself and my household with the blood of Jesus Christ.
11. My prayers today will not go in vain; my prayers will produce the desired results in the name of Jesus Christ.
12. I humble myself before you Lord; forgive me of any sin that may stand on my way, in the name of Jesus.
13. Holy Spirit help me this year, I don't want to run ahead of you, guide me in the way o righteousness, in the name of Jesus.

14. Power from above to start a journey and to complete it fall upon my life, in the name of Jesus.
15. O God arise and position my life for uncommon victory in my journey this year, in the name of Jesus.
16. Power to start with faith and to end with praise, fall upon me, in the name of Jesus.
17. Every bad trait in my family line, I shall see you no more in my life, in the name of Jesus.
18. Let the stars in their causes rise and fight for me this year, in the name of Jesus.
19. I receive this year fresh anointing from above to disgrace any form of opposition, in the name of Jesus.
20. Darkness shall not rule over the light of my life, in the name of Jesus.
21. This year and all my days: my head reject every evil load, in the name of Jesus.
22. Any power anywhere hired to pull me down fall down and die, in the name of Jesus.
23. This year and all my days: my eyes shall not see corruption in the name of Jesus.
24. Arrows of affliction, arrows of infirmity shall not locate me and my family, in the name of Jesus.
25. Blood of Jesus connect me with those that matter this year, in the name of Jesus.
26. I electrify my destiny, my life and my family with the Holy Ghost fire against any attacks, in the name of Jesus.
27. I receive the anointing to move forward, in the name of Jesus.
28. Blessed Holy Spirit have your way in my life, my family, my ministry this year, in the name of Jesus.

29. Anointing to breakthrough beyond any human limitations, fall upon my life afresh this year, in the name of Jesus.
30. Peace of God Most High, be my companion this year and all my days, in the name of Jesus.
31. My life, my ministry, my family shall glorify the name of the Lord this year and all my days, in the name of Jesus.
32. In the midst of adversity this year; O Lord be my help and my comforter, in the name of Jesus.
33. My past years mistakes, will not hinder my miracles this year in the name of Jesus.
34. This year as the Spirit of God is alive; I shall not labor in vain, in the name of Jesus.
35. This year, I shall not build for the enemy to inhabit in the name of Jesus.
36. This year, I shall not plant for the enemy to harvest, in the name of Jesus.
37. This year, I shall not go to the journey of no return, in the name of Jesus.
38. This year, my enemies will not rejoice over me, in the name of Jesus.
39. This year, I shall not beg to buy bread, in the name of Jesus.
40. With your great mercy O Lord; add riches to riches in my life and my family's lives, in the name of Jesus.
41. This year, O Lord of host; when the plan or arrangement of man call for battle/war, let your heavenly program of victory appear in my life, in the name of Jesus.
42. This year, O Lord, according to your mercy lift up my head and empower me to achieve greatness, in the name of Jesus.

43. O Lord, since the heaven and the earth is full of your glory; let your glory envelope me and my family this year and all our days, in the name of Jesus.
44. Lord Jesus by your mercy that endures forever, move me from where I am this year to where you want me to be, in the name of Jesus.
45. Anointing of power and fire to do the right thing at the right time fall upon my life, in the name of Jesus.
46. By the mercy of God, I decree whatsoever my enemy has planned to confuse me, and to discourage me with this year, will not have an impact in my life, in the name of Jesus.
47. My life will not listen to the enemy's instructions, in the name of Jesus.
48. Bewitchment from household wickedness shall not confuse my life this year, in the name of Jesus.
49. Bewitchment from church old wickedness shall not pollute my live this year, in the name of Jesus.
50. Environmental bewitchment shall not cut my life off this year, in the name of Jesus.
51. Whatsoever my God does not want for my life and my destiny, it shall not come to pass in my life this year, in the name of Jesus.
52. Anointing to know what is important and good in the presence of God for my life fall upon me this year, in the name of Jesus.
53. In this year I shall not journey on the road that leads to disaster and tragedy, in the name of Jesus.
54. This year I shall not travel on the road that leads to failure, frustration and disappointment, in the name of Jesus.

55. Every decision I shall make this year, will not lead to regret and sorrow, in the name of Jesus.
56. Holy Ghost Power incubate me, direct me, in all my decision making, in the name of Jesus.
57. Anointing for sound mind to make right decisions and to pass the right judgment, come upon me afresh this year in the name of Jesus.
58. Blessed Holy Spirit I thank because you are my helper and I know you will see me through to the end.

SPECIAL PRAYER FOR THE MONTH OF FEBRUARY

Passages To Read Before You Pray:
Isaiah 43:19, Habakkuk 1:5, Joel 2:21-27, Psalms 19, 29, 42

I have come today to fellowship with my heavenly Father, and make my requests and needs known unto Him. I cannot be hindered nor delayed because I know who I am in the Lord. I am a child of the Kingdom, born of the Spirit, redeemed by the blood of Jesus Christ. I walk in authority, living life without any apology because the power and authority has been given to me according to the Word of God in the book of Luke 9:1.

As I have come to pray today and to fellowship with my heavenly Father, I cover myself in the blood of Jesus Christ, and I put on the whole armor of God. I hereby come against every Prince of Persia that wants to hinder my prayer, I arrest you by the power in the blood of Jesus Christ, and I bind you and cast you down into the pit of hell.

I come against principalities and powers that wrestle with me and my prayers, I arrest you today by the power in the name of Jesus Christ, and I bind you and cast down into the pit of hell. I come against the rulers of the darkness of this world, against spiritual wickedness in high places, I arrest you all by the power in the name of Jesus Christ, and I bind you and cast you down into the pit of hell. I come against weakness and weariness, I arrest you today by the power in the name of Jesus Christ, and I bind you and cast you out of my life. I come against wondering

spirit and distractions, I arrest you today by the power in the name of Jesus Christ, and I bind you and cast you out of my life.

Today I receive the anointing to pray and get results, my prayers cannot be hindered nor delayed because Jesus is my Lord, I will pray today and get the desired results, I decree open heavens upon my prayers. I baptize myself in the fire of the Holy Ghost; therefore I have become too hot for the enemy to handle. My prayers today will attract divine intervention to every situation in my life; signs and wonders will follow my prayers today, testimonies will follow my prayers today and the name of God alone will be glorified, in Jesus name. Amen!

PRAYER POINTS:

1. O God my Father, thank you for being my God, my Father and my friend.
2. O God my Father, thank you for the privilege to know you and the power of the resurrection of Jesus Christ.
3. O God my Father, thank you for always being there for me and with me.
4. O God my Father, thank you for the great and mighty things that you are doing in my life.
5. O God my Father, thank you for your provision and protection over me and my household.
6. O God my Father, thank you for always answering my prayers.
7. I confess my sins before you today and I ask you to forgive me on the basis of your mercy, in the name of Jesus Christ.

8. Wash me clean today O Lord by the blood of Jesus Christ.
9. I cover myself and my household with the blood of Jesus Christ.
10. My prayers today will not go in vain; my prayers will produce the desired results in the name of Jesus Christ.

11. Ask for the baptism of the Holy Ghost to come upon your life and your household, in the name of Jesus.
12. O Arm of God that cannot fail; arise and lift me up from the valley of sickness and infirmity, in the name of Jesus.
13. Thou everlasting arm of God that cannot fail; arise, fight for me and deliver me, in the name of Jesus.
14. O arm of God that cannot fail; arise and break me loose from ancestral bondage, in the name of Jesus.
15. O arm of God that cannot fail; arise and set me free from the oppression of the enemy, in the name of Jesus.
16. O arm of God, deliver me from the grip of witchcraft power attack, in the name of Jesus.
17. O arm of God, arise give me joy and let sorrow depart from my life, in the name of Jesus.
18. O Lord let your divine favor encompass me and my household this month, this year and all our days, in the name of Jesus.
19. O Lord my father, by your power that cannot fail let all my Herods receive spiritual and physical decay, in the name of Jesus.
20. By the power in the blood of Jesus, I reject any demonic limitations and restrictions to my progress, in the name of Jesus.

21. By the power in the blood of Jesus, I decree that nothing shall be impossible for me this month, this year and all my days, in the name of Jesus.
22. Every satanic trap set for my sake; catch your owner, in the name of Jesus.
23. Every dark power affecting my destiny in the dream die by fire, in the name of Jesus.
24. Every anti-progress dream die, by fire in the name of Jesus.
25. My dream of success: manifest by fire, in the name of Jesus.
26. Every satanic traffic of bad luck operating in my life be arrested by fire, in the name of Jesus.
27. Witchcraft power assigned to destroy my peaceful dream you're a liar fall down and die, in the name of Jesus.
28. I shall not die but live to declare the good works of the Lord, in the name of Jesus.
29. The joy of the Lord is my strength, in the name of Jesus.
30. Holy Spirit, I have not journeyed in this month before therefore go with me and guide me and my family, in the name of Jesus.
31. Every physical and spiritual barrier to my joy this month be removed by fire, in the name of Jesus.
32. Every wall of hostility erected against my family this month, be pulled down according to the order of the wall of Jericho, in the name of Jesus.
33. O God arise and remove the reproach of house hold wickedness from my life, my marriage this month, in the name of Jesus.
34. Any evil eye monitoring the affairs of my family this month, receive permanent blindness, in the name of Jesus.

35. My miracle this month be invisible to the power of darkness, in the name of Jesus.
36. My testimony this month, defy logical explanation, in the name of Jesus.
37. Power of unity and harmony rest upon my life/ family, this month and all the days of my life, in the name of Jesus.
38. I receive divine wisdom to run the affairs of my home/ marriage successfully, in the name of Jesus.
39. You demon of disunity and hostility, I chase you out of my life/ marriage, in the name of Jesus.
40. Lord Jesus, you are the prince of peace, take total control of my life, home and marriage in the name of Jesus.
41. This month my testimony will make people to look at me with amazement and follow me to my God, in the name of Jesus.
42. By the power in the blood of the Lamb: This month my story shall change to the best, in the name of Jesus.
43. This month any power or wicked personality laughing with me in the day time and selling my information to the enemies at night , be disgraced, be exposed and be destroyed, by fire and thunder of God, in the name of Jesus.
44. By the power in the blood of Jesus: I shall arise above my root, in the name of Jesus.
45. By the power in the blood of the Lamb I shall see my afflictions no more, in the name of Jesus.
46. By the power of resurrected and glorified Jesus Christ: I shall rise and shine, in the name of Jesus.
47. Begin to thank the name of the Lord for answering your prayers. Glory be to His Holy name in the highest.

48. Holy Spirit be my companion this month, guide me in all my ways, let my thoughts be of you, in the name of Jesus.
49. Power of God be with me this month in all that I will do and let the name of the Lord be glorified, in Jesus name.
50. Presence of the Living God, go ahead of me this month, be the light unto my path and a lamp on my feet, in the name of Jesus.
51. This month I decree I will not outrun God in the affairs of my life, in the name of Jesus.
52. O Lord, rekindle my life with your fresh-fire, in the name of Jesus.
53. Holy Ghost Fire, burn to ashes every seed of failure in my life, in the name of Jesus.
54. Every impurity in my life, be washed away by the Blood of Jesus, in the name of Jesus.
55. Lord Jesus, hold me in the palm of your hands by your mercy, in the name of Jesus.
56. O God my Father, enrich me this month with your heavenly gifts, in the name of Jesus.
57. O God my Father, God of abundance bless me with the untold riches of the gentiles this month, in the name of Jesus.
58. O God my Father, re-align my life to suit your purpose, in the name of Jesus.
59. Lord Jesus create in me holy hunger, thirst for righteous living this month and all my days, in the name of Jesus.
60. Lord Jesus, quicken my spirit and increase my desire for the things of heaven, in Jesus name.
61. Lord Jesus, give me a new generous heart, in the name of Jesus.

62. Blood of Jesus, Holy Ghost Fire refresh every dry area of my life, in the name of Jesus.
63. My labor shall not enrich the enemies of God this month and all my days, in Jesus name.
64. Holy Spirit, have your way in my life this month and all my days, in the name of Jesus.
65. O God of Elijah; the God that answered by fire on Mount Carmel, fight my battle in an unusual way this month, in the name of Jesus.
66. O God of Elijah, arise in your power and scatter every evil gathering against my breakthrough this month, in the name of Jesus.
67. Anger of the Lord arise and scatter every witchcraft gathering organized for my sake, in the name of Jesus.
68. I command every evil tongue anointed by satan to curse me this month, be silenced forever, in the name of Jesus.
69. Every evil unity against the plan of God for my life this month, scatter unto desolation, in the name of Jesus.
70. I receive the anointing to disgrace every plan of the wicked assigned against my breakthrough, in the name of Jesus.
71. Any invisible chain on my hand and legs preventing me from moving forward, break asunder in the name of Jesus.
72. Witchcraft habitations from my place of birth conspiring to destroy my life; be destroyed by fire in the name of Jesus.
73. Congregation of the witches and wizards gathering for my sake scatter unto desolation, in the name of Jesus.
74. Powers and principalities rising against my progress, vanish in the name of Jesus.

75. Coven powers assigned to destroy me, be destroyed by fire, in the name of Jesus.
76. Arrows of discouragement fired into my life jump out and locate your sender, in the name of Jesus.
77. Any power or principalities making life difficult for me in the land of opportunity die, in the name of Jesus.
78. My full time enemies receive full time disgrace and shame, in the name of Jesus.
79. I shall not labor in vain, in the name of Jesus.
80. The work of my hands shall not become a reproach in my life, in the name of Jesus.
81. I shall not struggle to death, in the name of Jesus.
82. My glory, arise and begin to shine according to the divine agenda of the almighty, in the name of Jesus.
83. Glory be to the name of the Lord in highest for answering my prayers, in the name of Jesus.

SPECIAL PRAYER FOR THE MONTH OF MARCH

Passages To Read Before You Pray:
Isaiah 43:19, Habakkuk 1:5, Joel 2:21-27, Psalms 19, 29, 42

I have come today to fellowship with my heavenly Father, and make my requests and needs known unto Him. I cannot be hindered nor delayed because I know who I am in the Lord. I am a child of the Kingdom, born of the Spirit, redeemed by the blood of Jesus Christ. I walk in authority, living life without any apology because the power and authority has been given to me according to the Word of God in the book of Luke 9:1.

As I have come to pray today and to fellowship with my heavenly Father, I cover myself in the blood of Jesus Christ, and I put on the whole armor of God. I hereby come against every Prince of Persia that wants to hinder my prayer, I arrest you by the power in the blood of Jesus Christ, and I bind you and cast you down into the pit of hell.

I come against principalities and powers that wrestle with me and my prayers, I arrest you today by the power in the name of Jesus Christ, and I bind you and cast down into the pit of hell. I come against the rulers of the darkness of this world, against spiritual wickedness in high places, I arrest you all by the power in the name of Jesus Christ, and I bind you and cast you down into the pit of hell. I come against weakness and weariness, I arrest you today by the power in the name of Jesus Christ, and I

bind you and cast you out of my life. I come against wondering spirit and distractions, I arrest you today by the power in the name of Jesus Christ, and I bind you and cast you out of my life.

Today I receive the anointing to pray and get results, my prayers cannot be hindered nor delayed because Jesus is my Lord, I will pray today and get the desired results, I decree open heavens upon my prayers. I baptize myself in the fire of the Holy Ghost; therefore I have become too hot for the enemy to handle. My prayers today will attract divine intervention to every situation in my life; signs and wonders will follow my prayers today, testimonies will follow my prayers today and the name of God alone will be glorified, in Jesus name. Amen!

PRAYER POINTS:

1. O God my Father, thank you for being my God, my Father and my friend.
2. O God my Father, thank you for the privilege to know you and the power of the resurrection of Jesus Christ.
3. O God my Father, thank you for always being there for me and with me.
4. O God my Father, thank you for the great and mighty things that you are doing in my life.
5. O God my Father, thank you for your provision and protection over me and my household.
6. O God my Father, thank you for always answering my prayers.
7. I confess my sins before you today and I ask you to forgive me on the basis of your mercy, in the name of Jesus Christ.

8. Wash me clean today O Lord by the blood of Jesus Christ.
9. I cover myself and my household with the blood of Jesus Christ.
10. My prayers today will not go in vain; my prayers will produce the desired results in the name of Jesus Christ.
11. Holy Spirit my comforter, be with me on my journey this month and all my days, in the name of Jesus.
12. Lord Jesus, empower me to stand for the truth of your word, in the name of Jesus.
13. Every chariot and horse of trouble and tribulations assigned against my progress this month, be destroyed by the fire of God, in the name of Jesus.
14. Evil congregation organized against me this month, scatter unto desolation, in the name of Jesus.
15. Blessed Holy Spirit, even in the midst of turmoil, empower me to hear your voice and obey you, in the name of Jesus.
16. O God of Abraham, Isaac and Jacob, you are the God of Covenant, bring your Word to pass in my life this month, in the name of Jesus.
17. Every wicked power, delegated to break my staff of bread, with the rod of iron I break your back bone, in the name of Jesus.
18. Every troubled water, water of affliction roaring against my peace dry up by the fire of God, in the name of Jesus.
19. The wickedness of the wicked shall not prevail over my life and my family, in the name of Jesus.

20. Every arrogant and rebellious power challenging the authority of God in my life, be silenced forever, in the name of Jesus.
21. Witchcraft verdict against my progress be cancelled by the blood of Jesus.
22. Witchcraft decree over my life, be revoked by the blood of Jesus.
23. My life; my destiny; reject every witchcraft burial arrangement in the name of Jesus.
24. I shall not die but live to declare the works of the Lord, in the name of Jesus.
25. Arrow of prayerlessness fired into my life in the dream, get out of my life and locate your sender in the name of Jesus.
26. I withdraw the timetable of my life from the hands of the powers of the night, in the name of Jesus.
27. This month and all my days the enemy shall not harvest my labor, in the name of Jess.
28. This month and all my days I shall live above every limitation and restriction of the enemy, in the name of Jesus.
29. Blood of Jesus, defend my cause and protect my interest in every way, in the name of Jesus.
30. O Lord light my way this month and all my days that I may not journey into destruction, in the name of Jesus.
31. Every satanic ambush awaiting my arrival this month, this year and all my days: be consumed by the fire of God, in the name of Jesus.
32. I overthrow every obstacle on my way to breakthrough this month, this year and all my days, in the name of Jesus.

33. By the fire of God, I overthrown any evil king or dominion ruling my land of Canaan, in the name of Jesus.
34. Every satanic lion roaring in my land of breakthrough /my land of possession: you are a liar, die today by the fire of God, in the name of Jesus.
35. Every wicked power assigned to waste my efforts this month, this year and all my days, be destroyed by the fire of God, in the name of Jesus.
36. Destruction from the almighty God; visit the camp of my unrepentant enemies as you did for the Egyptians, in the name of Jesus.
37. Strange voices scaring away my helpers: I command you to be silenced forever, in the name of Jesus.
38. Strange fire prepared for my sake by the household witchcraft, backfire and destroy your owner, in the name of Jesus.
39. In this month and all my days; my body, soul and spirit reject the arrow of sickness, in the name of Jesus.
40. In this month and all my days, my life rejects the call of untimely death, in the name of Jesus.
41. Let the chastisement inflicted upon my savior Jesus Christ stand against any power of infirmity in my life, in the name of Jesus.
42. I attack every attacker of my divine connection this month, this year and all my days, in the name of Jesus.
43. I oppose every opposition to my greatness by the sword of fire, in the name of Jesus.
44. This month O God, arise and turn my point of ridicule to my point of rejoicing, in the name of Jesus.
45. Living waters from the throne of mercy quench my thirst today and forever, in the name of Jesus.

46. I overcome every battle against my progress this month and all my days by the fire of God, in the name of Jesus.
47. I reject failure at the edge of success this month, this year, and all my days, in the name of Jesus.
48. Holy Ghost fire, ignite my prayer life and set me on fire for God, in the name of Jesus.
49. O God my Father, arise in your mercy and help me in my journey with you this month, in the name of Jesus.
50. Holy Spirit divine, guide me and direct my path in this month, in the name of Jesus.
51. My life, my destiny jump out of every cage of sorrow, in the name of Jesus.
52. O hand of the living God, arise and deliver me from every witchcraft attack, in the name of Jesus.
53. O Mighty hand of the Lord that parted the red sea, arise! Separate my life from failure and defeat, in the name of Jesus.
54. Every wall of separation between me and my breakthroughs, be destroyed by the fire of God, in the name of Jesus.
55. Every wall of division between me and my spouse, be removed by the fire of God, in the name of Jesus.
56. Every wall of separation between me and my children, be destroyed by the fire of God, in the name of Jesus.
57. Every evil imagination against my life this month, scatter by fire, in the name of Jesus.
58. I pull down every stronghold of marital failure and marital distress, in the name of Jesus.
59. I pull down every stronghold of financial failure, in the name of Jesus.
60. Power of God, power of transformation; come upon my life afresh, in the name of Jesus.

61. Wherever I have been knocked down spiritually, O God my Father, lift me up by your mercy, in the name of Jesus.
62. Wherever I have been knocked down matrimonially; O God my Father, lift me up by your mercy, in the name of Jesus.
63. O God of Elijah, arise and disappoint my enemies, disgrace my oppressors, in the name of Jesus.
64. Any weapon of destruction fashioned against me and my family this month, backfire by fire, in the name of Jesus.
65. Goliath of my destiny, I command you to die by your own sword, in the name of Jesus.
66. Any wicked power, evil authority, that hate to see me rejoicing, die in sorrow in the name of Jesus.
67. I thank you Lord for your love towards me, I give you praise for answering my prayers. Glory be to your holy name in the name of Jesus.

SPECIAL PRAYER FOR THE MONTH OF APRIL

Passages To Read Before You Pray:
Isaiah 43:19, Habakkuk 1:5, Joel 2:21-27, Psalms 19, 29, 42

I have come today to fellowship with my heavenly Father, and make my requests and needs known unto Him. I cannot be hindered nor delayed because I know who I am in the Lord. I am a child of the Kingdom, born of the Spirit, redeemed by the blood of Jesus Christ. I walk in authority, living life without any apology because the power and authority has been given to me according to the Word of God in the book of Luke 9:1.

As I have come to pray today and to fellowship with my heavenly Father, I cover myself in the blood of Jesus Christ, and I put on the whole armor of God. I hereby come against every Prince of Persia that wants to hinder my prayer, I arrest you by the power in the blood of Jesus Christ, and I bind you and cast you down into the pit of hell.

I come against principalities and powers that wrestle with me and my prayers, I arrest you today by the power in the name of Jesus Christ, and I bind you and cast down into the pit of hell. I come against the rulers of the darkness of this world, against spiritual wickedness in high places, I arrest you all by the power in the name of Jesus Christ, and I bind you and cast you down into the pit of hell. I come against weakness and weariness, I arrest you today by the power in the name of Jesus Christ, and I

bind you and cast you out of my life. I come against wondering spirit and distractions, I arrest you today by the power in the name of Jesus Christ, and I bind you and cast you out of my life.

Today I receive the anointing to pray and get results, my prayers cannot be hindered nor delayed because Jesus is my Lord, I will pray today and get the desired results, I decree open heavens upon my prayers. I baptize myself in the fire of the Holy Ghost; therefore I have become too hot for the enemy to handle. My prayers today will attract divine intervention to every situation in my life; signs and wonders will follow my prayers today, testimonies will follow my prayers today and the name of God alone will be glorified, in Jesus name. Amen!

PRAYER POINTS:

1. O God my Father, thank you for being my God, my Father and my friend.
2. O God my Father, thank you for the privilege to know you and the power of the resurrection of Jesus Christ.
3. O God my Father, thank you for always being there for me and with me.
4. O God my Father, thank you for the great and mighty things that you are doing in my life.
5. O God my Father, thank you for your provision and protection over me and my household.
6. O God my Father, thank you for always answering my prayers.
7. I confess my sins before you today and I ask you to forgive me on the basis of your mercy, in the name of Jesus Christ.

8. Wash me clean today O Lord by the blood of Jesus Christ.
9. I cover myself and my household with the blood of Jesus Christ.
10. My prayers today will not go in vain; my prayers will produce the desired results in the name of Jesus Christ.

11. Blessed Holy Spirit come into my life, empower me and connect me to the throne of mercy in the name of Jesus.
12. O God my Father, in this month of April, visit my life in a new way, in the name of Jesus.
13. God of signs and wonders, arise and cause rivers to flow in my desert and make a way in my wilderness, in the name of Jesus.
14. Every gate of brass hindering my breakthroughs, be destroyed by the fire of God, in the name of Jesus.
15. Every iron under my feet or in my ground of cultivation, be melted by the fire of God, in the name of Jesus.
16. O God my Father, every good and perfect gift comes from you: bless me with the heavenly gifts this month, in the name of Jesus.
17. By the authority in the word of God I decree, season of sorrow and frustration depart from my life, season of joy and celebrations appear now by fire, in the name of Jesus.
18. The miracle that will speak for itself, manifest in my life this month, in the name of Jesus.
19. Any invisible wicked power holding me down from moving forward, wherever you are release me, in the name of Jesus.
20. By the power that parted the red sea, I separate my life from failure and frustration, in the name of Jesus.

21. O God my Father, let the blood of Jesus clear away every evil mark upon my body, in the name of Jesus.
22. Every curse of non-achievement or backwardness upon my life, brake by fire, in the name of Jesus.
23. Every satanic barricade against my progress, be destroyed by the fire of God, in the name of Jesus.
24. Witchcraft umbrella covering my glory, be destroyed by the fire of God, in the name of Jesus.
25. Satanic door keeper standing at my door of breakthrough; die by the fire of God, in the name of Jesus.
26. Any evil covenant from my foundation holding me down from moving forward, break by the fire of God, in the name of Jesus.
27. Arrows of darkness fired into my life, jump out now and locate your sender, in the name of Jesus.
28. Satanic delegate assigned to hurt me or harm me this month, you are a liar go back now and kill your sender and kill yourself, in the name of Jesus.
29. I release death sentence upon all my stubborn pursuers in the name of Jesus.
30. O Heavens, arise and write the obituary of my stubborn oppressors, in the name of Jesus.
31. I cover my life and my family with the blood of Jesus.
32. My testimony shall not die, in the name of Jesus.
33. I shall see the goodness of the Lord in the land of the living, in the name of Jesus.
34. Holy Spirit, take control of my life, in the name of Jesus.
35. Power of God, power of Pentecost come upon my life a fresh, in the name of Jesus.
36. By the power in the Blood of Jesus; let the rain of increase begin to fall, in the name of Jesus.

37. By the authority in the word of God, let my rain of divine connection begin to fall, in the name of Jesus.
38. By the power in the name of Jesus, which is above all name, let my rain of fruitfulness begin to fall upon me, in the name of Jesus.
39. My rain of promotion, begin to fall upon me now, in the name of Jesus.
40. Every satanic audience waiting to mock me this month, scatter by fire, in the name of Jesus.
41. Evil yoke of poverty/debt around my neck break by fire, in the name of Jesus.
42. Evil yoke of profitless hard work, upon my life, break by fire, in the name of Jesus.
43. Satanic chains of non-achievement tying me down, be destroyed by the fire of God, in the name of Jesus.
44. Viper of poverty attached to my hand, I shake you off into the lake of fire, in the name of Jesus.
45. Bondage of joblessness, bondage of business failure, break by fire, in name of Jesus.
46. Every embargo of failure upon my life, be lifted and be destroyed by the fire of God, in the name of Jesus.
47. You destiny vulture attached to my life, vomit my destiny and die by fire, in the name of Jesus.
48. Evil hands holding me down to one spot; wither by the fire of God, in the name of Jesus.
49. Witchcraft pronouncements upon my life and finances, be neutralized, in the name of Jesus.
50. Every ladder of failure erected at my destiny, be destroyed by the fire of God, in the name of Jesus.
51. In this month of April, I shall not fish in the Dead Sea, in the name of Jesus.

52. Witchcraft arrows of stagnancy fired at my destiny, I send you back by fire, in the name of Jesus.
53. You Lazarus of my breakthrough, come out of the grave and manifest by fire, in the name of Jesus.
54. Anointing for supernatural breakthrough fall upon my life, in the name of Jesus.
55. Any wickedness in my way, O God my Father, remove it by your mercy, in the name of Jesus.
56. Blessed Holy Spirit, have your way in my life, and make me your vessel of honor, in the name of Jesus.
57. Power of God come upon my life afresh, and direct my path in the name of Jesus.
58. Every organized wickedness set against my life this month, scatter by fire in the name of Jesus.
59. Wickedness of the wicked shall not prosper in my life this month and all my days, in the name of Jesus.
60. Witchcraft mirror set in place to monitor the affairs of my life, be shattered in the name of Jesus.
61. Any evil meeting set in the heavenlies for my sake, scatter by fire in the name of Jesus.
62. Any wicked power, evil association waiting to celebrate my failure, you are a liar, scatter by fire, in the name of Jesus.
63. Arrow of destruction will not locate me and every member of my family, in the name of Jesus.
64. Arrow of sudden death will not locate me and my family, in the name of Jesus.
65. Arrow of disaster will not locate me and my family, in the name of Jesus.
66. Every gate of prayerlessness, fired into my life, be destroyed by the fire of God, in the name of Jesus.

67. Enemy of prayer in my life, what are you waiting for fall down and die, in the name of Jesus.
68. Every evil attachment of darkness upon my life, be destroyed by the fire of God, in the name of Jesus.
69. Serpent of darkness attached to my life to suffocate my spiritual life, I command you to die by the fire of God, in the name of Jesus.
70. Every iron-gate challenging my breakthroughs, be destroyed by the fire of God, in the name of Jesus.
71. Every invisible hand holding me down from moving forward, wither by fire, in the name of Jesus.
72. Any wicked power from the waters, from the forest, from the heavenlies and from the earth, set up to mess me up this month, be destroyed by the fire of God, in the name of Jesus.
73. Any evil power set up anywhere to frustrate my efforts this month, perish by fire, in the name of Jesus.
74. O God my Father, arise and glorify your name in my life, in the name of Jesus.
75. O God my Father, let my heaven open and let the anointing of resurrection speak to my situation, in the name of Jesus.
76. I connect my spirit soul and body to the resurrection power of the Lord Jesus Christ, in the name of Jesus.
77. Every satanic agenda against my life and my destiny, scatter by fire, in the name of Jesus.
78. Any of my virtue in the grave, come out and live in the name of Jesus.
79. My life and my destiny are no longer a candidate of the grave, come alive and shine, live in the name of Jesus.

80. Because Jesus Christ is no more in the grave, therefore I terminate every premature journey into the grave , in the name of Jesus.
81. Every local satanic weapon fashioned against my life, be destroyed by the fire of God, in the name of Jesus.
82. In this month of April, I receive the mouth and the wisdom which my adversaries cannot withstand or contend against, in the name of Jesus.
83. By the power in the blood of the lamb: I receive deliverance from the power of the grave, in the name of Jesus.
84. I bind every power cursing my destiny into ineffectiveness, in the name of Jesus.
85. Let the resurrection power of the Lord come upon my life and revive my spiritual life, in the name of Jesus.
86. I bind the spirit of death and hell in my life and my family, and I cast it out to the lake of fire, in the name of Jesus.
87. I command every dead bone in my life to come alive by the resurrection power of the Lord Jesus, in the name of Jesus.
88. I receive life of God and I reject every spirit of death and hell, in the name of Jesus.
89. O God my Father, let the power of resurrection speak life to every dead situation in my life, in the name of Jesus.
90. By the power of resurrection, I break the hold of any evil power or evil force upon my life, in the name of Jesus.
91. Holy Spirit of God, arise and fulfill the purpose of Calvary in my life , in the name of Jesus.
92. I disgrace every evil wisdom working against the agenda of God for my life in the name of Jesus.

93. Lord Jesus, create in me thirst and hunger for righteousness and holiness, in the name of Jesus.
94. I bind all evil powers withholding my testimonies and my miracles, in the name of Jesus.
95. Holy Ghost, fulfill the purpose of resurrection in my life and my family, in the name of Jesus.
96. By the power in the blood of the lamb and by the anointing of resurrection, I move from bondage into liberty, in the name of Jesus.

SPECIAL PRAYER FOR THE MONTH OF MAY

Passages To Read Before You Pray:
Isaiah 43:19, Habakkuk 1:5, Joel 2:21-27, Psalms 19, 29, 42

I have come today to fellowship with my heavenly Father, and make my requests and needs known unto Him. I cannot be hindered nor delayed because I know who I am in the Lord. I am a child of the Kingdom, born of the Spirit, redeemed by the blood of Jesus Christ. I walk in authority, living life without any apology because the power and authority has been given to me according to the Word of God in the book of Luke 9:1.

As I have come to pray today and to fellowship with my heavenly Father, I cover myself in the blood of Jesus Christ, and I put on the whole armor of God. I hereby come against every Prince of Persia that wants to hinder my prayer, I arrest you by the power in the blood of Jesus Christ, and I bind you and cast you down into the pit of hell.

I come against principalities and powers that wrestle with me and my prayers, I arrest you today by the power in the name of Jesus Christ, and I bind you and cast down into the pit of hell. I come against the rulers of the darkness of this world, against spiritual wickedness in high places, I arrest you all by the power in the name of Jesus Christ, and I bind you and cast you down into the pit of hell. I come against weakness and weariness, I arrest you today by the power in the name of Jesus Christ, and I bind you and cast you out of my life. I come against wondering

spirit and distractions, I arrest you today by the power in the name of Jesus Christ, and I bind you and cast you out of my life.

Today I receive the anointing to pray and get results, my prayers cannot be hindered nor delayed because Jesus is my Lord, I will pray today and get the desired results, I decree open heavens upon my prayers. I baptize myself in the fire of the Holy Ghost; therefore I have become too hot for the enemy to handle. My prayers today will attract divine intervention to every situation in my life; signs and wonders will follow my prayers today, testimonies will follow my prayers today and the name of God alone will be glorified, in Jesus name. Amen!

PRAYER POINTS:

1. O God my Father, thank you for being my God, my Father and my friend.
2. O God my Father, thank you for the privilege to know you and the power of the resurrection of Jesus Christ.
3. O God my Father, thank you for always being there for me and with me.
4. O God my Father, thank you for the great and mighty things that you are doing in my life.
5. O God my Father, thank you for your provision and protection over me and my household.
6. O God my Father, thank you for always answering my prayers.
7. I confess my sins before you today and I ask you to forgive me on the basis of your mercy, in the name of Jesus Christ.

8. Wash me clean today O Lord by the blood of Jesus Christ.
9. I cover myself and my household with the blood of Jesus Christ.
10. My prayers today will not go in vain; my prayers will produce the desired results in the name of Jesus Christ.
11. Holy Spirit, have your way in my life, in the name of Jesus.
12. O God my Father, arise and show your raw power in my life, in this month of grace, in the name of Jesus.
13. O God my Father, arise and disgrace my enemies in a new way in this month of Grace, in the name of Jesus.
14. In this month of Grace, O God my Father, empower me to hear your voice and be able to recognize your voice, in the name of Jesus.
15. Every agreement of the enemy for my life in this month of May shall not stand, in the name of Jesus.
16. O God my Father, let your mercy deliver me from every satanic litigations and allegations, in the name of Jesus.
17. O God my Father, arise and proclaim your glory over my life in a wonderful way, in the name of Jesus.
18. Anything in the kingdom of darkness standing against my life and against my greatness, be dismantled today, in the name of Jesus.
19. Any ancestral mark of rejection upon my life, be washed away by the blood of Jesus, in the name of Jesus.
20. O God my Father, arise and fight for me as you fought for Daniel in the lion's den, in the name of Jesus.
21. Evil associations that gather around to mock the name of God in my life; scatter by fire in the name of Jesus.

22. Any genetically originated problems affecting my life, receive permanent solution today, in the name of Jesus.
23. In this month of Grace, O God my Father, empower me to be at the right place at the right time doing the right thing, in the name of Jesus.
24. Any power keeping me behind from getting to my heavenly ordained goal scatter by fire, in the name of Jesus.
25. Yoke of perpetual failure upon my life, break by the fire of God, in the name of Jesus.
26. Any witchcraft pillar standing as a hindrance to my greatness, be destroyed by the fire of God, in the name of Jesus.
27. Every environmental witchcraft agent monitoring my life for destruction, be destroyed by fire, in the name of Jesus.
28. Evil water of sorrow flowing in my family line, dry up now, in the name of Jesus.
29. My head, hear the word of the Lord, reject the arrows of death, in the name of Jesus.
30. Progress arresters, you will not arrest my progress, in the name of Jesus.
31. My destiny, receive divine acceleration and begin to move forward, in the name of Jesus.
32. Every witchcraft deposit in my body, be flushed away by the blood of Jesus Christ, in the name of Jesus.
33. You troublers of my Israel; God of Elijah shall trouble you, in the name of Jesus.
34. Any power anywhere using evil authority over my life, die by fire, in the name of Jesus.

35. Witchcraft broom sweeping away good things out of my life, be destroyed by the fire of God, in the name of Jesus.
36. I shall not die in the battle of life, in the name of Jesus.
37. In this month of grace; O God my Father, be an enemy to my enemies, in the name of Jesus.
38. I claim long life and prosperity this month and all my days in the name of Jesus.
39. I paralyze every power of death and hell assigned against me and my family this month, this year, and all my days, in the name of Jesus.
40. Any power on assignment to terminate my life this month, be terminated by fire, in the name of Jesus.
41. Any satanic arrow of death targeted against my life or any member of my family this month, backfire in the name of Jesus.
42. This month, this year and all my days; let the angels of the Living God encamp around me and my family and deliver us from all evil, in the name of Jesus.
43. Any evil plantation in my life and my family, be uprooted by the fire of God in the name of Jesus.
44. I declare the labor of the enemy over my life fruitless this month, this year and all my days of my life, in the name of Jesus.
45. Any evil device and scheme of the enemy over my life this month, this year, and all my days, be frustrated in the name of Jesus.
46. Anointing of an overcomer fall upon my life afresh, in the name of Jesus.
47. O God my Father, arise and move me to a higher ground this month in the name of Jesus.

48. By the power in the blood of Jesus; I decree nothing shall stop me from moving up to higher heights, in the name of Jesus.
49. O God my Father, give me the grace to forget my past failures and the power to look up to you for my better future, in the name of Jesus.
50. O God my Father, let your rain of divine mercy begin to fall upon my life, in the name of Jesus.
51. In this month of May, my ladder of greatness shall not break, in the name of Jesus.
52. Anything planted in my life scaring my helpers away, be destroyed by the fire of God, in the name of Jesus.
53. O God my Father, let my prayer altar receive fresh fire, in the name of Jesus.
54. Every evil cage that has refused to let me go: be destroyed by fire, in the name of Jesus.
55. Every satanic violence set up against my life and against the mercy of God for my life, scatter by the fire of God, in the name of Jesus.
56. Every power robbing me of the mercy and favor of God, your time is up, release me now and die, in the name of Jesus.
57. By the mercy of God, I decree that the hand of the enemy shall not prevail over my life, in the name of Jesus.
58. You wicked power delaying the manifestation of my divine mercy, loose your hold over my life, in the name of Jesus.
59. Every enemy of my progress within and without, I have obtained the mercy of God therefore die in shame in the name of Jesus.

60. By the mercy of God, I receive the miracle for supernatural breakthroughs, in the name of Jesus.
61. Any wicked power delegated to waste my destiny, be wasted by fire, in the name of Jesus.
62. Wherever the enemy has knocked me down, let the mercy of God lift me up and restore me, in the name of Jesus.
63. Every arrow of wickedness preventing my rain of mercy, be destroyed by the fire of God, in the name of Jesus.
64. If I am behind my heavenly ordained destiny, let the mercy of God move me forward to where I am supposed to be, in the name of Jesus.
65. By the mercy of God I shall not fish in the Dead Sea, in the name of Jesus.
66. By the mercy of God, let there be a way for me in the wilderness, in the name of Jesus.
67. By the mercy of God, let every valley in my life bring forth water, in the name of Jesus.
68. By the mercy of God, I shall not build for another to inhabit, in the name of Jesus.
69. By the mercy of God, I shall not labor for another to enjoy, in the name of Jesus.
70. By the mercy of God, I shall not plant for another to harvest, in the name of Jesus.
71. By the mercy of God, I shall not be unseated from my place of blessing and fulfillment, in the name of Jesus.
72. By the mercy of God, I shall not be a negative example in the house of God, in my family, in my community and to the nation at large, in the name of Jesus.
73. By the mercy of God, I shall obtain uncommon favor this month, this year and all my days, in the name of Jesus.

74. By the mercy of God, this month and all my days I shall not see disgrace, I shall not see shame, and I shall not see disappointment, in the name of Jesus.
75. By the mercy of God: I shall be watered from the garden of the Lord this month and all my days, in the name of Jesus.
76. By the mercy of God, I shall live in abundance and in good health this month and all my days, in the name of Jesus.
77. By the mercy of God, I shall be blessed and highly favored this month and all my days, in the name of Jesus.
78. By the mercy of God, where others have failed I shall succeed this month and all my days, in the name of Jesus.

SPECIAL PRAYER FOR THE MONTH OF JUNE

Passages To Read Before You Pray:
Isaiah 43:19, Habakkuk 1:5, Joel 2:21-27, Psalms 19, 29, 42

I have come today to fellowship with my heavenly Father, and make my requests and needs known unto Him. I cannot be hindered nor delayed because I know who I am in the Lord. I am a child of the Kingdom, born of the Spirit, redeemed by the blood of Jesus Christ. I walk in authority, living life without any apology because the power and authority has been given to me according to the Word of God in the book of Luke 9:1.

As I have come to pray today and to fellowship with my heavenly Father, I cover myself in the blood of Jesus Christ, and I put on the whole armor of God. I hereby come against every Prince of Persia that wants to hinder my prayer, I arrest you by the power in the blood of Jesus Christ, and I bind you and cast you down into the pit of hell.

I come against principalities and powers that wrestle with me and my prayers, I arrest you today by the power in the name of Jesus Christ, and I bind you and cast down into the pit of hell. I come against the rulers of the darkness of this world, against spiritual wickedness in high places, I arrest you all by the power in the name of Jesus Christ, and I bind you and cast you down into the pit of hell. I come against weakness and weariness, I arrest you today by the power in the name of Jesus Christ, and I

bind you and cast you out of my life. I come against wondering spirit and distractions, I arrest you today by the power in the name of Jesus Christ, and I bind you and cast you out of my life.

Today I receive the anointing to pray and get results, my prayers cannot be hindered nor delayed because Jesus is my Lord, I will pray today and get the desired results, I decree open heavens upon my prayers. I baptize myself in the fire of the Holy Ghost; therefore I have become too hot for the enemy to handle. My prayers today will attract divine intervention to every situation in my life; signs and wonders will follow my prayers today, testimonies will follow my prayers today and the name of God alone will be glorified, in Jesus name. Amen!

PRAYER POINTS:

1. O God my Father, thank you for being my God, my Father and my friend.
2. O God my Father, thank you for the privilege to know you and the power of the resurrection of Jesus Christ.
3. O God my Father, thank you for always being there for me and with me.
4. O God my Father, thank you for the great and mighty things that you are doing in my life.
5. O God my Father, thank you for your provision and protection over me and my household.
6. O God my Father, thank you for always answering my prayers.
7. I confess my sins before you today and I ask you to forgive me on the basis of your mercy, in the name of Jesus Christ.

8. Wash me clean today O Lord by the blood of Jesus Christ.
9. I cover myself and my household with the blood of Jesus Christ.
10. My prayers today will not go in vain; my prayers will produce the desired results in the name of Jesus Christ.
11. Holy Spirit divine empower me to pray right and get good results, in the name of Jesus.
12. Holy Spirit of God, come into my life and manifest your power in the name of Jesus.
13. I frustrate every evil network against the purpose of God for my life, in the name of Jesus.
14. O God my Father, open my eyes to see your glory in every area of my life this month, in the name of Jesus.
15. Agent of discomfort assigned against my life; wherever you are I withdraw your peace, in the name of Jesus.
16. Every satanic decree of failure over my life, be revoked by the fire of God, in the name of Jesus.
17. Witchcraft cobwebs over my life, be destroyed by the fire of God, in the name of Jesus.
18. Holy Ghost fire, destroy and burn to ashes every witchcraft gadget erected for my sake, in the name of Jesus.
19. Every work of darkness in my life, be destroyed by the fire of God, in the name of Jesus.
20. My life, you will not be tied down under the control of any witchcraft power, in the name of Jesus.
21. I release the judgment of fire upon any witchcraft power tormenting my life, in the name of Jesus.
22. O God my Father, arise and let your glory envelope my life and my family, in the name of Jesus.

23. O God my Father, command your divine favor upon my life and my family, in the name of Jesus.
24. O God my Father, arise and convert my point of rejection to celebration, in the name of Jesus.
25. O God my Father, arise and expose the nakedness of my enemies, in the name of Jesus.
26. Every ancestral chain of failure holding down my progress, break by the fire of God, in the name of Jesus.
27. Foundational marital bondage, be destroyed by the fire of God, in the name of Jesus.
28. The voice of the enemy will not overrule the voice of God in my life, in the name of Jesus.
29. The voice of man will not be the final in my life, in the name of Jesus.
30. Men shall not determine my altitude in life, in the name of Jesus.
31. Let every organ in my body become too hot for any evil animal to inhabit, in the name of Jesus.
32. I cover my life with the blood of Jesus and surround my house with the fire of the Holy Ghost, in the name of Jesus.
33. Enemies will not rejoice over my life, in the name of Jesus.
34. My head, you must not cooperate with failure this month and all my days, in the name of Jesus.
35. Any form of imperfection in my life, be made perfect by the power in the Blood of Jesus, in the name of Jesus.
36. Every chariot of trouble assigned against my life in this month of June, be destroyed by the fire of God, in the name of Jesus.

37. Holy Spirit of God, in the midst of trials, empower me to hear your voice, and lead me to make the right decision, in the name of Jesus.
38. O God my Father, arise in your power and let my enemies know that you are God indeed, in the name of Jesus.
39. I receive divine assistance to recover what the enemy has stolen from me, in the name of Jesus.
40. Every door of opportunity shut against my life, open now by the fire of God, in the name of Jesus.
41. Blood of Jesus, go into the water and strangulate to death any marine power holding unto my key of promotion and recover for me all that has been taken, in the name of Jesus.
42. Any form of sickness or infirmity or disease, challenging the name of God in my life, receive divine healing now, in the name of Jesus.
43. Every satanic roadblock to my greatness, clear away by the fire of God, in the name of Jesus.
44. O God my Father, arise and break the teeth of the ungodly challenging your authority in my life, in the name of Jesus.
45. Every horn of wickedness assigned to scatter my harvest, break by the fire of God, in the name of Jesus.
46. Lord Jesus, bring honey out of the rock for me this month, in the name of Jesus.
47. Begin to thank God for answering your prayers, and for His mercy and for his quick response.

SPECIAL PRAYER FOR THE MONTH OF JULY

Passages To Read Before You Pray:
Isaiah 43:19, Habakkuk 1:5, Joel 2:21-27, Psalms 19, 29, 42

I have come today to fellowship with my heavenly Father, and make my requests and needs known unto Him. I cannot be hindered nor delayed because I know who I am in the Lord. I am a child of the Kingdom, born of the Spirit, redeemed by the blood of Jesus Christ. I walk in authority, living life without any apology because the power and authority has been given to me according to the Word of God in the book of Luke 9:1.

As I have come to pray today and to fellowship with my heavenly Father, I cover myself in the blood of Jesus Christ, and I put on the whole armor of God. I hereby come against every Prince of Persia that wants to hinder my prayer, I arrest you by the power in the blood of Jesus Christ, and I bind you and cast you down into the pit of hell.

I come against principalities and powers that wrestle with me and my prayers, I arrest you today by the power in the name of Jesus Christ, and I bind you and cast down into the pit of hell. I come against the rulers of the darkness of this world, against spiritual wickedness in high places, I arrest you all by the power in the name of Jesus Christ, and I bind you and cast you down into the pit of hell. I come against weakness and weariness, I arrest you today by the power in the name of Jesus Christ, and I bind you and cast you out of my life. I come against wondering

spirit and distractions, I arrest you today by the power in the name of Jesus Christ, and I bind you and cast you out of my life.

Today I receive the anointing to pray and get results, my prayers cannot be hindered nor delayed because Jesus is my Lord, I will pray today and get the desired results, I decree open heavens upon my prayers. I baptize myself in the fire of the Holy Ghost; therefore I have become too hot for the enemy to handle. My prayers today will attract divine intervention to every situation in my life; signs and wonders will follow my prayers today, testimonies will follow my prayers today and the name of God alone will be glorified, in Jesus name. Amen!

PRAYER POINTS:

1. O God my Father, thank you for being my God, my Father and my friend.
2. O God my Father, thank you for the privilege to know you and the power of the resurrection of Jesus Christ.
3. O God my Father, thank you for always being there for me and with me.
4. O God my Father, thank you for the great and mighty things that you are doing in my life.
5. O God my Father, thank you for your provision and protection over me and my household.
6. O God my Father, thank you for always answering my prayers.
7. I confess my sins before you today and I ask you to forgive me on the basis of your mercy, in the name of Jesus Christ.

8. Wash me clean today O Lord by the blood of Jesus Christ.
9. I cover myself and my household with the blood of Jesus Christ.
10. My prayers today will not go in vain; my prayers will produce the desired results in the name of Jesus Christ.
11. Blessed Holy Spirit; I cannot walk alone in the journey of this month: therefore Holy Spirit go with me, direct my path to the glory of the Lord most high, in the name of Jesus.
12. O Lord God of Elijah, Arise today and advertise your goodness in my life this month in a special way, in the name of Jesus.
13. In the journey of this month, I shall not regret, I shall not sorrow, I shall not fail in all my endeavor, in the name of Jesus.
14. O God my Father, establish your perfect will in my life this month, in the name of Jesus.
15. By the power that parted the red sea; I shall not regret any journey I will undertake this month, in the name of Jesus.
16. I shall not travel under the direction and supervision of the enemy this month and all my days, in the name of Jesus.
17. The perfect will of God shall be established this month in my life, in the name of Jesus.
18. I command every mountain of impossibility in my life, be melted away in the name of Jesus.
19. Every fountain of sickness in my life, dry up by the fire of God, in the name of Jesus.
20. Every foundation of wickedness in my life, die to the root in the name of Jesus.

21. Every ordinance of failure and rejection, be wiped off by the blood of Jesus, in the name of Jesus.
22. Every contrary wind blowing in my life; be silenced forever, in the name of Jesus.
23. In the presence of those who hate me for no reason, O God arise and glorify your name in my life, in the name of Jesus.
24. O God my Father, arise and scatter unto desolation every witchcraft network organized for my sake this month, in the name of Jesus.
25. Every witchcraft standing order at the gate of my breakthrough this month, scatter unto desolation, in the name of Jesus.
26. Any foundational strong man standing at the gate of my success; fall down and die, in the name of Jesus.
27. Holy Spirit, in this month of perfection be my companion, and lead me in the right path, in the name of Jesus.
28. The journey of this month shall not be difficult for me, in the name of Jesus.
29. Month of July is the second half of the year, therefore I declare today that anything that I have been denied since the beginning of this year begin to manifest this month by the fire of God, in the name of Jesus.
30. My imprisoned benefits, come out and locate me, in the name of Jesus.
31. Power of God that parted the red sea, arise and fight my battles for me, in the name of Jesus.
32. In this month of July, I shall not appear to disappear, in the name of Jesus.
33. The journey of this month in my life shall not end in sorrow or disaster, in the name of Jesus.

34. O God my Father, let my life and destiny receive divine rearrangement, in the name of Jesus.
35. Every evil association organized for my sake this month, this year and all my days: scatter by the fire of God, in the name of Jesus.
36. Serpent and scorpion of affliction will not bite me and my family, in the name of Jesus.
37. Every dangerous meeting organized for my sake this month, scatter unto desolation, in the name of Jesus.
38. Any evil monitoring gadget set in place for my sake this month, be destroyed by the fire of God, in the name of Jesus.
39. O God my Father, let my life receive divine order from above and begin to yield good fruits, in the name of Jesus.
40. Every good thing that has been stolen from my life since the beginning of this year: be replaced by fire, in the name of Jesus.
41. Anointing for outstanding success fall upon my life, in the name of Jesus.
42. In this month of July, O God arise and fight for me in an unusual manner, in the name of Jesus.
43. Every red sea situation in my life, I command you to give way to my promise land, in the name of Jesus.
44. O Lord my father, you are perfect in all your ways; perfect your will in my life and let your name be glorified, in the name of Jesus.
45. O Lord let my enemies be engaged with useless assignments this month in the name of Jesus.
46. O God my Father, this month let my heaven of answered prayers open by fire, in the name of Jesus.

47. Angel of the living God, go before me in the journey of this month and make crooked places straight in the name of Jesus.
48. O God my Father, let your hand of mercy be upon my life and my household this month in the name of Jesus.
49. By the power in the blood of Jesus, I declare that I shall not eat the bread of sorrow this month and all the days of my life in the name of Jesus.
50. In this month of perfection, I reject evil verdict in the name of Jesus.
51. I decree by the power from above, every evil condition attached to my success, be totally and permanently eradicated in the name of Jesus.
52. Rain of sorrow, rain of affliction will not fall upon my life and my family in the name of Jesus.
53. Evil power, wicked power speaking demotion into my life and destiny, be silenced forever in the name of Jesus.
54. In this month of perfection, the Lord will perfect everything about my life. I shall move from glory to glory and from favor to favor in the name of Jesus.
55. O God my Father, by your never failing power, move my children forward in the name of Jesus.
56. Weapon of failure, weapon of destruction fashioned against the glory of my children, be destroyed by the fire of God in the name of Jesus.
57. Anointing to succeed where others have failed, fall on me and my family in the name of Jesus.
58. My head, receive the crown of unstoppable achievements in the name of Jesus.
59. Mighty hand of God that moved Joseph from the prison to the palace, move my children forward in the name of Jesus.

60. Power to triumph in the midst of adversity fall upon my children in the name of Jesus.
61. O God my Father, turn every opposition confronting my children to promotion in the name of Jesus.
62. O God my Father, turn every test to testimony for my children in the name of Jesus.
63. O God my Father, turn every point of ridicule to the point of rejoicing in the lives of my children in the name of Jesus.
64. O God my Father, turn ashes to beauty for my children in the name of Jesus.
65. Holy Spirit Divine have your way in my life, in the name of Jesus.
66. O God my Father, empower me to dwell in your secret place this month and all my life, in the name of Jesus.
67. I decree that in this month of perfection evil shall bow before me, in the name of Jesus.
68. I decree that where I have been knocked down, the hands of the Lord shall lift me up, in the name of Jesus.
69. In this month of perfection, my testimony shall cause my enemies to commit suicide, in the name of Jesus.
70. O God my Father, arise and destroy the foundation of wickedness in my life, in the name of Jesus.
71. Every altar of wickedness mounted against my destiny, be destroy by fire, in the name of Jesus.
72. My destiny and my life are attached to the Living GOD, therefore I decree that I shall not fall, I shall not fail, in the name of Jesus.
73. Any power set in place to derail my destiny, be destroyed by fire, in the name of Jesus.
74. Conspiracy of darkness against my life and destiny scatter by fire, in the name of Jesus.

75. I decree that in this month of perfection, fire of the enemy shall not burn me, in the name of Jesus.
76. O God my Father, let any power hunting for my life and destiny receive multiple frustrations, in the name of Jesus.
77. I decree that this month I shall have uncommon progress, in the name of Jesus.
78. This month I shall enjoy the peace of God in every area of my life, in the name of Jesus.
79. I shall be promoted this month and all my life beyond ordinary levels, in the name of Jesus.
80. I shall be protected from all evil and wickedness of men, in the name of Jesus.
81. I shall prosper in everything I lay my hands on in the name of Jesus.
82. I receive power from above over all my adversaries in the name of Jesus.
83. I shall live in the perfect will of God this month and all my days, in the name of Jesus.
84. Glory of my destiny, hear the word of the Lord, come out of the grave, rise up and shine, in the name of Jesus.
85. Anything in my life attracting failure and defeat, be destroyed by the fire of God, in the name of Jesus.
86. Every evil hand opening the door of defeat in my life, wither by fire, in the name of Jesus.
87. O God my Father, arise by your mercy and show me the beneficial secret of my life, in the name of Jesus.
88. O God my Father, arise and circulate my name around for divine favor, in the name of Jesus.
89. O God my Father, arise and expose every hidden agenda of the enemy for my life, in the name of Jesus.

90. The voice of man shall not override the voice of God in my life, in the name of Jesus.
91. Lord I thank you for answering my prayers: glory be to your holy name, in the name of Jesus.

SPECIAL PRAYER FOR THE MONTH OF AUGUST

Passages To Read Before You Pray:
Isaiah 43:19, Habakkuk 1:5, Joel 2:21-27, Psalms 19, 29, 42

I have come today to fellowship with my heavenly Father, and make my requests and needs known unto Him. I cannot be hindered nor delayed because I know who I am in the Lord. I am a child of the Kingdom, born of the Spirit, redeemed by the blood of Jesus Christ. I walk in authority, living life without any apology because the power and authority has been given to me according to the Word of God in the book of Luke 9:1.

As I have come to pray today and to fellowship with my heavenly Father, I cover myself in the blood of Jesus Christ, and I put on the whole armor of God. I hereby come against every Prince of Persia that wants to hinder my prayer, I arrest you by the power in the blood of Jesus Christ, and I bind you and cast you down into the pit of hell.

I come against principalities and powers that wrestle with me and my prayers, I arrest you today by the power in the name of Jesus Christ, and I bind you and cast down into the pit of hell. I come against the rulers of the darkness of this world, against spiritual wickedness in high places, I arrest you all by the power in the name of Jesus Christ, and I bind you and cast you down into the pit of hell. I come against weakness and weariness, I arrest you today by the power in the name of Jesus Christ, and I

bind you and cast you out of my life. I come against wondering spirit and distractions, I arrest you today by the power in the name of Jesus Christ, and I bind you and cast you out of my life.

Today I receive the anointing to pray and get results, my prayers cannot be hindered nor delayed because Jesus is my Lord, I will pray today and get the desired results, I decree open heavens upon my prayers. I baptize myself in the fire of the Holy Ghost; therefore I have become too hot for the enemy to handle. My prayers today will attract divine intervention to every situation in my life; signs and wonders will follow my prayers today, testimonies will follow my prayers today and the name of God alone will be glorified, in Jesus name. Amen!

PRAYER POINTS:

1. O God my Father, thank you for being my God, my Father and my friend.
2. O God my Father, thank you for the privilege to know you and the power of the resurrection of Jesus Christ.
3. O God my Father, thank you for always being there for me and with me.
4. O God my Father, thank you for the great and mighty things that you are doing in my life.
5. O God my Father, thank you for your provision and protection over me and my household.
6. O God my Father, thank you for always answering my prayers.
7. I confess my sins before you today and I ask you to forgive me on the basis of your mercy, in the name of Jesus Christ.

8. Wash me clean today O Lord by the blood of Jesus Christ.
9. I cover myself and my household with the blood of Jesus Christ.
10. My prayers today will not go in vain; my prayers will produce the desired results in the name of Jesus Christ.
11. Holy Spirit of God, have your way in my life, in the name of Jesus.
12. Holy Spirit of God, teach me to pray and connect me to the throne of mercy, in the name of Jesus.
13. O God my Father, arise and speak light to every spot of darkness in my life, in the name of Jesus.
14. O God my Father, arise and speak the word of light to the darkness, in my family, my marriage, in the name of Jesus.
15. Hour of darkness and sorrow, hear the word of the Lord, disappear from my life by fire, light of the Lord take over my life, in the name of Jesus.
16. Every evil gathering summoned to pull me down this month, scatter by the fire of God, in the name of Jesus.
17. O God of new beginnings, do a new thing in my life that will glorify your name and disgrace my enemies, in the name of Jesus.
18. O God of new beginnings, fight my battle in a new way that will catch my enemies unaware, in the name of Jesus.
19. O God of all righteousness, arise and let the power of enchantment and the enchanter set in place for my sake, destroy the owner in the name of Jesus.
20. O God my Father, release your fire to destroy every satanic barrier hindering my way to greatness, in the name of Jesus.

21. Every good thing that I have been chasing since the beginning of this year, this month I command you to manifest by fire, in the name of Jesus.
22. Any power assigned from the pit of hell to intimidate me this month, be consumed by the fire of God, in the name of Jesus.
23. By the power of the God of Elijah, I receive divine protection from the strife of evil tongue, in the name of Jesus.
24. Any satanic prophet assigned to curse my destiny this month and all my days, be silenced forever, in the name of Jesus.
25. Every obstacle that hinders people's progress in the neighborhood, in the town and in the city, you will not locate me and my household, in the name of Jesus.
26. Any wicked power or evil authority prolonging affliction in my life, your time is over die by fire, in the name of Jesus.
27. O God my Father, Arise and send forth your arrow and scatter the assembly of the ungodly gathering against me and my family, in the name of Jesus.
28. O God my Father, let my life receive fresh fire from above and begin to shine, in the name of Jesus.
29. O God my Father, arise and disappoint my adversaries and confound my oppressors, in the name of Jesus.
30. O God my Father, advertise your greatness in my life this month, in the name of Jesus.
31. O God of all possibilities, arise and bring honey out of the rock for me this month, in the name of Jesus.
32. I plead the blood of Jesus upon my body, soul and spirit, in the name of Jesus.

33. Every evil pronouncement upon my life, be revoked by the power in the blood of Jesus Christ, in the name of Jesus.
34. Every arrow of back to square one fired at my destiny, be destroyed by the fire of God, in the name of Jesus.
35. Mountain of opposition, mountain of impossibility in my life be rolled away by the fire of God, in the name of Jesus.
36. Every evil word of spoken into my life; be reversed now by the fire of God, in the name of Jesus.
37. Blood of Jesus, deliver me from the sword of the tongue, in the name of Jesus.
38. Every curse, every pronouncement of hardship and disappointment placed upon my life, break by the fire of God, in the name of Jesus.
39. Every curse of limitation and restriction upon my life, break by the fire of God, in the name of Jesus.
40. Every circle of repeated problems, repeated failure and repeated oppression, break by the fire of God, in the name of Jesus.
41. Witchcraft pronouncements upon my life, be neutralized by the blood of Jesus Christ, in the name of Jesus.
42. Every evil meeting summoned for my sake to make me fail, scatter by the fire of God, in the name of Jesus.
43. Every organized wickedness against my success, scatter by the fire of God, in the name of Jesus.
44. Evil predictions, evil prophecies against my life, be nullified by the power in the Blood of Jesus, in the name of Jesus.
45. Power of misfortune over my life, fail woefully in the name of Jesus.

46. Anything in my foundation that has subjected my life to be under evil prophecy, die with all your roots, in the name of Jesus.
47. My life, you will not dance to the music of the enemy, in the name of Jesus.
48. I release my destiny from any form of limitations and restrictions, in the name of Jesus.
49. Blood of Jesus, arise and retrieve my lost glory, in the name of Jesus.
50. By the word of prophesy, I prophecy into my life; my life, begin to yield fruit of success, fruit of joy, fruit of Godliness, fruit of holiness, in the name of Jesus.
51. By the authority in the word of the Living God, I decree that I shall not die before my day of glory, I shall not die before my day of celebration, in the name of Jesus.
52. Holy Spirit of God, connect me to the socket of power, in the name of Jesus.
53. My prayers today shall hit the target, I shall not pray amiss, in the name of Jesus.
54. Let the finger of God remove every strongman of prayerlessness from my life, in the name of Jesus.
55. Every strongman assigned to weaken my faith be destroyed by fire, in the name of Jesus.
56. You evil ancestral strongman attached to my destiny fall down and die, in the name of Jesus.
57. I disconnect my life and my destiny from every power of bad luck and misfortune, in the name of Jesus.
58. Any ancestral strongman having my goods in his possession, release it now by the fire of God, in the name of Jesus.
59. Every cloud of darkness preventing my sun to rise, clear away in the name of Jesus.

60. Ancestral covenant of failure and defeat operating in my life, break by fire, in the name of Jesus.
61. O God of new beginnings, arise and advertise your goodness in my life, in the name of Jesus.
62. In this month of new beginnings, the Lord shall bring honey out of the rock for me, in the name of Jesus.
63. Where others have failed; I shall succeed in the name of Jesus.
64. What caused others to fall shall be my platform to greatness, in the name of Jesus.
65. In my desert O Lord, let water begin to flow continually, in the name of Jesus.
66. When I sit in the dark the Lord shall be a light unto me, in the name of Jesus.
67. Any power anywhere trying to restructure my destiny, you are a failure, receive multiple disgrace in the name of Jesus.
68. Every wicked authority contending with my glory; be dethroned by the fire of God, in the name of Jesus.
69. Today I recover all that has been stolen from my life even when I was in my mother's womb, in the name of Jesus.
70. My life and destiny, arise and shine, do not cooperate with the spirit of demotion, in the name of Jesus.
71. Goodness and mercy of the Lord envelope my destiny, in the name of Jesus.
72. Glory of the Lord, cover and protect my destiny from every witchcraft attack, in the name of Jesus.
73. I shall not come to this world in vain, in the name of Jesus.
74. Righteousness of the Lord shall exalt my glory, mercy of God cover my destiny, in the name of Jesus.

75. I seal my prayers with the blood of Jesus, in the name of Jesus.
76. I thank you Lord Jesus for answering my prayers, glory be to your name, in the name of Jesus.

SPECIAL PRAYER FOR THE MONTH OF SEPTEMBER

Passages To Read Before You Pray:
Isaiah 43:19, Habakkuk 1:5, Joel 2:21-27, Psalms 19, 29, 42

I have come today to fellowship with my heavenly Father, and make my requests and needs known unto Him. I cannot be hindered nor delayed because I know who I am in the Lord. I am a child of the Kingdom, born of the Spirit, redeemed by the blood of Jesus Christ. I walk in authority, living life without any apology because the power and authority has been given to me according to the Word of God in the book of Luke 9:1.

As I have come to pray today and to fellowship with my heavenly Father, I cover myself in the blood of Jesus Christ, and I put on the whole armor of God. I hereby come against every Prince of Persia that wants to hinder my prayer, I arrest you by the power in the blood of Jesus Christ, and I bind you and cast you down into the pit of hell.

I come against principalities and powers that wrestle with me and my prayers, I arrest you today by the power in the name of Jesus Christ, and I bind you and cast down into the pit of hell. I come against the rulers of the darkness of this world, against spiritual wickedness in high places, I arrest you all by the power in the name of Jesus Christ, and I bind you and cast you down into the pit of hell. I come against weakness and weariness, I arrest you today by the power in the name of Jesus Christ, and I

bind you and cast you out of my life. I come against wondering spirit and distractions, I arrest you today by the power in the name of Jesus Christ, and I bind you and cast you out of my life.

Today I receive the anointing to pray and get results, my prayers cannot be hindered nor delayed because Jesus is my Lord, I will pray today and get the desired results, I decree open heavens upon my prayers. I baptize myself in the fire of the Holy Ghost; therefore I have become too hot for the enemy to handle. My prayers today will attract divine intervention to every situation in my life; signs and wonders will follow my prayers today, testimonies will follow my prayers today and the name of God alone will be glorified, in Jesus name. Amen!

PRAYER POINTS:

1. O God my Father, thank you for being my God, my Father and my friend.
2. O God my Father, thank you for the privilege to know you and the power of the resurrection of Jesus Christ.
3. O God my Father, thank you for always being there for me and with me.
4. O God my Father, thank you for the great and mighty things that you are doing in my life.
5. O God my Father, thank you for your provision and protection over me and my household.
6. O God my Father, thank you for always answering my prayers.
7. I confess my sins before you today and I ask you to forgive me on the basis of your mercy, in the name of Jesus Christ.

8. Wash me clean today O Lord by the blood of Jesus Christ.
9. I cover myself and my household with the blood of Jesus Christ.
10. My prayers today will not go in vain; my prayers will produce the desired results in the name of Jesus Christ.
11. Holy Spirit of God, empower me, teach me to pray and get results, in the name of Jesus.
12. Every unrepentant enemy that has stubbornly followed me into this month, perish by the rod of judgment of God, in the name of Jesus.
13. O God my Father, arise and bring honey out of the rock for me in the name of Jesus.
14. Any power holding my hands down from moving forward, you are a liar, release me now and perish in the name of Jesus.
15. By the power that parted the red sea, O God my Father, arise and separate my life from affliction and tribulation in the name of Jesus.
16. By the majesty of your name, O God my Father, arise and raise an advocate for me in heaven, in the name of Jesus.
17. Any evil record of failure and disappointment in my life, be wiped off by the blood of Jesus, in the name of Jesus.
18. Any evil handwriting against my moving forward this month, be erased completely in the name of Jesus.
19. Any evil power in my father's house challenging the authority of God in my life, you are wicked, I challenge you by heavenly authority, die by fire in the name of Jesus.

20. O God my Father, arise and bring solution to every difficult situation apposing my greatness in the name of Jesus.
21. I cancel every evil report concerning my life and my family in the name of Jesus.
22. O God my Father, arise and let my season of favor manifest in the name of Jesus.
23. O God of divine provision, prove yourself in my life as the all sufficient God, in the name of Jesus.
24. Fire of Holy Ghost, break the yoke of wickedness in my foundation and set me free in the name of Jesus.
25. Avenger of blood, you will not locate me and my family in the name of Jesus.
26. Ancestral avenger of blood you will not know my dwelling place in the name of Jesus.
27. Family avenger of blood, my life is not for you, you will not drink my blood in the name of Jesus.
28. Environmental avenger of blood, my life is not for you, my family is not for you, you will not destroy me, in the name of Jesus.
29. National and continental avenger of blood, my life is not for you, you will not destroy me and my family, in the name of Jesus.
30. The hands of the wicked shall not prevail over my life, in the name of Jesus.
31. Man shall not determine my altitude in life, in the name of Jesus.
32. Any evil record of failure and disappointment, be wiped off, by the blood of Jesus, in the name of Jesus.
33. Any evil handwriting against my moving forward this month be erased completely, in the name of Jesus.

34. Any evil power in my father's house challenging the authority of God in my life, you are wicked I challenge you by the heavenly authority; die by the fire of God, in the name of Jesus.
35. O God my Father, arise and bring solution to every difficult situation opposing my greatness, in the name of Jesus.
36. I cancel every evil report concerning my life and my family, in the name of Jesus.
37. O God my Father, arise and let my season of favor manifest, in the name of Jesus.
38. Fire of Holy Ghost, break the yoke of wickedness in my foundation and set me free, in the name of Jesus.
39. Holy Spirit of God, I commit the journey of this month into your hand, walk with me, guide me, and glorify your name in everything I will do, in the name of Jesus.
40. O God my Father, arise and let your rod of judgment rest upon every opposing power to my breakthrough, in the name of Jesus.
41. O God my Father, establish me in your righteousness and in truth this month and all my days, in the name of Jesus.
42. By the decree of heaven, I decree that the rod of the wicked shall not rest upon my life this month and all my days, in the name of Jesus.
43. O God my Father, faithful and just God, arise and let the oppression of the wicked come to an end in my life, in the name of Jesus.
44. O God my Father, arise in your power and let the wickedness of the wicked come to an end in my life, in the name of Jesus.

45. O God my Father, arise in your power and let the association of the wicked around me scatter unto desolation, in the name of Jesus.
46. O anger of the Almighty God, arise and locate the camp of my enemies and destroy them, in the name of Jesus.
47. O God my Father, let your name which is a strong tower be a shield over my life and my family, in the name of Jesus.
48. Any evil hand holding down my soul in captivity of prayerlessness, wither by the fire of God, in the name of Jesus.
49. Any power or force of darkness hindering the move of God in my life, I arrest you by the power in the name of Jesus Christ, in the name of Jesus.
50. Any power saying it is not yet my time to manifest, you are a liar, you will not escape the judgment of God, in the name of Jesus.
51. Now is my time to manifest; my glory, hear the word of the Lord, arise and manifest by fire, in the name of Jesus.
52. Any strange king of poverty ruling my world of riches, be dethroned by force, in the name of Jesus.
53. You evil king of barrenness ruling my world of fruitfulness, be dethroned by force, in the name of Jesus.
54. O God my Father, arise and show yourself as a mighty man in battle in my life, in the name of Jesus.
55. Any evil standing order against my breakthrough, be revoked by the fire of God, in the name of Jesus.
56. By the power in the Blood of Jesus, I receive the anointing to break every evil yoke, in the name of Jesus.
57. I will arise and shine in the name of Jesus.

SPECIAL PRAYER FOR THE MONTH OF OCTOBER

Passages To Read Before You Pray:
Isaiah 43:19, Habakkuk 1:5, Joel 2:21-27, Psalms 19, 29, 42

I have come today to fellowship with my heavenly Father, and make my requests and needs known unto Him. I cannot be hindered nor delayed because I know who I am in the Lord. I am a child of the Kingdom, born of the Spirit, redeemed by the blood of Jesus Christ. I walk in authority, living life without any apology because the power and authority has been given to me according to the Word of God in the book of Luke 9:1.

As I have come to pray today and to fellowship with my heavenly Father, I cover myself in the blood of Jesus Christ, and I put on the whole armor of God. I hereby come against every Prince of Persia that wants to hinder my prayer, I arrest you by the power in the blood of Jesus Christ, and I bind you and cast you down into the pit of hell.

I come against principalities and powers that wrestle with me and my prayers, I arrest you today by the power in the name of Jesus Christ, and I bind you and cast down into the pit of hell. I come against the rulers of the darkness of this world, against spiritual wickedness in high places, I arrest you all by the power in the name of Jesus Christ, and I bind you and cast you down into the pit of hell. I come against weakness and weariness, I arrest you today by the power in the name of Jesus Christ, and I bind you and cast you out of my life. I come against wondering

spirit and distractions, I arrest you today by the power in the name of Jesus Christ, and I bind you and cast you out of my life.

Today I receive the anointing to pray and get results, my prayers cannot be hindered nor delayed because Jesus is my Lord, I will pray today and get the desired results, I decree open heavens upon my prayers. I baptize myself in the fire of the Holy Ghost; therefore I have become too hot for the enemy to handle. My prayers today will attract divine intervention to every situation in my life; signs and wonders will follow my prayers today, testimonies will follow my prayers today and the name of God alone will be glorified, in Jesus name. Amen!

PRAYER POINTS:

1. O God my Father, thank you for being my God, my Father and my friend.
2. O God my Father, thank you for the privilege to know you and the power of the resurrection of Jesus Christ.
3. O God my Father, thank you for always being there for me and with me.
4. O God my Father, thank you for the great and mighty things that you are doing in my life.
5. O God my Father, thank you for your provision and protection over me and my household.
6. O God my Father, thank you for always answering my prayers.
7. I confess my sins before you today and I ask you to forgive me on the basis of your mercy, in the name of Jesus Christ.

8. Wash me clean today O Lord by the blood of Jesus Christ.
9. I cover myself and my household with the blood of Jesus Christ.
10. My prayers today will not go in vain; my prayers will produce the desired results in the name of Jesus Christ.
11. Holy Spirit divine, the journey of this month is in your hands; direct my path, order my steps and fashion my life according to your purpose in the name of Jesus.
12. I receive divine wisdom from above to journey this month and all my days without sorrow and regret in the name of Jesus.
13. O God my Father, let the blood of Jesus be a mark of distinction upon my life, my household this month and all my days in the name of Jesus.
14. As the Lord disgraced the enemies of Esther and the Jews, let all my enemies turn back with shame and disgrace this month and all my days in the name of Jesus.
15. O God my Father, arise and fight my battle this month and all my days in the name of Jesus.
16. Every conspiracy in the heavenlies, on earth, and in the sea against the purpose of God for my life this month and all my days, scatter by the fire of God, in the name of Jesus.
17. O God my Father, arise and let my Haman hang on the gallows he has erected for my sake in the name of Jesus.
18. This month O Lord, arise and convert all my past failures to success in the name of Jesus.

19. Every weapon of destruction fashioned against me and my family this month and all my days, be destroyed by the fire of God in the name of Jesus.
20. Every root of rebellion in my life and my household be uprooted by the fire of God in the name of Jesus.
21. This month and all my days, I refuse to disobey the word of God in the name of Jesus.
22. This month and all my days, fire of the enemy shall not burn me in the name of Jesus.
23. Favor of God that redeemed Esther and the Jews from mass destruction, come upon me and my household in the name of Jesus.
24. Contrary wind blowing affliction into my life and into my marriage, be silenced in the name of Jesus.
25. O God my Father, let the blood of Jesus wash away every evil mark of untimely death upon my life and my family in the name of Jesus.
26. I shall not die but live to declare the works of the Lord in the name of Jesus.
27. Every step of the enemy to pull me down this month and all my days shall turn to my advancement in the name of Jesus.
28. O God my Father, arise and convert my ashes to beauty in the name of Jesus.
29. O God arise and convert my ridicule to rejoicing this month in the name of Jesus.
30. O God my Father, in this month and all my days, let me drink from the well of salvation in the name of Jesus.

31. Lord I thank you because I know you will surprise me with all the heavenly blessings this month and this year in the name of Jesus.
32. I claim victory of the cross upon my life and my household in the name of Jesus.
33. Ten is the number of perfection. Lord Jesus perfect your will in my life this month in the name of Jesus.
34. Holy Spirit come upon my life afresh this month, lead me and direct my path, in the name of Jesus.
35. This month I shall arise and shine, my eagle shall soar high above every wicked manipulation, in the name of Jesus.
36. By the power in the word of God, by the authority in the name of Jesus, I trample over satanic schemes and devices and I declare my victory, in the name of Jesus.
37. Any evil passenger that has entered into the vehicle of my life, I chase you out by fire, in the name of Jesus.
38. Any evil passenger that has entered into the vehicle of my destiny, I chase you out by fire, in the name of Jesus.
39. The boat of my life will not sink in the ocean of life, in the name of Jesus.
40. The vehicle of my life shall not go on reverse gear, in the name of Jesus.
41. O God my Father, let my life hear the word of the Lord and move foreword by fire in the name of Jesus.
42. O God my Father, let my destiny hear the word of the Lord and move foreword by fire in the name of Jesus.
43. O God my Father, let my Life experience divine visitation this month, in the name of Jesus.
44. Any power that wants to waste my life be wasted by fire, in the name of Jesus.

45. Anything in my life cooperating with failure and frustration, I withdraw your cooperation now, in the name of Jesus.
46. Anything in my life hindering the plan and purpose of God for my life, come out now and die in the name of Jesus.
47. You power of error limiting my potentials, my life is no more for you, release me now by the fire of God, in the name of Jesus.
48. Any power calling my name from the grave, be silenced forever, in the name of Jesus.
49. Any power that wants me to fail, you are a liar, I am not a candidate of failure, I command you to be destroyed by the fire of God, in the name of Jesus.
50. The Lord has lifted me, I shall not fall, I shall not fail, I shall not falter, in the name of Jesus.
51. This is my season of recovery; everything I have lost in the past, I shall recover back fully, in the name of Jesus.
52. This month I shall not hear or receive bad news; evil report shall not be about me and family, in the name of Jesus.
53. Today I arise out of the dust of poverty by the power in the blood of the lamb, in the name of Jesus.
54. O God my Father, let the blood of Jesus magnetize my life to my divine breakthrough, in the name of Jesus.
55. By the power in the blood of Jesus, I forbid reoccurrence of evil in my life and in my family; I decree that as from today, the peace of God shall reign in my life, in my home, in my business in the name of Jesus.
56. Holy Spirit purge me, purify me and prepare me for battle, in the name of Jesus.

57. I receive the armor of fire to confront and conquer the enemy of God in my life, in Jesus name.
58. I paralyze every host of darkness assigned against my vision this month, in the name of Jesus.
59. O God of Elijah, you fought by fire for Elijah on Mount Carmel, fight for me this month in an unusual way, in the name of Jesus.
60. I reject every appointment with failure and defeat this month, in the name of Jesus.
61. I renounce and cancel every appointment with disappointment and frustration, in Jesus name.
62. O God my Father, pass through the land of the wicked in your violent anger and slay every power opposing your purpose in my life, in the name of Jesus.
63. O God my Father, arise in your power and remove from my life anything living or non-living blocking my way to success, in the name of Jesus.
64. O God my Father, arise in your mercy and plant into my life this month anything that will make me become your vessel of honor, in the name of Jesus.
65. Any power from my foundation assigned to monitor my life for evil this month, I render you powerless, in the name of Jesus.
66. O God my Father, if I have been walking opposite to your direction and plan for my life, redirect me by your mercy, in the name of Jesus.
67. Any wicked power assigned to swallow my efforts and labor this month, you are a liar, be destroyed by the fire of God, in the name of Jesus.
68. Spiritual armed robbers and physical bandits, you will not locate me and my family, in the name of Jesus.

69. O God my Father, let the blood of Jesus be a wall of protection around me and my children, in the name of Jesus.
70. Every evil plan or program of the enemy for my children this month shall not prosper, in the name of Jesus.
71. Agenda of the wicked shall not come to pass in the life of my children, in the name of Jesus.
72. O God my Father, let my land yield fruits of joy this month, in the name of Jesus.
73. Every door of fruitfulness shut against me, open now by the fire of God, in the name of Jesus.
74. O God my Father, let my womb/loins hear the word of the Lord, come alive and bear fruits of joy, in the name of Jesus.
75. O God my Father, arise in your mercy and connect me to my heavenly ordained helper, in Jesus name.
76. I refuse to fish in a dead sea; I refuse to labor for nothing, in the name of Jesus.
77. I bind every work of the flesh in my life and I render it impotent in the name of Jesus.
78. Serpent and scorpion of spiritual laziness, I set you ablaze in the name of Jesus.
79. Every plantation of darkness in my life, be destroyed by fire in the name of Jesus.
80. Plantation of darkness preventing the seed of joy to germinate in my womb/ life, be destroyed by the fire of God in the name of Jesus.
81. Agent of darkness assigned to monitor my life, receive blindness in the name of Jesus.
82. O God my Father, let your fire consume every plantation of infirmity in my body, in the name of Jesus.

83. Foundational witchcraft attacking my destiny, die by the fire of God, in the name of Jesus.
84. Every yoke of lateness in marriage and child bearing, break by the fire of God in the name of Jesus.
85. I stand against every agreement and covenant of sudden death in my life in the name of Jesus.
86. My life and destiny come out of the cage of familiar witchcraft, in the name of Jesus.
87. Blanket of darkness covering my glory, be destroyed by the fire of God in the name of Jesus.
88. Powers that sponsor one to hell, I stand against you, I curse you out of my life in the name of Jesus.
89. I refuse to be a causality in the battle of life, in the name of Jesus.
90. O God my Father, let your glory cover my destiny in the name of Jesus.
91. O God my Father, I thank for answering my prayers.

SPECIAL PRAYER FOR THE MONTH OF NOVEMBER

Passages To Read Before You Pray:
Isaiah 43:19, Habakkuk 1:5, Joel 2:21-27, Psalms 19, 29, 42

I have come today to fellowship with my heavenly Father, and make my requests and needs known unto Him. I cannot be hindered nor delayed because I know who I am in the Lord. I am a child of the Kingdom, born of the Spirit, redeemed by the blood of Jesus Christ. I walk in authority, living life without any apology because the power and authority has been given to me according to the Word of God in the book of Luke 9:1.

As I have come to pray today and to fellowship with my heavenly Father, I cover myself in the blood of Jesus Christ, and I put on the whole armor of God. I hereby come against every Prince of Persia that wants to hinder my prayer, I arrest you by the power in the blood of Jesus Christ, and I bind you and cast you down into the pit of hell.

I come against principalities and powers that wrestle with me and my prayers, I arrest you today by the power in the name of Jesus Christ, and I bind you and cast down into the pit of hell. I come against the rulers of the darkness of this world, against spiritual wickedness in high places, I arrest you all by the power in the name of Jesus Christ, and I bind you and cast you down into the pit of hell. I come against weakness and weariness, I arrest you today by the power in the name of Jesus Christ, and I

bind you and cast you out of my life. I come against wondering spirit and distractions, I arrest you today by the power in the name of Jesus Christ, and I bind you and cast you out of my life.

Today I receive the anointing to pray and get results, my prayers cannot be hindered nor delayed because Jesus is my Lord, I will pray today and get the desired results, I decree open heavens upon my prayers. I baptize myself in the fire of the Holy Ghost; therefore I have become too hot for the enemy to handle. My prayers today will attract divine intervention to every situation in my life; signs and wonders will follow my prayers today, testimonies will follow my prayers today and the name of God alone will be glorified, in Jesus name. Amen!

PRAYER POINTS:

1. O God my Father, thank you for being my God, my Father and my friend.
2. O God my Father, thank you for the privilege to know you and the power of the resurrection of Jesus Christ.
3. O God my Father, thank you for always being there for me and with me.
4. O God my Father, thank you for the great and mighty things that you are doing in my life.
5. O God my Father, thank you for your provision and protection over me and my household.
6. O God my Father, thank you for always answering my prayers.
7. I confess my sins before you today and I ask you to forgive me on the basis of your mercy, in the name of Jesus Christ.

8. Wash me clean today O Lord by the blood of Jesus Christ.
9. I cover myself and my household with the blood of Jesus Christ.
10. My prayers today will not go in vain; my prayers will produce the desired results in the name of Jesus Christ.
11. Holy Spirit of God, come upon my life and lead me to pray right, in the name of Jesus.
12. I renounce satan's involvement in my prayers, in the name of Jesus.
13. O God my Father, let the Holy Ghost fire incubate me and empower me to fight and win the battle of life, in the name of Jesus.
14. O God my Father, let the Holy Spirit empower me to be a victor in the battle of life and not a victim, in the name of Jesus.
15. I receive divine mandate from above, to confront, to attack, and to defeat every foundational power attacking my destiny, in the name of Jesus.
16. O God my Father, let the Holy Spirit be my guide in the journey of this month that I will not walk into trouble, in the name of Jesus.
17. O God my Father, let the Holy Spirit empower me this month to open the gate of my breakthroughs, in the name of Jesus.
18. Every evil wall or satanic barricade erected against my success, be pulled down today by the fire of God, in the name of Jesus.
19. I receive unchallengeable anointing to excel in every area this month, in the name of Jesus.

57. O God my Father, arise and let the wickedness of the wicked come to an end in my life, in the name of Jesus.
58. O God my Father, arise and break the arm of the wicked troubling my life, in the name of Jesus.
59. Witchcraft lion assigned to eat my flesh, die by the fire of God, in the name of Jesus.
60. By the power in the name of Jesus Christ, I arrest every witchcraft delegate assigned to waste my life, in the name of Jesus.
61. Powers that hindered my parents now attacking my progress, lose your hold over my life, in the name of Jesus.
62. O God my Father, let the sword of the wicked go back on their heads, in the name of Jesus.
63. I remove my name from the ancestral register of failure and defeat, in the name of Jesus.
64. The horn of the wicked shall not prevail over my life, in the name of Jesus.
65. The purpose of God for my life shall not be frustrated, in the name of Jesus.
66. I shall not appear to disappear, in the name of Jesus.
67. O God my Father, I thank you for answering my prayers, blessed be your holy name, in the name of Jesus.

45. Any evil power, authority or kingdom, contending with the power of God in my life, fire of God consume them all, in the name of Jesus.
46. Any contrary handwriting against my progress in the heaven, on the earth, underneath the earth, in the sea, and underneath the sea, be blotted out by the power in the blood of Jesus, in the name of Jesus.
47. O God my Father, keep me and my family under your everlasting arm, far above principalities and powers, in the name of Jesus.
48. My time of favor, appear and manifest now, in the name of Jesus.
49. My season of celebration, appear and manifest now, in the name of Jesus.
50. Where I have been rejected, I shall be honored, in the name of Jesus.
51. O Lord that caused Daniel to be celebrated after rejection, by your mercy secure my celebration this month, in the name of Jesus.
52. O God my Father, you destroyed the garment of shame assigned to blind Bartimaeus: arise, frustrate and destroy shame and disgrace out of my life, in the name of Jesus.
53. O God my Father, as you gave Abraham and Sarah testimony at the time of no hope; by your mercy I decree that I shall have testimony, in the name of Jesus.
54. Evil foundational tree shading my glory, be uprooted by the fire of God, in the name of Jesus.
55. Ancestral evil tree bringing forth evil fruit into my life; I set you ablaze, in the name of Jesus.
56. Axe of God, cut down to the root of every evil tree planted in my life, in the name of Jesus.

20. As darkness cannot contend against light, no power of darkness shall be able to stand or contend against my glory, in the name of Jesus.
21. Any evil programmed against my glory in the heavens, scatter by the fire of God in the name of Jesus.
22. Any power in the valley pulling me down, you are a liar, I am for the top, therefore leave me alone and die in your valley in the name of Jesus.
23. I shall not miss my appointed time of breakthrough in the name of Jesus.
24. I fire back satanic arrows of spiritual laziness, in the name of Jesus.
25. I refused to be enslaved by any evil habit in the name of Jesus.
26. Witchcraft projections for my life and family this month, receive multiple failure, in the name of Jesus.
27. My destiny is attached to God, therefore I decree with assurance that I cannot fail, I will not fail, I will succeed whether the enemy likes it or not, in the name of Jesus.
28. Anointing of an overcomer, come upon my life now, in the name of Jesus.
29. Anointing of fire and power come upon my life now, in the name of Jesus.
30. Pentecostal anointing, come upon my life now, in the name of Jesus.
31. Undefeatable anointing, come upon my life now, in the name of Jesus.
32. Unchallengeable anointing, come upon my life now, in the name of Jesus.
33. Anointing to seek and find, descend upon me now, in the name of Jesus.

34. Anointing to ask and receive, come upon my life now, in the name of Jesus.
35. Anointing for Open heavens, come upon my life now, in the name of Jesus.
36. O God my Father, by your mercy, renew my mind/heart to be in line with your purpose for my life, in the name of Jesus.
37. Lord Jesus, you are the good Shepherd; empower me to trust you in all my ways, in the name of Jesus.
38. O God my Father, deliver me from the confusion of the mind that war against my spiritual growth, in the name of Jesus.
39. O God my Father, let the heavenly sunlight arise, expose and shakeout every pothole of darkness and every den of wickedness in my life and my family, in the name of Jesus.
40. Every chariot of hell, every spirit of deception and distraction assigned to derail me from the way of truth; be consumed by fire, in the name of Jesus.
41. O God my Father, let my love for you and your kingdom be renewed by fire, in the name of Jesus.
42. Every stone of limitation and restriction to my advancement spiritually, physically, maritally, financially, be rolled away by fire, in the name of Jesus.
43. Holy Ghost, advertise yourself in my life this month in an unusual way, and let the world know that I serve a living God, in the name of Jesus.
44. Every gate of breakthrough that the enemy has shut against me, open now by the fire of God, in the name of Jesus.

SPECIAL PRAYER FOR THE MONTH OF DECEMBER

Passages To Read Before You Pray:
Isaiah 43:19, Habakkuk 1:5, Joel 2:21-27, Psalms 19, 29, 42

I have come today to fellowship with my heavenly Father, and make my requests and needs known unto Him. I cannot be hindered nor delayed because I know who I am in the Lord. I am a child of the Kingdom, born of the Spirit, redeemed by the blood of Jesus Christ. I walk in authority, living life without any apology because the power and authority has been given to me according to the Word of God in the book of Luke 9:1.

As I have come to pray today and to fellowship with my heavenly Father, I cover myself in the blood of Jesus Christ, and I put on the whole armor of God. I hereby come against every Prince of Persia that wants to hinder my prayer, I arrest you by the power in the blood of Jesus Christ, and I bind you and cast you down into the pit of hell.

I come against principalities and powers that wrestle with me and my prayers, I arrest you today by the power in the name of Jesus Christ, and I bind you and cast down into the pit of hell. I come against the rulers of the darkness of this world, against spiritual wickedness in high places, I arrest you all by the power in the name of Jesus Christ, and I bind you and cast you down into the pit of hell. I come against weakness and weariness, I arrest you today by the power in the name of Jesus Christ, and I

bind you and cast you out of my life. I come against wondering spirit and distractions, I arrest you today by the power in the name of Jesus Christ, and I bind you and cast you out of my life.

Today I receive the anointing to pray and get results, my prayers cannot be hindered nor delayed because Jesus is my Lord, I will pray today and get the desired results, I decree open heavens upon my prayers. I baptize myself in the fire of the Holy Ghost; therefore I have become too hot for the enemy to handle. My prayers today will attract divine intervention to every situation in my life; signs and wonders will follow my prayers today, testimonies will follow my prayers today and the name of God alone will be glorified, in Jesus name. Amen!

PRAYER POINTS:

1. O God my Father, thank you for being my God, my Father and my friend.
2. O God my Father, thank you for the privilege to know you and the power of the resurrection of Jesus Christ.
3. O God my Father, thank you for always being there for me and with me.
4. O God my Father, thank you for the great and mighty things that you are doing in my life.
5. O God my Father, thank you for your provision and protection over me and my household.
6. O God my Father, thank you for always answering my prayers.
7. I confess my sins before you today and I ask you to forgive me on the basis of your mercy, in the name of Jesus Christ.

8. Wash me clean today O Lord by the blood of Jesus Christ.
9. I cover myself and my household with the blood of Jesus Christ.
10. My prayers today will not go in vain; my prayers will produce the desired results in the name of Jesus Christ.

11. Holy Spirit of God, have your way in my life in the name of Jesus.
12. Holy Spirit of God, open my understanding to the knowledge of God and eternity in the name of Jesus.
13. Holy Spirit of God, lead me, teach me and empower me to pray and get results, in the name of Jesus.
14. O God my Father, open my understanding to see, and know where and how the enemy is taking advantage of me, in the name of Jesus.
15. O God my Father, let your fire expose every hidden secret of the enemy in my life, in the name of Jesus.
16. Every handwriting of sickness and infirmity upon my life since the beginning of this year; O God my Father, let the blood of Jesus wash it away, in the name of Jesus.
17. Any stubborn sickness in my body contending with the power of the Great Physician, come out by fire, in the name of Jesus.
18. Any agreement I have consciously or unconsciously made with the devil to afflict me with infirmity; I cancel and revoke it by the blood of Jesus Christ, in the name of Jesus.
19. O God my Father, deliver me from any form of sickness today by your healing power, in the name of Jesus.
20. Garment of emotional infirmity upon my body, be destroyed by the fire of God, in the name of Jesus.

21. Power of spiritual sickness upon my life; be destroyed by the fire of God, in the name of Jesus.
22. Strange powers and familiar enemies working together to torment my life; be destroyed by the fire of God, in the name of Jesus
23. Every power assigned to drain my life and my purse with infirmity, I command you to release me now, in the name of Jesus.
24. I release the fire of destruction upon any power troubling my life with any form of infirmity, in the name of Jesus.
25. The Lord is my portion; therefore I shall not die but live to declare the good works of the Lord, in the name Jesus.
26. What the enemy has taken away or denied me since the beginning of this year; I recover back by the fire of God, in the name of Jesus.
27. O God my Father, by your name Alpha and Omega, put an end to suffering and lack in my life, in the name of Jesus.
28. By the Power in the Blood of Jesus and by the authority in the word of God, I declare that any bad experience of the past shall not repeat itself in my life again, in the name of Jesus.
29. By the authority in the name of Jesus Christ, I command the spirit of rejection to depart from my life, in the name of Jesus.
30. By the power in the Blood of Jesus, I command every repeated oppression in my life to die permanently, in the name of Jesus.
31. Witchcraft affliction and oppression, your time is up in my life and in my family, in the name of Jesus.

32. By the Power in the Blood of the Lamb, I move away from the realm of lack and want into the fullness and abundance of God, in the name of Jesus.
33. Let the terror of the Almighty torment my tormentors, in the name of Jesus.
34. I receive power from above, and I move out of any position of failure, frustration and discomfort in the name of Jesus.
35. By the Power of God that set Paul and Silas free from the prison, I move out of any bondage I have ever got into by my ignorance or by the act of household wickedness, in the name of Jesus I am out completely.
36. Every curse of financial limitation and restriction in my life, break by the fire of God, in the name of Jesus.
37. I stand in the righteousness of the Living God, and I stand against every opposition to my greatness, in the name of Jesus.
38. O God my Father, let the blood of Jesus destroy every seed of sickness and infirmity in my body, in the name of Jesus.
39. By the Power in the Blood of Jesus, I reject evil carry over into the New Year, in the name of Jesus.
40. Any power contending with my peace, I hold the Blood of Jesus against you, in the name of Jesus.
41. O God my Father, let the blood of Jesus be a shield around my life, protect me and my family from every attack, in the name of Jesus.
42. By the Power in the Blood of Jesus, I am an overcomer, I am more than a conqueror, in the name of Jesus.
43. Arrows of failure and frustration fired into my life, get out and locate your sender in the name of Jesus.

44. Locust of darkness eating the labor of my hands, be destroyed by the fire of God, in the name of Jesus.
45. Holy Ghost fire, come upon my life and burn to ashes the serpent of failure and frustration in the name of Jesus.
46. Holy Ghost fire, descend upon my life and consume the serpent of poor finishing, in the name of Jesus.
47. I started this year well, O God my Father, empower me to end it well, in the name of Jesus.
48. My delayed benefits since the beginning of this year, come out and locate me in the name of Jesus.
49. Any snake or scorpion of failure that has entered into my life since the beginning of this year, I set you on fire, in the name of Jesus.
50. Every power of poor finishing assigned against me, be rendered useless and powerless, in the name of Jesus.
51. Every power from the pit of hell fueling problems in my life, die by the fire of God, in the name of Jesus.
52. Every negative agreement standing against my success, be nullified in the name of Jesus.
53. Every mountain of satanic confrontation in my life, be destroyed by the fire of God, in the name of Jesus.
54. Every occultic consultation against my life, be frustrated by the fire of God, in the name of Jesus.
55. Every evil river of backwardness flowing in my life and my family line, dry up now in the name of Jesus.
56. Holy Spirit of God, transform my weaknesses to strengths in the name of Jesus.
57. Every financial coffin fashioned against my finances, be destroyed by the fire of God, in the name of Jesus.
58. O God my Father, let all my delayed miracles manifest now by the fire of God, in the name of Jesus.

59. Holy Spirit, perfect the will and purpose of God in my life, in the name of Jesus.

CREDITS

Spiritual Warfare: Earth-Moving Prayer is an extract from an article written by Pastor Flo Shaw, International Coordinator of World Network of Prayer.

Used by permission.